THE
WORLD
IN
1776

THE HORIZON HISTORY OF

THE WORLD
IN
1776

BY MARSHALL B. DAVIDSON

and the Editors of HORIZON

Published by American Heritage Publishing Co., Inc., New York

Book Trade Distribution by McGraw-Hill Book Company

Staff for this Book

EDITOR
Marshall B. Davidson

ART DIRECTOR
Murray Belsky

PICTURE EDITOR
Douglas Tunstell

ASSOCIATE EDITORS
Anne Moffat
Kaari Ward

CONTRIBUTING LIBRARIAN
Laura L. Masters

CONTRIBUTING WRITER
Bruce Bohle

EDITORIAL ASSISTANTS
Diane Koszarski
Donna F. Whiteman

EUROPEAN BUREAU
Gertrudis Feliu, *Chief*
Christine Sutherland, London

AMERICAN HERITAGE PUBLISHING CO., INC.

PRESIDENT AND PUBLISHER
Paul Gottlieb

GENERAL MANAGER, BOOK DIVISION
Kenneth W. Leish

EDITORIAL ART DIRECTOR
Murray Belsky

Library of Congress Cataloging in Publication Data

Davidson, Marshall B
The Horizon history of the world in 1776.

Half title: The world in 1776.
Includes index.
1. History, Modern—18th century. I. Horizon (New York, 1958–   ) II. Title. III. Title: The world in 1776.
D289.D35   909.7   75–17844
ISBN 0-07-015430-9
ISBN 0-07-015431-7 deluxe.

909.7

Above: Jean Huber's engraving, The Philosophes at Dinner, *features the leading figures of the Enlightenment in France. Voltaire, born François Marie Arouet, has his hand raised; Denis Diderot, creator of the* Encyclopédie, *is seated at his left; the brilliant mathematician Jean d'Alembert is in the left foreground.*
BIBLIOTHEQUE NATIONALE

Title page: A detail from "America," one of a set of four tapestries ordered by Louis XVI as a gift for George Washington. Fame is shown fastening a profile of the American leader to a marble pillar; Liberty, holding a flag of thirteen Stars and Stripes, is attended by Peace and Plenty; in the foreground a confused and battered Britannia is shielding herself from America's ally, France.
SOTHEBY'S, LONDON

Endsheets: "The World, Agreable to the latest Discoveries" was published by Thomas Jefferys, an English mapmaker, in 1773. The map does not include the findings of Captain James Cook's first voyage, along the coasts of New Zealand and eastern Australia, which were also published in 1773. Within a decade Cook's other voyages — to the Antarctic Ocean, the South Pacific, along the coastlines of Siberia and Alaska — changed the outline of the known world.
NEW YORK PUBLIC LIBRARY, MAP DIVISION

The calligraphic designs appearing with the chapter titles were drawn by Ferdinand von Freisleben for Calligraphia Latina, *published in 1756.*
OSTERREICHISHE NATIONALBIBLIOTHEK, VIENNA

CONTENTS

PROLOGUE TO THE PAST

"It was the best of times, it was the worst of times, it was the age of wisdom, it was the age of foolishness, it was the epoch of belief, it was the epoch of incredulity, it was the season of Light, it was the season of Darkness, it was the spring of hope, it was the winter of despair."

In those unforgettable opening lines of *A Tale of Two Cities*, quoted at left, Charles Dickens described Europe on the eve of the French Revolution. Actually, the shape of that world of extraordinary contrasts and puzzling contradictions, of apparently irreconcilable forces and contentions, had already been drawn on the eve of the American Revolution thirteen years earlier. Then, as never before, thoughtful men throughout the Western world were united by a common body of ideas that recognized no national boundaries, while their separate governments were rivaling one another in nationalist fervor. England and France, for instance, were never more in cultural rapport than in the years of the eighteenth century when the two nations were so often at war. Even during hostilities English visitors flocked to Paris, where they were cordially received. Voltaire returned to France from a highly rewarding exile in England praising almost everything he had witnessed in that land. (It has been said that he was "England's best gift to France.") England, on the other hand, read with avid interest whatever French writers were producing, even as the military machines of the two nations lined up for battle. Across the Atlantic the individual colonies which were finally uniting in a common cause against the parent government had in many ways closer cultural ties to England than to each other. The tidewater Virginia planter felt more akin to the English country gentleman than he did to the Boston merchant; the cosmopolitan citizen of Charleston who had studied law at the Inns of Court was at least as close in outlook to his London colleagues as he was to graduates, of whatever colonial origin, of the provincial little college at Princeton in New Jersey.

Voltaire, who in 1776 was approaching the end of his years, was in a sense a living paradox in those paradoxical times. As one of his compatriots remarked, he "incessantly undermined the ground on which despotism was ever building." Yet this tireless and peerless champion of the oppressed paid flattering attentions to the most despotic monarchs of his day. Among other equally fulsome encomiums, he wrote Russia's Catherine the Great that she was the "benefactress of Europe" and, with almost obscene flattery, that he wished he might kiss her hands and feet, "which are as white as the snows of Russia." (To secure her hold on the crown, Catherine reportedly had had her husband, the Czar Peter, first dethroned and then murdered.)

He paid fawning tribute to Frederick the Great of Prussia, described by one contemporary English observer as "the completest tyrant God ever made, for the scourge of an offending people." Voltaire died with the conviction that in his day and with his help the Age of Reason had prevailed, yet he wrote Frederick (that "Solomon of the North," as Voltaire called him) that he must consider no limitations to his despotic powers on the part of his subjects; "once the populace begins to reason," argued the Prince of Reason, "then everything is lost." Voltaire's concern for the unenlightened man, it might be added, was never great.

No doubt our own world two hundred years later can be charged with as many contradictions as the world of 1776. Both could be termed worlds in transition: times of change and resultant confusion, as stubbornly held traditional values face radically new concepts stemming from the pressing needs of the day. Differences in viewpoints and opinions at times could be absolute. It was in 1776 that Edward Gibbon published the first volume of *The Decline and Fall of the Roman Empire,* one of the greatest historical works in English literature, and in those magisterial pages found reason to congratulate his privileged contemporaries on the fact that the age of great political and social disruptions was safely past. Even in the unlikely event that barbarian hordes might again overrun Europe as they had in the Dark Ages, he observed, "ten thousand vessels would transport beyond their pursuit the remains of civilized society; and Europe would revive and flourish in the American world which is already filled with her colonies and institutions." (That statement recalls the remark to the same effect made by Winston Churchill in the darkest days of World War II.)

In that same year Thomas Paine issued his brilliant and inflammatory pamphlet *Common Sense,* in which he pronounced, directly contrary to Gibbon's conclusion, that a new social and political order must be wrought by whatever violent means might be necessary and that America was at that moment the place to undertake such action; the principles of contemporary government in general and Britain's in particular, he insisted, must be challenged and changed. Hereditary absolute monarchies were a useless evil, supported neither by scripture nor common sense and condemnable by historical experience —a burden humanity should no longer suffer.

Both publications had resounding successes. The entire first impression of Gibbon's book was exhausted in a few days. *Common Sense* sold as many as a hundred thousand copies in the first six months. (In a handsome gesture Paine devoted all the proceeds from that enormous sale to the American cause.) As General George Washington was pinning down the British expeditionary forces in Boston from the neighboring heights he read that radical tract and praised its "sound doctrine and unconscionable reasoning." At the same time Washington's officers' mess was still toasting the health of King George III, in the spirit of liberty-loving Englishmen. But the pace of events was fast. Less than six months later, on July 4, the "good People" of the United States of America in a formal document renounced "all Allegiance to the British Crown," and declared that "all political Connection between them and the State of Great-Britain, is and ought to be totally dissolved."

Since World War II many new and independent nations have been conceived and born in various parts of the world. However, in 1776, when the duly appointed representatives of the thirteen American colonies declared that those colonies were and ought to be "Free and Independent States," the birth of a new nation was an uncommon event. In retrospect it seems to have been a sensational development. But at the time news of the Declaration was received with mixed feelings, where it was heeded at all. There were those who thought the document proclaimed a turning point in the history of human affairs. Others, Americans among them, doubted that the proposed experiment in self-government would succeed. Still others paid no attention whatever to the emergence of a new state so far removed from the main centers of politics and civilization, if indeed they were aware of it. As many as twenty-one years after the Declaration was signed, John Quincy Adams in Prussia, representing his country as American minister to that state, met one officer of the guards who admitted without a blush that he had never so much as heard of the United States.

In the Declaration of Independence, Americans had defined their cause with rare eloquence; in the following years they fought, endured, and won the long struggle to free themselves from old and binding ties. But they still had to prove that their novel experiment in republicanism was a practical and viable system of self-government. Nothing like it had been attempted on such a scale since the days of ancient Rome, and the temper of the times was generally not favorable to another deliberate move in that direction. Or so it seemed in the courts and capitals of the rest of the world. Frederick the Great argued that the very size of the new country made disunion or monarchy inevitable.

With a few minor exceptions, in 1776 all the advanced and settled nations on earth were monarchies; the practical advantages of royal absolutism as a system of government seemed clear from long experience, Paine's injunction to the contrary notwithstanding. Except for the distant rumblings from America, there was at the moment no serious indication that such venerable traditions might soon be threatened. Barely a decade before the outbreak of hostilities at Lexington and Concord, even such highly spirited patriots as the Sons of Liberty assumed that, should the colonists ultimately part from Great Britain—a prospect that then filled them with the "darkest Gloom and Horror"—they would go about "erecting an Independent Monarchy here in America."

Those rumblings were, to be sure, the portent of a worldwide storm, but a portent that was scarcely meaningful to most prophets of the day. As a gifted agent of Louis XVI, the author and dramatist Beaumarchais did indeed warn his king that this overseas disturbance might divide the world and that he had better look sharply to his own interests—and to his own head, Beaumarchais might have added. A descendant of Louis XIV, the glorious "Sun King," and an absolute ruler in his own right could hardly be expected to rejoice in a rebellion based on the theory that governments derive "their just Powers from the Consent of the Governed." Nevertheless, it seemed to be in the best interest of the crown for France to aid the colonists in their struggle, first covertly and then openly, following the great American victory at Saratoga in 1777. It was also self-serving, to be sure, for it took advantage of a prime opportunity to undermine Britain's imperial power; but that expensive action left the royal coffers empty. The striking irony was that in thus supporting the cause of American freedom the French monarchy virtually, if unintentionally, committed suicide, as events of succeeding years would reveal.

For the better part of a century the nations of Europe had been engaged in a conflict that has been called the Second Hundred Years' War. In a series of shifting alliances, beginning about 1689, the ruling families had been jostling one another in what seemed like a perpetual maneuver to decide whose kingdom would become the greater power, or to prevent another state's becoming such, or at least to preserve some balance of power among them all that could be accepted with regal dignity and a measure of security. The highborn Aragonese Pedro de Bolea, count of Aranda, who was the true head of the Spanish government from 1766 to 1773, summarized such attitudes in a manner that his contemporaries easily understood. International diplomacy, he explained, had resolved itself "into recognizing the strength, the resources, the interests, the rights, the fears and the hopes of the different powers, so that as the occasion warrants it, we may appease these powers, divide them, defeat them, or ally ourselves with them, depending on how they serve our advantage and increase our security."

Wars played a dominant part in the history of Europe in the eighteenth century. It was not war as we have so unhappily come to know it. Contests were between or among political bodies rather than peoples, governments rather than men. Except in the American wilderness and in India, to which distant areas the conflicts ultimately spread but where peculiar conditions prevailed, civilians were hardly affected. Because governments deemed it prudent to disrupt the economy of a state as little as possible, the rank and file of armies was generally conscripted from the least productive elements of the population. In order to make up those armies, wrote the comte de Saint-Germain, distinguished war minister of France under Louis XVI, the nation must inevitably call up "the scum of the people" and "all those for whom society has no use." (Three British regiments in the American Revolution were composed solely of reprieved criminals.) Toward the same end, mercenary troops were recruited from other nations (as Britain hired Hessians to help fight the colonists). Still others were enlisted from enemy deserters. Military leaders, in turn, were to a large extent drawn from the nobility, that social class which alone, it was felt, possessed the sense of personal honor required of a good officer—men, it might be added, who could afford to buy their commissions. For the most part, those wars aroused relatively little popular interest or national feeling. Great causes and principles were not in question, merely the prestige or practical interests of the ruling elements of the separate states.

Compared to wars of later times, those of the eighteenth century were usually not destructive, and they were rarely conclusive. Battles were fought not to destroy enemy forces but to outmaneuver them and to gain a position of strength from which to negotiate. One year's foe might be next year's ally. Armies were expensive to train and maintain, and it was a reckless or a heedless monarch or general, or indeed a desperate one, who committed his troops to an engagement which might prove costly in lives and equipment. (Navies were still more expensive, but in terms of worldwide strategy more important, a point to which this story will later return.) To paraphrase J. F. Bielfeld, inspector general of Prussian universities under Frederick the Great, wars gave rise to treaties and treaties were the source of new wars in a constant, oscillating sequence. It almost seems they might have gone on indefinitely without inflicting any great catastrophe on mankind.

Several times during its colonial history America had been engaged on the perimeter of such hostilities—hostilities that spread not only to the New World, but as far east as India and, in the end, to Africa and the Philippines. Twenty years to the day before the signing of the Declaration of Independence, young George Washington, colonel of the Virginia militia, lost a frontier skirmish to French forces in western Pennsylvania. Of that wilderness encounter Voltaire wrote: "Such was the complication of political interests that a cannon shot fired in America could give the signal that set Europe in a blaze." That tiny spark did, in effect, ignite the international rivalries that resulted in the Seven Years' War (known in America as the French and Indian War) and that soon involved—along with the American colonists and native Indian factions in Asia—France, Austria, Russia, Saxony, Sweden, and Spain on one side and Prussia, Great Britain, and Hanover on the other. It was, in short, a world war, and this time a bloodier and more destructive war than others had been.

In 1763 the last of the war-weary powers, their resources spent in the long struggle, laid down their arms and signed still another treaty establishing still a new balance of power. As Voltaire had suggested, it was now apparent that any balance of power in Europe could be disturbed by events and circumstances thousands of miles distant. The "shot heard round the world" in 1775 did not immediately recall that truth to those in high positions, but it was another signal from America that the world would once again be ablaze. By then the uneasy and tense truce abroad had lasted twelve welcome years, but major and minor princes alike remained ready to pounce on their neighbors at any sign of weakness among them.

The new balance of power that emerged from the Seven Years' War presented problems that were more subtle and more involved than those faced by the previous generation. Dr. Samuel Johnson once shrewdly observed that the international politics of Europe in the eighteenth century were too complicated for any man to understand, and the diplomatic confusion of the period immediately following the war supports that view. However, from a distance of more than two hundred years a number of important developments loom high above the welter of intrigue of the times. It seems clear, for example, that the relatively rapid rise of Prussia and Russia as political and military forces in the European scheme of things was of enormous significance to the future history of the world. Together with a rebirth of Austrian power under the Hapsburgs, this shifted the center of gravity of European diplomacy toward the east, with immediate consequences. It was during this period, in 1772, that these three states effected the first partition of hapless Poland, an operation they completed soon thereafter, and only a few years later that Russia took from Turkey the steppelands on the north shore of the Black Sea and then the Crimea. A century and a half earlier the Ottoman Turks had ruled over the world's largest empire, but that day of glory was now fast fading.

In western Europe, with the peace of 1763, Great Britain had obtained vast territories which extended from the Gulf of Mexico to the Arctic barrens. This now constituted the world's largest empire, and included all lands in North America east of the Mississippi River as well as lucrative islands in the West Indies, parts of West Africa, and important holdings in India. Great Britain ruled the ocean seas, and its merchant marine was supreme. Much of that success was won at the expense of France, which, beaten and humiliated, remained vengeful and determined to restore its power and its lost prestige—with fateful results in the years soon to come.

However, Britain had paid dearly for its own success, which had aroused fears throughout western Europe that its sea power might lead to a monopoly of overseas trade and might preclude whatever dreams other nations had of their own overseas expansion. In the face of such widespread jealousy, resentment, and apprehension, Great Britain found itself virtually isolated politically, without allies, and as the year 1776 approached, probably in a weaker position in the international world than at any other time in the eighteenth century.

Even in triumph, Britain's finances were depleted in waging the Seven Years' War. The national debt had practically doubled as a result of the conflict. Most of the other European states that had been involved were closer to bankruptcy. Whether they had participated or not, nearly all governments recognized an urgent need to overhaul and "modernize" the administration of their internal affairs if they were to survive competition with their neighbors and rivals. Reforms long under way must now be accelerated, new ones undertaken.

The need was all too obvious. Domestic trade was often discouraged by innumerable customs barriers set up as collection points for fees due on commodities passing from one province to another within a single country. Rates varied from one checkpoint to the next, and smuggling flourished as a consequence. Even such basic matters as weights and measures were differently gauged from one region to another. A "league" might be considered the equivalent of 2,000 yards in one place and 3,000 yards elsewhere. There was no such thing as a common measure for a carafe of wine, even from one village to the next. Nor was there indeed any common standard of justice. "In France," Voltaire remarked, "a traveler changes his laws as often as he changes his horses." In Russia many decrees were proclaimed without being printed or published. In America, Benjamin Franklin observed, each colony even had its "peculiar expressions, familiar to its own people, but strange and unintelligible to others."

Almost everywhere the attempts by the central government to standardize and unify rules, laws, and procedures conflicted with deeply entrenched local rights and privileges—conflicts leading to dramatic developments that had international repercussions and that were, in the end, revolutionary in consequence. Circumstances varied with every nation, and it would be tedious to recount in detail how each met its separate problems. The situation in France differed radically from that in Great Britain and sharply in other directions from that in Russia; and so, in kaleidoscopic fashion, the picture changes as we look toward Sweden and Prussia, the Low Countries and Spain, Italy, Switzerland, and, with a long glance westward, America, which was both figuratively and literally a world apart from the others. Whatever those differences, however, in every case the basic issues centered on the need of increased revenues without which the state could not be adequately administered and could not equip its military machinery and thus maintain or enlarge its area of influence. Taxation must provide a major share of the necessary revenue, and it was clear that a maximum yield from that source depended upon the efficiency of the collection organization and some sensible, practical distribution of the tax load among the different elements of society. As often as not, however, the government officials charged with these and other responsibilities had traditionally been non-professional administrators serving without salary, men who may have purchased their posts, who lived off the perquisites of their offices, and who considered those jobs private property of which they could not be deprived without due compensation. What records they kept were their own private affair, unavailable to those who might draw helpful lessons from them.

Matters were further complicated by the widespread fact that some individuals, groups, organizations, and localities claimed long-standing rights and privileges that exempted them either from all taxation or from any amounts that could be considered commensurate with their means. Some members of the nobility were exempt on principle; they considered taxation a degradation of their favored status in society. There were autonomous bodies intermediate between the state and the individual, constituent bodies that historically were privileged to assess and tax by their own authority according to customs that varied in different areas. From medieval times, guilds of tradesmen and artisans had collected taxes from their own membership, turning over to the state a sum that bore no necessary relationship to the amounts that they might have justly exacted. Towns and whole districts enjoyed certain ancient privileges that did not apply equally to neighboring or surrounding areas. Conspicuously, the Church traditionally maintained that its vast holdings were not subject to taxation by the state (as is still true in the United States), although it might make "free gifts" in recognition of its stake in the welfare of society in general.

The reluctance of individuals and groups to surrender their established privileges impeded or complicated the process of reform. It was another paradox of the age that although France had the richest resources of any country in Europe, its government was chronically poor because it could not effectively tap the sources of wealth within the kingdom. Every effort by the crown to replenish the national coffers through tax reforms was frustrated by the regional *parlements*, or assemblies, whose members enjoyed exemptions they were not prepared to yield, a stand in which they were supported by members of the nobility, who were no less eager to retain their own exemptions.

Great Britain, standing astride a huge empire, faced separate problems arising from a similar predicament. "There has been nothing of note in Parliament," wrote Horace Walpole in February, 1765, "but one slight day on the American taxes." That was the day yawning members of the House of Commons passed the Stamp Act with a heavy majority and with scarcely a word of debate or show of serious intent. The expenses of the French and Indian War had put a heavy strain upon the British taxpayer, and the ministry had decided to call upon the American colonies to bear some equitable share of the further burden of defending the empire's wilderness frontiers. Since the colonial delegates could not guarantee any such grants by voluntary acts of their constituent assemblies, Parliament had proceeded to impose a solution that would help to assure the immediate needs. "We might as well have hindered the sun's setting," wrote Benjamin Franklin from London to a fellow Philadelphian. "That we could not do. But since 't is down, my friend, and it may be long before it rises again, let us make as good a night of it as we can. We may still light candles."

The night was indeed a long one, but it was lighted by more than candles. With the passage of that act, all unwittingly, the complacent members of Parliament had put a torch to the times. Even Franklin was surprised at the vehemence of the Americans' resistance to this step which they felt violated their own long-established privileges. Colonial legislatures returned strong resolutions of protest as quickly as these could be properly formulated; mobs—mob-fashion—did violence to the property of unpopular persons to demonstrate their patriotism; secret organizations of more solid worth sprang up throughout the colonies to co-ordinate resistance to oppression.

The American colonists were far from alone in thus vaunting their imprescriptible and unalienable rights. On the European continent, everywhere west of Russia and Turkey, there were also political entities within the separate states that rushed to put a stop to any intrusion by central authorities of what they considered their historic constitutional liberties. Hungary, Belgium, and France also knew such agitation as was aroused in America by the Stamp Act. The large province of Brittany in France, for example, zealously and persistently defended those special privileges and liberties which had been conceded when the area had long before first come under the crown. Bretons paid the lowest per capita tax in the kingdom, less than half that of neighboring Normandy, and "consented" to make "gifts" of their own discretion to the king.

When the royal governor of Brittany undertook a program of needed internal improvements in that relatively undeveloped area, to be effected by a tax in the form of conscription of local labor, he met with immediate and militant resistance. In his efforts to discipline the province through special royal courts set up for the purpose, the king aroused the resentment of parlements in Paris and in other provinces which now claimed as a group that no laws or taxes could be imposed without their approval. In 1766, harassed to the limits of his patience by years of such brash remonstrances, Louis XV hastily assembled the members of the Paris parlement and presented the strongest assertion of royal absolutism ever made by a French king. "In my person only," he read in part, "does the sovereign power rest. . . . From me alone do my courts derive their existence and their authority. . . . To me alone belongs legislative power. . . . By my authority alone do the officers of my courts proceed. . . . Public order in its entirety emanates from me. . . ."

That was a brave utterance on the part of the monarch who was no longer "well-beloved" as once he had been. However, the parlements paid it small due, and continued their remonstrances and protests with undiminished determination. The troubles in Brittany also continued. Louis finally realized that either he or the parlements must rule France, and stirred out of his customary apathy, in 1770 he simply abolished those hereditary bodies and sent their members packing. "For myself, I think the king is right," Voltaire observed. "and since it is necessary to serve, I would rather do so under a lion of good pedigree . . . than under two hundred rats of my own kind." But Louis had little time left to recapture lost ground. He died, largely unlamented, in 1774.

Despite the many difficulties, Louis bequeathed a much more efficient government to his young successor than he himself had inherited from the powerful "Sun King" almost sixty years earlier. Over the decades leading to 1776 most of the other leading European nations had also succeeded in converting archaic survivals of government management into more systematic procedures. By one means or another, individual officials with vested interests in their jobs were being replaced by impersonal agencies or by salaried individuals with fixed responsibilities. More uniform laws, more equitable taxation, sounder fiscal programs, and more orderly administration generally were replacing the irregularities of earlier years. Official records were kept in central archives, where they could be studied to determine the state of public business, a matter that previously had been subject to uninformed guesswork. Warfare, it was recognized, had become too complex to be left entirely to generals and to officers who bought their commissions for the sake of prestige. In France, as it prepared to wage its vengeful war against Britain, the navy was rebuilt and massively enlarged and the army reconstituted. Regular troops were recruited and trained to replace the old militia. Scholarships were provided at military schools, where less than affluent lads could learn the arts of war. (One recipient was to be a Corsican youth named Bonaparte.)

All this was not accomplished quickly or at an even pace in the separate nations. As a small but striking instance of the survival of outworn patterns, in 1787 upon his release from a two-day stay in an Edinburgh jail, a debtor was confronted with a demand for 17 pounds 6 shillings $5\frac{1}{2}$ pence in fees. His jailer insisted that the charge was necessary since in running the prison he received no salary and was put to unavoidable expenses which somehow he must pay off. However, in general the modern bureaucratic state was beginning to consolidate its forces.

In the late decades of the eighteenth century most sovereigns—those of western Europe, in any case—had dispensed with the pretense that they ruled by divine right. As early as 1748 Montesquieu's great work, *L'Esprit des lois* (*The Spirit of the Law*), in which he searchingly questioned the nature of government, did not bother to mention the matter at all. Such justification was hardly necessary at a time when the principle of royal authority was firmly established on other grounds. Even the remonstrating parlements and most of the liberal thinkers of the day agreed on that principle. As already seen, in most countries the actual power of kings and queens was indeed conditioned by binding traditions and historical circumstances which could not be disregarded. But within the state the monarch was, and was expected to be, the ultimate force that drove the machinery of government. The sovereign was the supreme superintendent over the lives of his subjects. In theory at least he owned his country. In international affairs he was the symbol of his nation's power and repute. Where the monarch and his ministry were weak, the state suffered accordingly in its relations with contending states. This was pitifully the case of Poland, at one time one of the largest European states. As a consequence of royal impotence, that country was simply taken over by and divided among its more powerful neighbors. Since the Polish crown was elective, that unfortunate nation was sometimes deemed to be a republic, and its collapse added weight to Frederick the Great's contention that bigness and republicanism were incompatible factors in the structure of a state.

Where it was successfully accomplished, the systematic organization of civil and military procedures enormously increased the power of government. Traditionally, the internal politics of a state were the politics of monarchy—a matter of personal relations within the court. Now, for the personal allegiance to the king was substituted a more impersonal bond of loyalty to the crown as an institution. Much as they complained of royal encroachments, the constituent bodies could not impede the increasing authority of the crown. By 1776 monarchy had prevailed almost everywhere—emphatically so in such despotisms as Prussia, Russia, and Austria, and as well in Hungary, Sweden, France, some of the Italian states, and even to a degree in England, which in so many other ways provides exceptions to the pattern of developments elsewhere in Europe. While the American Revolution was still in progress, the House of

Commons in committee passed a famous resolution complaining "that the influence of the Crown has increased, is increasing, and ought to be diminished." A motion to that effect was carried by a narrow margin on April 6, 1780.

By then the king's authority in America had been practically demolished and his imperial interests elsewhere in the world were being seriously challenged. America was already far on its way to securing its own independent destiny. The men who had led America to independence quite naturally based their case for separation from England upon the differences rather than the likenesses between the two countries. Yet, however important those differences may have seemed to be, in so many vital ways the new nation that was forming revealed a natural kinship with the old world it professed to reject—not only with England, but with numerous other countries. In his *Common Sense* Thomas Paine castigated the "false, selfish, narrow, and ungenerous" notion that England was the parent, or mother country of America. "Europe, and not England," he protested, "is the parent country of America." The New World had for years, he added, offered asylum to the persecuted lovers of civil and religious liberty "from every part of Europe." That observation was heartily endorsed just a few years later by Michel-Guillaume Jean de Crèvecoeur, former French soldier and sometime resident of New York, in his *Letters from an American Farmer*. "What then is the American, this new man?" he asked in a widely quoted passage from that book. "He is either an European, or the descendant of an European, hence that strange mixture of blood, which you will find in no other country. . . . Here individuals of all nations are melted into a new race of men, whose labours and posterity will one day cause great changes in the world."

Such observations were justified. One-third of the men who signed the Declaration of Independence were of non-English stock, eight being first-generation immigrants. It was in recognition of the mixed European background of so many Americans that John Adams, Benjamin Franklin, and Thomas Jefferson later proposed that the official seal of the United States bear the national emblems of Scotland, Ireland, France, Germany, and Holland as well as of England, thus "pointing out the countries from which these States have been peopled." (This idea was abandoned.) The list might well have been much longer. There were Jews from eastern Europe and from Spain and Portugal (via South America), Swedes, Walloons, Swiss, and still others. Many came, as Paine stated, in search of asylum. But they also came with an intent to preserve and refresh in the free air of the New World those aspects of life in their homelands which they best remembered and most highly valued.

In the world of 1776, despite its highly combustible international contentions, Europe boasted a rich civilization, alive with dynamic ideas and with flourishing arts, with promising new concepts and methods in the sciences. The rudiments of modern industry and business administration were well founded and social reforms were being undertaken. These original and powerful gifts Europeans took with them as they colonized and traded about the world. They had come in contact with the great civilizations of the East, above all, with that of China, and this experience added significantly to the cosmopolitan culture of the Continent. The Pacific Ocean had been explored and Australasia discovered, and the new knowledge gleaned from such expeditions was accelerating an ecological revolution of universal importance. This abundance of experience and knowledge that characterized the world of 1776 as outlined in the following pages, was the inheritance America shared as a birthright.

A TIME OF

"There is something exceedingly ridiculous in the composition of Monarchy; it first excludes a man from the means of information, yet empowers him to act in cases where the highest judgment is required. The state of a king shuts him from the World, yet the business of a king requires him to know it thoroughly...."

Thomas Paine in *Common Sense*

The reigning sovereigns who exercised such ultimate authority in the world of 1776 were a mixed bag of individuals. Their separate monarchical dictates stamped the times with bold and variegated designs that all but covered the globe. The most absolute of those rulers and in some ways the outstanding personage among them was Frederick the Great of Prussia. He was, Goethe wrote with an admiration that was widely shared, "the polar star, who seemed to turn about himself Germany, Europe, nay the whole world." There were others, as we have seen, who acknowledged the the man's accomplishments, but who found little to admire in them.

Nothing in his childhood remotely suggested that Frederick would in his maturity become a warrior-despot of fearsome reputation. Indeed, his father, Frederick William I, long despaired even of making a man of the small, delicate, and studious boy who loved to play his flute and yearned, against his parent's proscription, to learn Latin and ancient history. To the king's extreme disgust the lad also showed an early liking for Frenchified ways, for French literature and music. The father was a decidedly sick man with the temperament of a sadistic army sergeant. He was the first king habitually to wear a military uniform, and he indulged a monomaniacal passion for drilling his regiment of hand-picked giants, all more than six feet tall, whom he recruited and dragooned into his service from all over Europe. (One Irishman of enviable height was kidnaped in the streets of London; a very tall Austrian diplomat was seized as he was entering a hackney cab, but he managed to extricate himself

16

ABSOLUTISM

from that surprising and highly undiplomatic situation before being obliged to march in rank for the Prussian monarch.)

Although the 275-pound king repeatedly beat his small son for any or no disciplinary reason, knocked him down or dragged him through the mud by his hair, by his father's whimsical standards the boy remained incorrigible. In 1730, when the prince was eighteen years of age, he conspired with a loyal and sympathetic friend to flee to England for refuge from such punishing treatment. When their plan was discovered, both were charged with desertion and sentenced to death. Through the intervention of the Austrian ambassador, Frederick's life was spared, although he was cast into prison; however, not before being forced to watch as his faithful comrade's head fell to the executioner's axe while the young conspirator was waving adieu to his beloved prince—who fainted at the gruesome sight.

Yet this was the youth who succeeded to the throne in 1740 and who soon began to prove himself a far greater military commander than his father had ever been before him—a man whose exploits in the field Napoleon later studied and admired. In his first military adventure as king, undertaken almost before his father was cold in the grave, Frederick invaded and occupied the rich neighboring Austrian province of Silesia, whose resources he needed to bolster the economy of his country—without bothering to declare war and without regard for his country's pledge to support the sovereignty of the new young Hapsburg empress Maria Theresa. With this act of "selfish rapacity," wrote the British

When Frederick the Great of Prussia invaded and captured Silesia from Austria in 1740, the result was years of warfare. Punctuated by several truces and one formal treaty of peace—signed at Aix-la-Chapelle in 1748—the hostilities continued until 1763. The plate seen above commemorated the Treaty of Aix-la-Chapelle, which awarded control of Silesia to Prussia.

METROPOLITAN MUSEUM OF ART

historian Thomas Macaulay, Frederick was responsible for setting all Europe on fire. His brazen act did indeed trigger a new wave of hostilities that not only spread across the Continent, but, by bringing France and Great Britain once more into conflict, reached to far places. Thus, continued Macaulay, because of that one quick maneuver by Frederick, "black men fought on the coast of Coromandel and red men scalped each other by the Great Lakes of North America." But Frederick kept Silesia, and the world learned that he was to be feared and not to be trusted.

Shortly thereafter, in the Seven Years' War, he was faced by a formidable coalition of enemies, but by brilliant strategy and with some good luck Frederick again emerged victorious. At more than one point in the conflict his cause seemed so hopeless that he considered suicide. In his desperation he had to commit his precious army without regard for losses. If Russia had not withdrawn from the enemy coalition at the last moment, Frederick's empire would have been extinguished. (In January, 1762, the Empress Elizabeth of Russia had a fatal stroke on leaving church, and her successor, the demented Peter III, who idolized Frederick and called him "the king my master," immediately reversed Russia's role in the war and neutralized his troops in the field. Only a few months later Peter was done away with in a coup d'état, but meanwhile Prussia was saved.) The cost in both men and resources proved unbearably high, and in the future Frederick shied from further warfare to spare his means. "Henceforth," he wrote, "I would not attack a cat except in self-defense." However, he kept his superb army always at the ready, as a weapon held in respect by rival states. With his least move, Frederick remarked later in his life, he was suspected of planning to upset the balance of power in Europe.

By the peace of 1763 Frederick retained and consolidated earlier territorial gains, and he would soon add to them, without going to war, through the first partition of Poland, as earlier mentioned. His successful challenge to Austrian leadership among the German states was one of the most important political developments in eighteenth-century Europe, one that held major significance for the future as the two great houses of Hapsburg in Austria, caretakers of the ancient Holy Roman Empire, and the upstart Hohenzollern monarchs of Prussia vied for hegemony over the miscellaneous assemblage of German principalities. (A century later Otto von Bismarck, "the Iron Chancellor," had William I of Prussia proclaimed emperor of Germany. The subsequent history of Prussia was that of Germany.)

When Frederick returned in triumph to Berlin in 1763 he was a battle-weary, weather-beaten, prematurely gray man of fifty-one, habitually dressed in a worn and faded uniform and three-cornered hat—"Old Fritz," as his subjects familarly dubbed him. Freed from the demanding chores of warring, he immediately immersed himself in the internal affairs of state, which seriously needed attention. Compared to its neighbors, Prussia was a very small country, but in terms of military power and administrative efficiency, it became a model for the others. Building on foundations laid by his father, Frederick ran the nation through the most rigid of bureaucracies, which he personally supervised with tireless vigilance. With the heavy burden of his military machine to carry, he watched every penny and every move; there was no room for even the smallest waste. He demanded and received total loyalty from the Junkers, members of the landed aristocracy who provided the officers for his army and incorruptible, if highly privileged, civil servants for the government.

Frederick himself was Prussia's most devoted servant. The remaining peaceful years of his life gave him the opportunities he craved to transform the country into a "modern" state. He undertook to reform the judicial system and the courts that administered the laws of the land. The promptness and efficiency of Prussian justice soon surpassed anything that had been known on the Continent. He improved the educational system and graced Berlin with palaces and public buildings, although he himself preferred his relatively modest rococo palace, Sans Souci, at Potsdam. There he continued to play his flute and, following the obsequious editorial guidance of Voltaire, to indulge his taste for French literature and culture.

To the advanced intellectuals of the time Frederick seemed the enlightened despot par excellence. He was cynical and pragmatic, ruling his land by his own self-constituted authority with no nonsense about divine right. He scarcely disguised his opinion that all religious orthodoxies were fraudulent or, what was worse, stupid. In the Age of Reason it seemed that Frederick was ruling his subjects in a highly rational manner, industriously, realistically, and with no idle show of traditional pomp and ceremony. His subjects did not all feel so heartened by his rule. His primary interest was in the state as a power, and that state was, in effect, the private estate of the Hohenzollerns, that power enhanced the glory of the Hohenzollerns. Frederick owned it as he owned his subjects. For those subjects he felt on the whole only contempt. With the gross favoritism he showed the Junkers who served him well as functionaries of the state, Frederick remained largely indifferent to the lot of the mass of peasants, or serfs, upon whom the economic burdens of the country fell, as of old. "Let somebody raise his voice for the rights of subjects or against exploitation and despotism," wrote the contemporary German dramatist and writer Gotthold Lessing, "and you will soon see [in Prussia] which is the most slavish land in Europe."

Actually, Frederick had little true affection for anything German—German culture, German speech, German literature. There was some truth in Vol-

In the first half of the eighteenth century Poland was the third largest state in Europe; by the end of the century it no longer existed. Poland was weak and vulnerable because the king was chosen and controlled by the nobles. The painting above shows the election of Stanislas Poniatowski outside Warsaw in 1764. Just four years later Stanislas, unable to suppress fighting between Catholics and non-Catholics, called in Russian troops to restore order. Poland's political chaos and military impotence made it an inviting target for the surrounding monarchs, who used religious persecution to justify their first partition in 1772. Prussia, Russia, and Austria grabbed additional territory in 1793 and completed the liquidation of Poland two years later.

NATIONAL MUSEUM OF WARSAW

taire's caustic taunt that in Frederick's kingdom Germans used their native tongue only to address servants and animals. When critics complained that his rule did not provide the progressive freedom enjoyed by, say, Englishmen, Frederick retorted with small respect for his countrymen that after all he ruled over Prussians not Englishmen. His autocratic measures built an impressive superstructure on foundations that, lacking his commanding presence, would crumble under any serious pressure from without. So it happened within twenty years after his death when Napoleon's troops surged across the Prussian borders. As Madame de Staël remarked from the scene at that time, Germany seemed to lack any national spirit. Frederick had seen to that. However, in his cynical conviction that the moral rights and human needs of the individual must be sacrificed to the interests of the state, he had established in the German mind and heart the doctrine of *realpolitik*, which in the future would bring so much misery to mankind.

In neighboring Austria, Maria Theresa, archduchess of Austria, queen of Hungary and Bohemia, and wife of the Holy Roman Emperor, did more to improve the lot of the serf than any other eighteenth-century ruler in eastern Europe, except for her own son Joseph II. Whatever humane motives persuaded her to do so, they were coupled with a shrewd perception that in relieving this large mass of the population from its ancient feudal bondage to noble landlords she was creating another source of tax revenue. She was here far more enlightened and progressive than Frederick.

When she came to the throne in 1740 (the same year that Frederick's rule began) she was young—twenty-three years old—beautiful, and inexperienced. She was also intelligent, strong-willed, courageous, and extremely resourceful. Although forthright and sincere, she instinctively understood how to exploit her charm in the game of power politics. She knew when to plead rather than command. In 1741 when, following Frederick's seizure of Silesia, her king-

Frederick the Great (above) and Maria Theresa were lifelong enemies (below, they play diplomatic chess as Mars looks on); but in his book on the Seven Years' War Frederick revealed his admiration for the empress. She had brought order and economy to her country's finances, he wrote; she improved and supervised the discipline of her army, and established a well-staffed military academy in Vienna. "This woman's achievements," Frederick concluded, "were those of a great man."

dom was assailed from all sides by hostile forces, the young queen made a dramatic appearance in Hungary to accept the crown of St. Stephen and to seek Hungarian support for her cause. Although Hungary was nominally a dependency of Austria, the Hungarians were volatile, turbulent, and fiercely defensive of their independent privileges. Only forty years earlier they had been in open rebellion against Hapsburg suzerainty and still had not forgotten their crushing defeat at that time. The queen's advisers warned her not to go through with the planned visit.

However, instead of asserting her royal will, Maria Theresa implored the Hungarian constituents to defend her, an outraged woman, from her assailants. The story was that as she eloquently pleaded with the dour Magyars, she held aloft her infant child to emphasize her role as a young and tender mother in need of succor. "Forsaken by all," she cried, "we place our sole resource in the fidelity, arms and long-tried valour of the Hungarians. . . ." Whatever the facts of the occasion, she inflamed the chivalrous feelings of her audience (as no man could have done), and the Hungarian nobles pledged their "blood and life" to support her, and provided one hundred thousand soldiers. In later years, returning from the opera one evening, Maria Theresa remarked to her husband that the singer they had heard was the greatest of all actresses; to which he replied, "except yourself, Madam."

For forty years, from her accession to the throne until her death in 1780, Maria Theresa played a vigorous and significant part in the wars and politics of Europe. Her family, the Hapsburgs, had been the ruling house of Austria since 1282 (and would continue to be until 1918). By tradition the head of the house had been elected Holy Roman Emperor since 1438. In the sixteenth century Hapsburgs ruled an empire "where the sun never set," reaching from Peru to the Carpathians. However, by the time of Maria Theresa's accession the family holdings had shriveled to a relatively paltry, sprawling domain peopled by

This lead statue commemorated Maria Theresa's coronation in 1741 as queen of Hungary ("queen" to everyone else; to the proud Magyars, unable to accept the idea of a female sovereign, "our Mistress and King"). While she was still in Hungary for the coronation, the French army threatened Vienna. Maria summoned the Hungarian Diet and spoke to them in Latin. The Diet voted to raise and equip an army to defend Maria and so played a critical role in ensuring Austria's survival.
OSTERREICHISCHE GALERIE, VIENNA

many discordant elements (Germans, Magyars, Czechs, Slovaks, Slovenes, Croats, Italians, and Flemings) without common interests, loosely held together only by traditional attachments to Hapsburg Austria, and surrounded by vigilant and intriguing powers—powers that saw in the new young queen a likely victim of their plans for aggrandizement.

With that unpromising inheritance Maria Theresa proceeded to demonstrate that she was one of the most capable in all the long line of Hapsburg sovereigns. At the very beginning of her reign she lost the precious province of Silesia to Frederick, to be sure, and this early, very harsh lesson in forceful "diplomacy" she could not forget. But by wile and intelligence, through experience and shrewdly chosen advice, she held off her other enemies as she methodically consolidated control over her own lands—all this while bearing sixteen children. Throughout years of intense strain, even while she was battling with half of Europe and until the weight of years slowed such activities, she indulged her irrepressible high spirits by dancing, playing cards, and in other festive pursuits. Meanwhile, once her rule was firmly secured over the challenge of her enemies, she attended to the completion of her great palace of Schönbrunn, with its 1,441 rooms, 139 kitchens, and other accommodations. (It was here that the boy Mozart astonished his royal audience with his great virtuosity.) When the English, who helped finance her war with France, complained that she was wastefully extravagant with their funds, Maria Theresa replied, in perfectly good faith, that all their money went to the military; for palace-building, she explained, she turned to the Jewish moneylenders.

For all her gaity and extravagance, Maria Theresa was a virtuous, devout, and conscientious queen. Her court was the most moral in Europe. (At one point she went so far as to establish a "Chastity Commission" through which to discipline those ladies whose sexual morals did not accord with her own lofty standards.) Like Frederick and other contemporary sovereigns, she realized that to survive, the administration of her country must be reformed, that she must replace the territorial controls of nobles in their various diets with power centralized in her own queenly office, that local governments of traditional patterns must be converted into an impersonal, responsible bureaucracy. Courses for training bureaucrats were instituted, and in good season Austria became the most completely bureaucratic state in Europe, a measure that enveloped the multilingual, heterogeneous mass of her subjects with a semblance of uniformity. To further that end, German was made the official language.

Maria Theresa, and Joseph after her, had in Wenzel Kaunitz an adviser who was one of the most astute statesmen of the times. Frederick the Great described Kaunitz as "a solemn, arrogant, mouthing, brow-beating kind of man, with a clear intellect twisted by perversities of temper, especially by a self-conceit and arrogance which are boundless." He had reason to resent him, for it was Kaunitz who negotiated an alliance with France, Austria's traditional enemy, thus reversing three hundred years of Hapsburg diplomacy and winning badly needed support in contesting the power of Prussia. It was to further secure that alliance that in 1770 Maria Theresa married her fifteen-year-old daughter Maria Antonia to the French dauphin as Marie Antoinette, to become queen of France when her husband was crowned as Louis XVI. Even her maternal feelings were subordinated to the interests of the state. For all her moral scruples, Maria Theresa advised the girl to be polite to the mistresses of Louis XV in order that the relations between the two courts might remain ami-

Count Wenzel Anton von Kaunitz, a close adviser to the Austrian crown, brilliantly directed government policies for forty years.

cable. In 1775 when Marie Antionette was queen, her mother cautioned her to behave more sensibly than had been her wont. "Your luck can all too easily change," the empress wrote, prophetically, "and by your own fault you may well find yourself plunged into deepest misery. . . . One day you will recognize the truth of this, but then it will be too late."

The reforms instituted by the queen were achieved with the earnest support of her first-born son who, as Joseph II, in 1765 became her co-regent and the emperor. Joseph's zeal outstripped his mother's determination, which led to bitter altercations between the two. He carried Maria Theresa's humane principles to idealistic extremes. Her late adored husband, the Emperor Francis I, had been irresolute and ineffectual, although she loved him none the less for that; following his death she went into widow's weeds, which she wore for the rest of her life. Her son, on the other hand, was single-minded, high-minded, and excessively self-willed. He was the epitome of the benevolent despot, both more autocratic and less realistic than his mother.

Joseph loathed ignorance, and gave Austria the finest educational system in Europe, although that system was regimented to a degree that was almost intolerable to the professors and students alike. To the Marquis de Mirabeau it seemed that "even their souls" were put in uniform. Although a devout Catholic in matters of dogma, Joseph secularized the schools and ordered religious toleration throughout the state, except for atheists and deists. He granted Jews some civil rights and even created Jewish nobles, to the dismay of the blooded aristocrats. For the well-born and the rich he held only contempt and, withdrawing their immunities, insisted that the nobles of the land pay taxes on an equal footing with everyone else. He also decreed that they must suffer punishment for their crimes like everyone else. One titled personage accused of committing forgery was chained to common convicts and forced to sweep the Vienna streets.

Thus Joseph proceeded in the most arbitrary fashion to convert his state into his image of what a state should be. "The state," he remarked, in advance of his time, meant "the greatest good for the greatest number." Much that he did was

TEXT CONTINUED ON PAGE 26

"Her person was formed to wear a crown, and her mind to give luster to the exalted dignity of her position; she possessed a most commanding figure, great beauty . . . and an intrepidity above her sex."

British ambassador to
the court of Maria Theresa

Voltaire and Frederick the Great corresponded frequently with each other; these excerpts span a period of thirty years

From Frederick

Although I have not the satisfaction of knowing you personally, you, are none the less known to me by your works. They are treasures of the mind, if the expression may be allowed, and compositions elaborated with so much taste, delicacy, and art, that their beauties appear new each time they are reread. I feel I have discovered in them the character of their ingenious author, who does honour to our age and to the human mind. The great men of modern times will one day be obliged to you, and to you alone. . . . If among your manuscripts there should be any which, with necessary prudence, you think fit to hide from the public eye, I promise you to keep it secret and to content myself with applauding it in private.

From Voltaire

Be certain there have been no truly good kings except those who began like you, by educating themselves, by learning to know men, by loving the truth, by detesting persecution and superstition. Any prince who thinks in this way can bring back the golden age to his dominions. Why do so few kings seek out this advantage? You perceive the reason, Monseigneur; it is because almost all of them think more of royalty than of humanity: you do precisely the opposite.

From Voltaire

In vain does human reason perfect itself by philosophy, which makes such progress in Europe; in vain, great prince, do you strive to practise and to inspire this humane philosophy; in this very age, when reason lifts her throne on the one side, we see the absurd fanaticism still build its altars on the other.

From Voltaire

I know not how to behave with a king, but I am perfectly at ease with a real man, with a man who has the love of the human race in his head and in his heart.

From Frederick

We are not the masters of our fate, my dear Voltaire. We are borne along by the whirlwind of events and we must allow ourselves to be carried with them. I beg you will see in me nothing but a zealous citizen, a rather sceptical philosopher and a really faithful friend. For God's sake, write to me as a man and, like me, scorn titles, names and all exterior pomp.

From Frederick

I began by increasing the forces of the state by 16 battalions, 5 squadrons of hussars and a squadron of body-guards. I have laid the foundations of our new Academy. I have acquired Wolff, Maupertuis, Vaucanson and Algarotti. I am awaiting replies from s'Gravesande and Euler. I have established a new college for commerce and manufactures; I am engaging painters and sculptors; and I am just leaving for Prussia to receive the homage, etc., without the holy ampulla and without the useless and frivolous ceremonies established by ignorance and superstition and supported by custom.

From Voltaire

It seems to me obvious that God meant us to live in society, even as He gave bees the instinct and instruments proper to make honey. Since our society could not exist without the ideas of justice and injustice, he gave us the means of acquiring them.

From Frederick

I am now reading or rather devouring your *Age of Louis the Great*. If you love me, send me what you have added recently to this work; 'tis my sole consolation, my amusement, my recreation. You who only work from choice and genius, have pity on a political labourer, who only works from necessity.

From Voltaire

Yes, Sire, setting aside heroism, throne, victories, all that imposes the most profound respect, I take the liberty, as you know, to love you with all my heart; but I should be unworthy of loving you to that extent and of being loved by your Majesty if for the sake of the greatest man of his age I should desert another great man who it is true, wears a mob-cap [Madame du Châtelet], but whose heart is as masculine as yours and whose courageous and unshakable friendship during ten years imposes upon me the duty of living near her.

From Frederick

You protest because I think you have a passion for the Marquise du Châtelet. . . . In any case, you have promised to sacrifice some of your days to me; and that is sufficient for me. The more I think that to be absent from the Marquise costs you some effort, the more grateful I shall be to you. Beware of undeceiving me.

From Voltaire

Experience and reason convince me that we are machines made to run a certain time and as God pleases.

From Frederick

In society tolerance should guarantee to everyone the liberty to believe what he likes; but this tolerance should not be extended so far as to authorise the effrontery and licence of young scatter-brains who audaciously insult what the people revere. These are my sentiments, which are in conformity with that which assures liberty and public safety, the first object of every legislation.

AMERICAN NUMISMATIC SOCIETY

Catherine the Great indefatigably wrote down her thoughts on everything—from personal feeling to matters of state.

From the Memoirs

Happiness and unhappiness are in the heart and soul of everyone: if you are unhappy, put yourself above this unhappiness and arrange for your happiness not to depend on any outside factor. This was the disposition of mind with which I had been born; I was endowed with great sensibility and a face that was at least interesting and pleasing at first glance, without any artifice or pretence. My spirit was so conciliatory that no one ever spent a quarter of an hour with me without being at their ease and conversing as though they had known me for a long time.

Naturally tolerant, I easily attracted the confidence of those who had anything to do with me, because they felt that meticulous honesty and goodwill were the qualities that I evinced most readily. If I may venture to be frank, I would say about myself that I was every inch a gentleman with a mind much more male than female; but together with this I was anything but masculine and combined with the mind and temperament of a man, the attractions of a lovable woman. I pray to be forgiven for this description which is justified by its truthfulness and which my vanity admits without any pretence at false modesty.

Besides, all that I have been writing should be sufficient proof of what I say about my brain, my heart, and my temperament.

I have just said that I was attractive. Consequently one half of the road to temptation was already covered and tis only human in such situations that one should not stop halfway. For to tempt and to be tempted are closely allied; and in spite of all the finest moral maxims buried in the mind, when emotion interferes, when feeling makes its appearance, one is already much further involved than one realizes, and I have still not learnt how to prevent its appearance. Perhaps escape is the only solution, but there are situations, circum-

stances, when escape is impossible, for how can one escape, be elusive, turn one's back, in the atmosphere of a Court? Such an act might give food for talk. And if you do not run away, nothing is more difficult, in my opinion, than to avoid something that fundamentally attracts you. Statements to the contrary could only be prudish and not inspired by a human heart. One cannot hold one's heart

in one's hand, forcing it or releasing it, tightening or relaxing one's grasp at will.

On moral ideals

Study mankind, learn to use men without surrendering to them unreservedly. Search for true merit, be it at the other end of the world, for usually it is modest and retiring. Virtue does not shine through a crowd, it is neither eager nor greedy and remains easily forgotten.

Do not allow yourself to become the prey of flatterers; make them understand that you care neither for praise nor meanness.

Have confidence in those who have the courage to contradict you if necessary and who place more value on your reputation than on your favour.

Be gentle, humane, accessible, compassionate, and liberal-minded: do not let your grandeur prevent you from condescending with kindness towards the small and putting yourselves in their place. See that this kindness, however, does not weaken

your authority nor diminish their respect. Listen to anything which seems to deserve attention. Behave so that the kind love you, the evil fear you, and all respect you.

Preserve in yourself those qualities of the spirit which form the character of the honest man, the great man and the hero; reject all artificiality, do not allow the world to contaminate you to the point of making you lose the ancient principles of honour and virtue. Great men do not know duplicity, they despise it.

I swear by Providence to stamp these words in my heart and in the hearts of those who will read them after me.

On law making

It is the greatest Happiness for a Man to be so circumstanced, that, if his Passions should prompt him to be mischievous, he should still think it more for his Interest not to give Way to them.

The Laws ought to be so framed, as to secure the Safety of every Citizen as much as possible.

The Equality of the Citizens consists in this; that they should all be subject to the same Laws.

This Equality requires Institutions so well adapted, as to prevent the Rich from oppressing those who are not so wealthy as themselves. . . .

In a State or Assemblage of People that live together in a Community, where there are Laws, Liberty can only consist *in doing that which every One ought to do,* and *not to be constrained to do that which One ought not to do.*

A Man ought to form in his own Mind an exact and clear Idea of what Liberty is. *Liberty is the Right of doing whatsoever the Laws allow:* And if any one Citizen could do what the Laws forbid, there would be no more Liberty; because others would have an equal Power of doing the same.

The Russian empire ranged from Armenia to Lapland, from the Ukraine to Siberia, encompassing many diverse peoples. Catherine the Great commissioned the engravings reproduced above for a book about traveling through Russia.

in conflict with his mother's policies, or went far beyond her more orderly approach to problems. Where she had judiciously regulated serfdom, he simply abolished it. He challenged the pope and expelled the Jesuits from Austrian territory (as was also done in France, Spain and Portugal) and used some of the large endowments of their schools and monasteries to subsidize education, hospitals, and public works. (The foundations of Vienna's reputation as a medical center were laid by such measures.)

In the end, it must be added, Joseph's reforms were too many, too drastic, and too abrupt for the public to accept and abide by. What his mother accomplished was permanently gained. From the end of the Seven Years' War until her death in 1780, Austria was a revolutionary and dynamic force in German affairs, as Prussia remained quiescent and by Frederick's policy conservative. What Joseph attempted in his zeal finally brought his empire close to a general rebellion. He attempted a social revolution by edict, and failed. Revolutions, it appeared, would not be imposed from above; they would erupt from the public will. Such were the limitations imposed on even the most despotic and enlightened power by tradition and circumstance.

Shortly before she died, Maria Theresa wrote Marie Antoinette to complain that Catherine the Great, "that Russian monster of depravity," was incessantly plotting against both France and Austria in her imperial schemes. To Maria, Catherine was a godless whore. "I cannot describe the horror and aversion she inspires in me," she wrote her daughter. But Joseph rather admired the Russian empress as a successful empire builder. Over the protestations of his mother, but supported by Kaunitz, he had joined both Catherine and Frederick in the first partition of Poland in 1772. (Maria Theresa had sincere moral objections to the rape of this friendly and helpless Catholic neighbor and did not particularly covet the territory thus gained, which added further heterogeneous elements to Austria's already complex ethnic structure. However, she was persuaded to accede to the take-over. Frederick observed with customary cynicism, "She weeps, but she takes.")

As a young girl Catherine showed as little promise as Frederick had in his youth of becoming a militant and forceful ruler. She was born to an obscure German princeling with little hope of grandeur in her future. However, as a teenager this Princess Sophie Frederica Augusta of Amhalt-Zerbst, known in the family as "Figgy," was summoned to St. Petersburg by Elizabeth of Russia, who had seen the girl's portrait, to be looked over as a possible bride for that

empress' nephew and heir, the Grand Duke Peter, himself but a lad, notorious for his boorishness and bad manners. Nevertheless, as prospective emperor of Russia, the German-born boy was the most eligible bachelor in all Europe. The girl's father was in the pay of Frederick, who looked to such a match to further his interests at the Russian court where he had many enemies. He had little idea what a formidable empress his child-candidate would one day become.

In Russia the buxom girl passed muster. "Her health is known to be good," observed the Empress Elizabeth. "I want them to have a large family." The wedding ceremony was duly performed, but the marriage was never consummated. The Grand Duke was not only childish, he was also impotent. He liked to play with his toy soldiers or, when drunk, to torture his pets. He was deficient in both mind and body. The virgin bride put up with him, and with his obsessively suspicious aunt who for a time had the young couple virtually imprisoned in their quarters and Catherine ("Figgy" had changed her name with her marriage) held incommunicado.

"For eighteen years," Catherine recalled in her memoirs, "I lived a life that would have rendered ten other women mad, and twenty others in my place would have died of a broken heart." But she persevered. She accepted the orthodox faith, and in other respects metamorphized herself into a Russian. "God is my witness," she wrote, "that the glory of this country is my glory." She read widely and as circumstances permitted took lovers to her bed and had children by several of them. Then, in 1762, Peter succeeded to the throne and Catherine became czarina.

It took Peter III a mere six months to earn vast unpopularity with all manner of Russians. One of his first monumental mistakes was to make peace with Russia's "bitterest enemy" but Peter's own hero, Frederick the Great, returning all territory Russian troops had won and permitting Frederick to emerge from the Seven Years' War with his nation miraculously intact. Such were the various grievances held against Peter that in June, 1762, Catherine's current lover, Grigori Orlov, could accomplish a bloodless palace revolt, depose the emperor, and proclaim Catherine "autocrat" of Russia in his stead. Peter went off to exile, sneered Frederick, "like a child being sent to sleep." Within several weeks he died under mysterious circumstances. A statement was issued that a seizure of "hemorrhoidal colic" had done him in, which led the French philosopher d'Alembert to snicker that hemorrhoids were a serious malady in Russia. The

"Liberty, the core of everything, without you there would be no life! I want the laws to be obeyed, but I want no slaves. My general aim is to create happiness, without all the whimsicality, eccentricity, and tyranny which destroy it."

Catherine the Great

more common rumor was that Catherine had had her husband murdered. (Ivan VI, who had briefly ruled a score of years earlier, was still alive in prison, and after a short while Catherine also had him murdered as a further precaution.) In his overt adulation of the empress Voltaire brushed aside Peter's homicide as inconsequential. "People blame her for a few trifles in regard to her husband," he wrote the celebrated bluestocking Madame du Deffand, "but that is a domestic issue with which I have no concern."

The belief prevailed that Catherine's reign would be brief. So Frederick was advised by his ambassador in Russia. She had no valid claim to the throne she occupied; a "godless foreign usurper," as one adversary within the state called her. The nobility had, in effect, put her there, as they had raised other Russian monarchs in past palace revolutions—and they could take her down, as they had deposed other monarchs in Russia's turbulent history. She had assumed control of a sizeable area of the globe peopled by heterogeneous and discordant elements. She was still a relatively young woman. Outside the capital, public opinion was hostile to her, and outside Russia, the world was tensely concerned over the precarious balance of power which a new and untried monarch might so easily upset to the hazard of all.

Actually, Catherine would rule her land for thirty-four years, until her death in 1796—a reign charged with important events and developments, all of which bore the imprints of her majestic will. She may have been the greatest woman ruler of all time. Her first proclamation as empress denounced Peter's peace treaty with Frederick, whom she characterized as "a disturber of the peace," although she maintained an overtly amicable relationship with the Prussian king as a security measure. She needed peace in that quarter of Europe if she was to proceed with her imperial plans.

Before beginning the partition of Poland in which Frederick would join her, she made that country a virtual Russian protectorate by putting one of her former lovers, Stanislas Poniatowski, on the throne as Stanislas II. (Eventually, in the final partition, she received the lion's share of Polish territory without regard for Stanislas, who ended his unhappy days in a St. Petersburg prison.) Then, in 1768, Catherine went to war with Turkey, concluding that struggle with a treaty signed in 1774, which made Russia the dominant power in the Middle East. By also acquiring territories to the west she extended the Russian frontiers into the heart of central Europe. At one point during the American Revolution a report reached Detroit by way of Montreal that Russian troops, twelve thousand strong, had surged as far west as New York. That unlikely story stemmed from the well-known fact that George III had asked Catherine for mercenaries to help suppress his rebellious colonies, but the empress had no intention of becoming involved in the far distant west—except, to be sure, to encourage settlements in Alaska.

In all she did, Catherine's intention was to establish her absolute rule in the empire she had taken over. This she accomplished, although like all other monarchs, she had to acknowledge that there were limits to absolutism. Like her fellow rulers, Catherine was to a degree a prisoner of precedent and of history. She learned that she could not discreetly abrogate or alter the traditional privileges of the nobility, for example, in particular their total, feudal command over the serfs of the land—that is, over by far the largest part of the population of the enormous, conglomerate state. Indeed, by her lavish gifts of crown lands to her lovers and favorites, Catherine even extended the scope of the nobles' authority

After suffering severe defeats in the second of the Russo-Turkish wars with Catherine the Great, Selim III, sultan of the extensive Ottoman empire, made peace in 1792. Russia obtained the Black Sea coast between the Bug and Dniester rivers and the Crimea.

over her oppressed subjects, who sank ever deeper into virtual slavery.

However, in 1766, with a fine gesture, Catherine offered a prize for the best essay on the emancipation of the serfs. Whatever ideas she may have entertained in that direction were given a violent jolt just before the commencement of the American Revolution. For years past there had been spasmodic outbursts by peasants, desperately protesting their miserable life. Within little more than a decade, from 1762 to 1773, there were forty revolts within the empire, but these had been summarily quashed by government forces. Then, in 1773, a Cossack veteran of the Seven Years' War and the Turkish war, Emilyan Pugachev, gathered around him a horde of the discontented, and started a march on Moscow. He proclaimed that he was really Peter III, miraculously saved from Catherine's attempt to murder him. As he forged triumphantly onward, thousands flocked to his standard—Cossacks, escaped criminals, fugitive serfs, and renegades of every stripe—burning and pillaging village after village with savage zest as they went.

Catherine tried to pass the trouble off as a minor disturbance. "Do not, I beg of you, believe all you read in the papers," she wrote her correspondents abroad. "That *marquis de Pougacheff* has been rather tiresome, but I mean to settle the business very soon. It is a purely local rebellion. . . ." Actually, the struggle dragged on for two years before Catherine, alarmed by the scale and intensity of the conflict, sent a full-fledged, disciplined imperial army to put a very bloody end to the matter. Pugachev was brought to Moscow in an iron cage, was beheaded and quartered. His head was stuck on a pole and shown about the city as a warning to others who might be tempted to question the empress' final and absolute authority.

That unpleasant episode dampened some of Catherine's fondest dreams of reform and intensified her passion to govern as the complete autocrat. As another by-product, that revolt had strengthened her alliance with the nobles. Among them she found many councilors—but none were counselors. She might well have said with Louis XIV, "*L'état, c'est moi.*" Her system for choosing ministers was unique. She chose as her bedfellows men who were not only physically impressive, but trusted and capable in other matters of state. Each in his turn served as her prime minister until he was dismissed, usually bearing away costly gifts from the empress, and replaced by her next favorite. "I am serving the Empire in educating competent youths," she once wrote in explaining the nature of her amorous routine.

In principle Catherine was conspicuously one of those so-called enlightened despots who gave European monarchy a remarkable cast in the eighteenth century. She read the works of such advanced minds as Montesquieu, Diderot, d'Alembert, Grimm, and, of course, Voltaire; and through her correspondence and association with some of these *philosophes*, as they were called, managed to use them as publicity agents to improve her image beyond Russia. She turned to them and to others like them for advice on the political, legal, and social reforms she hoped to undertake in Russia. It all made excellent propaganda, but such bright prospects of rational and progressive changes in Russian life remained largely on paper. However, in thus exposing her countrymen to the liberal thoughts of Western Europe, Catherine was giving a fresh direction to Russian history. To read Voltaire and the other contemporary French writers was to be apprised that individual freedom was every person's birthright, that autocratic and arbitrary power was tyranny,

Catherine (above) named her grandsons Alexander and Constantine, expressing her dream to create a new Christian empire based in Constantinople and subservient to Russia. She never conquered Constantinople, but her victories over Turkey left her power unquestioned.

that slavery was the most degraded condition of man—notions flatly contrary to the deeply rooted traditions of Russian life. To converse about liberty and equality and to continue the ruthless exploitations of the serfs, by which the ruling class in Russia gained its livelihood, was to open a sore in the Russian conscience that would fester at least until the Bolshevik Revolution of 1917. That was inescapably one part of Catherine's legacy to her adopted country. In the end the empress herself became aware of the mischief caused in her land by the circulation of radical ideas. The works of Voltaire were proscribed along with those of other French writers, and Catherine relegated her once-treasured busts of these visionaries to a lumber room where sight of them could no longer distract her from the pragmatic and immediate pursuit of her imperial designs.

At the creative center of this intellectual ferment, in France, those intellectuals also came under official censure. In 1758, to escape molestation by both French and Genevese authorities, Voltaire took up residence at Ferney, just outside Geneva and just inside the French border, and here he remained for twenty years, long exiled from the Paris he so loved. Diderot, whose monumental encyclopedia included contributions from a whole constellation of brilliant minds and embodied all the advanced thought of the eighteenth century, was repeatedly imprisoned, and his great work was twice suppressed because it called attention to the abuses of officialdom and the clergy. Actually, the *Encyclopédie* found its way to all quarters of the state and of Europe. The small southern town of Périgord alone boasted forty subscribers—twenty-four of them priests. Whenever Louis XV himself wanted information on any subject, were it a formula for gunpowder or for lip rouge, Madame de Pompadour would bring him her copy of the forbidden work for his consultation. "The king would find what he was looking for," André Maurois wrote, "and regret the suppression."

No stretch of the imagination could see a despot in either Louis XV or his grandson and successor, Louis XVI. Both were too ineffectual to dominate their administrations; nor did they care to. They reigned, but they did not rule. Louis XV could and did proclaim his absolute power as monarch before the Paris parlement, but that was about as far as he chose to go. He was too cynical and too distracted to enforce those claims, and preferred to leave the direction of his kingdom to his ministers, or to his mistress, Madame de Pompadour, the "prime minister in petticoats," as she was derisively called by those who deplored her influence. She was in regular communication with generals of the army in the field; and it was long believed that it was she who altered France's traditional alliances with the German states against Austria because Frederick the Great had lampooned her in one of his verses whereas Maria Theresa had written her a friendly letter—a diplomatic reversal that led to the disasters of the Seven Years' War. But this probably exaggerates the importance of her privileged and intimate role by the king's side.

The extravagance of the court at Versailles was monumental. In one year a fourth of the government's revenue went to the support of the royal household, with its thousands of horses, hundreds of carriages, armies of servants, and costly rounds of pleasure. Such a burden on the state together with the king's scandalous lechery and the profligacy of his mistresses made Louis an increasingly unpopular monarch. One day he was even stabbed on the streets of Versailles by a malcontent, an assault which apparently astounded no one but Louis himself. He felt obliged to build a special road to take him from Fon-

Both Madame de Pompadour (above), as King Louis XV's maîtresse en résidence, and Marie Antoinette (below), as the wife of Louis XVI, had weighty influence in French political affairs.

tainebleau to Versailles without passing through Paris, where he feared the reception he might get. Neither did Pompadour dare show herself on the streets of that city. When she died in 1764 there was rejoicing. Such was the state of affairs that in 1765 Horace Walpole reported that Parisians had "no time to laugh. There is God and the King to be pulled down first; and men and women, great and small, are devoutly engaged in the demolition." However, when complaints reached Louis that all was not well in his kingdom, he reportedly observed that things as they were would probably last at least through his time. Pompadour had recognized the truth of the times with her memorable and sinister prophecy, "*Après nous le déluge.*"

Louis quickly found other mistresses to help him spend the people's taxes, and he continued to find hunting more engrossing than matters of state. It was said that he knew more about his hounds than he did about his ministers, and that a day without hunting was the day the king did nothing. He had some capable ministers, among them the great Duc de Choiseul, who reorganized the French fighting forces, instituted numerous reforms in the government, and who even supported the publication of Diderot's *Encyclopédie*. At times he overruled and intimidated his royal master. (He had the advantage of Pompadour's friendship.) He remained the king's principal adviser from 1758 to 1770. Most of that time he was preparing France for its coming war of revenge against Great Britain. One of his last acts in office that worked in that direction was to negotiate the marriage of Marie Antoinette with the dauphin. Madame Du Barry was then the reigning mistress at Versailles, and in 1770 a clique surrounding that former prostitute persuaded the king to dismiss Choiseul summarily. Louis still commanded that much power, which he exercised erratically and for reasons not necessarily associated with the welfare of his kingdom.

However, even the voluptuous Du Barry did not satisfy all the king's lust. In 1774 he chose as an additional bedmate a barely nubile youngster. From her Louis contracted smallpox and soon died of that dread malady. His successor, Louis XVI, was barely twenty years of age when he came to the throne, a very young king with not enough will to rule and with an even younger, foreign queen who acted irresponsibly. She referred to her adopted countrymen as "my charming naughty subjects," lacking all understanding of their problems. Her famous solution to the bread shortage, "Let them eat cake," is an apocryphal quotation, but it fairly suggests her attitude. Louis himself truly wanted to be loved by his people, but he was utterly incapable of governing them or guiding their destiny. He spent happy hours riding to the hunt and practicing locksmithing, diversions to which he was passionately attached, while his kingdom seethed with discontents. It was not so much because the general lot was miserable—most of the population was, in fact, relatively well-off—but because there were good reasons why it should be improved. Changes were wanted that would lead in that direction.

Repeatedly in the past the nation had turned to the king to heal its wounds and restore its well-being, to reform abuses and defend the mass of people against oppressive, privileged factions. As a symbol, at least, Louis remained the hope of his subjects, but a fading hope. For the first two years of his reign that hope had flickered more brightly as the immensely capable and reform-minded Anne Robert Turgot served in Louis' ministry as comptroller general of finances. It was a powerful post, and Turgot shared the advanced ideas of the philosophes. (He had been a contributor to the *Encyclopédie*.) He saw nothing

Louis XVI authorized the distribution of engravings such as this one, which shows him plowing a field, to create an image for himself as a man of the people.
BIBLIOTHEQUE NATIONALE

31

anomalous in having the civil and political liberties he envisioned ordained by princely fiat. In fact, he yearned for five years of despotism in France so that he could enlist the ancient prestige of the crown to set men free. Such was the tenacious belief that only absolute monarchical power could guarantee good government. But Louis could never rise to such a challenge. Turgot had earned the hostility of the queen by not favoring her protégés, and she, with other inimical groups jealous of their special privileges, worked for his downfall. Under such dubious pressures from within the court, in 1776 Louis regretfully dismissed Turgot from his cabinet, and the monarchy lost its best chance to cure the ills of France through an enlightened administration. In his retirement Turgot received news of the American Revolution. He wrote to his English liberal friend, the Reverend Dr. Richard Price, that the nation aborning overseas was "the hope of the human race." It might become the model, he wrote, that would show the world that man can be free and yet peaceful, that would compel other governments by its very example to be just and enlightened.

The Spanish ambassador to France in 1776, the brilliant count of Aranda, went even further than Turgot by predicting that the American colonies would in time become one of the great world powers. A dedicated reformer and a convinced encyclopedist, Aranda had done everything in his power to free Spain from its traditional shackles and make it a "modern" European state, and it seemed for a time that the reforms he and other like-minded officials attempted might have a chance of succeeding. The Bourbon king Charles III who had come to the throne in 1759 was, as it was later claimed, "the paradigm of enlightened despotism" in Spain. He had inherited a faith among his subjects that he was "the absolute lord of the lives, the possessions and the honor of us all"; to doubt that credo was in the nature of sacrilege. In the eyes of all but the most skeptical of his people, he ruled by divine right in that most Catholic country.

However, the best intentions of this most liberal monarch could only with difficulty budge his backward state toward the future. Agriculture was still the mainstay of the Spanish economy, and the two largest landholding groups in Spain, the Church and the aristocracy, were entrenched in a complacency that resisted any alien notion of change or progress. The mass of the illiterate peasantry, bound to these groups by ancient custom and authority, had no choice but to live in the unalterable past, and for all his absolute rights, the king could do little enough about it. In 1775 and 1776 an English traveler in Spain remarked of the peasants he observed there: "They feel little or no concern for the welfare of a country, where the surface of the earth is engrossed by a few overgrown families, who seldom bestow a thought on the conditions of their vassals. The poor Spaniard does not work, unless urged by irresistible want, because he perceives no advantage from [his] industry." Even today when asked "How are things?" Spaniards will answer *"No hay novedad"*—a phrase that means "There's nothing new" and implies everything is fine. When Charles compelled the people of Madrid to stop emptying their slops out of windows, the populace objected. (The king observed that they were like children who cried when their faces were washed.) At one point Charles was forced to flee Madrid for his very life before an infuriated Madrid populace, but Aranda came to the rescue and saved the situation. Yet, even in the face of such resistance, aided by his well-chosen officials of state, before he died in 1788 Charles III managed to renovate the economy and general welfare of Spain to a degree that under the circumstances was amazing.

Charles III, king of Naples and Sicily (1735-59), returned to Spain after a twenty-seven-year absence, to succeed his half-brother, Ferdinand VI, as king. About 1785 the Spanish artist Francisco Goya portrayed Charles in his hunting garb.

In the meantime, as the approaching American rebellion generated new international problems and possibilities, Charles' government proceeded with caution, a policy that Aranda with diplomatic nicety termed "dissimulation and serenity." Mindful that he also had important colonies in the New World, and in spite of the enmity he felt for Great Britain, Charles did not openly embrace the cause of the North American colonists, although in June, 1776, he surreptitiously sent them funds through French intermediaries. But when France took up arms in that cause, and as the worldwide stakes grew greater, with its large and staunch fleet Spain joined forces in the struggle to humiliate Britain and divest it of coveted territories in both the Old World and the New.

England confronted this advancing storm under the rule of a king who, whatever else may be said about him, was truly stupid. George III was the first Hanoverian king of England who was born in his kingdom, both his predecessors having been German by birth. He was educated in England and spoke the English language without a foreign accent. His father, Frederick, who died before the death of his own father, George II, was despised not only by his friends and enemies, but, more pathetically, by his parents. George II had married this son of his, "my half-witted coxcomb" as he called the youth, to a princess of Saxe-Gotha, and from that drab union issued a surprising number of children and grandchildren who turned out to be congenital idiots, fitfully insane, or simply odd or wicked. The future George III may have been the best of the lot, but he had obvious limitations. In any case, it was with such a dubious pedigree that he ascended the throne in 1760 at the age of twenty-two.

The year before had been that "year of miracles" when England had won such smashing triumphs over the French toward the end of the Seven Years' War. "In no one year since she was a nation," reported the Annual Register for 1759, "has she been favored with so many successes, both by sea and by land, and in every quarter of the globe." The victories of those times did, in fact, mark a major turning point of history, one which would give direction to the destinies of the world for the centuries to come. In 1757 with England's help the Prussians defeated the French and Austrians at Rossbach, which began the history of modern Germany. That same year at Plassey in distant India Robert Clive's little army, about 3,000-strong, defeated an opposing native force numbering about 64,000, and with that astonishing triumph the history of Britain's empire in the East had its historical beginning. Europe for the first time since the days of Alexander the Great would now have some determining influence on the nations of the Orient. Finally, when Wolfe defeated Montcalm on the Plains of Abraham at Quebec in 1759 and removed the menace of France, the American colonies could breathe their native air more freely. The history of the United States was all unwittingly conceived.

In the realization of its remarkable successes, England flushed with pride and satisfaction. It was a time of greatness—and a time for greatness in the king. The new young monarch, insecure and emotionally immature, was awed by his responsibilities to God and his countrymen for the administration of what had become the world's greatest empire since the fall of Rome. (He shortly suffered the first of those bouts of insanity that in the end would incapacitate him.) However, he was determined to play a part in English politics, an aim not considered by the first two Georges. And he was resolved to rule his empire with the regal majesty that was his birthright.

Since his adolescence George had been exposed to the factional politics that bristled about the English throne. In 1762, just before he began his monumental *Decline and Fall*, Gibbon witnessed this contemporary scene with something like despair. "I should shrink with terror," he wrote, "from the modern history of England, where every character is a problem, and every reader a friend or an enemy; where a writer is supposed to hoist a flag of party, and is devoted to damnation by the adverse faction." Such a political atmosphere of hatred and betrayal might well have daunted the most gifted monarch, no less one of George's untried and questionable capacities. To advise him, he chose as his first prime minister John Stuart, the earl of Bute, an intimate friend of his widowed mother who had guided him as a youthful prince. Within a very few years, however, Bute told the king that even the angel Gabriel would find it hard to govern the country under the circumstances. He soon collapsed under the fire of his adversaries, and, reluctantly, George had to depend upon his own devices. Yet every year his concept of kingship grew stronger. He stubbornly opposed the entrenched parliamentary opposition with his will to establish the supremacy of the crown.

Viewed from across the Channel, England appeared to be an exception in the world congress of monarchies. More than a century earlier, in 1649, those island people had risen up and deliberately and methodically tried their king for disloyalty and treachery, had condemned and killed him in the person of Charles I for his felonies. By the standards of monarchical absolutism in the Continent such dedication to liberty was close to anarchy, and it had sent chills

Lacking self-confidence, George III (here caricatured by James Gillray) was jealous of the ability and independence exhibited by some of his capable advisers—a trait which led him to dismiss the able William Pitt the Elder.

of horror through all the courts of Europe. It was like a crime against nature; as if, H. G. Wells has observed, a committee of deer had taken and killed a jungle tiger. Long before, in 1721, Montesquieu had seen in England "liberty rising ceaselessly from the fires of discord and sedition, a prince constantly trembling on an unshakable throne, a nation which is . . . wise in its very madness. . . ." With such historical precedents George III had to come to terms.

He also had to contend with a press that enjoyed more freedom in England than was true anywhere else in Europe at the time. The studied insolence of John Wilkes in his journal, the *North Briton*, is but one example of the outspoken criticisms that could not be suppressed. "The King is only the first magistrate of this country . . . ," wrote Wilkes in 1763, "responsible to his people for the due exercise of the royal functions in the choice of ministers." Legal actions were brought against him, but Wilkes ultimately won his case and in doing so confirmed important liberties that no English monarch could abrogate. However, as he took the throne, George had much working for him in his stubborn aim to rule by his own majestic will. "I am happy to think that I have [at] the present the real love of my subjects," he wrote Bute in November, 1760, "and lay it down for certain that if I do not show them that I will not permit ministers to trample on me, that my subjects will in time come to esteem me unworthy of the Crown I wear." The English monarchy was on the whole a popular institution, one that in normal circumstances could expect the support of all loyal and patriotic subjects and in questionable matters the benefit of any doubt.

At a purely political (and venal) level, a sizeable proportion of the members of both the House of Commons and the House of Lords held offices, pensions, or contracts that they owed to the crown, and were thereby susceptible to royal influence. Beyond that, in his diatribes Wilkes had called attention to the notoriously unrepresentative nature of Parliament, to its corruption and prejudice in favor of special privilege, which tended to deflect public favor toward the support of royal authority where the general welfare was concerned. However, George himself contributed to that corruption by his extravagant bribery of parliamentary members through patronage and preferments, that he might thus weaken opposition to his purposes. Public opinion was confounded by such developments and political tensions exacerbated.

For ten years George had to make do with one makeshift ministry after another as Parliament contested any further aggrandizement of royal prerogatives. He even tried William Pitt, "the Great Commoner," whom he hated and whom he had earlier forced from office. The times needed a man of unassailable honesty and of proven ability. More than any other person, Pitt had been responsible for England's spectacular victories in the Seven Years' War. He loomed as a man of destiny, and he prided himself on being above party. But very soon he, too, succumbed to the strains of an almost impossible office, resigned, and became an ardent supporter of the American cause, thus earning the king's renewed hatred.

Through this time of political chaos George never lost sight of his right and duty to rule his kingdom personally and in the light of his own reason. Unfortunately, his reason was very limited. In his ignorance he could not dissassociate his constitutional position as ruler from his own mortal person. Any criticism of royal authority, any suggestion of change and reform, became for him a personal affront, to be overruled. When, with the passage of the Stamp Act, Pitt warned that America was almost in a state of open rebellion, the king disdain-

Like George III, William Pitt (here caricatured by George Townshend) resented criticism; he was arrogant and obstinate, and would not serve a king unless he could control him. Ironically, Pitt's son became George III's prime minister.

COLLECTION OF LORD TOWNSHEND
RAYNHAM HALL, NORFOLK, ENGLAND

35

fully brushed his protests aside. The Stamp Act was repealed within a year, and in America, wrote John Adams, that reversal hushed the public clamor and "composed every wave of popular disorder into a smooth and peaceful calm." It seemed that mother and child had resolved their quarrel, that America had quietly settled back into the bosom of the imperial family. But George deplored that settlement. The first duty of Americans was to obey the king. Pitt's claim that the colonists' rights should be recognized George castigated as a "trumpet of sedition." "All men feel," the king remarked, "that the fatal compliance of 1766 has increased the pretensions of the Americans to absolute independence." He simply could not believe that any injustice, provocation, or legal or moral argument could possibly justify the awful treason of the Americans in breaking up that empire which it was his holy trust as king to keep intact for posterity. His fixed purpose became to undo that compliance at the first opportunity, which came too soon for the good of everyone concerned. In the late spring of 1776 the largest expeditionary force ever assembled by Great Britain—some two hundred vessels carrying more than thirty thousand trained professional soldiers—arrived at New York harbor to ensure that the king's will be done in his rebellious American colonies.

The king was swimming ineptly and unavailingly against the tide of events. Had he been a much wiser man he could not have prevented America from going its separate way. With his inborn obstinacy he attempted to fulfill honorably duties that were far beyond his capacities. When the long battle for independence was finally over and the definitive treaties of peace were signed, John Adams presented himself to the king as the first minister of the United States of America accredited to England. The king explained the situation with almost endearing candor. "I wish you to believe, and that it may be understood in America," he told Adams, "that I have done nothing in the late contest but what I thought myself indispensably bound to do by the duty which I owed to my people. I will be very frank with you. I was the last to consent to the separation: but the separation having been made and having become inevitable, I have always said, as I say now, that I would be the first to meet the friendship of the United States of America as an independent power."

That was close to the end of his dream of undisputed sovereignty. For a time, by political trickery and with able support of his "friends" in the government, he had provided England with the closest formal approximation to enlightened despotism it was ever to know. But now George was teetering on the brink of madness. On one occasion a few years later he stepped down from his coach to address an oak tree, which he chose to consider his eminent cousin, Frederick the Great of Prussia. On another occasion he tried to throttle his worthless son, the prince of Wales, and was put in a strait jacket. In 1811 he went irrevocably mad, and all pretense of his authority was abandoned. By then there was scarcely a monarch in Europe who claimed authority as an enlightened ruler. The success of the American Revolution had given a decisive blow to the royal system. In this new and growing nation across the Atlantic the ideas of the Enlightenment, to which the European despots had paid lip service for several generations, were actually realized, institutionalized for the first time on a large and practical scale, and all trace of monarchy had been eliminated in the process. It was something to wonder at.

The crown of Catherine the Great

THE POWER STRUCTURE

In 1776 monarchy was accepted by nearly everyone as the natural form of government. Voltaire had asked, "Why is almost the whole earth governed by monarchs?" and supplied his own answer, "Because men are rarely worthy of governing themselves." With so little questioning of their right to rule, the reigning sovereigns—kings, emperors, czars, sultans, dukes, counts—could wield enormous power. In Europe monarchs who appeared to conform to the philosopher-king ideal of the Enlightenment began to institute reforms in more than a dozen states. Few seemed to sense that the Enlightenment would undermine the very structure of absolutism.

CÉRÉMONIE DU SACRE
DE LOUIS XVI
le 11 Juin 1775.

LOUIS XVI OF FRANCE

The coronation ceremony for Louis XVI at the Reims Cathedral (shown at left) carried with it the high hopes that d'Alembert—and most of his fellow Frenchmen—had for the new ruler: "He loves goodness, justice, economy, and peace. . . . He is just what we ought to desire as our king, if a propitious fate had not given him to us." Louis, however, proved unwilling or unable to impose his will on the nation, the 6,000-person court at Versailles, or even his wife, Marie Antoinette. She emerged as the most extravagant member of an extravagant court in financially troubled times. Tied to an impotent husband, she amused herself with costly gems, operas, and plays. The king disapproved, but indulged her. He ordered buildings erected in her honor, like the Temple of Love (above), completed in 1777. That same year Marie's brother, Joseph II of Austria, disturbed by the gossip in European court circles, visited Versailles and tried to warn her: "I really tremble for your happiness, for it cannot turn out well in the long run, and there will be a cruel revolution unless you take steps against it." He also persuaded Louis to have an operation to correct his impotence, and Marie Antoinette gave birth to their first child in 1778. However, Louis XVI was incurably irresponsible as a ruler, dominated by an effete, self-destructive court.

SCHLOSS SCHONBRUNN

MARIA THERESA OF AUSTRIA

KUNSTGEWERBE MUSEUM. VIENNA

Maria Theresa was not brilliant, but she did have sound judgment, a generous spirit, and numerous children (sixteen in twenty years), whom she shrewdly married off for her diplomatic purposes. One marriage was not arranged—Marie Christine to Duke Albert of Saxony—and it proved the happiest. The porcelain group (opposite left) commemorated the couple's engagement. The portrait at opposite, top shows Maria and her dearly loved husband, Francis, with eleven of their thirteen surviving offspring. Maria delighted in the spectacular Hapsburg court life (above, a ladies' riding tournament at the Hofburg), while Francis often sought his pleasures elsewhere. His death in 1765 upset both Maria and his mistress; Maria cut off her hair, gave up her wardrobe and jewelry for mourning clothes, turned over the kingdom to her son Joseph, paid off the mistress' debts, and considered retiring to a convent. Within a few months, however, Joseph's plans for reform, which Maria thought ill-considered, led her to reassume supreme authority over internal affairs.

41

CATHERINE THE GREAT OF RUSSIA

"I tell you that my aim is to be joined in bonds of friendship with all powers, in armed alliance, so that I may always be able to range myself on the side of the oppressed, and so become the arbiter of Europe," wrote Catherine the Great (opposite) to one of her ambassadors. She launched her foreign policy by taking Russia out of the Seven Years' War—in effect, ensuring Prussia's victory. Shortly thereafter she and Frederick signed a treaty that led to the partition of Poland. In 1779 Catherine served as the arbiter between Frederick and Joseph II at the Peace of Teschen. The next year she bound Denmark, Sweden, Prussia, Austria, and Portugal with Russia in a league of armed neutrality to protect their ships in the war between England and America. Two successful wars with Turkey gave Russia access to the Black Sea and control of the Crimea. Before the end of her reign, Catherine's aggressive foreign policy had clearly established Russia as a dominant force in European politics (subject of the contemporary cartoon above).

FREDERICK
THE GREAT
OF PRUSSIA

Frederick the Great opened his reign by invading and conquering the mineral-rich Austrian province of Silesia. For the next forty-six years his words and deeds provoked both fear and admiration on the Continent. He built up the Prussian army until it was capable of defeating half of Europe united against him, and for security kept it strong in peacetime as well. Above, Frederick—near the end of his reign—and his generals return from maneuvers. After Maria Theresa arranged an alliance with Elizabeth of Russia and Madame de Pompadour against him, Frederick referred to them as the "three whores." His well-known distaste for the trio led to speculation that a statue of three daughters of Zeus (right), atop a palace built during the 1760's, actually represented Madame de Pompadour and the two empresses. Voltaire, who first labeled him "the Great," rationalized Frederick's warmaking and praised him for his domestic reforms and cultural pursuits. Frederick composed a number of concertos for the flute, and played the instrument at frequent concerts at Sans Souci palace in Potsdam (opposite).

GEORGE III OF ENGLAND

By 1776 the English Parliament had evolved into a strong bicameral legislature with broad lawmaking powers. No bill could become law unless passed by both houses and signed by the king, and since 1714 no king had withheld assent from a bill approved by Parliament. However, the House of Commons (above) was not a truly representative body; only one-fifth of its members were popularly elected. George III's ministers, with his consent, continued and expanded the tradition of governing by cajoling, or browbeating, or bribing the legislators. (In 1770 over 190 members of Commons held remunerative appointive positions in the administration.) In the early, chaotic years of his reign George III was often caricatured as a despot. Although inept and mentally unstable, the king revered the constitution and made no efforts to usurp power. He did remodel Windsor Castle to accommodate his large family (opposite, a 1771 portrait of George with Queen Charlotte and six of their fifteen children), but measured against the contemporary monarchs, he was notoriously frugal.

CHARLES III OF SPAIN

Led by two capable ministers, Charles III made a valiant effort to bring the Enlightenment to Spain. In an attempt to exert some control over the Catholic Church, he expelled the Jesuits in 1767, and tempered the Inquisition somewhat by granting toleration to

Protestants and Moslems, although not to Jews. Significant changes were made in agriculture and commerce; Spain's income from America rose 800 per cent and export trade tripled. But wars consumed much of the new revenue, and Charles was not able to overcome the opposition of Spain's powerful conservative forces. In the romantic painting reproduced above, churchmen and nobles remain standing as Charles III, seated alone, is served lunch; only the king's beloved hunting dogs were permitted to sit in the royal presence.

POPULAR MONARCHIES: SWEDEN & HOLLAND

For much of eighteenth century, republican and monarchist groups vied for power in Sweden and the United Provinces (or Holland, so called after the most prosperous of those seven provinces). The Swedish constitution had made the king subject to the will of the Riksdag. However, Gustavus III (opposite, his coronation in 1773), along with sympathetic army officers, forced the popular assembly to grant him nearly absolute powers. Six years later Gustavus' reforms won the unanimous approval of the Riksdag. However, prolonged wars with Russia and his increasingly autocratic ways cost him his subjects' support, and he was assassinated by a disgruntled nobleman at a masked ball. Each of the United Provinces chose its own stadholder, or governor. Together they could elect a general stadholder, who became, in effect, a limited monarch (below, a meeting of the estates of Holland and West Friesland). Forty years of republican dominance ended in 1747, when William IV was elected general stadholder. His son, William V, aided by the Prussian army, stifled republican opposition, forcing 40,000 democrats to emigrate; thereafter the House of Orange was established as a constitutional monarchy.

REPUBLICAN GENEVA & VENICE

Diderot's *Encyclopédie* (1757) listed federations, such as the United Provinces, and city-states, such as Geneva (below) and Venice (opposite), as republics—anomalies in an otherwise largely monarchical world. Venice had been a republic since the 1300's, when political power was vested in some 200 families, all of whom were involved in trade or commerce. Headed by a doge elected for life, Venice was a great political and economic success. By 1776, however, the political and economic systems were outmoded and corrupted. Increasingly, Venice was a city living on its past glory, still as today, dependent upon tourism for survival. Geneva, a small town of 25,000, was surrounded by powerful neighbors. The 1738 constitution that established the republic was guaranteed by France, Bern, and Zurich. Geneva was dominated by an aristocratic elite, but middle-class agitation resulted in a new constitution in 1768, granting its members increased political power. That still left three-quarters of the population without a voice in the government. Two years later the middle class branded groups meeting to demand rights similar to theirs as subversive and dissolved them. But in 1782 the Geneva aristocracy called for intervention by the French army and revoked the constitution of 1768.

At its height in the sixteenth and seventeenth centuries the Mogul empire controlled territory from Afghanistan to the Bay of Bengal. Even then it was beset by native factions—namely the Sikhs and Marathas. By the 1770's, however, no semblance of a strong central government remained, and India's southern provinces were in a state of constant warfare. Around the edges of this decaying empire, European traders, who had established outposts in the 1660's in places like Bombay, Madras, and Calcutta, seen below in the 1760's, waited for the chance to seize still more power and wealth. One ploy was to buy the loyalty of local noblemen, like the one shown above, who then became puppets of the French or the British in order to maintain their elaborate courts.

THE MOGUL &

OTTOMAN EMPIRES

In 1600 the Ottoman empire was the largest in the world. Nearly all Arab lands from Iraq to Algiers as well as Christian lands in the Balkans and the Danube Valley owed their allegiance to Istanbul. Dominated by military and religious cliques, the empire remained a medieval state politically, economically, and socially (above, a scene from a late eighteenth-century court). It was customary to keep the heirs to the sultan's throne in virtual solitary confinement until their turn came, by which time they were often hopeless lunatics or alcoholics. Abdul-Hamid I's mind was considerably weakened by his forty-three years of incarceration prior to becoming sultan in 1774. His short reign was taken up by two wars that resulted in the loss of the Crimea.

CH'ING DYNASTY IN CHINA

In the middle of the seventeenth century a Manchu clan from beyond the Great Wall overthrew the decadent Ming dynasty; the "foreign" Ch'ing dynasty would rule China for more than two and one half centuries. Emperor Ch'ien Lung, who came to the throne in 1736, inherited an empire with a strong central government, well-disciplined officials, and a large treasury surplus. During his sixty-year reign China grew to be the richest and most populous nation on earth and reached its maximum territorial expansion. In the late 1750's the Manchus put down a Moslem rebellion south of Ili and transformed the entire Turkestan region into Sinkiang, or the "New Dominion." The paintings seen above are details from a scroll by the Jesuit artist-priest Castiglione honoring that Manchu victory. (Above, Mohammedan captives kneel at the entrance to the Purple Light Hall, waiting the arrival of Ch'ien Lung, seen above right making his entrance in a sedan chair, for a victory dinner.) Later, Manchu armies conquered Mongolia, Nepal, and Yunnan. Expeditionary forces were sent to put down disturbances in Vietnam, Burma, and to conquer Taiwan. Opposite, a Manchu fleet lands cavalry in an attack on the Vietnamese. Ch'ien Lung was not unknown in Europe; Castiglione and other Jesuits in residence at his court wrote letters praising his support of the arts and his imaginative, enlightened domestic policies—for instance, fighting hard times with vast public works programs. However, in the last two decades of his reign Ch'ien Lung delegated authority to a man who used the power to accumulate a personal fortune; at the emperor's death corrupt civil and military bureaucracies, internal revolt, and a depleted treasury threatened China's stability.

THE TOKUGAWA SHOGUNATE IN JAPAN

From the early seventeenth century shoguns ("generalissimos") from the Tokugawa clan ruled Japan for more than 250 years. Tokugawa society was rigidly divided into classes—feudal barons (the daimio), professional soldiers loyal to particular daimio (the samurai, seen at right), peasants, artisans, and merchants. The shogun (opposite, receiving officials at his court) operated a centralized, efficient, repressive system of government. Although the daimio were permitted to rule their own lands, they owed their allegiance to the shogun. He required them to make biennial visits to his headquarters at Edo (modern Tokyo) and remain there for the entire year at great expense (above, a daimio with his entourage on the way to pay his respects at the shogun's castle). When the daimio returned home they had to leave members of their families behind in Edo—in effect, hostages of the shogun. The Japanese emperor possessed hereditary authority and a strong religious aura, but for centuries had exercised no political power. Most retired to Buddhist monasteries and served as figureheads for policies promulgated by the ruling shogun.

59

THE BUSINESS

In the years leading up to 1776, the world was swarming with commerce as never before. Reduced to a chart, that intricate global traffic would show currents of trade coursing from all directions to deposit new wealth on the nations of western Europe, principally on Britain, France, and Holland. In terms of the resources and services it could command, that relatively small area facing the Atlantic, with its myriad ocean routes leading to Asia, Africa, and the Americas, had become incomparably more wealthy than any other portion of the earth.

There was nothing particularly new in this driving activity except its heightened pace and its extended range. Europe had long been oriented toward a global economy by the pathfinding ventures of navigators from Portugal and Spain in the sixteenth century, and by the worldwide trading interests that developed in the wake of their discoveries. The rest of the states watched with envy as those two powers fattened on the proceeds of their overseas enterprise; and virtually from the beginning of that enterprise the other maritime states, eager to share in the spoils, began to harass the Portuguese and Spanish fleets on the high seas, and soon established trading stations of their own in faraway lands. That was a costly business, generally beyond the resources of most government treasuries. To float such undertakings, chartered companies were formed with private capital—and they reaped profits for their investors. The three great East India companies—Dutch, English, and French—were all joint-stock companies. The French *Compagnie*

OF EMPIRE

des Indes did depend heavily upon support from the crown (which was interested in creating a merchant marine that would enhance France's naval power); but for all intents and purposes it was private initiative that generated the company's activities. In every case it was assumed that the success of the chartered organization would contribute to the ultimate advantage of the state in its international rivalries.

The Dutch East India Company was founded in 1602 with the avowed purpose of breaking the Portuguese monopoly of the Asia trade. To accomplish this, the basic objective was to acquire such trading bases as would enable the company to establish a monopoly of its own in specific commodities. With that end in view, Dutch vessels found their way to corners of the earth that had never even interested the Portuguese. By the early eighteenth century the Dutch held the Cape of Good Hope, posts on the Malabar and Coromandel coasts and in Bengal, Ceylon, the Malay Straits, Cambodia, Japan, among other places. Then, nineteen years later, in 1621, the Dutch West India Company was founded, with authority to prowl the western Atlantic and plunder whatever Portuguese and Spanish ships they might find there. The company pursued its mission with such zeal that within a few years 545 ships, with cargoes valued at ninety million florins, had been captured. When, off Havana, in 1628, the Dutch admiral Piet Hein, with a few small ships, captured a Spanish fleet loaded with precious metals, pearls, spices, and drugs, twelve million florins worth in all, the company's goal seemed within reach. (The commander of the ill-fated Spanish flotilla was executed as soon as he reached Spain.) However, that was an unusually rewarding exploit, which netted the shareholders a seventy-five per cent dividend payment.

England, too, was quick and eager to find Spanish carracks, gorged "with rubies, carbuncles, and sapphires," fair game on the open sea. As early as 1580 Francis Drake returned to England in the *Golden Hind*, after spreading terror for almost three years along both coasts of Spain's American and other distant colonies, and after rifling, among others, the great Spanish treasure ship *Nuestra Señora de la Concepción*, "the chiefest glory of the whole South Sea." (Drake entertained its amazed and defeated admiral with violin music and "all possible kinds of delicacies" served on silver plate.) Briefly hesitating because of the political consequences of such a gesture, Queen Elizabeth publicly approved Drake's great plundering expedition and knighted him in recognition of his services in Britain's cause. Spain's lifelines had taken deep cuts, and as Spain bled, other countries were more free to project their own overseas enterprise. "My very good Lord," Drake wrote Lord Burleigh, Queen Elizabeth's chief adviser, "there is now a very great gap opened, very little to the liking of the King of Spain." And through that gap the first English colonists found their way to permanent homes in the New World. One incident in their gradual expansion along the Atlantic coast of North America was the takeover of the Dutch West India Company's colony at New Netherland in 1664, "without a blow or a tear." The Dutch put up no resistance. The gains in silks, tea, and spices from the Orient had far more appeal to that trading nation than bargaining for pelts with greasy native hunters from the American forests. The French seem to have been more concerned. "The King of England grasps at all America!" one French officer remarked with astonishment.

On New Year's Eve in 1600 a company of London merchants was chartered under the seal of Queen Elizabeth as the London East India Company. The queen's seal represented namely her assent to this purely mercantile venture designed to tap the wealth of the Orient by trade in gems, indigo, camphor, and spices. No thought of empire was considered, save for the profitable contribution such activity would make to the strength and the prestige of Britain.

France, too, joined the ocean traffic and created its own East India Company in 1664, under the administration of Jean Baptiste Colbert, for more than a score of years Louis XIV's remarkably able and powerful minister for finance and economic affairs. Fort Dauphin in Madagascar was France's first port of call. Like its British counterpart, the French company established its agents at points along the Indian coast, where they built forts, maintained armies, coined money, and entered into treaties with native rulers, all under charter of their home government.

Directives given at London and Liverpool, at Paris and Bordeaux, and at Amsterdam set in motion the machinery of empire around the world. To fuel that machinery, increasing numbers of Indians were set to spinning cotton, Chinese to raising tea, Malays to gathering spices, and Africans of the Gold Coast to unearthing precious metals and to hunting out ivory, and in places far from their homeland, to tending sugar cane and the tobacco crop.

Each of these companies was chartered for the same purposes—to develop a monopoly of the trade with the East for its own country and to eliminate competition between individual merchants of that country, thus to assure the

largest possible return on the invested capital. In the event a company did not succeed and became insolvent, the state was obliged to lend it financial aid or to take over its establishment. On the other hand, if through its very success a company developed into an important territorial power, a government might be tempted or obliged to step in and reclaim its own political powers. Because of financial failures, both the Dutch and French companies had to turn over their assets to their respective state governments during the course of the eighteenth century. In that same period the English company started to serve as the government for an increasingly large area of India, and it survived in such a role until 1858.

Lord Haversham, admiral of the British navy at the end of the seventeenth century, had early advised his countrymen, "Your trade is the mother and nurse of your seamen; your seamen are the life of your fleet, your fleet is the security of your trade, and both together are the wealth, strength, and glory of Britain"; and the advice was well taken in war and peace. The middle decades of the eighteenth century witnessed a series of demonstrations, staged on four continents and along the seaways of the world, of England's "wealth, strength, and glory." In 1759 alone, during the course of the Seven Years' War, almost every month brought tidings of Britain's triumphs over the hostile powers—notably France—that contested its authority. The first of August of that year was one of the brightest days in the history of the British army when, in a daring assault at Minden in Westphalia, a British infantry brigade (followed by some battalions from Hanover) put to rout the advancing French cavalry and its supporting infantry, although the line of approach was covered by a crossfire from batteries of French artillery. "I have seen what I never thought to be possible," observed a French officer, "—a single line of infantry break through three lines of cavalry, ranked in order of battle, and tumble them to ruin!" The enemy left ten thousand men and forty-five guns on the field as the remainder of his forces retreated in a demoralized mass; and Louis XV was obliged to recast his dreams of conquest on the Continent.

Earlier that same year, in May, the British admiral Edward Boscawen had intercepted and defeated a French fleet at Lagos Bay, off the coast of Portugal, taking three large ships, burning two others, and returning to England triumphantly with his prizes and two thousand prisoners. Those French vessels had been on their way from Toulon to Brest to join others gathered there for a proposed invasion of England—a possibility that had caused some panic among the English, not yet as confident in the prowess of their navy as they were soon to become.

The French fleet at Brest under Admiral de Conflans left that port nevertheless in November, but was carefully watched by British warships under the command of Admiral Edward Hawke. Defying the worst of weather, Hawke pursued the French vessels along one of the most dangerous coasts in the world to the Bay of Quiberon in Brittany, the most westerly part of France. The swift tides in that area can reach heights of more than forty feet, and the sea can be savage. (At one point along that treacherous coast the shock of storm waves pounding against the rocks can be felt almost twenty miles inland.) There, in the dark of night, and disregarding the hazardous circumstances, Hawke effectively put the French fleet out of commission, although his ships ran out of provisions toward the end of that campaign. The distress of his crewmen was recorded in a contemporary jingle addressed to their countrymen:

> Ere Hawke did bang
> Monseer Conflang
> You sent us beef and beer;
> Now Monseer's beat
> We've nought to eat,
> Since you have nought to fear.

Once again the menace from French rivalry was sharply reduced.

The Seven Years' War continued to rage also on the far side of the Atlantic, in America. On July 25, 1759, the English-born colonist Sir William Johnson with his Indian allies had captured Fort Niagara on New York's western frontier; it had been a guard of the coveted gateway to France's rich fur lands in the interior of the continent. In a parallel campaign the French bastions at Crown Point and Ticonderoga fell to Lord Jeffrey Amherst at the end of July. The road northward from the American colonies to the French provincial capital at Quebec was now wide open. On the thirteenth of September that vital citadel was attacked by a British force led by General James Wolfe. Several days before that decisive event Wolfe, a seriously sick man and fearful that he would not be able to lead his troops in person, had consulted his physician. "I know perfectly well you cannot cure me," he said, "but pray make me up so that I may be without pain for a few days, and able to do my duty; that is all I want." In the battle that took place on the Plains of Abraham before Quebec, he was wounded three times. As he lay dying, an aide, viewing the continuing encounter, exclaimed, "They run; see how they run!" "Who run?" Wolfe asked, like a man aroused from his sleep. "The enemy, sir," was the answer. "Egad, they give way everywhere." Turning on his side Wolfe murmured with his last breath, "Now, God be praised, I will die in peace." His adversary, the French general Montcalm, was also mortally wounded in the same engagement and was carried to rest in a rough box, a few boards nailed together to serve as a coffin, which was then lowered into a cavity made by a bursting enemy shell.

Montcalm's funeral was the funeral of New France. In the peace settlement

The mortal wounding of the French general Montcalm at the battle of Quebec in 1759 foreshadowed the end of France's empire in North America.
NATIONAL GALLERY OF CANADA, OTTAWA

that followed, half the North American continent passed to the British crown. Voltaire contemptuously referred to the defeat as the loss for France of "a few acres of snow," but his perspective was remarkably shallow. With the mopping up that followed the victory on the Plains of Abraham, the American colonies for the first time in generations felt free from the threat of French envelopment—as some contemporaries conjectured, freed from the need to depend on the mother country for their further development.

Halfway around the world in that same year the British were consolidating their position in India at the expense of the Dutch and the French, hurrying to a climax an old international rivalry among Western agents for profitable control of that vast subcontinent. The gradual assumption of territorial control of India that led from success in that rivalry significantly changed the course of British imperialism in the East and set a model for the future development of other European colonial empires in Asia, Africa, and the Pacific.

In his *History of the English People,* John Richard Green wrote that it was "no exaggeration to say that three of many victories [of the Seven Years' War] determined for ages to come the destinies of mankind. With that of Rossbach [where Frederick the Great won a crucial battle], began the re-creation of Germany . . .; with that of Plassey [in India] the influence of Europe told for the first time since the days of Alexander on the nations of the East. . . . With the triumph of Wolfe on the heights of Abraham began the history of the United States." To celebrate England's triumphs in that "wonderful year," the noted actor David Garrick wrote a masque whose words were put to music by William Boyce. It read, in part:

> Great Britain shall triumph, her ships plough the sea;
> Her standard is Justice; her watchword, "Be free!"
> Then cheer up, my lads, with one heart let us sing,
> Our soldiers, our sailors, our statesmen, our King.
>> Heart of oak are our ships,
>> Jolly tars are our men,
>> We always are ready,
>> Steady, boys, steady!
>> We'll fight and we'll conquer
>> Again and again.

Such victories, wrote Thomas Babington Macaulay, were merely "instruments which received their direction from one superior mind. It was the great William Pitt [the Elder] who had vanquished the French marshals in Germany and French admirals on the Atlantic—who had conquered for his country one great empire on the frozen shores of Ontario and another under the tropical sun near the mouth of the Ganges."

The scale and finality of Britain's victories in the Seven Years' War stunned the world. There was ample occasion for the ringing of bells and the lighting of bonfires which signaled rejoicing throughout the island. France offered peace in 1760, if England would desert its Prussian ally; but Pitt would have none of it. Indeed, he urged an additional new war with Spain, hoping to seize the treasure fleet from the Indies and to occupy the Isthmus of Panama. But there were others of different counsel, and to these the newly enthroned George III gave heed. To some, the increasing cost of the war, and the mounting taxation that resulted, had become intolerable. (In his first speech to the

Privy Council the king spoke of this "bloody and expensive war"—an invidious expression apparently directed at Pitt.) Others were fearful that the very completeness of Britain's victories and, with its extraordinary sea power, its domination of the world's trade routes would gain it the envy, if not the hatred, of much of the rest of the world—leave it without friends and a prey to some grand alliance of hostile European powers intent on reducing its overbearing greatness. It was not an unjustified fear, as events were to prove.

Pitt's enemies shrank from his aggressive plans, and the king supported their call for peace. In October, dismayed by such opposition, the "Great Commoner" resigned his office. "Pitt disgraced!" exulted a French philosopher. "It is worth two victories to us!" The English subsidies to Frederick the Great, which had measurably helped to sustain Prussia during these war years, were withdrawn, and Frederick was reduced to despair. (As noted in the first chapter, with the sudden withdrawal of Russia from the war Frederick was in the end spared from defeat.)

Three weeks after Pitt's fall Spain, as an ally of France, declared war on Britain, justifying Pitt's earlier plan of attack on that nation's commercial structure. Such was the momentum of Britain's sea power, as Pitt could have advised, that in 1762 both Cuba and the Philippines—wealthiest of Spain's holdings in the Caribbean and the Pacific—along with several important French West Indian islands, fell to British fleets. With these victories, England went to the peace table in 1763 to end the long conflict.

On the open sea and in colonial lands it had been almost entirely a commercial war, which England had won hands down. British trade was increasing enormously in both East and West. Of at least equal interest was the fact that Britian's seaborne commerce was safe in peace and war, whereas that of France and other nations was dependent upon Britain's political objectives. In France the Duc de Choiseul found that situation intolerable. "While pretending to protect the balance on land which no one threatens . . . ," he observed, "the British are entirely destroying the balance at sea which no one defends." To correct that imbalance, he started to rebuild the French fleet with a vengeful determination.

The peace settlement enraged Pitt. The important sugar islands of Guadeloupe and Martinique were returned to France. France was also given its old rights to fish on the Grand Banks and was permitted to retain its five main bases in India, provided that they were not fortified. "We retain nothing," Pitt ranted in the Commons debate, "although we have conquered everything." That was not quite true, since India had been secured and Canada acquired. However, Pitt's basic policy had been violated by the terms of the peace. To deliver his speech Pitt, suffering from a severe attack of gout, had to be carried to the House. He talked with passionate conviction for three hours, interrupted at times by paroxysms of pain. "France is chiefly, if not solely, to be dreaded by us in light of a maritime and commercial power," he exhorted before the House of Commons: "and therefore by restoring in her all the valuable West India islands, and by our concessions in the Newfoundland fishery, we have given her the means of recovering her prodigious losses and of becoming once more formidable to us at sea." It was a prophetic utterance as the next two decades would make abundantly clear.

Pitt was not forgotten. After his dismissal from office Londoners hung on his carriage, embraced his footman, and even kissed his horses. He had been,

"The terms of the proposed treaty [the Seven Years' War] meet with my most hearty disapprobation. I see in them the seeds of a future war. The peace is insecure, because it restores the enemy to her former greatness. The peace is inadequate, because places gained are no equivalent for places surrendered."

William Pitt

as Dr. Samuel Johnson averred, a minister given by the people, who adored him, to the king. England's great achievements were considered to be Pitt's achievements, by foreigners and most Englishmen alike. "England," announced Frederick the Great, "has been a long time in labor and has suffered a great deal to produce Mr. Pitt, but she has at last brought forth a Man." One Frenchman, who had fought against England in India and had been sent to London as a prisoner of war, concluded that he had become "historically acquainted with but two men in the world, the King of Prussia and Mr. Pitt." When Voltaire was preparing to put out an edition of the works of the French playwright Corneille, he begged for the honor of being allowed to place Pitt's name at the head of the list of subscribers.

England's hold on India, which had been tightened during the period of the Seven Years' War largely through the agency of the East India Company, was

During the Seven Years' War, England supported Frederick the Great with vast subsidies made available in silver. Sending ships laden with silver was a risky proposition during war, and Frederick required only a small percentage of the subsidy in silver, for paying his soldiers and officials; his main need was arms and foodstuffs, and a highly profitable triangular trade developed, organized by merchants in Hamburg (above, the city's seal). They exchanged the silver earmarked for the king of Prussia while it was still in England for sugar, rum, coffee, and tobacco, and made arrangements for shipment to Hamburg (left, the trading card of an eighteenth-century English shipping broker). On the Continent the merchants traded the English commodities for whatever the belligerents required—foodstuffs, raw materials, weapons, and ammunition. When the war ended, Hamburg merchants continued their trade; by the end of the century Hamburg was Europe's third most important—after London and Amsterdam—trading center.

When this map of India was made in 1761, the once-great Mogul empire was wracked by internal dissension, and various European states, in posts along the coast, were poised to take over. The French-British rivalry was strongest along the Coromandel coast, where France controlled Pondicherry, and England held Madras and Fort St. David.
BRITISH MUSEUM

finally secured by the same means. As has been suggested, the course of events that stemmed from those developments tell an epic story of the growth of empire. In the eighteenth century India presented a great temptation to fortune seekers with power and skill to direct their energies in a gigantic treasure hunt. More than a century earlier, Sir Thomas Roe, English ambassador under James I to the Mogul court at Ajmir, had reported with awe the enormous wealth of that land. "In revenue," he wrote, "the Moguls doubtless exceed either Turk, Persian, or any Eastern Prince: the sum I dare not name." He and other early visitors wondered at the profusion of jewelry and the gorgeous costumes they saw, the hoards of precious metals they heard of. During the long reign of Shah Jehan (1628–58), the empire reached its greatest extent and the height of its glory—a glory symbolized by the unsurpassably beautiful Taj Mahal that he had built near Agra, and at Delhi by a superbly carved alabaster palace in which he placed the Peacock Throne, made of solid gold and studded with gems.

As a footnote to that conspicuous opulence, during his residence in India, Thomas Pitt, grandfather of William Pitt, bought a fabulous diamond in 1701, which he later sold to the regent of France at a staggering profit. (It eventually ended up among the British crown jewels.) With that fortune, along with the fruits of other singularly successful Eastern ventures, "Diamond Pitt," as he was called, had established a prosperous base for the careers of his illustrious grandson and great-grandson. Pitt was a private adventurer competing as an individual with the company's business—a pirate, in the company's eyes; but such a successful one that the company retaliated by taking him into its fold and making him the governor of Madras. Madras was then being administered under a charter from England as a foreign-based municipality. The first of its governors had been Boston-born Elihu Yale, who had won enduring fame by making a sizeable donation from the private fortune he had accumulated to a little colonial college in New England, which took his name as a tribute to his generosity.

With the death of Jehan's son, who had deposed and imprisoned his father,

the Mogul empire fast fell apart into discordant elements commanded by provincial viceroys and feudal princes eager for their good share of power and the
wealth that went with it. With much the same end in view, the French and
British East India companies from their stations along the coast, each in its
own interest, played one native faction against another, offering military support in return for territorial concessions and tribute, and even taking over governmental authority where that proved possible and promised the greatest
rewards. In the contest for trading advantages, French and British forces were
themselves frequently involved in direct warfare with varying fortunes at different times and places. There is no need to trace the complicated developments which saw Britain gradually oust its rivals and ultimately win domination over the land; but it is of particular interest to recall the part played by
Robert Clive in assuring that outcome.

After a turbulent youth, Clive had gone to India in 1743 at the age of eighteen as a clerk in the service of the East India Company, to the relief of his
friends at home, who were glad to be quit of this unruly, moody lad. (Once he
had organized a Mafialike protection racket which terrorized local shopkeepers.) Shut off from his associates in India by his haughty, shy temperament,
according to the legend, in a fit of depression he twice pulled the trigger of a
pistol at his head in vain. Baffled by that failure to end his life, he somewhat
reluctantly concluded that he had been spared for higher things to come—
and such was to prove true. He was to become the first of a century of those
so-called soldier-politicals who were to assure the conquest and consolidation
of the greatest dependency in Britain's imperial domain.

Shortly after his arrival, Clive quit the company's civil service for a commission in the company's military, and here he found an ideal exercise for both
his talent and temperament. In 1751, given the rank of captain in the absence
of his superior officer, he took command of a meager force of two hundred Europeans and three hundred sepoys (paid native soldiers),
equipped with but three fieldpieces and directed by eight officers, six of whom
had never seen action before. He was determined to assail the town of Arcot,
capital of an Indian puppet governor installed in that position by the French.
Clive hoped to replace the ruler with a puppet governor of his own. With this
handful of supporters, he marched toward his objective, during the monsoon
rains, when such roads as there were had been washed away. His swift advance, "unconcerned through a violent storm of thunder, lightning and
rain," took the adversary forces completely by surprise and so frightened
them that they fled from their position in a major fort, leaving behind guns
and a considerable supply of powder and shot. Clive then withstood a siege of
fifty-three days until his reinforced enemies finally fled the scene, their panick-
ing armored elephants leading the rout. It was such a demonstration of stubborn valor and inspired leadership as led Pitt to refer to Clive as a "heaven-
born general." Clive was then just twenty-seven years old, and he had already
won enormous respect from the Indians as both a heroic warrior and a skilled
administrator. He had, as well, taught the English a lesson. The governor of
Madras wrote his employers in London that Clive had revealed how unsub-
stantial Indian resistance was to European power. "'Tis certain," he wrote,
"any European nation resolved to war on them with a tolerable force may
overrun the whole country."

After a several years' sojourn in England, Clive returned to India, and soon

*In 1765 Emperor Shah Alam granted the
fiscal administration of Bihar (Bahar,
on map), Bengal, and Orissa (Orixa) to
Robert Clive of the East India Company in return for a regular subsidy.*
OFFICE OF THE INDIES

won a more spectacular victory for his country—or for the company, it might better be claimed. The Indian nawab (viceroy) of Bengal had decided to throw the English out of that province before the English threw him out, and he had seized the company's settlement at Calcutta. The English were completely unprepared for this attack and were quickly overcome. Most of the inhabitants had already fled in confusion when the viceroy's troops swarmed into the citadel. The surviving and defeated remaining members of the English garrison proved somewhat obstreperous, and the viceroy suggested they be temporarily locked up to keep them out of harm's way, and to prevent their escape. Upon advice, and without realizing the circumstances, he had all of them confined to the "Black Hole" of Calcutta. There were sixty-four of them, including one woman, and their overnight prison was an airless room about eighteen by fourteen feet, with but two small openings barricaded by iron bars—a room often used to detain drunken soldiers. Without water and in ghastly heat most of them died overnight of asphyxiation and heat prostration; the rest were trampled or stabbed to death by those struggling toward the little windows for a breath of air. The horror of the scene, as described by one of the few survivors of that night, is almost unbelievable: in their agonizing thirst men sucked the sweat off one another's clothing or drank their own urine; others were held upright in ghastly postures because in the crush they could not fall down, even after they had suffocated and died. In the morning when the viceroy heard of the gruesome episode, he had the living prisoners released from their torture; there were only twenty-three of them.

The next year the company took action to retrieve its prestige and recapture this most profitable center of its trade. A contingent of royal troops had recently arrived in India, at Madras, but their officers looked with contempt on the company's soldiers and refused to join the march on Calcutta. Leadership was assigned to Clive. "This expedition," he wrote his father, "if attended with success, may enable me to do great things. It is by far the greatest of my undertakings. I go with great forces and great authority." (His expedition was attended by four warships of the royal navy.) Without the government's commanders, on June 23, 1757, at the head of nine hundred European and two thousand three hundred native troops, Clive routed a force of fifty thousand men at Plassey. With this ridiculously easy defeat of a vastly larger Indian army Clive demonstrated with finality England's military authority in India. The incident of the "Black Hole" was avenged. Eighty-four years later writer and statesman Macaulay wrote of the Indian viceroy who had so unwittingly caused that night of horror "on the eve of the battle of Plassey, gloriously in his tent, haunted—as the Greek poet would have said—by the furies of those that cursed him with their last breath in the Black Hole." After Calcutta was retaken, the viceroy was deposed and a new, friendly, and grateful native prince in charge of the administration of Bengal was installed in his place.

Clive had become a "kingmaker." When he entered the capital as a conqueror Clive believed it to be larger than London, and wealthier. He saw there an almost blinding accumulation of rupees, jewels, gold, silver, and other treasures. Invited by the new viceroy to name his reward, Clive asked £160,000 for himself, £500,000 for his army and navy, £24,000 for each member of the company's governing board, and £1,000,000 for damages to the company's Calcutta property. Not only were those staggering sums forth-

In this contemporary engraving prisoners trapped in a dungeon, the "Black Hole" of Calcutta, fight for a drink.

coming, but Clive received an additional £200,000 in lavish presents from the viceroy.

The French continued their opposition as best they could, but Clive had made it clear that their position in India was now hopeless. He had also made it quite clear that colossal fortunes could be made more easily by strength of arms than by humdrum trading, rewarding as that was. He had, almost accidentally, created an Eastern British empire, but when he finally returned home in 1767, his health shattered by the demands he had made upon it, the means by which he had achieved so much were the subject of critical official inquiry. The whole matter of Britain's presence in India was wide open to question. Incorporated under Queen Elizabeth, the East India Trading Company had been no more than a company of sea adventurers. By degrees the company found itself dealing not merely in spices and dyes and tea and jewels, but in the government and destiny of millions of alien peoples occupying a vast territory, an empire far greater and more populous than all the rest of Britain's domain. Acting in their own private interest as well as corporately, agents of the company, even clerks and soldiers, could with reasonable luck quickly accumulate a fortune and return to England to live in gentlemanly ease on their spoils. With their conspicuous wealth such nabobs, as they were called, invited the envy and the suspicion of their stay-at-home compatriots. As the English author Horace Walpole was later to say, "no man ever went to the East Indies with good intentions."

In 1772 two parliamentary committees investigating Indian affairs revealed details of cruelty and exactions which they found outrageous. "We have outdone the Spaniards in Peru!" Walpole expostulated. "We have murdered, deposed, plundered, usurped. Nay, what think you of the famine in Bengal, in which three millions perished, being caused by a monopoly of provisions by the servants of the East India Company?"

The next year Clive was called before one of the committees to justify his conduct. When challenged on the fabulous tribute he had taken from the Indian factions he had supported in their struggle for supremacy over their rivals, Clive exclaimed: "Consider the situation in which the battle of Plassey had placed me. A great prince was dependent on my pleasure; an opulent city lay at my mercy; its richest bankers bid against each other for my smiles; I walked through vaults which were thrown open to me alone, piled on either hand with gold and jewels. By God, Mr. Chairman, at this moment I stand amazed at my own moderation." Parliament passed a vote of censure, but conceded that Clive "did at the same time render great and meritorious service to his country." At one point in the interrogation, stung by the questions being put to him, Clive retorted to Lord North: "My situation, sir, has not been an easy one for these twelve months past, and though my conscience could never accuse me, yet I felt for my friends who were involved in the same censure as myself. . . . I have been examined by the select committee more like a sheep-stealer than a member of this House." The next year, at the age of forty-nine, Clive took his own life. His volatile temper had been tried beyond its limits.

It was, in fact, a strange and unprecedented situation in world history that found Parliament nominally ruling over a London trading company, which was, in turn, ruling a distant and exotic empire very much on its own corporate terms; a company which by this time was asking for financial aid from

"[Those] who had yet some strength and vigour left made a last effort for the windows, and several . . . got hold of the bars, from which there was no removing them. Many to the right and left sank with the violent pressure, and were soon suffocated."

John Howell, a survivor

Parliament to bail it out of its difficulties. Those difficulties stemmed in good part from the fact that the host of civil servants and soldiers the company employed were less interested in the company's profits than in their own salaries and perquisites. According to one report, those agents constituted an "immense number of Idle Sycophants" who were intercepting substantial amounts of revenue before it could reach the public treasury. It was strangely like piracy on a vast scale. In 1773 Parliament passed the Regulating Act, designed to regulate the British subjects in India, whom no Indian government could control. Although the company remained independent, it was obliged to inform the British government of all its financial, administrative, and military affairs in India. The next year Warren Hastings was sent to the company headquarters at Calcutta as the first British governor general, appointed by the company, but responsible to His Majesty's government—a post he held until 1785. After Clive, Hastings was the principal agent of British supremacy in India.

If Clive had been an empire builder by accident, Hastings was an empire builder by design. In the course of carrying out his duties as governor general he was charged by a multitude of enemies both in India and at home. As a consequence, in 1786, he was impeached and subjected to a trial in the House of Lords—a trial that he endured for seven years before he was finally acquitted. The term of his administration had coincided with the most critical period in the history of Britain in the East. India was at the time experiencing the worst stages of political anarchy. Meanwhile, the directors of the company at home were divided among themselves and at the same time were often at odds with Parliament. Nevertheless, Hastings could truly claim, as he did at his trial, that he had saved all that Clive had gained and laid the firm foundation of British sovereignty in India.

The seven-year impeachment trial of Warren Hastings inspired editorials and cartoons from both sides. This cartoon, favorable to Hastings, pictures his leading opponents—from the left, Edmund Burke, Lord North, and Charles James Fox—as "political banditti."

In this 1775 French engraving the world watches in anticipation as a magic lantern projects an image of a teapot exploding, symbolizing the uproar caused by Boston's tea party.

In 1784, with the India Bill, introduced by William Pitt the Younger, the administration of India had been made part of the general system of the English government. Although the company retained its commercial rights and functions, a board of directors was formed from members of the Privy Council for the approval or annulling of the company's acts. Under this dual control, the governor general would thenceforth rule the growing British sphere in India virtually as an absolute monarch. Whatever else might be said, under the control of the ministry and the Parliament of Great Britain, the land enjoyed better government, greater security of persons and property, than it had known for at least a century past.

Meanwhile, Indian goods, including opium, were exported not only to Europe but to China, where they helped to pay for the rapidly growing imports of tea by the Occident. Profits from the tea trade came to surpass the company's losses elsewhere, and saved it from bankruptcy. In 1773, to help alleviate the financial distress of the company, it was permitted to sell tea directly to the American colonies without first auctioning it off in England. The Tea Act that made that possible alienated powerful colonial interests at the crucial stage of the constitutional conflict. This ill-considered step threatened those independent merchants whose welfare was based on the transatlantic carrying trade. "America," wrote one of them, "would be prostrate before a monster that may be able to destroy every branch of our commerce, drain us of all our property, and wantonly leave us to perish by the thousands." Such fears may have been groundless, but they were neverthelesss powerful. The Boston Tea Party of December 16, 1773, (and other such demonstrations along the seaboard) was one consequence. "The American colonists," Edmund Burke announced, "augur misgovernment at a distance, and sniff the approach of tyranny in every tainted breeze." However, in spite of an erratic display of royalism by George III, there was at the time a trend to centralize all British territories under the authority of Parliament, a policy that changed the course of empire. Until the events of 1776 proved otherwise, it also seemed to the London authorities that the American colonists were incapable of ruling themselves responsibly.

Charter companies contributed to the English settlement of North Ameri-

After failing miserably as a military cadet in 1769, William Hickey, a perennial ne'er-do-well, returned to India in 1777 and quickly amassed a fortune.

From the Memoirs

On 1st May [1769] we made the coast of Coromandel, a few miles to the southward of Pondicherry.... when falling calm, we came to an anchor, to wait the land breeze, which would carry us into Madras roads by daylight of the following morning. At the usual hour I went to my cot; but the thoughts of being so near the place of our destination entirely banished sleep, and finding all my efforts were in vain, I put on my clothes and went upon deck. Just as I got my head above the companion ladder, I felt an indescribably unpleasant sensation, suddenly, as it were, losing the power of breathing, which alarmed me much; for I supposed it to be the forerunner of one of those horrid Indian fevers of which I had heard so much....

Whilst worried by this idea, my friend Rogers, whose watch it was, said to me, "Well, Bill, what do you think of this? How do you like the delightful breeze you are doomed to spend your life in?" Enquiring what he meant, I found that what had so surprised and alarmed me was nothing more than the common land wind blowing as usual at that hour directly offshore, and so intensely hot that I could compare it only to standing within the oppressive influence of the steam of a furnace. At daybreak ... we heard that ... the ship's carpenter, a strong-made, vigorous man, was taken suddenly and violently ill with universal cramp in his limbs and stomach ... in one hour from his first being seized, he was no more. This quick death, added to the horrible land wind, gave me a very unfavourable opinion of the East Indies....

[in August 1769]

We arrived at Canton about noon. The view of the city, as you approach it, is strikingly grand, and at the same time picturesque. The magnitude and novelty of the architecture must always surprise strangers. The scene upon the water is as busy a one as the Thames below London Bridge, with this difference, that instead of our square-rigged vessels of different dimensions, you there have junks, which, although in the

middle of the fair weather season they navigate all along the coast of China and even to the Straits of Malacca, yet they never go out of sight of land, and for this plain reason they are wholly ignorant of navigation and all its advantages....

About half a mile above the city suburbs, in going from Whampoa, is a wharf, or embankment, regularly built of brick and mortar, extending more than half a mile in length, upon which wharf stands the different factories or place of residence of the supercargoes, each factory having the flag of its nation on a lofty ensign staff before it. At the time I was in China, they stood in the following order: first, the Dutch, then, the French, the English, the Swedes, and last, the Danes. Each of these factories, besides admirable banqueting, or public, rooms for eating, etc.,

have attached to them sets of chambers, varying in size according to the establishment. The English being far more numerous than any other nation trading with China, their range of buildings is much the most extensive. Each supercargo has four handsome rooms; the public apartments are in front looking to the river; the others go inland to the depth of two or three hundred feet, in broad courts, having the sets of rooms on each side, every set having a distinct and separate entrance with a small garden, and every sort of convenience.... The Americans (whom the Chinese distinguish by the expressive title of Second Chop Englishmen) have also a flag....

[1777]

At the time I arrived in Bengal, everybody dressed splendidly, being covered with lace, spangles and foil. I, who always had a tendency to be a beau, gave into the fashion with much goodwill, no person appearing in richer suits of velvet and lace than myself. I kept a handsome phaeton and beautiful pair of horses, and also had two noble Arabian saddle horses, my whole establishment being of the best and most expensive kind....

I lived so dissipated a life in point of drinking and late hours, no man laboured harder. I was always at my desk before seven in the morning and, with the break of half an hour for breakfast, never ceased work until dinner; after which, unless upon emergencies, I never took pen in hand. I had sufficient business to occupy myself and three native clerks. Money consequently came in fast, so that I never bestowed a thought about the price of an article. Whatever I wanted was ordered home; I made it a rule, however, to discharge every demand upon me the 1st of each month.

ca, but their role proved to be relatively brief and of minor consequence. Before any such organizations were formed for the exploitation of the New World, hapless ventures were undertaken by gentlemen adventurers; men less interested in profit than in extending the Christian queen's domain—in transferring the western wilderness into a feudal domain in which the social and political aristocracy of old England would be reproduced, with its lords and landed gentry surrounded by freeholders and tenants, its counties, boroughs, and parishes. It was in that idealistic and militant spirit that in 1587 Sir Walter Raleigh, the last of the great Elizabethan adventurers, attempted to found a colony in Virginia. His tiny settlement disappeared without a trace, and Raleigh had exhausted his fortune to no avail.

Several years earlier Sir Humphrey Gilbert, another visionary knight, had lost his life in a pathetic attempt to establish an English colony in Newfoundland. With such failures in mind, subsequent adventurers, aware that the East India Company was then netting one hundred per cent profit from its investments, briefly turned to the charter company as a device for exploiting the resources of the New World. Two groups of capitalists were organized, the one centering in Bristol and the other in London, dividing between them the English claim to North America. The first American commonwealth was planted by the London group at Jamestown, Virginia, in 1607. Two years later, needing more capital, the company was reorganized as an incorporated joint-stock company under the title "The Treasurer and Company of Adventurers and Planters of the City of London for the First Colony of Virginia." The enterprise was widely promoted, and when its charter was sealed, shares had been subscribed by 659 individuals, including 21 peers, 96 knights, 58 gentlemen, 110 merchants, and 282 citizens—and by 56 of the companies of the City of London. Its first president, Sir Thomas Smythe, was also the first president of the India Company. However, as a financial speculation the enterprise turned out to be a disaster, and in 1624 the charter was annulled and Virginia became a royal province.

Northern Virginia, renamed New England in 1620, fell to the Bristol group. In 1620, with a grant from the company and financed by some hopeful English merchants, the Pilgrims set sail for America. A decade later, seventeen vessels carrying close to one thousand men and women representing the Massachusetts Bay colony, under a royal charter granted by Charles I, sailed for New England. The company brought its charter along with its membership and its own government to the New World, thus establishing a colony that was virtually independent of England, free of controls by either king or Parliament. As the century advanced, the Lords of Trade became increasingly irritated by the independent ways of the colony, and in 1684 recommended annulling its charter. In 1686 New England also became a royal province.

The proprietary province succeeded the charter company as a device to build England's American empire. Royal grants of territory, bestowing broad jurisdiction on a lord proprietor, or lords proprietors, were responsible for the founding of most of the other colonies, including Maryland, Pennsylvania, Delaware, New York, New Jersey, and the Carolinas. Most of these, plagued by administrative problems, in the course of time sold out to the crown. At the outbreak of the Revolution, Pennsylvania, Delaware (in the hands of the Penn family), and Maryland (in the hands of the Calvert family) were the only remaining proprietary colonies. Connecticut and Rhode Island were incorporated colonies, with charters from the royal hand. All the other colonies had become royal provinces, governed theoretically by the king's instructions to his governors, but with their own legislative assemblies and a lively awareness of their rights and interests.

Both the English and the French also used the proprietary method of colonization in the islands of the West Indies, where immense profits were to be made in the cultivation of sugar. The sugar islands of Guadeloupe and Martinique had been returned to France largely because English merchants, who had long thrived on the profits of Britain's own sugar islands in the West Indies, feared that incorporation into the British economic empire of the French islands, with their large and efficient production, would disrupt the long-standing mercantile advantage English traders had enjoyed by excluding French sugar from English markets. In the global economy of the eighteenth century sugar was one of the most precious commodities. It was the ideal colonial product. It could not be grown in Europe, black labor could produce it cheaply in the New World, and Europe craved it. Thanks in good part to sugar, the Americas at the time played a larger role than Asia in the trade of western Europe. During the Middle Ages the princes and prelates of Europe had been able to sample the sweet delights of sugar as it had trickled through the trade routes from East to West. Then, in the seventeenth century, the cane had been brought in quantities from the East and planted in the West Indies, and within a few decades a whole new economic system had evolved, with large plantations worked by black slaves brought from Africa to provision what became an almost inexhaustible market in the Western world. "The profits of a sugar plantation in any one of our West Indies colonies," wrote Adam Smith, "are generally much greater than those of any other cultivation that is known either in Europe or America."

Important merchants and brokers who controlled the sugar trade of the West Indies enjoyed seats in the House of Commons, from which they could guide legislation that would protect or advance their interests. It was estimated that in 1775 property in those islands to the value of £14,000,000 was owned by persons living in England. One of the great sugar fortunes was amassed in Jamaica by William Beckford, a merchant who entered Parliament in 1747 and who became lord mayor of London. He was only the most famous of those who influentially represented the plantation owners and their corresponding merchants and traders—and who soon became all-powerful in "the City." Although ministers spoke reverently of His Majesty's government and bowed to the king in his presence, it was well known that the fortunes of the realm were in the hands of such large property interests, which buttressed an unstable throne.

In passing, such were the ramifications of imperial design that Beckford's son, heir, and namesake, orphaned at the age of eleven, was put under the guardianship of Pitt. Privately educated (he studied music under Mozart) and widely traveled, the younger Beckford both amused and scandalized his contemporaries by the eccentricities he could afford to indulge through his immense wealth. At Fonthill-Gifford, Wiltshire, he built a huge and fantastic "folly," a Gothic extravagance called Fonthill Abbey, surrounding his property with a high wall to exclude fox hunters and unwelcome guests. (One matron who called, uninvited, to press the interest of her marriageable daughter was royally entertained by servants for several days, but never set eyes on the

For the London Mag.

ATLANTIC

Trade Winds

OCEAN

CARIBBY

Explanation.
Eng. English.
Fr. French.
Sp. Spanish.
D. Dutch.
Dan. Danish.

Samana I.
C. Raphael
HISPANIOLA
Bayaqana OR Seibo
St. DOMINGO
Alta Gratia
Saona I.
G. ANTILLES

Zachco
Monguin Mona
Jaunico
Guadianilla
I. PORTO RICO to Spain
Passage
St. Juan de Porto Rico
P. S. Germano
St. Thomas Dan.
Tortola Eng.
Crab I. Eng. & Fr.
St. Cruz Dan.
St. Croix Dan.
Anegada Eng.
Virgin Gorda Eng.
Sombrero Desert
Anguilla Eng.
Vergera Eng.
St. Eustatia
St. Martin Sp. & Fr.
St. Bartholomen Sp. & Fr.
Ft. Lewis
St. Christopher
Barbuda Eng.
Saba D.
Ft. Charles Basseterre Eng.
Nevis Eng.
St. Johns Town
Redonda Eng.
Montserrat Eng.
North Pt.
Seal I.
Ft. St. Peter
GUADELOUPE to Fr.
St. Lewis
lx. Desirade Fr.
Pet. Terre Fr.
Marie les Saints
Mariegalante Fr.
F. de la B. Terre
Old Ft. Point
te Camp du Roi
Dominica neutral & desert
ANTEGO Eng.
Falmouth

Ares I.

NORTH

Trade Winds

SEA

LEEWARD Is.

WINDWARD Is.

An ACCURATE MAP
of the
CARIBBY ISLANDS,
with the Crowns, &c.
to which they severally belong.
By T. Kitchin Geogr.

Basse Pt. la Trinite
Ft. St. Pierre
C. Tourmente
MARTINICO Fr.
Ft. Royal
Pt. des Salinas
Pt. Diamant

BARBADOS Eng.
Speights Town
Bridge Town
Ostins Town

St. Lucy Claimd by king & Fr. but seized by the Fr.

St. Vincent neutral

Bequia neutral
Canouan
Cariouacon
Grand Union
le Fort
Grenada Fr.

British Statute Miles 69 to a Degree
10 20 40 60 80 100 120 140

LITTLE ANTILLES

St. Pierre
Curasao D.
Buen Ayre D.
I. de Aves Sp.
Rocca Sp.
Urchilla Sp.
I. Blanca Sp.
The 7 Ages
MARGARITA Sp.
Tortuga Sp.
Frayles
Cola
Testigos
Tabago desert
C. Galera
C. Redondo

Sicco Pt.
Triste Gulf
C. Blanco
Farillao
Perrilu I.
Nra Sra de Carvalleda
St. Jago de Leon
Comanagotta
Comana
Cubagua
Pt. St. Jago
G. of Cariaco
Macanao
Coeta
C. of 3 Points
C. Salinas
Boca del Drago
St. Joseph
TRINIDAD I. Sp.
Pt. Redondo
G. of Paria
Pt. Gallo

CARACCAS
SOUTH AMERICA
COMANA
PARIA

Longit. W. from London

68 67 66 65 64 63 62 61 60

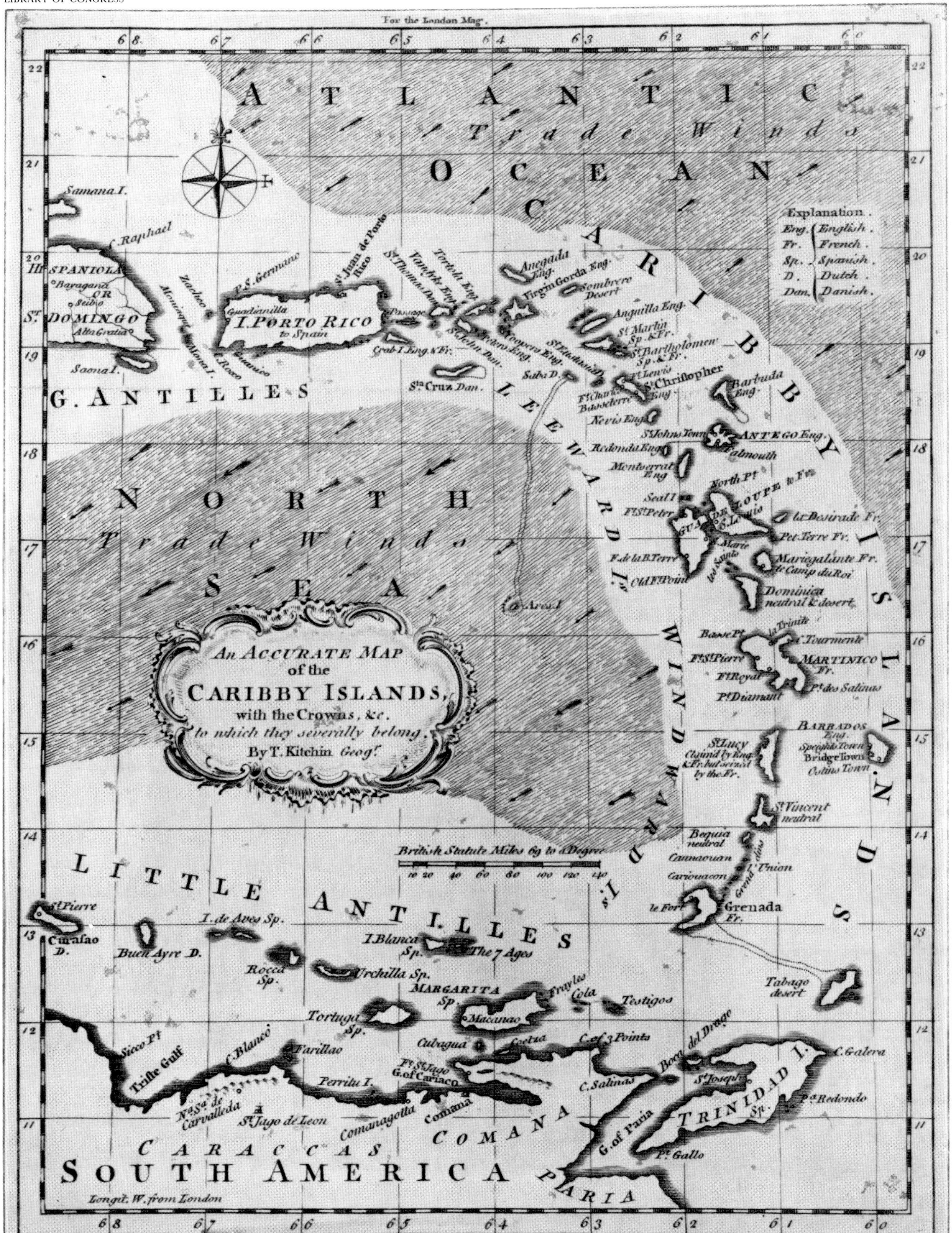

master of the house.) There he lived in magnificent seclusion, and assembled an impressive art collection that included works by—or attributed to—Raphael, Murillo, Claude, Holbein, Dürer, Callot, Van Dyck, Bellini, and Van Eyck. He gathered together a large library of rare books and manuscripts, and at one point purchased the entire collection of books of Edward Gibbon at Lausanne, sight unseen, so that he might have something to read in case he happened to be passing through that city. Along his travels he paused long enough at Sintra, in Portugal, to build on its outskirts a palace of pure white stone in the Moorish style, now known as Montserrat, with a surrounding park with high-lying lawns, as perfect as any in England, systematically cultivated by subsequent British owners with rare plants, giant tree ferns, and other flora assembled from all corners of the earth. With income from sugar plantations, Beckford outdid the nabobs from India in the conspicuous display of his wealth. For some years he was a member of Parliament but, unlike his father, he seldom attended the House. He was a precious fruit of British imperialism.

French fortunes were also made in sugar. With money he gleaned through international trade, Jean Joseph Laborde, born of a bourgeois family in the south of France, bought huge sugar plantations in San Domingo (later Haiti). With the additional, enormous wealth realized from those holdings he became one of the foremost bankers of Paris and for a time acted as Voltaire's investment agent. He owned a number of chateaux near Paris and as a large-scale real estate operator developed that part of Paris now known as the Chaussé d'Antin. His daughter married the Comte de Noailles, a member of one of France's very distinguished and old families (Lafayette also married into the Noailles family). Laborde gave generously to charities and substantially underwrote the construction of new hospitals. With his influence and reputation he was able to raise the money the French government needed to help pay the French army and navy that were dispatched to aid the Americans in their war for independence. Later, he also helped finance the insurrection that introduced the French Revolution. With all those good deeds in the background, in 1794 he lost his head to the guillotine.

"The chief and fundamental support" of the American plantations, in the islands and on the mainland, was the slave trade. Up until the beginning of the American Revolution that infamous traffic had been expanding continuously for several centuries—and it continued to do so. A Dutch frigate landed the first twenty Negro slaves on the mainland of North America at Jamestown, Virginia, in 1619, a year before the Pilgrims arrived at Plymouth. The price of the rapid colonization of North America in the years that followed was in good part paid for by Africa through the increasing exportation of black chattels. By the time the War of Independence broke out, there were about half a million slaves in the colonies. Time and again some American colonists had protested against the traffic in human flesh that was maintained, for a time at least, chiefly in the interest of the Royal African Company and its successor, the Regulated Company; but it was in vain. Colonial laws prohibiting the practice were disallowed by the Privy Council. In 1770 George III forbade the governor of Virginia "to assent to any law by which the importation of slaves should be in any respect prohibited or obstructed," and even as late as 1776 William Legge, Lord Dartmouth, denounced the colonies for their attempts "to check or discourage a traffic so beneficial to the nation."

A sugar planter on the island of Martinique introduces his two latest purchases to slaves he has owned for a time.
BIBLIOTHEQUE NATIONALE

Nevertheless, by the 1770's the debate on slavery was intense, not only in England, but also in France, Denmark, and America as well.

Meanwhile, in spite of that moral climate, colonial merchants were growing rich in the so-called triangular trade, in which an essential element was traffic in slaves. In this notorious three-way commerce New England ships exchanged farm products of the middle and northern colonies for West Indian sugar and molasses, which was brought home to be converted into rum by local distilleries. The rum was then shipped to Africa, where it was bartered for slaves, which were then in turn brought to the islands and mainland of the Americas for sale to plantation owners and others who could use such forced labor. Among the seafarers who took part in such business were Esek Hopkins, who later became commander in chief of the continental navy, and John Paul Jones, who was to be the most celebrated naval hero of the Revolutionary War. After a brief experience Jones quit what he referred to as this "abominable" trade in human bodies.

All in all, it has been estimated, as many as fifteen million slaves, including the significant percentage who died under the ghastly conditions of the middle passage, or sea voyage, and were thrown into the sea, were shipped out of Africa to the New World before that hideous traffic was ended. (The statistics do not include the uncounted number of Africans who must have been killed during the wars and raids in which their fellow men were rounded up.) The western coast of Africa was lined with forts and "factories" that served as depots for the human cargoes assembled from inland tribes for shipment overseas—assembled for the most part, it must be recalled, by the ruling black aristocracy who waged wars, organized raids, and passed judgment on criminals and debtors to provide the "capital" they needed to buy European goods they wanted. To pay for spirits, tobacco, firearms, gunpowder, and other such lethal luxuries, they were obliged to sell away their fellow men. As one French trader observed, "the trade in slaves is the business of kings, rich men, and prime merchants." The economy of all western Africa was dominated by this sorry exchange. Most of the European maritime nations played their part—Dutch, Portuguese, French, Spanish, Danish—although it was Britain that led the way, supplying not only its own American colonies but those of France and Spain; hawking such "black gold" wherever there was a demand for it, to man the silver and copper mines as well as the sugar, indigo, tobacco, and cotton plantations.

It was, as Lord Dartmouth said, a very "beneficial" enterprise for those who were in a position to reap the profits. From the ready supply of the commodities unearthed and cultivated by slave labor grew the industries which contributed so substantially to Europe's, and America's, growing wealth—the textile, distilling, sugar-refining, metallurgical, and, indirectly, shipbuilding industries. "The founding of industries, private fortunes, public opulence, the rebuilding of towns, the social glories of a new class," wrote one French historian; "great merchants eager for public office that should reflect their economic importance and impatient to be rid of what they called with careless exaggeration, 'the shame of servitude'; such were the sum of the essential consequences for eighteenth-century France of the African slave trade."

For Africa it was, of course, a sadly different story. The slave trade brutalized everyone involved in it, white and black alike, but particularly the traditional rulers in West Africa and all who served them in their greedy com-

A detail from the frontispiece of the second volume of Abbé Raynal's six-volume history of Europe in the Indies
LIBRARY OF CONGRESS

merce. Beyond that, the massive removal from their home districts of millions of Africans in the prime of life depopulated the land. Others were distracted from their traditional trades, to participate in the sordid and profitable business of selling their brothers (and sisters). By violently shifting village economies from ancient, firmly based patterns to the pursuit of baubles and spirits, standard exchange for slaves, the character of life in a very considerable area of the world was disastrously changed. The economic and cultural development of that part of Africa was delayed for centuries to come. In the process, the art and sculpture of the people of Benin, Ife, and Oyo, for example, virtually disappeared, a loss that has been recognized only in recent years as art dealers and collectors assiduously search for rare reminders of those ancient arts and crafts.

One part of Africa that remained outside the limits of the sickening trade in slaves, and the only considerable European settlement on the continent, was in the extreme south. There the Netherlands East India Company had in the seventeenth century established a strategic base as a half-way station on the sea route from Europe to the Orient; a port of call where merchantmen could be provisioned with grain, meat, and wine. In 1772 one visitor wrote of the Cape that it "may with propriety be stiled an inn for travellers to and from the East Indies, who, after several months' sail may here get refreshments of all kinds, and are then about half way to the place of their destination, whether homeward or outward bound." Unfortunately, a grim proportion of the men who shipped out of Dutch ports for the East never reached the refreshments of the Cape. In 1782 more than forty-three per cent of the crews of one fleet of East Indiamen died before reaching the "half-way house," and almost as many had to be hospitalized on their arrival there.

French Huguenots and Germans came to settle at the Cape and, along with the permanent Dutch population, developed a distinctive and expanding colony whose frontiers pushed constantly farther into the interior of the continent. These mixed peoples, to become known as Boers, were unified by their Afrikaans language and the widespread influence of the Dutch Reformed Church, and were to have a strong impact on the course of South African history in centuries to come. Also, they shared a common irritation from the au-

tocratic and often corrupt administration of the company's representatives. As American patriots were taking up arms to achieve and secure their independence, leading Boers were reading the revolutionary literature of Locke, Adam Smith, Grotius, and others, forming their own patriot movement. However, in the years immediately to follow, during the Napoleonic Wars when France invaded the Low Countries, England found an excuse to take over the South African colony—and redirect the course of its history.

The Boers were already well acquainted with the English, whose merchant ships put in at the Cape and contributed handsomely to the colony's prosperity. "Nothing can be more agreeable to the people of this place," wrote one English lady visitor in 1764–65, "than the arrival of an English ship, as it causes a circulation of money, and indeed it is chiefly by the English that most people in town are supported; not only by taking the captains, passengers, etc., to board at their houses, but by furnishing the ships with provisions. A great many French ships likewise stop here, and all the Dutch passing to and from India; but for the last they are obliged to provide according to certain prices, stipulated by the Dutch Company, and as neither the Dutch nor the French spend their money so freely as the English, of course they are not so desirable guests. The custom is to pay a rix-dollar daily for each person's board and lodging, for which they are provided with everything; the tables are plentiful, the houses are clean, and the people obliging, and what makes it extremely comfortable, is, that most of them speak English. French is likewise spoken by many; so that foreigners find themselves more at home in this port than can be imagined."

Trade beyond the Cape to the Far East faced special problems. Europe wanted more from Asia than Asia wanted from Europe. In technical skills China and India, in particular, were in many ways more advanced than any of the Occidental countries, and the cost of Eastern labor was lower. Europe could not match the quality of the silks, cottons, lacquers, porcelains, and rugs, for example, that in the early days of the trade could be bought in the Orient and that were coveted in the West. (The very names given to cotton fabrics in Western nations suggest the places from which they were said to have come: "madras" and "calico" from Madras and Calicut in India; "muslin'' from the Arab city of Mosul. "Gingham" is derived from a Malay word meaning "striped"; "chintz" from a Hindustani word meaning "spotted.") The principal acceptable commodity the West could offer in exchange for such Oriental goods was precious metal drawn from Spanish-American mines or from those of Africa's Gold Coast—a price that was reluctantly paid at a time when economic theory held that the gold and silver retained in a nation's coffers provided the basis of its security and power. Before the use of credit was widely developed, the issues of war were likely to depend upon the gold and silver a ruler could command, either directly from the treasury or through the hands of tax collectors. Such viewpoints were passing as the eighteenth century advanced, but they had affected the operations of generations of statesmen and merchants, and the structures of colonies about the globe.

Also, as the century advanced, tea became the single most important export from Asia to Europe. Tea had been introduced to the Western world in the seventeenth century, but at first its merits were disputed and its peculiar delights barely savored. Some thought of it as a medicinal drink (or as an herb to be chewed), good for, among other ailments, a "cold and defluxions" and "the Headache, giddiness and heaviness thereof." (One Dutch doctor prescribed up to two hundred cups of the beverage a day for his unfortunate patients.) Others considered it a "damned weed," a "rank poison farfetched and dear bought." In the beginning it was indeed a costly drink. In 1664 the British East India Company presented Charles II with slightly over two pounds of tea as an appropriately princely gift. However, as the price dropped, consumption went up until tea became practically an everyday necessity in certain areas of Europe and America, notably in England and the colonies; and the China trade boomed. In the years just preceding 1776 the average annual shipment of tea to England alone rose to more than ten million pounds.

For centuries Canton remained the sole official port for foreign trade with China. The Arabs had a trading community there as early as the seventh century, and from the sixteenth century on, this port was the goal of Europe's fleets. Trading rules and regulations were rigidly set and controlled by Chinese officialdom. Business dealings were restricted to a small section of the city's waterfront where warehouses, or hongs, were leased to foreign nations. A powerful group of Chinese merchants, who were imperial appointees, was held responsible for the credit and deportment of their clients. As soon as the European dealers had transacted their business, they were supposed to retire from Canton to the Portuguese settlement at Whampoa, about twelve miles down the river. European women were strictly forbidden to enter the hong area. To the Chinese, all foreigners trading at Canton were *fan kwaes*, or "foreign devils"; and like all devils, they needed the closest watching.

The system was awkward and often humiliating for the Europeans. However, China disdained to "recognize" any European country as either friend or foe on the haughty assumption that they were all composed of barbarians and were of relatively minor importance in the scheme of things as seen from Peking. Late in the eighteenth century a British ambassadorial mission was sent to the court of the Chinese emperor Ch'ien Lung with the aim of revising the conditions which English traders were obliged to suffer, so that they might live and work in a manner compatible with the dignity to which they were accustomed in their own nation. The entourage was led by Chinese carrying banners inscribed "Tribute Bearers." Ch'ien Lung condescended to send a

Holland, or as it is also called Horan, or Komo (*lit.* "Red-hair") is the name of one of the provinces of the Netherlands. Now the Netherlands lie in the extreme N.W. of Europe. This territory has seven Provinces and seventeen Daimyo. Holland is one of these seven Provinces. This may be compared, in our country, with Shikoku and Kyushu, etc. forming provinces out of the whole of Japan. Holland lies between 50° & 53° from the North Pole. It is a very cold country. These people have five outstanding features; they have high noses, blue eyes, red hair, white skins, and tall bodies. Their characters are called retteru (letter) and they are written horizontally; they cannot be read by Japanese, Chinese or similar people. Their *buruku* (broeck = breeches) corresponds to and is worn like the Japanese *momohiki*. Their coat is called *rokko* (rock) which answers to our *Jiban*. Their officials are called mandarins, and on ceremonial occasions wear a cloak corresponding to our *maru-kappa*. Their food is bread and wheaten flour, made like a *mochi* (rice-ball) and eaten roasted. Besides this, they are fond of fowls, meat and greasy foods. Furthermore they eat lots of raw *daikon* (radishes).

This country lies a long way from Japan, — 13,000 *ri* by our reckoning. Of this distance from Japan to Java is 3,000 *ri*, whilst from Java to Holland is 10,000 *ri*. Now the Hollanders who come every year to Japan, all come from Java and none from Holland. Java has been conquered by the Hollanders who have their chief fortress at Batavia; this corresponds to the Red-hair settlement of Deshima in Japan. Java lies due South of Japan. Therefore they come in the rainy season of the fifth month with the South wind, and, after importing their products, leave again

The Dutch ship Shellach *docked at Deshima in 1782, and a Japanese artist named Hayashi Shihei did a woodcut of the ship (below) and wrote an explanatory inscription, quoted here, to his print. (The Japanese weights and measures he mentions are: 1* ri, *or 3,937 meters; 1* jō, *or 3,030 meters; 1* shaku, *or 0.303 meters; 1* kwan, *or 3.75 kilograms; 1* kin, *or 0.6 kilograms.)*

with the North wind in the ninth month. This is done regularly.

Now the Hollanders call their ships *skippu* (schip). Their build is very imposing. To begin with they make the ship's hull from big timbers; next they fix in crosswise, square blocks of chestnutwood; then they caulk up the seams with pitch and tar. All the hull below the waterline is sheathed in lead. The ship's beam is 3 *jō*; length, 15 *jō*; draught, 3 *jō* 8 *shaku*. All are 3-decked ships, distance between decks, 9 *shaku*. Altogether there are 4 masts. The height of the main mast is 19 *jō*. There are 17 sails altogether, and 12 flags. The ship mounts more than 30 guns. Each gun fires a shot weighing 3 *kwan*.

Now the crew of these ships usu-

ally amount to 100 or more persons. Amongst them are the officers called Captain, Factor, skipper, koopman, pilot etc. who are all upper-class Hollanders. The people under them are called *matorosu* (matrozen) who are very low class. Furthermore one lot of these lower-class people is called *swardo jongo* (swaerte jongen) being *kurombo* or blacks, and not natives of Holland. Coolies from Jacatara (Batavia), Boegis, Boutin, Timor, etc. are bought by the Hollanders and used as slaves. As they all come from tropical countries they are all very black. Again, every ship has her own name, such as *Zeedoin* (*Zeeduin*), *Sutabenissu* (*Stavenisse*) *Hoisutesupiki* (*Huis te Spijk*) and so forth.

Now the goods imported by these ships include sugar, sappanwood, rattans, woollens, velvets, San Thomé (calicoes), *kaiki*, incense, drugs, cloves, jasmine, pepper, and also glass and spectacles. Besides these, curios, strange birds, and animals are also imported. Their provisions include oxen, pigs, poultry, geese and the like in enormous quantities. Furthermore, the goods they export from Japan include a million *kin* of copper (annually), regularly. In addition, oil-paper, umbrellas, pottery, lacquered wares, copper kettles, copper cash, dry goods, clothes, as well as *saké*, mustard, pickled *daikon* and fruits, etc., for provisions, all in large quantities. The ship with the cargo weighs about ten million *kin*.

Now that country has been in existence for 5,400 years. From the date of the first Hollander rule till the present day, is 1776 years. There has been no change in the dynasty of the rulers. From Kwanei 17 (*i.e.* 1640) when trade was first allowed, unbroken intercourse has continued for 143 years till this year. Written in the 2nd year of Tenmei (1782).

Lord Macartney's mission to China in 1793 failed to achieve its goal—an easing of the trade restrictions imposed by Ch'ien Lung on the East India Company. As is seen in this James Gillray cartoon, the Chinese were not impressed with Macartney's gifts (among them a jackdaw in a cage, a mousetrap, and the illustrated works of Shakespeare).

message to George III without relinquishing an iota of his own "celestial" dignity. "As the Requests made by your Ambassador militate against the Laws and Usages of This Our Empire," the message read, "and are at the same Time wholly useless to the End proposed, I cannot acquiesce in them. I again admonish you, O King, to act conformably to my Intentions. . . ."

Ch'ien Lung had called the tune. But the increasing amounts of opium from India and Persia, used to supplement European payments in precious metals, led to portentous developments. Opium smoking was centuries old in China, although until the late eighteenth century the addiction had not been widespread. By then, however, the Chinese had at last come to need the drug, and this growing demand could be met from the vast fields of opium poppies in Bengal; and over the produce from those fields the British East India Company had a monopoly. Opium was the only commodity from the outside world which the Chinese did crave. Finally, the English had found something that would help them balance a trade that had always been in China's favor. So the British became drug pushers, bribing their way past local officials who were charged with discouraging the traffic. The profits from this illicit trade were so great that they helped in large measure to save the company from bankruptcy. (The trade had been developed by Hastings who, recognizing the disastrous effect of opium on the Indian peasantry, had insisted on its export to China.) The necessity of this trade, however nefarious, was not even debated. Without the profits derived from it, British rule in India was in grave danger of collapsing. Looking far beyond the limits of this story for a moment, in the 1840's and 1850's, after the Chinese government tried to control trade in the drug, the British government went to war over the issue, and Chinese relations with the outside world were abruptly changed. For the better part of a century to come, Europeans would then call the tune where their interests in China were concerned.

Europe's exposure to Oriental cultures, particularly the Chinese, had a wide variety of rewards far beyond the profits from trade. Merchants returning from the East, like earlier missionaries, brought back reports of the astonishing things they saw and heard in those remote climates. As will be told in more detail in a later chapter, the West was seized with a mania for things Chinese, and for things that seemed to be Chinese. That land was sufficiently remote from Western civilization to induce free speculation about its customs, its arts, its institutions, and its religion. As the French man of letters Baron von Grimm remarked in 1776: "The Chinese Empire has become in our time the object of special attention and of special study. The missionaries first fascinated public opinion by rose coloured reports from that distant land, too distant to be able to contradict their falsehoods. Then the philosophers took it up, and drew from them whatever could be of use in denouncing and removing the evils they observed in their own country. Thus this country became in a short time the home of wisdom, virtue, and good faith, its government the best possible and the longest established, its morality the loftiest and most beautiful in the known world; its laws, its policy, its art, its industry were likewise such as to serve as model for nations of the earth."

One of the most familiar and engaging forms of social criticism in eighteenth century Europe was in the adventures of an imaginary Eastern visitor whose perplexed and amazed accounts of the European scene, as he witnessed it, artfully revealed the follies and conceits of civilization in the Western world. Early in the century Montesquieu published his *Lettres persanes*, which was a satire and criticism of French institutions in the guise of letters purportedly written by two Persians traveling in France and commenting on their experiences in that land of very strange ways. (The publication won Montesquieu immediate notoriety.)

But the Chinese were the preferred characters for such a literary device, since they represented what many intellectuals chose to believe was a truly superior civilization, as Grimm pointed out. In 1762, in England, Oliver Goldsmith published (anonymously) *The Citizen of the World*, in which one Lien Chi Altangi, in letters written to a friend at home, describes Europe as a disorderly and dismaying stage for avarice, ambition, and intrigue of men. By extolling the virtues of another, remote culture, the author could expose the deficiencies of his own society clearly enough to reach a literate audience, but in a manner that spared him official censorship.

The influence of China on Western philosophy (and religion) was more remarkable and more durable. At the University of Halle, one German philosopher raised a tempest by implying that there was greater wisdom in the writings of Confucius than in all the tenets of Christianity. In France, Voltaire was an outspoken admirer of China's ancient culture, its tolerant government, and its sage philosophy, from all of which he believed Christian Europe had much to learn. In praising Confucianism as an enlightened deism he relied heavily on writings of the early Jesuits in China, who also had emphatically praised Chinese civilization (and who were as a consequence accused of compromising with paganism. "I have read his [Confucius'] books with attention," Voltaire wrote, "I have made extracts from them; I found that they spoke only the

Indian workers carrying opium, neatly packaged for shipment to Canton, China
VICTORIA AND ALBERT MUSEUM

This building, designed for a Roman celebration of Chinese culture in 1772, provides some measure of Europe's enthusiasm for chinoiserie. Wealthy Europeans furnished homes with silk wall hangings, lacquered furniture, and dainty tea services, all preferably made in China.
MUSEO DI ROMA

purest morality. . . . He appeals only to virtue, he preaches no miracles, there is nothing in them of religious allegory." "One need not be obsessed with the merits of the Chinese," he further observed, "to recognize at least that the organization of their empire is in truth the best the world has ever seen, and moreover the only one founded on parental authority." What, Voltaire asked, should European princes do when they hear of such examples? "Admire and blush, but above all imitate." (Such notions did not die; as late as 1901 a Cambridge philosopher would write in his *Letters from John Chinaman* still another attack on Western civilization from an Oriental viewpoint.)

Voltaire was attracted by the religions of India as well. He wondered whether India might have been the cradle of civilization and Vedic Hinduism, the primitive religion of mankind. Here he was informed by the writings of certain members of the East India Company who had delved into Hindu and Moslem laws as well as religions and who stressed the depth and subtlety of Hindu doctrine. One of the company's servants, Charles Wilkins, founded a tradition of Oriental scholarship in Great Britain by translating the Bhagavad-Gita, a sacred Hindu text.

There were others who believed that greater wisdom and virtue were to be found among the so-called more primitive peoples with whom Europeans became associated in their trading and colonizing. The very influential philosopher Denis Diderot was an extravagant advocate of the Tahitians, about whom Captain Cook also wrote in a report of his travels there in 1769, and whom Diderot thought to be superior beings because they lived in close harmony with nature. In their mouths he put the words of experienced philosophers viewing life with a refreshing simplicity and honesty long lost to sophisticated Europeans. Among other things they contrast the sexual repressions of the

Christian world with the open sensuality of their own country. The "noble" red man of the American forests also came in for his share of praise. In one of the early books of travel in the back country of the North American continent the talented young Baron de Lahontan made a Huron chieftain the mouthpiece of his own cynical thoughts about European society. Lahontan had roamed over a large part of the American wilderness and developed an admiration for the native Indians that he exaggerated into a fierce purpose. "Really, you weary me with your talk of gentlemen, merchants, and priests!" remarks the rhetorical savage Adario. "Would you see such a thing were there neither *thine* nor *mine*? You would all be equal, as the Hurons are . . . those who are only fit to drink, eat, sleep, and amuse themselves would languish and die; but their descendants would live like us." It was revolutionary talk that anticipated some of the arguments of the philosophes.

One of the most persuasive dissidents from such points of view was the Abbé Raynal, a renegade disciple of the Jesuits whom Benjamin Franklin met in Paris in 1776. Raynal was then engaged in revising and augmenting a work he had prepared with the help of Diderot and others and had first published in about 1770 (the exact date is uncertain). In a number of ways this was one of the most unusual, if not the best informed, of those compilations of knowledge that flowed so abundantly from the presses in the eighteenth century. It carried the very descriptive title *A Philosophical and Political History of the Settlements and Trade of Europeans in the Two Indies.* In the words of Baron von Grimm, Raynal's publication was designed "to consecrate the progress of our enlightenment." It was the first attempt to trace the history of European expansion about the world, and the first to give fair consideration to other races. It condemned slavery and preached that colonization was iniquitous and war immoral; that the Church had betrayed religion; and that people had a right to revolt against tyranny. Nothing quite like this had ever before appeared in print, and it attracted enormous interest. Franklin read and criticized it. Jefferson replied to its arguments in his *Notes on Virginia.* Crèvecoeur dedicated his *Letters from an American Farmer* to Raynal. Gibbon admired the work, and Frederick the Great threw it into the fire when he found that it disparaged the wars he had fought. It was banned, burned, and put on the Index—and read everywhere. Before the excitement subsided, Raynal's *History* had grown to twelve volumes since its first appearance, and it was issued in scores of editions, legitimate and pirated.

One curious contention of his initial thesis was that not only did Europeans corrupt the natives in lands they colonized, but they themselves deteriorated in those backward places of the earth, so distant from the stimulating climate of the civilized old world. Even the English who settled in North America had "visibly degenerated," he claimed. In short, Raynal concluded, the founding of America had been an unfortunate mistake. This sort of judgment from a widely esteemed "philosopher" amused Franklin. One evening he gave a dinner party at his residence at Passy to which Raynal and some of his compatriots were invited, along with an equal number of Franklin's American acquaintances. When the Abbé launched his favorite theory, Franklin suggested that they try the question by the fact before them. "We are here one-half Americans and one-half French," he remarked, "and it happens that the Americans have placed themselves on one side of the table, and our French friends are on the other. Let both parties arise and we will see on which side

This illustration first appeared in Baron de Lahontan's book about North America, which helped popularize the "noble savage" and "natural man" themes.
NEW YORK PUBLIC LIBRARY

nature has degenerated." By chance the Americans were all tall and stalwart men, and the Frenchmen—especially the Abbé—remarkably small. According to Thomas Jefferson, Raynal parried this demonstration by admitting that there were notable exceptions to his thesis, among which, he graciously conceded, Franklin himself was a conspicuous example. Obviously, even among the elite all was not reasonable in the Age of Reason.

Were any further proof needed to demonstrate how wrong Raynal was on that point, it was provided in abundance by the character and deportment of the men who were at that time leading and fighting the American Revolution. Indeed, it seems almost paradoxical that a relatively small society of three million people, far removed from the main centers of learning and culture, hemmed in by a vast wilderness, and with no tradition of high politics, should have produced in one generation a galaxy of statesmen as distinguished as any to be found in the eighteenth century—or perhaps of any other time. In his *Notes on Virginia*, Jefferson made precisely this point: on the basis of its much larger population France should have had eight Washingtons and eight Franklins (for modesty's sake not to mention eight Jeffersons).

Elsewhere in his writings Raynal was at once contradictory and singularly prophetic. In referring to the discovery and exploitation of the East and West Indies, he remarked: "This great event hath improved the construction of ships, navigation, geography, astronomy, medicine, natural history, and some other branches of knowledge; and these advantages have not been attended with any known inconvenience. It has procured to some empires vast domains, which have given splendor, power, and wealth, to the states which have founded them. But what expenses have not been lavished to clear, to govern, or to defend these distant possessions. When these colonies shall have acquired that degree of culture, knowledge, and population which is suitable for them, will they not detach themselves from a country which has founded its splendor upon their prosperity? We know not at what period this revolution will happen; but it must certainly take place."

At another point he observed that if the American colonists "once ceased to have Negroes for slaves, and kings who live at a distance from them for masters, they perhaps would become the most astonishing people that have ever appeared on earth. The spirit of liberty which they would imbibe from their earliest infancy; the understanding and abilities which they would inherit from Europe; the activity, which the necessity of repelling numerous enemies would inspire; the large colonies they would have to form; the rich commerce they would have to found on an immense cultivation; the ranks and societies they would have to create; and the maxims, laws, and manners they would have to establish on the principles of reason: all these springs of action would, perhaps, make, of an equivocal and miscellaneous race of people, the most flourishing nation that philosophy and humanity could wish for the happiness of the world." He went on to predict that "if ever any fortunate revolution should take place in the world, it will begin in America. After having experienced such devastation, this New World must flourish in its turn and, perhaps, command the Old. It will become the asylum of our people who have been oppressed by political establishments, or driven away by war."

Raynal obviously wrote these lines before his meeting with Franklin and his friends, but by coincidence they were translated into English in 1776.

The American Revolution was only the most immediate of those changes in

The Paris parlement exiled the controversial Abbé Raynal, shown above in a contemporary engraving, in 1781.

the colonial world that Raynal predicted. An epoch in colonialism was ending. Within the coming generation, under the leadership of Toussaint L'Ouverture, the Negro republic of Haiti freed itself from French control. Spain's hold on its vast dominions in South America was at last loosening; they would be broken up into a group of separate nations. Within another generation Brazil would repudiate the authority of Portugal. In the West Indies voices of sympathy for the cause of independence were raised, although those islands generally did not have the capability to overthrow imperial controls. The Boer farmer of South Africa, the New England merchant, the Peruvian Creole, and the emancipated Negro were all animated by the same spirit, which looked to freedom from Europe's authority.

It was also in 1776 that Adam Smith published his *Inquiry into the Nature and Causes of the Wealth of Nations,* a brilliant book of revolutionary portent and one deeply concerned with the business of empire. The revolt then stirring in America, partly because of British restrictions on colonial trade (Smith termed them "mean and malignant expedients"), provided the background of Smith's theories. Recent historians have conjectured, not implausibly, that had the proposals regarding free trade advanced by Smith been then put to actual practice by the British government, there might have been no American Revolution, at least at that time. As one sidelight to his arguments, Smith wrote that he expected the American nation beyond the sea to become one of the foremost nations in the economy of the world; that within little more than a century it might indeed become the seat of the British empire.

But Smith's ideas did not completely capture the imagination of his generation, even in England, which was in its economy the most advanced European nation in the second half of the eighteenth century. A centuries-old faith in the mercantilist system, which had its roots in the Middle Ages, persisted until the end of the century, and in many states beyond that. Actually, the mercantilist system was not a coherent system at all, but rather a mixed bundle of loosely held beliefs and attitudes—beliefs and attitudes that had everywhere in the Western world guided the trade of nations and the colonial enterprise of empires for at least two hundred years. The unquestioned and fundamental maxims of mercantilism were that commerce should be regulated in the interest of the state; that no nation should be dependent upon rival countries for staple commodities, for this, it was believed, would threaten at once the prosperity of the trading class and the strength of government; and that the supply of precious metals, most basic of staple commodities, should be zealously hoarded, within the control of the individual state. To be economically self-sufficient in order to be politically independent was the cardinal doctrine. "That Realme is most compleat and wealthie," wrote one Englishman in the sixteenth century, "which either hath sufficient to serve itselfe or can finde means to exporte of the naturall comodities [more] than it hath occasion necessarily to import." Thus stated, this was merely the old feudal and municipal ideal adapted to the demands of a national state.

In mercantile terms the balance of trade was the equivalent of the balance of power in political terms. It was when England found itself increasingly dependent upon imports from foreign (and hostile) states that it turned to India and America to alleviate that menace to its security. "Our monies and wares that nowe run into the hands of our adversaries or cowld frendes," it was early observed, "shall pass into our frendes and naturall kinsmen and from them likewise we shall receive such things as shall be most available to our necessities, which intercourse of trade maye rather be called a home bread traffique than a forraigne exchange." Once gain a footing in India and America, in other words, and the commerce of England, grown so alarmingly foreign, would be diverted back into national channels to the benefit of all (Englishmen) concerned.

To exploit these large possibilities, involving long ocean voyages by expensive fleets and traffic with alien and often inimical people, required resources beyond the reach of any individual, and it called for authority backed by a king's government. It was under such circumstances that the joint-stock company was devised, assisted or sometimes controlled by the state and provided with monopolistic privileges which would discourage competition. The main purpose of this endeavor was neither to raise the standards of living of its own people nor, certainly, to contribute to the well-being of other countries, but to regulate commerce and industry and to control policy so that in the end the power of one state would be increased relative to that of any other state.

It was these hoary notions that Adam Smith challenged in his epochal book. He practically backed into writing it, or at least into starting the undertaking. While traveling in France as private tutor for the duke of Buccleuch he became bored. As he wrote his friend David Hume, the Scots philosopher, from Toulouse, "I have begun to write a book to pass away the time." And thus came into existence the modern science of economics. Smith himself thought of it as but a part of a large study for a comprehensive ethical system. (Some years earlier, in 1759, he had published his ethical conclusions in *Theory of Moral Sentiments*, which one contemporary pronounced "the most important work that has ever been written on this important subject.") However, it is *The Wealth of Nations* that will continue to be remembered as his signal contribution to modern thought. It presented a not altogether original thesis. The French physiocrats François Quesnay, Robert Turgot, and Pierre Samuel du Pont de Nemours had already declared that governmental controls along mercantile principles discouraged economic growth. They had already coined the phrase that would become the universal and standard slogan for a new economic liberalism: *Laissez faire, laissez passer* ("Let men act freely, let goods move freely"). But Smith, well aware of their contributions, provided a systematic summary of these and related ideas, fired by penetrating economic insight, that became the classic expression of principles from which the liberal economic individualism of the future would grow—the primary statement of the new capitalism.

Smith was preaching a kind of economic democracy that was contrary to contemporary theory and practice. Wealth, he urged, came not from the gold and silver that states managed to store in their treasuries; it stemmed from the labor of the people who produced it and who consequently should benefit from it proportionately. "No society can surely be flourishing and happy," he wrote, "of which the far greater part of the members are poor and miserable. It is but equity, besides, that they who feed, cloath and lodge the whole body of the people, should have such a share of the produce of their own labor as to be themselves tolerably well fed, cloathed and lodged." Their own self-interest in this end would benefit society at large and themselves in particular. In such a statement there were premonitions of Marxism as well as of democracy.

Adam Smith, shown lecturing, was a professor of moral philosophy at the University of Glasgow before he gained wide recognition as a political economist.

Smith was aware that the division of labor increased the special skill of a worker and hence his productivity; but he was also aware that increasing specialization had its own disadvantages to the workman, with forewarnings of the dilemmas that face today's mass-production techniques. "In the progress of the division of labour," Smith wrote, "the employment of the far greater part of those who live by labour, that is, of the great body of the people, comes to be confined to a few very simple operations, frequently to one or two. But the understanding of the greater part of men are necessarily formed by their ordinary employments. The man whose life is spent in performing a few simple operations, of which the effects are perhaps always the same, or very nearly the same, has no occasion to exert his understanding or to exercise his invention in finding out expedients for removing difficulties which never occur. He naturally loses, therefore, the habit of such exertion, and generally becomes as stupid and ignorant as it is possible for a human creature to become."

As a classic example, Smith cited the manufacture of pins by "modern" mechanical means. "One man draws out the wire, another straights it, a third cuts it, a fourth points it, a fifth grinds it at the top for receiving the head; to make the head requires two or three distinct operations; to put it on is a peculiar business, to whiten the pins is another; it is even a trade by itself to put them into the paper; and the important business of making a pin is, in this manner, divided into about eighteen distinct operations, which, in some manufactories, are all performed by distinct hands, though in others the same man will sometimes perform two or three of them."

Smith deplored the institution of slavery since, as he declared, "the work done by free men comes cheaper in the end than that performed by slaves." In the case of any conflict of interest, he sided with the workman against the employer who, Smith wrote, had "generally an interest to deceive, and even to oppress, the public. . . ." He spoke out for higher wages, which he claimed would benefit both employer and employee. At a time when the law in England forbade employees to organize to protect their interests (although employers might do so), Smith advocated the organization of labor to secure its rights, among other things, to those higher wages.

Excepting David Hume, who much admired his work, Smith was the greatest figure in the Scottish enlightenment. His advocacy of free, competitive enterprise without undue governmental influence and restriction, as a spur to business and trade, heralded the new era in commercial history; and with that, new concepts regarding the administration of colonial empires. In the meantime, the American colonists were taking matters into their own hands. Smith proposed that if they resisted taxes imposed to help support the British empire, they should be granted independence forthwith. "By thus parting good friends," he observed, "the natural affection of the colonists to the mother country . . . would quickly revive. It might dispose them . . . to favor us in war as well as in trade, and instead of turbulent and factious subjects, to become our most faithful . . . and generous allies."

In a relatively stationary society, in which it was assumed that the total sum of goods was constant, the tenets of mercantilism could be rationalized. With that assumption, it seemed obvious that one state could not grow rich and powerful unless another state grew poor and weak—just as it seemed natural for the individual to believe that money in his pocket must come out of some-

"Plenty of good land, and liberty to manage their own affairs their own way, seem to be the two great causes of the prosperity of all new colonies."

Adam Smith in *The Wealth of Nations*

The coal industry was the first to adapt to steam power. This late eighteenth-century view of a British mine shows the Newcomen engine (center) lifting coal from the shafts (far left and right).
WALKER ART GALLERY, LIVERPOOL

one else's pocket. But in Smith's day, in large areas, the world was rapidly changing, and nowhere more rapidly than in England. Wealth was making more wealth. "The age is running mad after innovation," grumbled Samuel Johnson, "all the business of the world is to be done in a new way. . . ." He had in mind those early stirrings of the Industrial Revolution (and of an agricultural revolution) which, as it gathered force, would transform the structure of society as well as the nature of trading among nations. And it was against the background of these developments as well as the political revolution in North America that Smith prepared his thesis.

The most radical of these developments were in technology, in transport, and in methods of industrial organization. Within less than a decade on either side of 1776, a number of profoundly important inventions revolutionized the textile industry, introducing an age of golden prosperity that lasted for a quarter of a century to come. In earlier days it was not possible for the spinning process to keep up with the weaving; it took at least five spinners to keep one weaver supplied with yarn. With the newly introduced mechanization, spinning more than met the needs of the weavers, reversing the traditional imbalance. Then, in 1785, in a crescendo of production, a practical mechanical loom was invented that made it possible for the weaver to keep up with the flow of yarn and thread. Cotton fabrics had never before been produced in Europe at a price to compete with the sheer muslins and bright calico prints made in India; these enjoyed the public favor to the point where many governments, to protect their old textile industries, simply forbade importation of the Oriental fabrics altogether. With the introduction of power machinery that situation was reversed; local enterprises could now undersell foreign competition. It was ironical that Liverpool, the main port of Lancashire where the modern factory system was born, had derived the wealth that supported its innovative mechanization from the trade in slaves, the most primitive source of energy known.

In mining, metallurgy, and engineering, technical advancement affected the development of English industry even more profoundly than did progress in the textile field. The perfection of methods of smelting iron with coal made the production of cast iron rapid and cheap. Iron was produced in greater quantities than ever before, and the new machinery built with it assured finer and more accurate work in the making of all manner of things. John Wilkinson, greatest of all the English ironmasters, had faith that iron would soon replace stone and wood as a more practical and durable material. In 1767 he produced railroads for mines and a dozen years later built the first iron bridge in the world over the Severn River. He built an iron chapel for Wesleyans and was to see the first iron boat afloat in 1787. Appropriately, when he died he was buried in an iron coffin.

Many of the new factories were powered by the steam engine perfected by James Watt, with the financial assistance of the manufacturer Matthew Boulton. After preliminary trials, a steam engine based on Watts' principle had become a commercial reality in 1776. In that year James Boswell visited Boulton's Soho foundry to inspect the new machinery. Boulton proudly declared to him: "I sell here, Sir, what all the world desires to have—POWER." The great revolution was well launched. For the first time in all the ages man was freed from his dependence upon the natural sources of power.

Up until about this time the growth of industry was severely hampered by the wretched condition of roads and the inadequacy of the riverways; cheap or rapid transit of materials and wares was impossible. But in 1761 Manchester was joined with its port of Liverpool by a canal that for part of its way was carried on a lofty aqueduct; and the lesson learned, other canals soon joined depots to depots, rivers to rivers, quickening and easing transportation and communication to an unprecedented degree. Every canal cut through the land cheapened the cost of goods and helped raise the standard of living. Josiah Wedgwood, the famous potter, estimated that one tow horse could pull as much merchandise on a canal barge as could forty horses on land—and with less breakage of cargoes. In 1777 a canal linking the Trent and the Mersey rivers brought a world market to Wedgwood's potteries at Etruria, which eclipsed similar enterprises in Holland or France. As the historian J. H. Plumb has written, industry was no longer the handmaid of commerce, but its mistress.

Industry and agriculture were interdependent. To set up their mills and factories, many of the new industrialists used money they or their fathers had made from their cultivated fields. Now, in turn, much of the capital generated by the new industries was used for the improvement of the land and methods

TEXT CONTINUED ON PAGE 96

Josiah Wedgwood opened his new factory at Etruria (below) in 1769. The factory's canal was part of the Grand Trunk Navigation system financed by Wedgwood. Completed by 1777, the system linked the Mersey and Trent rivers, carrying inexpensive water communications from west to east across the heart of the new industrial England.
ELIZA METEYARD, *The Life of Josiah Wedgwood*, 1865

Heavy Industry

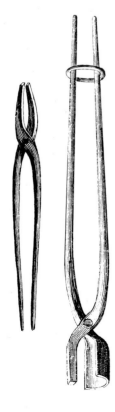

Although Diderot's *Encyclopédie* was controversial because of the "radical" philosophy it presented, its popularity rested on its wealth of technological information. The *Encyclopédie* included some 2,900 engraved plates, mainly on arts and crafts, but also on the sciences, engineering, and industry. The three engravings reproduced here related to the iron industry and were keyed to lengthy descriptions in the *Encyclopédie*. The forge represented a midpoint in the progression from the medieval smith to the steel plant; it was also the culmination of one line of development—its product is still iron whereas the future for malleable metal in the next century lay with steel. First, ore was smelted in a blast furnace to produce pig iron or direct castings. Pig iron could then be remelted in a foundry to produce cast iron products or fined in a forge to be wrought into goods made of malleable metal. The two engravings at top depict the latter process. Items too bulky to be handled by the available machinery, such as the ship's anchor illustrated opposite bottom, were forged by hammer and manpower. Left and right, implements used by the ironworkers.

Fig. 1.

fig. 7.   fig. 4.   fig. 6.

"Land cultivated in cut-up parcels by the small farmer requires more men and expenses, and the profits are much more limited. . . . We do not now look upon the rich farmer as a worker who personally tills his land. He is an entrepreneur who administers and increases the value of his enterprise by his intelligence and wealth."

from the *Encyclopédie*

of cultivation. One of the most fundamental developments in agricultural reform evolved from the enclosure of fields and of common lands, converting these areas into units that could be worked individually. Although this had been going on for about three hundred years, the pace of enclosure remark-ably accelerated between 1750 and 1780, giving the English countryside something like the appearance it has today, with its hedges, fields, and scat-tered farms. So long as the lands were held in common, with herds mingling in the pastures, any prospect of improving cattle and crops by regulating breeding and cultivating was all but hopeless. Now, each farmer was inde-pendent of the others and free to introduce attempts at improving the land he tilled and the animals that fed on it.

The wealthy landowners, who substantially controlled Parliament and who also served locally as justices of the peace, were primarily responsible for the enclosure act. From their large holdings, let out to responsible farmers, they looked for the increased revenues that would be assured by more advanced methods.

The results were, in fact, electrifying. Between 1710 and 1750 there had been but 114 enclosure acts; between 1750 and 1780 there were 1,222. In 1710 the average weight of oxen was 370 pounds, of calves 50 pounds, and of sheep 38 pounds. Toward the end of the century the average weights were 800, 150, and 80 respectively. They had more than doubled and tripled. One Thomas Coke of Holkham, by strictly insisting that his tenants follow the most up-to-date methods of production, increased their annual yield and raised the ren-tals he received from them almost tenfold in forty years. His well-deserved success made him something of a celebrity in Europe, and inspired others to follow his lead. Progressive farming in England became a fashionable pursuit. Landed heirs and younger sons, country parsons, nabobs—even the king himself, "Farmer George"—all turned to farming with a fresh enthusiasm. By improving breeding, Robert Bakewell of Leicestershire transformed the English sheep from a scrawny, small beast into the plump, fleece-covered

animal we know today. His experiments with nutritious grass and root crops assured his cattle adequate fodder during the winter months, and the roast beef of England became legendary.

The farmer's yield was measurably increased, and a smaller proportion of the population was needed to produce it. The persons displaced from the rural scene by these changes presented a distressing social problem, which Oliver Goldsmith pondered in *The Deserted Village*:

> Ill fares the land, to hastening ills a prey,
> Where wealth accumulates, and men decay.
> Princes and lords may flourish, or may fade . . .
> But a bold peasantry, their country's pride,
> When once destroyed, can never be supplied.

That "bold peasantry," who had been the economic, military, and moral background of the English, did, in fact, virtually disappear as a class. Many of them became the wage earners of a new day, as hired hands in field or factory. However, now that wheat could be grown almost anywhere in England, even the poor could eat white wheat bread. This, along with the consumption of roast beef and beer, was considered one indication of an Englishman's superiority over a Frenchman. In France—and wherever it was noticed abroad—the progress of agriculture in England was greatly admired, but only slowly followed. It deserved admiration. The agricultural and industrial changes that took place during these revolutionary years were as great a step forward as had been made by mankind since the neolithic revolution millenniums earlier, when man first learned to domesticate animals and grow crops.

England, and to a considerable degree France and Holland, continued to prosper from the Asian and American trade. But the routes that led to their ports from the far places of the world did not stop there. Holland was too small to sustain any large manufacturing enterprise. But its role in commerce, shipping, and finances diminished only slightly in the face of commercial

The breeding of farm animals as a systematically controlled process began during the eighteenth century. The results were remarkable, but not so remarkable as suggested by the painting of the "Pangborn Hog" (above) from Tidmarsh Farm in Berkshire. Robert Bakewell was the most successful breeder in England. Sheepbreeding was his specialty, and sheep like the one seen above helped make his farm at Dishley famous.
AGRICULTURAL RESEARCH INSTITUTE, OXFORD
MUSEUM OF ENGLISH RURAL LIFE, UNIV. OF READING

prominence of the two other nations. The Dutch remained the most active middlemen in distributing goods from the rest of the world to European countries that had no direct access to them, and fattened on the business of being common carriers for such trade. (They also smuggled tea, that essential ingredient of American independence, into the colonies, relieving them of the onerous matter of paying duties.) Until the end of the century Amsterdam remained the financial center of Europe. In the middle of the eighteenth century a third of the capital of the Bank of England was owned by Dutch shareholders. Significantly, in 1780 John Adams was commissioned to go to Holland to secure recognition of the United States as an independent government and to negotiate a loan that would help guarantee its existence in its earliest years. He succeeded on both counts, arranging the first of such treaties of amity and commerce between the United States and a foreign power following the French alliance of 1778.

The British, along with the Dutch and the French, sold the products of the New World and Asia to central and eastern Europe. As they became "Europeanized," the upper-class Russians, for instance, wanted sugar, tobacco, and tea, which they could only get through the great maritime nations; and these they could pay for with grain, timber, and naval stores. Britain sold Russia six times as much merchandise in 1790 as in 1700, and imported fifteen times as much from Russia. The North American colonists also wanted goods that because of restrictive trade regulations imposed by Parliament they could obtain only by way of England—or through smuggling, to be sure. As a matter of practice and principle they contested these regulations through various nonimportation agreements. At one point importations from England fell off by one-half in Boston, by two-thirds in Philadelphia, and by four-fifths in New York. The most dramatic incident in such embargoes was the memorable Boston Tea Party of December 16, 1773. With that radical gesture the colonists finally challenged the time-worn contention that government-sponsored monopoly could serve the best interests of empire.

It was with an eye to such disturbing consequences that Adam Smith wrote the concluding paragraph of *The Wealth of Nations*: "The rulers of Great Britain have, for more than a century past, amused the people with the imagination that they possessed a great empire on the west side of the Atlantic. This empire, however, has hitherto existed in imagination only. It has hitherto been, not an empire, but the project of an empire; not a gold mine, but the project of a gold mine; a project which has cost, which continues to cost, and which, if pursued in the same way as it has been hitherto, is likely to cost, immense expense, without being likely to bring any profit; for the effects of the monopoly of the colony trade, it has been shown, are, to the great body of the people, mere loss instead of profit. It is surely now time that our rulers should either realise this golden dream, in which they have been indulging themselves, perhaps, as well as the people, or that they should take it away from themselves, and endeavour to awaken the people. If the project cannot be completed, it ought to be given up. If any of the provinces of the British empire cannot be made to contribute towards the support of the whole empire, it is surely time that Great Britain should free herself from the expense of defending these provinces in time of war, and of supporting any part of their civil or military establishments in time of peace, and endeavour to accommodate her future views and designs to the real mediocrity of her circumstances."

The first London headquarters of the British East India Company

A WORLD OF TRADE

By the middle of the eighteenth century a good portion of the New World was ruled by Spain, Portugal, England, France, and Holland. In Africa and Asia a small number of European inhabitants controlled the numerous coastal trading bases; there was little sign, however, that any of these would develop into colonies. Eastward European expansion had been directed almost exclusively by private companies, founded for the express purpose of acquiring wealth through trade. By 1776 it had become evident that in order to trade profitably, some degree of government intervention and even territorial control would be necessary.

THE EUROPEAN MARKETPLACE

At the beginning of the eighteenth century nearly every European statesman subscribed to the economic theory known as mercantilism. It held that a nation's wealth was measured by the gold and silver it possessed. Aside from owning gold and silver mines or stealing the precious metals enroute, an obvious way for any state to amass gold and silver was for the exports to exceed the imports. With governments encouraging trade, inter-European commerce increased dramatically during the eighteenth century (opposite bottom, French imports at an English port; below, the Amsterdam bourse, where a buyer could purchase almost every commodity needed in Europe and also speculate in precious metals and in stocks of Dutch and foreign companies). Business was hampered by the profusion of local weights, measures, and coins. Baden, for instance, had one hundred twelve separate measures for length. Sweden used copper money, including one "coin" weighing forty-three pounds. Not much progress was made in standardizing weights and measures before the end of the century, but a simplified money system was agreed upon (opposite top, a contemporary explanation of English money).

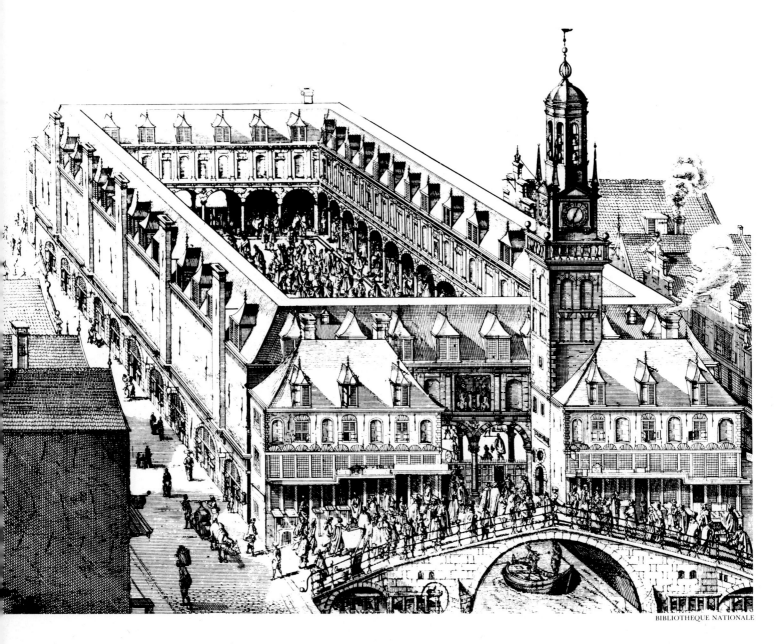

COINS	Weights			Value	Lawfull Money	Silver Coins	Weights			Value	
	OZ.	dw	Gr.	OLD TENOR	£ s		OZ.	dw	Gr.	£ s	grains is one penny, enny is one Ounce.
Guinea	0	5	9	10 10	28/	Eng Crown	0	19	8½	2 10	
Half D	2	16½	5 5		14/	Half Ditto		9	16¼	1 5	
Moidore	6	22	13 10		36/	Dollar		17	12	2 5	

The acquisition of overseas colonies fitted into the mercantilist scheme if they provided valuable raw materials or a market for the manufactured goods of the mother country. The economic regulations imposed on the American colonies reflected this philosophy: no foreign ships were permitted to enter colonial harbors; all imported goods had to be shipped from a British port, regardless of their place of origin; certain enumerated exports had to be shipped to England, regardless of their final destination. This "state of commercial servitude and civil liberty," as Edmund Burke labeled it, worked well for more than a century. English merchants profited from re-exporting colonial products (above, a 1775 engraving of a tobacco planter selling his cargo), and the colonies were an important market for British manufactured goods (left, a view of Philadelphia). Canada's importance to England was as a source of raw materials. The Hudson's Bay Company, chartered in 1670, maintained a prosperous fur trade (below), and with the expulsion of the French in 1763, anticipated even greater profits.

LE BEAU, *Adventures*, VOL. 1

Portugal and Spain were the first European countries to establish colonies in the New World. By the eighteenth century the Spanish empire in America was already some two centuries old. Although in Mexico and parts of Peru there existed an urbanized upper class living on the profits of large cattle-raising estates tended by the native peasantry, Spain's first and overriding interest in the New World was mining gold and silver (opposite below, a Spanish silver mine in Peru). No precious metals were found in Brazil until the 1690's, and so Portugal had developed a plantation colony. They imported slave labor from Africa to produce sugar (opposite, a sugar plantation in Pernambuco) and tobacco for the European market. Impressed by the Portuguese success in Brazil, France and Britain followed their model in establishing their Caribbean colonies. Jamaica was England's most valuable colony; altogether the British West Indies in the 1770's supplied one-fourth of England's imports. During the frequent European wars in the last half of the eighteenth century, colonies became pawns of strategy and diplomacy. Caribbean colonies, in particular, were almost helpless victims of whichever nation had the strongest navy. England occupied enemy colonies in order both to distract its rivals and to acquire negotiating chips for the peace conferences. In 1762 an English fleet attacked and captured Havana (below), but at the peace talks the next year Cuba was returned to Spain and Florida became a British territory.

SOUTH AMERICAN &
CARIBBEAN COLONIES

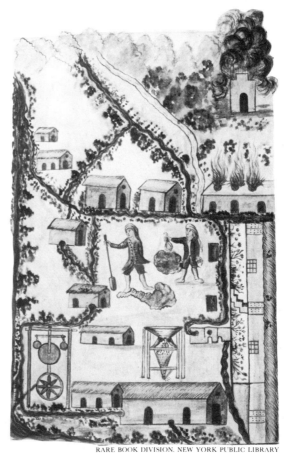

"BLACK GOLD"

European plantation colonies demanded a steady supply of slave labor. The first slave traders were the Portuguese; but by 1600 they had been joined by the Dutch, French, and English, followed by the Danes, Prussians, Swedes, and Genoese. Between 1768 and 1780 Portugal, Britain, and France controlled nearly ninety per cent of the trade (North American slave traders were included in the British total). They established permanent stations along Africa's west coast, with the purpose of monopolizing the trade in their immediate territories. The maintenance of these coastal outposts bankrupted private companies, and by the 1770's European governments subsidized their private traders. In some areas Africans, too, set up their own trading monopolies. At Xavier (below) each foreign company was restricted to a separate mud-walled compound. In exchange for the slaves (above), Africans received gold, iron or copper bars, firearms, gunpowder, steel blades, axes, or rum. The price at one port for "these valuable people" was 115 gallons of rum for a healthy man, 95 for a woman. Opposite, a French ship off Haiti after a successful voyage — only seven of the 340 slaves died enroute.

107

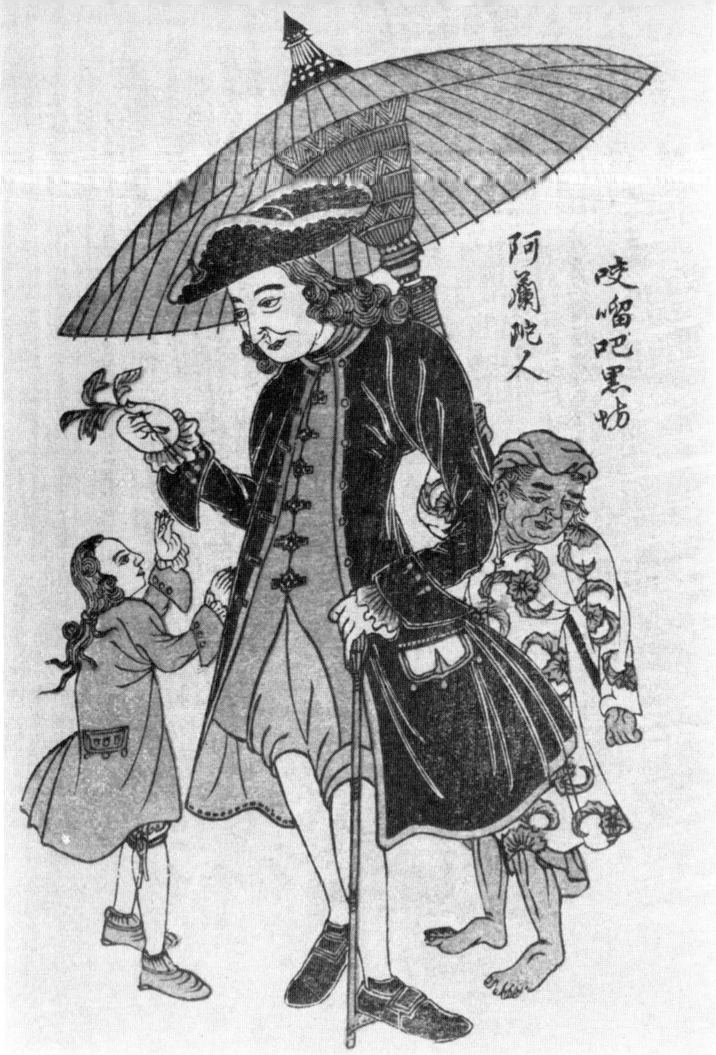

PRIVATE COLLECTION

PORTS OF CALL
IN THE
FAR EAST

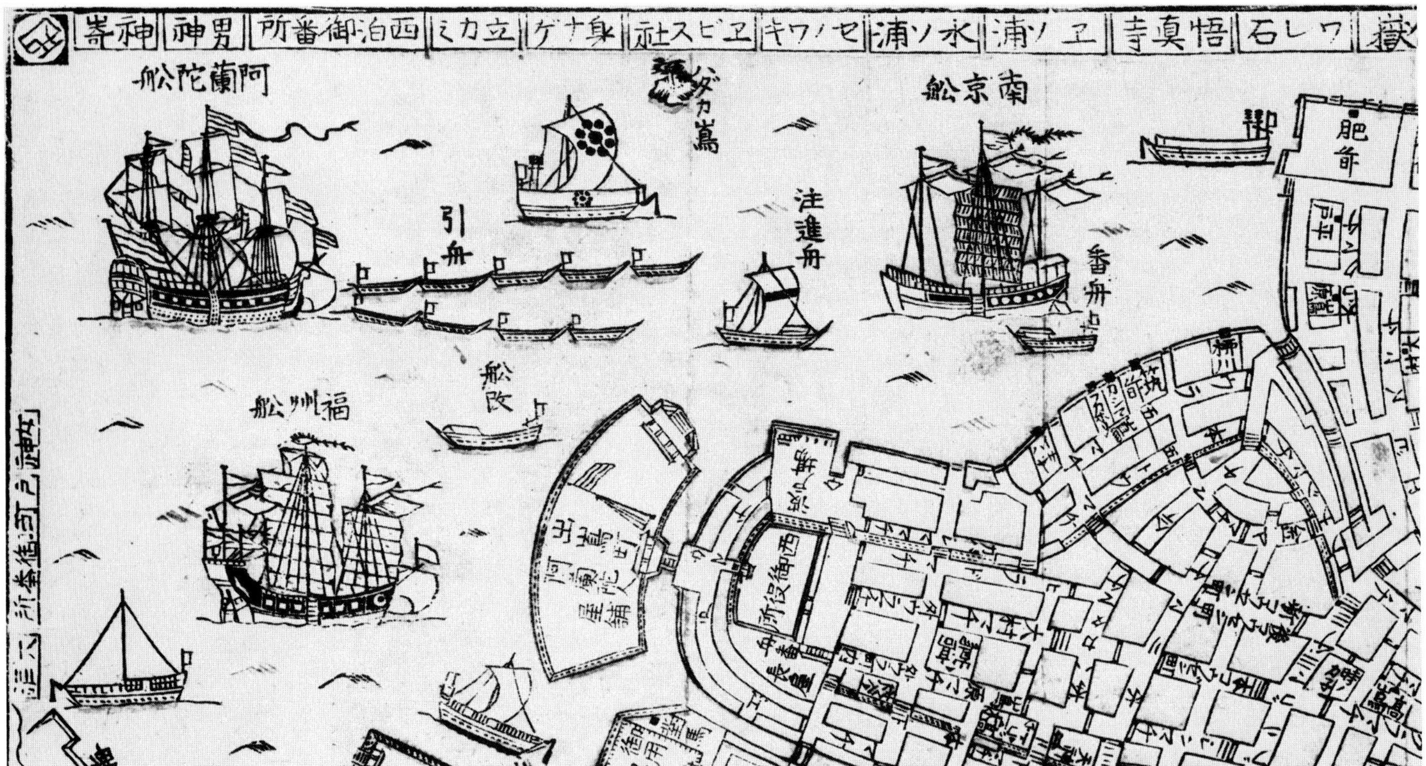

RICHARD C. RUDOLPH, UNIVERSITY OF CALIFORNIA, LOS ANGELES

VUE DU CAP FRANÇAIS
ET
DU N.º LA MARIE SERAPHIQUE DE NANTES
CAPITAINE GAUGY
LE JOUR DE L'OUVERTURE DE SA VENTE
TROISIEME VOYAGE D'ANGOLE
1772. 1773.

COUPE DU NAVIRE

The West African slave trade fell within the monopoly of the Dutch West India Company and was a necessary complement to the colonies it planned to establish in the Americas. The company rapidly took over a string of Portuguese bases and new territories (including New Netherland), but lost them almost as quickly. By 1700 it held only a few small Caribbean islands, Surinam, and a major slave-trading base at Elmina (below, a mid-eighteenth-century governor at Elmina with his slave). The majority of stockholders preferred trading illicitly with foreign colonies to maintaining their own. The Dutch East India Company was more of a financial success (opposite top, its headquarters in Amsterdam). Granted a monopoly of trade east of the Cape of Good Hope, the company was authorized to raise land and sea forces, erect forts and plant colonies, make war, arrange treaties, and coin money. By the early 1700's it held the Cape of Good Hope, "factories" along the Indian coast and in Southeast Asia, and much of the Indonesian Archipelago, with headquarters at Batavia (opposite bottom).

THE DUTCH TRADING COMPANIES

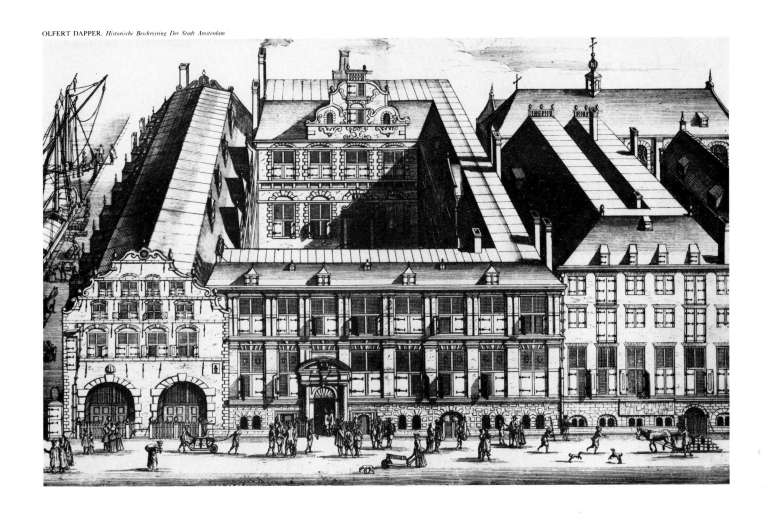

PORTS OF CALL

IN THE

FAR EAST

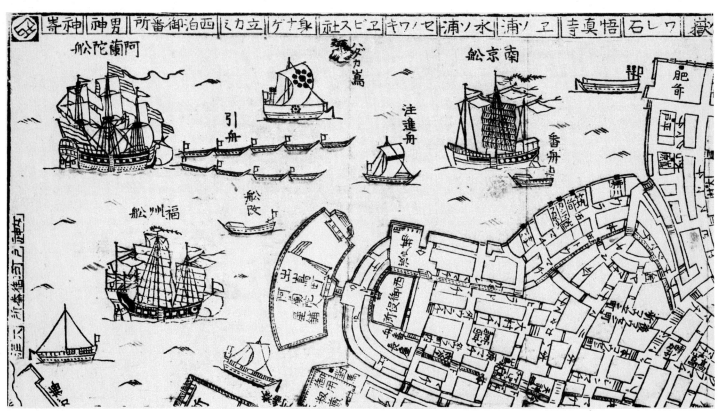

The Dutch East India Company planned to finance its European trade by monopolizing the interport trade in Asia. The Dutch never eliminated the competition from other companies, or from smugglers, but they did more interport Asian trading than any other Europeans. In addition to the spices, pepper, textiles, tea, coffee, and porcelain shipped to Europe from Batavia, the Dutch traded those products and indigo and saltpeter from India, elephants from Ceylon, slaves from Arakan, Butung, and Bali, and silver, gold, copper, and lacquered goods from Japan throughout Asia. They were the only Europeans to trade with the Japanese for more than two centuries (1640–1854); they were confined to the island of Deshima outside Nagasaki (opposite), and only a limited number of ships could enter the harbor each year (left, a Japanese print of a Dutch trader with his Balinese slave; above, a Japanese artist's view of Deshima's main street). Wars and increasing administrative costs so drained the resources of the company that it was taken over by the government in the 1790's.

OVERLEAF: European demand for tea increased spectacularly during the 1700's. This montage shows the raising, processing, and selling of tea at the harbor in Canton.
BERRY-HILL GALLERIES, NEW YORK

111

By 1700 the British East India Company had established a trade relationship with China. The French, Germans, Danes, and Dutch were there, too, to fill the tremendous demand for tea, silk, and porcelains (opposite, Chinese packing porcelain for export to Europe; right, a dish bearing Prussia's coat of arms and made in China for Frederick the Great around 1750). China was the only source of tea; none was grown in India or Ceylon at the time. The Chinese were economically self-sufficient; they neither needed nor desired Western goods and materials. Consequently, they demanded silver in payment, creating a deficit for the Europeans in the balance of trade. Fearing attempts at territorial acquisition, China strictly regulated the foreign trade. In 1759 Emperor Ch'ien Lung reaffirmed Canton as the only port for European trade (below, an early nineteenth-century view of Canton showing the headquarters of foreign companies). He further stipulated that foreigners be confined to living quarters just outside Canton, be permitted to live there only from September to March, when the tea crop was harvested, and be allowed to leave the compound only three times a month. Ch'ien Lung's regulations, however, said nothing about the importation of opium, which the British had begun to ship from Bengal. For centuries the Chinese had been using moderate amounts of opium for medical purposes and smoking. Addiction was not widespread and the trade was small. The rising demand for opium, however, soon reversed the balance of trade and enabled the British to capture much of the China market.

DEMAND FOR CHINESE GOODS

THE
COMPETITION
FOR INDIA

In the early 1700's the British East India Company had four trading stations along the coast in India; the French East India Company had two. At each station the company made treaties with local rulers for the sale of its manufactured goods in exchange for Indian-made goods. Relations between the British and French companies were fairly cordial; inter-European rivalries did not spill over to India so long as the Mogul political network remained fairly intact. As the Mogul empire deteriorated the French determined to support one local prince against another in return for favorable trading arrangements. The British, who had deliberately stayed out of Indian politics, had to choose to get involved or possibly lose their commercial advantages. The result, beginning in the 1740's, was nearly sixty years of bitter struggle between the two companies—battles punctuated by uneasy peaces. Robert Clive (above) won several important battles and installed a British puppet to rule Bengal. By 1773 the French company was bankrupt, its few remaining posts taken over by the crown; the British company, headquartered in Calcutta (opposite), ruled vast territories in India.

117

THE NOTORIOUS NABOBS

Robert Clive once remarked that the only real threat to the British in India was the "venality and corruption" of the company employees. Clive himself had amassed a fortune there. Private trading and payoffs from local rulers were perfectly legal. The British lived in "splendid sloth and languid debauchery." Sixty servants staffed one home (above); routine business was conducted with great pomp (below); grand events were devised for entertainment (opposite, Englishmen at a cockfight). After returning home, these nabobs became notorious for their tasteless flaunting of wealth. In 1772 the company asked Parliament for a loan. Noting the contrast between a bankrupt company and its wealthy employees, Parliament ordered an inquiry. The Regulating Act of 1773 gave the government some control over the worst abuses of company rule.

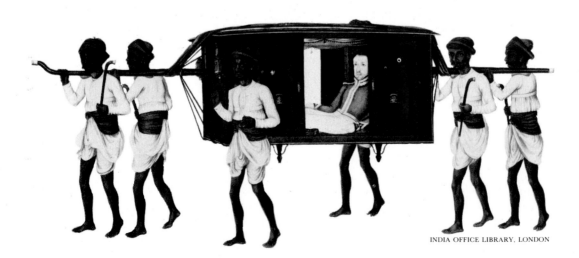

IMPACT OF EXPANSION

In Europe the expansion of overseas trade produced enormous, and often unforeseen, changes in the way people lived. When once exotic imports became necessities, production of inexpensive goods to trade had to be increased. French foreign trade nearly doubled between 1763 and 1787, and port cities like Marseilles (below) swelled with merchants, shippers, warehouses, new factories (soap, hat, glass), refineries, and tanneries. As a result of the slave trade, Liverpool emerged as a bustling commercial center. Between 1750 and 1775 its trade increased four times as fast as Britain's. Wealth was no longer the perquisite of landowners, but available to those who controlled industry, commerce, or finance as well. Thousands of people labored behind spinning machines and looms and in forging shops and gun factories to supply the overseas markets. In England during the 1770's the application of steam power enabled factories to produce goods in greater number and at a lower cost. The painting at left, by Joseph Wright, is a view of industrialist Joseph Arkwright's first powered cotton spinning mill at Cromford.

QUESTIONS OF

Every age is an age of transition, although this is more apparent in some periods than in others. For the currents of history run fitfully. At some points they turn sluggish, spreading out into what seem like stagnant pools of time, as in the Dark Ages. At other points they swirl about in active, changing patterns, until they merge to form a new mainstream, as in the years surrounding 1776. During those years the Enlightenment reached its apogee. Novel and radical ideas that had long been generating were now clearly and concisely formulated and presented to a literate public that was becoming constantly larger and more receptive to new doctrines. Fundamental issues had been opened to investigation and debate. The nature of monarchy, the privileges of aristocracy, the authority of the Church, the freedom of the individual, the quality of justice, the plight of the poor and the sick, and the very meaning of life were all critically examined and re-evaluated.

Such a disposition to pry into the state of society, so unreservedly and in all its aspects, was unprecedented in history. Even the men of the Renaissance had not probed the inner and outer worlds more industriously, more variously, and more skeptically than did the leading thinkers of the eighteenth century. Many of the ideas they advanced were openly and intentionally opposed to the old, established views; if translated into practice they would completely change the traditional structure of society and of government. But that would take time.

More than two thousand years earlier Plato had predicted that there would

ENLIGHTENMENT

be "no end to the troubles of states, or indeed, of humanity itself until philosophers became kings in this world, or until those we now call kings and rulers really and truly become philosophers." None of the kings or queens of the eighteenth century were "really and truly" philosophers, although a number of them pretended to be, and to bolster their claims to that distinction they courted the true philosophers. In the form of a mutual admiration society those monarchs patronized the intellectuals, who in return paid their tribute to the monarchs. Thus, as earlier mentioned, Frederick the Great persuaded Voltaire (and Diderot, among other intellects) to treat him—at least to his face—as a corresponding member of the international coterie of enlightened minds. Catherine the Great invited Voltaire to her court, although he never went there. She asked Diderot to prepare a model plan for education, which he did and which she promptly shelved—while she continued to countenance the slavery of Russian serfs.

If the monarchs were not true philosophers, the philosophers were far from being monarchs. In spite of his fame and his royal friends, Voltaire spent a substantial part of his life in exile or in hiding; Rousseau was habitually on the run from the authorities; Diderot was cast into jail for the unorthodox opinions he published in his great *Encyclopédie*, which was several times banned; and so on down a dreary list of attempted suppression and repression of advanced and liberal thought. Virtually everywhere, excepting America (and even there to a degree and for a while), the defenders of the old order, with its traditional authority, rallied to protect their established positions against reforms that might imperil the accustomed stability of social and political institutions.

The later years of the eighteenth century were years of confusion, leading up to the climactic confusion that resulted with the French Revolution. Until then, and in many areas for long afterward, the old order remained deeply entrenched in its prerogatives and accustomed practices in spite of the contrary intellectual atmosphere. Ancient and anachronistic privileges were still supported by rigid custom. Equally old injustices were still tolerated by those in society who did not have to suffer from them. But to defend its position the old order had to use the language of its critics, which had won currency even in reactionary circles; and this was the language of change, and of the future. In 1764 the liberal Milanese economist and jurist Cesare Beccaria proclaimed that the aim of government should be to provide the greatest good for the greatest number (*maggior felicitè divisa nel maggior numero*), and shortly thereafter his royal master, the Holy Roman Emperor Joseph II of Austria, repeated that statement with imperial authority in German. Within less than a generation the Holy Roman Empire had ceased to exist.

In our own day the concept of the greatest good for the greatest number has become a cliché to which devout lip service, at least, is paid throughout much of the world. But in the eighteenth century it had revolutionary connotations. In his *Thoughts on Government* issued in 1776, John Adams voiced the same thought in support of the American colonists' rebellious attitude. "Upon this point all speculative politicians will agree," he wrote, "that the happiness of society is the end of government, as all divines and moral philosophers will agree that the happiness of the individual is the end of man. From this principle it will follow that the form of government which communicates ease, comfort, security, or, in one word, happiness, to the greatest number of persons, and in the greatest degree, is the best."

Even in the America of that year such a pronouncement did not indicate the actual state of things. But it asserted what in the minds and hearts of right-thinking persons *should* be the case everywhere. In the regenerated society they outlined, hoped for, wrote about, and talked of, it *would* be so. For long centuries traditional Christian teaching had held forth a prospect of human happiness that could be achieved by good and God-fearing souls in a heavenly world of the hereafter. But this newly conceived dispensation for humanity would come about here on earth, not because it was divinely ordained but because it was ordered by the knowledge and wisdom of mortals who, to capture their vision, were prepared to boldly challenge the most firmly established and sacrosanct beliefs of the age.

Western Europe, where so much of the material and intellectual power of the world was then concentrated, was in the painful process of repudiating its own past; groping toward a distant democracy. The most vital ingredient in its vision of the future was the newly conceived and, by many intellectual leaders, firmly maintained conviction that mankind was continuously progressing toward some higher goal which, when reached, would free him from all the constraints of ignorance and superstition. Mankind, in short, was perfectible, given time and opportunity.

This doctrine of progress has become commonplace in our own day, a platitude we still accept, by and large, in spite of all evidence to the contrary that

"Experimental philosophy knows neither what will come nor will not come out of its labours; but it works on without relaxing. The philosophy based on reasoning, on the contrary, weighs possibilities, makes a pronouncement and stops short. It boldly said: 'light cannot be decomposed' : experimental philosophy heard, and held its tongue in its presence for whole centuries; then suddenly it produced the prism, and said, 'light can be decomposed.' "

Denis Diderot

has disturbed recent history. But it was an apocalyptic vision of the eighteenth century. Neither the long years of Christian teaching nor millenniums of pagan speculation before that had produced any such concepts. It came from the minds of men who had, they earnestly believed, an unprecedentedly clear understanding of the nature of the world they lived in, and of their own human nature in relation to that outer world.

In the preceding century, by elementary methods and fundamental reasoning, Isaac Newton had banished much of the mystery that throughout the past surrounded the workings of the universe. He had played rays of light through an ordinary glass prism, watched an apple fall from the branch of a tree, and by these and similar elementary procedures (and by very abstruse calculations, to be sure, although he claimed to dislike "mathematical trifles"), he had fixed laws that explained the basic workings of the universe; laws that applied to the governance of men and women in their lives on earth as well as to the gravitational pull of celestial bodies. With such newly discovered and immutable standards of reference the world could be re-ordered on purely rational grounds. These were "the Laws of Nature and of Nature's God" that Jefferson and his fellow congressmen propounded in the Declaration of Independence.

Newton's revelations captured the imagination of the eighteenth century, as Darwin's did that of the nineteenth and Einstein's that of the twentieth. As the noted historian Carl L. Becker suggested, "if the character of so intangible a thing as light could be discovered by playing with a prism, if, by looking through a telescope and doing a sum in mathematics, the force which held the planets could be identified with the force that made an apple fall to the ground, there seemed to be no end to what might be definitely known about the universe."

Without Newton's immeasurable contributions to knowledge it would be impossible to conceive of the Age of Enlightenment that was dawning during his later years. (Indeed, historians sometimes refer to this era as the Newtonian Age.) By the middle of the eighteenth century "Newtonian philosophy" was widely familiar in Europe and far from unknown in America. (Thomas Jefferson considered Newton one of three greatest men the world had ever produced, along with Bacon and Locke.) "Very few people read Newton," Voltaire explained, "because it is necessary to be learned to understand him. But *everybody talks about him.*" More or less popular versions of his theory appeared in a steady flow of publications, however, including one by Voltaire himself that could be read in either French or English. Suggesting the varied interest his writings excited, a year after Newton's death there appeared a book with the engaging title, *The Newtonian System of the World the Best Model of Government, an Allegorical Poem.* And in 1775 the great man was even eulogized, also in verse, in a popular American almanac.

France is customarily thought of as the birthplace and the main base of the Enlightenment, and not wrongly so

A London printseller, hoping to capitalize on the optimism of Alexander Pope's Essay on Man, *ordered this print and another,* Essay on Woman, *from engraver Valentine Green in 1769.*

125

In writing his Encyclopédie *Diderot was aided by many of the best think-ers of his day. This controversial project took twenty years to produce.*

From Diderot to his mistress Sophie
It is late and I must hurry off to Le Breton's to see our second volume of plates, which is due to appear very soon now. I hope it will be even better received than the first. The quality of the engraving is better and the subjects are more varied and more interesting. If our enemies were not the most despicable of men, they would die of shame and envy. . . . In time this work must certainly cause a revolution in the minds of men, and I hope it will not be to the advantage of tyrants, oppressors, fanatics and bigots. We shall have served the human race; but we shall have been reduced to cold unfeeling dust, long before anyone is grateful to us.

From the Encyclopédie
In truth, the aim of an *encyclopedia* is to collect all the knowledge scattered over the face of the earth, to present its general outlines and structure to the men with whom we live, and to transmit this to those who will come after us, so that the work of past centuries may be useful to the following centuries, that our children, by becoming more educated, may at the same time become more virtuous and happier, and that we may not die without having deserved well of the human race. I have heard it said that M. de Fontenelle's rooms were not large enough to hold all the works that had been published against him. Who knows the title of a single one of them? Montesquieu's *Spirit of Laws* and Buffon's *Natural History* have only just appeared, and the harsh criticism against them has been entirely forgotten. We have already remarked that among those who have set themselves up as censors of the *Encyclopedia* there is hardly a single one who had enough talent to enrich it by even one good article. I do not think I would be exaggerating if I should add that it is a work the greater part of which is about subjects that these people have yet to study. It has been composed with a philosophical spirit, and in this respect most of those who pass adverse judgment on us fall far short of the level of their own century. I call their works in evidence. It is for this reason that they will not endure and that we venture to say that our *Encyclopedia* will be more widely read and more highly appreciated in a few years' time than it is today.

Celebrités Françaises, VOL. III

From the Encyclopédie: natural rights
The only essential quality in your species is what you demand from all your fellow men for your happiness and for theirs. It is this conformity of you with all of them and all of them with you that will mark you when you go beyond or stay within the limits of your species. Therefore never lose sight of it; otherwise you will see the notions of benevolence, justice, humanity and virtue blurred in your understanding.

From the Encyclopédie: political authority
No man has received from nature the right to command other. Liberty is a gift from heaven, and each individual of the same species has the right to enjoy it as soon as he enjoys the use of reason. If nature has established any *authority*, it is paternal control; but paternal control has its limits, and in the state of nature it would terminate when the children could take care of themselves. Any other *authority* comes from another origin than nature. If one seriously considers this matter, one will always go back to one of these two sources: either the force and violence of an individual who has seized it, or the consent of those who have submitted to it by a contract made or assumed between them and the individual on whom they have bestowed *authority*.

From the Encyclopédie: government
If it happens that those who hold the reins of *government* find some resistance when they use their power for the destruction and not the conservation of things that rightfully belong to the people, they must blame themselves, because the public good and the advantage of society are the purposes of establishing a *government*. Hence it necessarily follows that power cannot be arbitrary and that it must be exercised according to the established laws so that the people may know its duty and be secure within the shelter of laws, and so that governors at the same time should be held within just limits and not be tempted to employ the power they have in hand to do harmful things to the body politic.

From Voltaire to d'Alembert, 1766
It seems to me that never have intelligent men been feared in Paris as much as they are today. The inquisition against books is severe; I am informed that the subscribers do not yet have the *Encyclopedic Dictionary*. That is not only being severe; it is being very unjust. If the circulation of this book is stopped, the subscribers will be robbed and the book dealers ruined. I should really like to know what harm a book costing a hundred écus can do. Twenty folio volumes will never create a revolution; the little thirty penny portable books are the ones to be feared.

when we consider the host of well-known French writers—*philosophes*, as they were generally termed—whose works present the leading thoughts of that age; men such as Montesquieu and Voltaire, Rousseau and Diderot, Turgot and Quesnay, Buffon and Condorcet, Helvétius and d'Holbach, among numerous others. But, as observed earlier in this book, the Enlightenment was an international phenomenon that ignored state boundaries just as the rulers of the time were most jealously guarding them against intrusions of a political nature. Germany was also the home of philosophes, where Lessing and Herder and Leibniz contributed to the intellectual ferment of the times; and England with Locke, Hume, Adam Smith, Priestley, and still others. So it was elsewhere in the Western world. In America, Jefferson and Franklin added fresh perspectives to the visions they shared with their European contemporaries.

The outlook of these widely different and scattered individuals was bound by a common faith; a faith in the basic power of human reason to reveal truths that had long been hidden. By its penetrating force reason would disclose all the laws of Nature which governed man and his universe, a possibility Newton had so magnificently demonstrated. With a passionate intensity, they set about classifying all the works of Nature, fitting them into the orderly patterns that revealed the master plan dictated by an omniscient deity at the time of creation. Nothing was too insignificant or too gigantic to earn their attention. Between 1734 and 1742 René Antoine de Réaumur published six weighty volumes devoted to the classification of insects, which tiny creatures in his gracefully written pages incidentally became almost as attractive as characters in romantic fiction. During the middle decades of the eighteenth century the Swede Carolus Linnaeus constructed a monumental system for the classification and nomenclature of all known forms of flora and fauna. (With some modification that nomenclature still prevails.) The greatest naturalist of the century, Georges Louis Leclerc de Buffon, devoted his long life to compiling a massive compendium of data on natural history, *Histoire Naturelle*, which finally ran to forty-four volumes; and so on.

The most impressive of all such compendiums was Diderot's enormous *Encyclopédie*, in which as editor and contributor he attempted nothing less than the organization of all useful knowledge. In the words of one critic, this work was "the great affair of its time, the goal to which everything preceding it was tending, the origin of everything that has followed it, and consequently the true center for any history of ideas in the eighteenth century." In a broad view it was not an encyclopedia as we think of such a reference work today—an objective summary of fact and record. Beyond seeking to give sound information on a multitude of subjects ranging from handicrafts to philosophy, from statecraft to theology, it sought to guide opinion in the direction of the advanced views of its distinguished contributors—such men as Diderot himself, Voltaire, d'Alembert, Rousseau, Montesquieu, Turgot, and others. Frequently disguised in devious ways to avoid censorship, the opinions it countenanced called attention to what its editor and authors considered social inequities, religious bigotry, political injustice and corruption, backwardness in economic practices, and other evils that the heavy hand of the past had laid upon the present. In its entirety it held a mighty dream of social progress and advancement. The understanding of Nature, and the faith in reason so proposed, comprised a cluster of ideas which were the equivalent of those that supported the traditional Christian concepts of grace, salvation, and predestination.

For promoting these and similar views Diderot was in almost continual trouble with the authorities of Church and state. Rarely has an editor been so hounded and so hindered in his work. In February, 1752, following the publication of the second volume, the Marquis d'Argenson noted in his journal: "This morning appeared an *arrêt du conseil* which had not been foreseen: it suppressed the *Dictionnaire encyclopédie*, with some appalling allegations, such as revolt against God and the royal authority, [and] corruption of morals. . . . It is said on this score that the authors of the dictionary . . . must shortly be put to death." All the material Diderot had amassed was confiscated, leaving him temporarily helpless. However, through the intercession of Madame de Pompadour and other influential friends of the project, the files were returned to him and he was permitted to continue, albeit under the watchful eyes of censors.

Six years later the work was again suppressed; by order of the Council of State no further volumes were to be printed and none that had been printed was to be sold in the future. Both Frederick and Catherine the Great offered to help Diderot complete his publication in their countries. However, he persevered in his little attic room in Paris, the French officials relented, and in 1780 the last volume was finally issued. The total enterprise consisted of twenty-seven volumes of text and eleven volumes of handsome engraved illustrations. The impact of the publication was tremendous and widespread. Costly as it was to produce, it went through forty-three editions in twenty-five years. Separate editions were issued in Switzerland, Italy, Germany, and Russia. (Jefferson urged James Madison to buy a set of the volumes.) Such an

The Paris salon, a guest explained, is where "we polish one another, and rub off our corners and rough sides by a sort of amicable collision." In this fanciful painting of Madame Geoffrin's salon by Charles Lemmonier, a bust of Voltaire oversees nearly every eighteenth-century philosophe. The wealthy hostess (right foreground), in a lace bonnet, listens to the actor Le Kain read to a gathering that includes d'Alembert, Raynal, Buffon, Diderot, Montesquieu, and Rousseau.

exhaustive airing of radical opinions had explosive potential. Among its many other appeals to reason and justice, the *Encyclopédie* called for the liberty of all peoples, without which "happiness is banished from states." All in all, Diderot had issued a forceful manifesto that fomented revolt in the minds of men everywhere the work was read. It was a herald of the French Revolution so soon to come.

Although Pompadour helped protect the authors of the *Encyclopédie* from their reactionary enemies at Versailles, her influence did little to enlighten King Louis XV and his dull and depraved court. Elsewhere, in the higher circles of French society, a more liberal spirit prevailed. The brightest and most adventurous minds of the capital held their own private, intellectual courts in the phenomenal Paris salons of such brilliant women as Madame Geoffrin, Madame du Deffand, Mademoiselle de Lespinasse, Madame Helvétius, and others. They made virtually an institution of these intimate gatherings. The king's chief ministers and other members of French officialdom and of the Church were in frequent attendance, and such distinguished foreigners as Horace Walpole, Stanislas Poniatowski (the future King Stanislas II of Poland), and the German Baron von Grimm came as occasional guests and participants. (As one consequence of his attendance at Madame du Deffand's salon, the crotchety, spiteful, cynical, and fashionable Walpole became the object of this lady's almost unbridled passion, although she was then sixty-eight years old—twenty years older than Walpole—and blind. Her letters to him expressing the pangs of her unrequited love have become classics of the French language.)

Although badinage and flirtation were essential to these ostensibly social occasions, there was also the most serious and stimulating conversation in which lucid presentation of the most abstruse topics was carefully cultivated —a discipline that had a beneficent influence on French writing then and in years to come. "Women accustom us to discuss with charm and clearness the dryest and thorniest subjects," wrote Diderot. "We talk to them unceasingly; we wish them to listen; we are afraid of tiring or boring them. Hence we develop a particular method of explaining ourselves easily, and this method passes from conversation into style." In the salons of Paris no topic was banned provided it was presented with wit and wisdom. Thence went the intellectual lions of the hour, the philosophes among them, to display their talents and to hone their ideas against other sprightly and brilliant minds. Here, among members or associates of the ruling class, none of them revolutionaries, was hammered out a revolutionary ideology. The privileged participants loved the world they lived in too much to advocate any violent upheaval. Nevertheless, in the words of Madame de Lambert, whose salon was one of the earliest of the eighteenth century, to philosophize was "to shake off the yoke of authority." As the century progressed, it seemed ever more clear that authority would somehow be replaced by the rule of reason.

Jean Jacques Rousseau was of a different mind. "What can be proved by reason," he wrote in a virtual declaration of war against the Age of Reason, "to the majority of men is only the interested calculation of personal benefit." In his other writings he gave another dimension to the Abbé Raynal's theory of human degeneration along the outer fringes of European civilization by finding the source of evil at the very center of that civilization. Society as Rousseau saw it at that focal point, in Paris particularly, denied man everything he needed to realize his God-given potential. Rousseau burst abruptly on the intellectual scene after he had passed the midpoint of his life. Little in his earlier days presaged his ultimate fame. His birth at Geneva in 1712 had cost his mother's life, and his childhood remained insecure. His elder brother ran away from home as a boy, and their father fled Geneva as the consequence of some fracas when Jean Jacques was ten. Shortly thereafter the youngster experienced his first sexual pleasure while he was being spanked for some naughtiness by the sister of the pastor with whom he was boarding. All his life he retained a perverse desire to repeat that experience, but was too shy to ask from a woman the thing he most desired. After miscellaneous wanderings and occupations he became for several years the bedmate and protégé of an older woman, a Madame de Warens, whom he significantly called *Maman*. Just before his death he recalled this period as the most contented of his life. Under her influence he was converted to Catholicism, but he soon reverted to Protestantism, and he continued his wanderings and the pursuit of odd jobs.

From that undistinguished, somewhat vagrant past, at the age of thirty-seven Rousseau achieved fame virtually overnight. He had found his way to Paris, where he met Diderot and other encyclopedists. Then, in 1749, the Academy of Dijon offered a prize for the best essay on the subject: "Has the restoration of the sciences and the arts contributed to corrupt or purify morals?" Diderot, at the time in prison at Vincennes (for having written an essay the authorities considered subversive), urged him to compete for the prize by taking the negative side of the issue. It would be a bold gesture and an odd one, for at Diderot's suggestion Rousseau would attack the arts and sciences

The political doctrine of Jean Jacques Rousseau was largely contained in his Social Contract _(1762); below are brief excerpts from various chapters._

Introduction

Man was born free, and everywhere he is in chains. Many a one believes himself the master of others, and yet he is a greater slave than they. How has this change come about? I do not know. What can render it legitimate? I believe that I can settle this question.

If I considered only force and the results that proceed from it, I should say that so long as a people is compelled to obey and does obey, it does well; but that, so soon as it can shake off the yoke and does shake it off, it does better; for, if men recover their freedom by virtue of the same right by which it was taken away, either they are justified in resuming it, or there was no justification for depriving them of it. But the social order is a sacred right which serves as a foundation for all others. This right, however, does not come from nature. It is therefore based on conventions. The question is to know what these conventions are.

The social pact

To find a form of association which may defend and protect with the whole force of the community the person and property of every associate, and by means of which each, coalescing with all, may nevertheless obey only himself, and remain as free as before. Such is the fundamental problem of which the social contract furnishes the solution.

Monarchy

One essential and inevitable defect, which will always render a monarchical government inferior to a republican one, is that in the latter the public voice hardly ever raises to the highest posts any but enlightened and capable men, who fill them honorably; whereas those who succeed in monarchies are most frequently only petty mischiefmakers, petty knaves, petty intriguers, whose petty talents, which enable them to attain high posts in courts, only serve to show the public their ineptitude as soon as they have attained them. The people are much less mistaken about their choice than the Prince is; and a man of real merit is almost as rare in a royal ministry as a fool at the head of a republican government.

Good government

All other things being equal, the government under which, without external aids, without naturalizations,

and without colonies, the citizens increase and multiply most, is infallibly the best. That under which a people diminishes and decays is the worst.

The abuse of government

In the vulgar sense a tyrant is a king who governs with violence and without regard to justice and the laws. In the strict sense, a tyrant is a private person who arrogates to himself the royal authority without having a right to it. . . .

To give different names to different things, I call the usurper of royal authority a _tyrant_, and the usurper of sovereign power a _despot_. The tyrant is he who, contrary to the laws, takes upon himself to govern according to the laws; the despot is he who sets himself above the laws themselves. Thus the tyrant cannot be a despot, but the despot is always a tyrant.

The body politic

The body politic, as well as the human body, begins to die from its birth, and bears in itself the causes of its own destruction. But both may have a constitution more or less robust, and fitted to preserve them a longer or shorter time. The constitution of man is the work of nature; that of the State is the work of art. It does not rest with men to prolong their lives; it does rest with them to prolong that of the State as far as possible, by giving it the best constitution practicable. The best constituted will come to an end, but not so soon as another, unless some unforseen accident brings about it premature destruction.

General will

So long as a number of men in combination are considered as a single body, they have but one will, which relates to the common preservation and to the general well-being. In such a case all the forces of the State are vigorous and simple, and its principles are clear and luminous; it has no confused and conflicting interests; the common good is everywhere plainly manifest and only good sense is required to perceive it. Peace, union, and equality are foes to political subtleties. Upright and simpleminded men are hard to deceive because of their simplicity; allurements and refined pretexts do not impose upon them; they are not even cunning enough to be dupes. When in the happiest nation in the world, we see troops of peasants regulating the affairs of the State under an oak and always acting wisely, can we refrain from despising the refinements of other nations, who make themselves illustrious and wretched with so much art and mystery?

of the day as corruptions of civilization, just as Diderot was exalting them in his encyclopedia. Returning from a visit to Diderot, Rousseau rested by the roadside to contemplate the matter and there experienced a vision, went into a trance apparently, from which he emerged sopping wet from the tears he had shed in his ecstasy. "Ah," he later wrote, "if ever I could have written a quarter of what I saw and felt under that tree, with what clarity I should have brought out all the contradictions of our social system! With what simplicity I should have demonstrated that man is by nature good, and that only our institutions have made him bad!"

He obviously recovered enough of those feverish thoughts to pour them into the essay he submitted to the Academy; it won him the prize of three hundred francs and a gold medal. With the subsequent publication of the essay, which Diderot arranged, Rousseau immediately became a controversial celebrity. "Your *Discours* is taking beyond all imagination," Diderot wrote him; "never was there an instance of a like success." Beyond that sudden development, in his vision and with his essay Rousseau had discovered the abiding theme of his future life's work. He would proceed in his subsequent writings to expose further what he considered the degrading evils of contemporary society—its artificiality and immorality, the gross deficiencies of the economic system that led to the pitiable contrasts of rich and poor, the callousness or the lack of justice, and the desiccation of the spirit through the replacement of religion and feeling with science and intellectualism.

Basically, what Rousseau appealed for was a society worthy of man in all his inherent goodness, and men worthy of that society. He offered no systematic program for realizing such a happy state of affairs, but the ideas he put forth to justify his vision—"taking men as they are and laws as they might be" —could not be brushed aside. In the words of one of his advocates, Rousseau's purpose "was not to propose practicable measures but to present great principles with force and energy." He utterly rejected the concept so fondly held by the majority of contemporary philosophers that the state was essentially a large family ruled by a more or less enlightened king who was father to his people. To Rousseau the idea of an absolute state, however benign, providentially created to guide and control the lives of its citizens without their active participation, was repulsive. "Do not talk to me any longer of your 'legal despotism,'" he once expostulated to a correspondent. "I could not stand it, let alone understand it, and for me these are only two contradictory words." For Rousseau the true sovereign must be the individual citizen acting in public association and common agreement with his fellow citizens to serve the general welfare—and the individual's own best interests.

Men would truly become masters of their fate through the enjoyment of civil liberties which they secured through a social contract entered into among themselves. In obedience to the laws thus prescribed by the general will, each would find his individual freedom. Unlike the philosophes, who for the most part spurned the masses, Rousseau was speaking in the name and the interest of the common man whose aspirations were so unhappily thwarted, everywhere, by the political and social structures. He issued a plea for individualism against the regulations imposed by the absolute state. He has been called the "first great spokesman of democracy" (the word "democracy," incidentally, was virtually unknown in his day). With his arguments he passed over the threshold into the modern world.

"Nature, to strengthen the body and make it grow, has means which must never be thwarted. A child must not be constrained to stay when he wants to go, nor to go when he wants to remain still. . . . They must jump, run, shout, when they want to. All their movements are needs of their constitution which is seeking to strengthen itself."

Jean Jacques Rousseau in *Emile*

The two unquestionable masterpieces of Rousseau's maturity were *Emile* and *The Social Contract*. The former is a treatise in which he developed his conviction that the true role of education was to safeguard the natural, healthy impulses of a child from the inhibiting and misleading influences of purely rationalist instruction; to emancipate him from the tyranny of adults as he learned of the world through his own experiences and sensibility; to permit him to recognize and respect the natural promptings of the heart before exposing him to intellectual rhetoric. *The Social Contract*, in turn, analyzes a society that could only be developed about a body of citizens so educated. Basically that society rests on the authority of responsible individuals, on the concept of individual worth. But that society did not exist. Something had gone wrong since the Supreme Being had originally endowed man with reason and with conscience to manage his affairs on earth. "Everything is good as it leaves the hands of the Creator," he wrote in *Emile*; "everything degenerates in the hands of man." And in the opening sentence of *The Social Contract* he asserted, "Man is born free, and everywhere he is in chains"—another formulation of the same thought. Here he offered new substitutes for the devil and original sin to explain the human plight; man is born good but society has corrupted him.

In its entirety Rousseau's message to his contemporaries—and to posterity —was of incalculable importance. His *Social Contract* alone went through innumerable editions in virtually all European languages. There were thirteen in French in 1762-63; three in English and one in German in 1763-64; and one in Russian in 1763. John Adams read the book in America in 1765, and ultimately had four copies in his library. It provided a justification of revolution and won fresh interest when revolution became a fact. There were thirty-two more French editions issued between 1789 and 1799—and four more in Russian in 1906-1907.

Rousseau's writings contained the most comprehensive and the most radical social criticism that had ever appeared in print, and the impact of that criticism is still felt in our own day. He has been misunderstood and misrepresented by his friends and enemies alike—and he had a perverse instinct for making enemies. During the course of his bizarre life he had been hunted like a criminal over the face of Europe and at the same time consulted like an oracle. Then and throughout the years since, even his most enthusiastic admirers have persistently distorted his thought. "They took from his writings only what they pleased," wrote the late J. Christopher Herold, one of the most perceptive of Rousseau's critics, "either to propagate or to attack what they chose to regard as his doctrine. He has been both claimed and damned by Marxists and conservatives, by atheists and mystics, by anarchists and totalitarians. He has been blamed with some plausibility for such disparate developments as the Reign of Terror, Hitlerism, progressive education, romantic love, liberation, communism, nudism, momism, and the revival of square dancing." "Indeed," Herold concluded, "it may perhaps be said that no man since Christ has had more follies committed in his name."

Rousseau himself did not make it easy to view his contribution in perspective. He was decidedly a neurotic person with curious sexual inhibitions and autoerotic tendencies. He also suffered from a variety of bodily ailments. Among other things, a malformation of the urethra caused urine retention. Afraid of wetting himself in the presence of His Most Christian Majesty, he

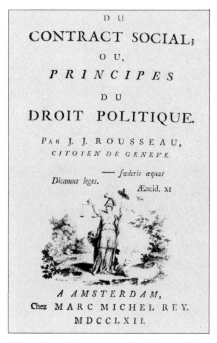

The frontispiece of the first edition of The Social Contract *by Jean Jacques Rousseau, published in* 1762

The eighteenth-century's idealization of the noble savage is shown in this detail from Tiepolo's fresco America (1752), *which adorns the ceiling of the Würzburg Palace. The Indian maiden, symbolizing America, is astride an alligator and surrounded by a melting pot of peoples.*
GUNDERMANN, WURZBURG

refused an invitation by Louis XV to come to his court. Typically, he made his refusal appear to be the proud gesture of a republican citizen. With that refusal he lost his chance of obtaining a royal pension, which emolument would have spared him from some of his miseries. He died a recluse in a state close to insanity. But the fact remains that he had produced several of the most influential works of modern times. In his *Confessions*, posthumously published, he performed a unique act of self-exposure designed to prove to the world that with all his many weaknesses he was, like all men, fundamentally good. However, that unreservedly candid revelation only added to the misunderstanding and misrepresentation that clung to his reputation.

Perhaps the most persistent misconceptions of Rousseau's ideas have been the beliefs that he preached a "return to nature" and that he extolled primitive man, the "noble savage." He did neither. To be sure, he found in nature a wholesome innocence that was at variance with the corruption he saw in existing social institutions, and he advised *turning* to nature (not *re*turning to it) as a guide in thinking through the problems of society. As he wrote late in his life, he had no thought of plunging "humanity back into its original barbarism." On the contrary, he aspired to convert existing institutions to the high levels of his expectations, not to eliminate them, which would leave the vices of the world and remove the means of their cure.

Rousseau died in 1778 at the age of sixty-six, Voltaire died that same year at the age of eighty-four. It has been fairly claimed that no two authors in the history of literature have ever exercised so powerful an influence on the thoughts and feelings of their contemporaries. For their critical writings both men were at different times exiled from Paris and from France by actions of the authorities. After those authorities were overthrown during the French Revolution, the bodies of both men were given honorable resting places in the Pantheon at Paris, that magnificent mausoleum of the illustrious. (With the restoration of the Bourbon monarchy, their bones were exhumed and thrown into a pit outside the city to be consumed by quicklime. The adherents of the ancien régime had taken their revenge.)

The parallel between their fortunes ends there. Rousseau spent so many of his years being hunted through Europe because he refused to flatter or to lie to those who were in a position to help him secure and maintain his independence. Voltaire gained his independence by flattering kings and queens and others in high positions, often with a fulsomeness that is embarrassing to contemplate, that he might freely publish wherever their authority reached. (Goethe observed that few writers had made themselves so dependent in order to be independent.) At other times he denied that he had written what he had obviously written that he might be free to write more. Ironically, at one point early in his life Voltaire served a prison term in the Bastille for certain offenses against the regent that he probably did not write.

However, that was not Voltaire's last experience with the Bastille. About ten years later he was returned to those "cool apartments" following an absurd quarrel with a decayed aristocrat who had started the trouble in the first case. From those uncomfortable experiences Voltaire learned to his cost the perils of openly confronting the hierarchic society of his day. He became a master of his own maxim on literary guerrilla warfare: "Strike and conceal your hand." It was after his second imprisonment that, full of rage, he fled to England, where he remained for nearly three years as a welcome guest in that open society. There he was immediately impressed by the comparative liberty enjoyed by men of letters, who could not be arbitrarily clapped into jail by the king and his minions; by the safeguards provided to individuals through the English Constitution. He later wrote, "We can well believe that a constitution that has established the rights of the Crown, the aristocracy, and the people, in which each section finds its own safety, will last as long as human institutions can last. He was also impressed by the fact that successful businessmen enjoyed equal status with members of the most noble and ancient families of the land and by the degree of religious toleration that he found so widespread and generally respected. He was especially attracted to the doctrines of the Quakers; he attended their meetings, and he stated that were it not for his horror of seasickness he would emigrate to Pennsylvania and settle there among their New World emissaries.

In England he also studied the works of Newton and of his contemporaries, the philosophers Thomas Hobbes and John Locke. Both Hobbes and Locke had reasoned that political authority was derived, or should be, from the consent of the governed and that its goal was the general welfare. Locke believed that in some circumstances revolution was not only a right but an obligation. Such checks and balances as were ultimately incorporated into the Constitution of the United States, he asserted, were essential to good government. Locke drew up the Fundamental Constitution of Carolina for the proprietors of that colony. It was a fantastic blueprint for life in America, composed in the quiet of an Oxford study, and quite impractical for settlements in the forests of the New World. Nevertheless, the theorists of the American Revolution drew heavily upon his political writings, as upon those of Hobbes, to rationalize their cause. In 1774 Josiah Quincy expressed a sentiment common among his compatriots when, in bequeathing the works of Locke to his son, he concluded, "May the spirit of Liberty rest upon him!"

That English statesman John Morley subsequently contended that Voltaire "left France a poet and returned to it [from this sojourn in England] a sage," a statement that in its exaggeration suggests the substantial gains that stay did contribute to Voltaire's ideology. When he returned to his native country he wrote a book, *Letters Concerning the English*, which in the guise of a panegyric of English ways was an attack on the establishments of state and Church in France. He did not dare publish the work, but a pirated edition was soon issued in Paris, and that was publicly burned by order of the Paris parlement. In fear of prosecution, Voltaire fled the city for a comfortable retreat near the border of Lorraine, whither he could escape should his freedom be threatened.

Over the next three decades Voltaire became the most prominent literary figure of his age. No one since the Humanist Desiderius Erasmus in the sixteenth century had enjoyed such unique eminence in the world of letters. Tirelessly and incessantly he produced a flow of poems, plays, and essays, histories, works of criticism, diatribes, and popularizations of scientific studies. He wrote with style and passion, with clarity and wit. He wrote with a vengeance directed at legal injustice, persecution, superstition, human folly in all its forms—and with deadly aim at what he considered the uninformed, deceptive, bigoted and repressive dogmas of all revealed religion, especially of the Roman Catholic Church. "Your Majesty will do the human race an eternal service," Voltaire wrote Frederick the Great of Prussia, "in extirpating

The English philosopher John Locke (seen here at age fifty-two) had a profound influence upon leaders of the Enlightenment and the American Revolution.
NATIONAL PORTRAIT GALLERY, LONDON

this infamous superstition [Christianity], I do not say among the rabble, who are not worthy of being enlightened and who are apt for every yoke; I say among the well-bred, among those who wish to think." For his part, that monarch declared that in his country "everyone must go to heaven his own way," and gave welcome to refugees from religious persecution in other countries.

Voltaire was not antireligious. Along with Rousseau, Franklin, Jefferson, and a very large group of other thoughtful men of the eighteenth century, he was a deist. He did not deny the existence of God, but like those others he conceived of the deity as a prime moving force, a sublime mathematician (as some termed him) who had created the universe and the laws by which it would be governed, and had then withdrawn to allow it to operate mechnically, clockwork fashion, according to those "natural" principles and regulations that had been originally established and which with diligent inquiry and clear reasoning could be properly understood and appreciated. All the formalities and mysteries that had since clustered around Christian beliefs and practices were to the deists obfuscations later interpolated by a self-serving and power-hungry and often quarreling clergy. Rational men needed no churches, prayers, saints, communion, priests, or miracles to respect or worship their God.

Rational men also might question the validity of traditional Christianity as they pondered over the significance of the great astronomical and geographical discoveries of the age. Christendom, it had been clearly revealed, was but a tiny fragment of the universe. Untold millions of human beings had never even heard of Jesus Christ or any of the Christian saints. Could all the Chinese, for example, be damned because they knew nothing of an event which, as far as they were concerned, might well have happened on the moon? The earth itself, as Newton had revealed, was but an atom in space. Were the entire human race, Christian and heathen together, to be totally destroyed, wrote the infamous Comte de Sade, it would afflict the cosmos so little that "it would no more interrupt its course than if the entire species of rabbits or hares

This contemporary German print projected the enormity of the Lisbon disaster on November 1, 1755, by showing everything happening at once—earthquake, fire, and tidal waves. Actually, the tidal waves struck only the lower portion of Lisbon, but the fires continued to smolder for a week. Thousands who luckily survived the earthquake perished in the holocaust and confusion that followed.

were extinguished." That speculation rudely shocked his readers, but it made a point that could not be ignored.

Voltaire and his entire world were profoundly affected by the cataclysmic earthquake and fire that practically destroyed Portugal's capital city of Lisbon in 1755 as its population was attending divine services on All Saints' Day. (It was said that the shock of that disturbance was felt from Scotland to Asia Minor.) The quake was followed by an enormous tidal wave that broke over the lower town. As many as forty thousand persons may have perished in the disaster. As the news spread about the world every variety of explanation was produced to account for this horrible demonstration of God's wrath. Members of the English clergy maintained that the city was demolished because its population was Catholic; survivors in Lisbon attributed the catastrophe to the fact that they had errantly harbored some Protestants in their midst. The religious convictions of others, including Voltaire, were shaken and confounded. If, as was so widely believed, God was omnipotent and benevolent, how could he have permitted or perpetrated such cruel punishment at the very moment the faithful were worshiping Him?

Voltaire was moved to write a poem on the subject, the most sincere one he had ever composed. Only God could explain the atrocity, he wrote, but He refused to do so, leaving His children as "bewildered atoms in a mass of mud." Following that, Voltaire created his literary masterpiece, *Candide*, a brilliant satire on the optimists of the age, Rousseau and Leibniz among them. His character, Candide, had been tutored to believe in the perfectibility of man and the loving kindness of God. However, Candide suffered one misfortune after another as he journeyed about the world. His fate had taken him to Lisbon just at the time of the earthquake. "If this be indeed the best possible of worlds," he asks, "then what must the other worlds be like?" He concludes that one should renounce fruitless speculation about the purposes of Providence, go about one's business, and stoically accept what comes. The tale of disillusionment end with the memorable words, "we must cultivate our garden."

By this time Voltaire was not only famous, he was a very rich old man. He had enjoyed the favor of kings and queens and been their adviser. His high station in the literary world was uncontestable. His cynical wit was applauded by his friends and admirers, and feared by those at whom it was directed. "I have never made but one prayer to God," he remarked, "a very short one: 'O Lord, make my enemies ridiculous.' And God granted it." In this the Deity had Voltaire's helpful assistance, it must be added. With a mocking eye to the military escapades of Frederick the Great, Voltaire once remarked, "It is forbidden to kill, therefore all murderers are punished unless they kill in large numbers to the sound of trumpets." One way or another Voltaire had amassed a large fortune, partly, it seems, through speculation on army contracts and partly by lending money at high rates of interest (also, during much of his life he had lived at the expense of others, and for the rest he was scrupulously stingy). About such matters he was altogether reticent. In *Candide* he suggested that the art of making money consists simply in having been born lucky.

In 1758 he purchased the considerable property of Ferney, on French soil, from which he had been technically banished, but within four miles of Geneva, a haven in case of trouble. There he spent the next twenty years of his life

Voltaire, shaken by the events in Lisbon, was moved to write a poem about it, and then Candide, *which rejected the* tout est bien *philosophy of Leibniz and Rousseau. Above, an illustration from* Candide, *first published in 1759*
BIBLIOTHEQUE NATIONALE

For the last thirty years of his life Voltaire (above) was passionately in love with Madame Denis (opposite), the daughter of his sister Catherine.

in the company of his dead sister's daughter, Madame Denis, an unattractive woman to whom he nevertheless was passionately attached. Almost incredibly, the love letters he wrote her—he the aging, sophisticated man of the world, rich in experience and wisdom—were like those of a mooning adolescent. Here again Voltaire presents a paradox. When Voltaire died Madame Denis quickly got rid of Ferney and sold her uncle's library to Catherine the Great.

During those twenty years, many of the most celebrated men of the world came to Ferney to speak with Voltaire, to hear him discourse. (Joseph of Austria passed him by, although he sought out Rousseau, and for this Voltaire never forgave him.) His own activity did not flag. All his life he had been a reformer. Now in his last sanctuary he became a full-time crusader, lashing out at the inequities of the French legal system, urging the abolition of torture, the provision of lawyers for defendants, the reduction of punishments; he campaigned to have blasphemy and homosexuality removed from the catalogue of crimes, to have court trials made public. The single most celebrated cause he espoused was that of one Jean Calas, a Huguenot whose son had been found hanged in the father's shop. Although suicide seemed evident, Calas was accused of having murdered his son to prevent him from converting to Roman Catholicism. The parent was cruelly tortured, found guilty, and executed by his Catholic judges. To Voltaire this apparently clear example of religious bigotry and persecution was intolerable. For three years he fought to have the verdict overturned, in his efforts enlisting the financial support of Catherine the Great, the king of Poland, and even George III, as well as a wide public. He gained the sympathy of Madame de Pompadour and high officials of the French government; finally the innocence of Calas was established by the Council of Paris.

That was only one of the battles against injustice that Voltaire waged from his frontier retreat, but it was the most conspicuous and it alone won him immortality as a champion of the oppressed. When he finally re-entered Paris in 1778 after an absence of twenty-eight years he returned in triumph, not so much as the famed author but as the hero of the Calas affair. He was not directly welcomed by the royal court, but his return was received with rejoicing by the public at large as well as by the Academy of Sciences. (It was said that nobles disguised themselves as tavern waiters to catch sight of him.) On the evening of April 29 at a meeting of the Academy both Voltaire and Benjamin Franklin were present, seated near one another on the platform in full view of the audience, which clamored that the two venerable sages must be introduced to one another, and then that they must embrace French fashion. John Adams witnessed the scene. "The two aged actors upon this great theater of philosophy and frivolity," he reported, "embraced each other by hugging one another in their arms, and kissing each other's cheeks, and then the tumult subsided. And the cry immediately went through the whole kingdom, and, I suppose, over all Europe, 'How charming it was to see Solon and Sophocles embrace.'"

During those later years at Ferney, Voltaire made peace of a sort with the Church, although he could never accept all the dogmas that went with formal religious observance, nor supernatural explanations of religious history. But he did believe in the existence of one mighty God.("As to Monsieur the Son and Madame his mother," Voltaire remarked, "that is another matter!") At Ferney he built a small church, the only one in the world, he claimed, that was dedicated to that single God, all the others being dedicated to saints. He wrote the pope asking for sacred relics, and was sent a piece of the haircloth worn by Saint Francis of Assisi. On the altar of the chapel he had installed a life-sized sculptured image of Christ—not Christ the divine son of God, but Christ the mortal sage. All this, his somewhat dismayed critics among the philosophes maintained, was actually a political gesture toward Versailles, a pretended show of piety to win him official remission of his sins against the court and the state. It was also, they suggested, a way of using God to police his servants and the peasants at Ferney through the moral scruples imposed by the Church. Nevertheless, in the end Voltaire died in the Catholic religion, and was buried in consecrated ground.

Victor Hugo once observed that "to name Voltaire is to characterize the entire eighteenth century." Considering the extraordinary range of the man's interests and writings, concerned as they were with religion, morality, philosophy, politics, government, science, economics, ethics, social questions, and literature in its many forms, Hugo's claim may seem justified. Voltaire's keen mind was never at rest. (All the while he kept up a continuous and voluminous correspondence with half the world.) Throughout his long career he had reasoned to a wide audience that superstition was ridiculous, sentiment absurd, fanaticism unintelligent, and oppression infamous. As earlier remarked, Voltaire died in the belief that his lifetime had witnessed the triumph of reason. "It is certain," he concluded, "that the knowledge of nature, the skeptical attitude toward old fables dignified by the name of history, a healthy metaphysic freed from the absurdities of the schools, are the fruits of that century when reason was perfected."

Voltaire's own customary skepticism is missing from that conclusive statement. Looking beyond his words with the light of historical perspective it can be seen that, at the time Voltaire so confidently wrote, those fruits were reserved for a small elite; that they were beyond the reach of the large majority. Voltaire himself referred to the mass of people as "a ferocious and blind monster" whom he had no hope of enlightening. That, he facetiously remarked, "was the job of the apostles," intimating that it might take an eternity to accomplish. But the majority also included privileged and favored members of society who could be as unreasonable as the lowliest peasant, although on a grander scale and in a more spectacular manner.

A good part of the fascination of the Age of Reason rests in the fact that it could be and often was utterly unreasonable. It was a golden age of fakes and charlatans whose antics made a mockery of rationalism and who found a responsive public at every level of society, royalty by no means excepted, as will be seen. Voltaire himself, along with others who thought like him, must bear some responsibility for this. By disparaging the well-organized disciplines of traditional religious belief and practice, the philosophes had created a spiritual vacuum which reasoning could not easily or quickly fill and into which all sorts of irrational notions were ready to flow. When creeds were abolished credulity crept in. What is more, if all conventions and institutions of the past were subject to question, the door was open to almost any form of speculation about better ways and means to meet and solve the problems of life or to hasten the pursuit of happiness. Reason, it had been made plain, could come masked in unexpected garb.

Voltaire was bemused by the hocus-pocus being practiced in the name of scientific reason. One of the persons who figures prominently in his correspondence, the so-called Comte de Saint-Germain, was one of the celebrated adventurers of the age, a highly sophisticated trickster who with his various talents found his way into a number of the courts of Europe and into other high circles where over a long span of years he exercised considerable influence with his claim to have discovered some extraordinary secrets of nature. As early as 1743, Horace Walpole reported that, after spending some time in Paris, Saint-Germain appeared in London, where he was arrested as a Jacobin spy and then released. "He is called an Italian, a Spaniard, a Pole," wrote Walpole, "a somebody that married a great fortune in Mexico and ran away with her jewels to Constantinople; a priest, a fiddler, a vast nobleman." Just who Saint-Germain really was or where he came from is uncertain. He is commonly believed to have been an illegitimately born Portuguese Jew; but there were also rumors that he was of royal birth. He spoke most of the European languages, he was a composer and capable violinist. "He sings, plays on the violin wonderfully," wrote Walpole, " . . . is mad and not very sensible." He had a comprehensive knowledge of history, and his accomplishments in chemistry were real and considerable. And, by whatever means, he was rich. Grimm thought him the best man of parts he had ever known.

Saint-Germain was also professedly an alchemist of rare gifts, and he claimed to be able to remove flaws from diamonds. By cabalistic rituals he could also summon the dead from the dark regions and had perfected an ointment which would spare women the awkwardness of growing old. He claimed that he himself was hundreds of years old, had been close to Alexander the Great, and once had an interesting conversation with Jesus Christ. A few years after his experience in London he appeared at Versailles, where he cast the horoscope of Madame de Pompadour, and through her interest was presented to Louis XV, who was convinced that he had actually seen Saint-Germain transmute three small diamonds into one large one. A special laboratory was set up in the royal chateau of Chambord in the Loire Valley, where Saint-Germain was expected to perform his magic and, through the transmutation of metals, among other devices, alleviate the king's financial woes. To the dismay of Louis' ministers, the king sent Saint-Germain to Holland as a secret agent to negotiate with the Dutch bankers and diplomats. By his own secret diplomacy the Duc de Choiseul effectively undermined that mission, and the *Wundermann*, as Saint-Germain was called, went by way of London to St. Petersburg, where, it is said, he conjured up a semblance of Peter the Great for Catherine of Russia, to assure the empress that she had been justified in having her husband murdered to gain the throne for herself. Saint-Germain ended his days in Schleswig-Holstein studying the "secret" sciences with the Landgrave Charles of Hesse. Meanwhile, according to the memoirs of his even more notorious contemporary Alessandro di Cagliostro, he had founded freemasonry in Germany and had initiated Cagliostro himself into that rite.

Guiseppe Balsamo, who assumed the name and title of Count Alessandro di Cagliostro as his fame mounted, was another imposter and fraud who found an eager reception for his infamous deceits in the capitals of Europe. As a youngster in his native Sicily he was expelled for misconduct from his monastery school and disowned by his relations. However, from such lowly and tawdry beginnings he improved his fortunes to the point where he was at one time welcomed at St. Petersburg by Catherine the Great's influential minister Potemkin (although Catherine herself refused him an audience) and where, among other recognitions of his importance, he won letters of recommendation from the Comte de Vergennes, minister of foreign affairs under Louis XVI, and that monarch's reputable and respected minister of war, the Comte de Ségur. At Strasbourg he gained the attention, the confidence, and the support of the great Cardinal de Rohan, who had been appointed to greet Marie Antionette on the steps of the cathedral of that city as she journeyed toward Paris for her nuptials with the dauphin. Rohan was certain he had seen Cagliostro perform miracles of alchemy, and that with his support the necromancer would make him the richest man in Europe. The cardinal-prince placed a bust of the favored magician in his large country palace, labeling it "The Divine Cagliostro."

Cagliostro ended his days in a Roman dungeon, charged with heresy and sorcery, but not before he had spent the better part of his life successfully and profitably fleecing the best society throughout most of Europe by selling them his love philtres, elixirs of youth, and other magical nostrums of absolutely no use, and by giving worthless promises of unlimited wealth to those who would trust his secret and miraculous formulas. As the Grand Copt of the order of Egyptian Masonry, he used his authority to organize many lodges in that influential fraternal organization.

Largely because of the salacious accounts of his experiences that were published in his memoirs, Giovanni Casanova is probably the best remembered of those eighteenth-century adventurers who preyed so brazenly on the credulity of the times. He was born in Venice but, as a young man, left there to pursue a colorful career that led him to all corners of Europe, often moving across borders from one country to another at the insistence of the police. Casanova made his way through the world by gambling, spying, writing, and, among other things, by seducing women. He was a man of learning and taste, and his personal charm gained him entry into high-ranking society. In Paris, where he won the favor of Marie Antoinette, he was made director of state lotteries, with which position he gained a financial reputation and a considerable fortune. At Rome the pope gave him the Order of the Golden Spur.

Casanova spent three nights with Voltaire on the Swiss border. Voltaire explained to him that all his life he had fought to exterminate "the hydra of superstition," to which Casanova impudently replied that this was hardly something to boast of. "If a people lost their superstitions," he dared to tell the older man, "they would all become philosophers and thereby also lose the gift of obedience. You should let the people keep their hydras, since they love them." It was a quarrelsome visit, and Casanova left with his vanity injured and with a lasting grudge against his acerbic host.

One of the more bizarre incidents in Casanova's life resulted from a duel over gambling debts in which he slightly wounded his adversary, a young count with aristocratic connections. The two men were immediately reconciled. As proof of his friendship, Casanova painted the count's wound and previously ailing thigh with a magical concoction he called the "talisman of Solomon." The count's afflictions were immediately cured and, in gratitude, he introduced Casanova to his aunt, the Marquise d'Urfé, a wealthy lady with a passionate interest in the occult. Casanova immediately proceeded to lead this new patron down the dark ways of spiritualism so that she might satisfy

Giovanni Casanova (above, in a portrait by Anton Raphael Mengs) won fame and fortune by catering to the needs of women and by playing the confidence game brilliantly with both sexes. In 1776, having either charmed or outraged much of European society, Casanova was back in his native Venice, employed as a spy by the government.
ARMANDO PREZIOSI, BOLOGNA

her longing to communicate with the elemental spirits. "I became arbiter of her soul," Casanova wrote, "and I often abused the power I exercised over her." Since those spirits she so ardently wished to approach would not communicate with a woman, the marquise must somehow change her sex, and this Casanova volunteered to accomplish by the most outrageous incantations and nostrums. He even persuaded her to write a letter to the moon, to which through an oracle Casanova managed to provide a satisfactory reply. The totally absurd scheme was finally abandoned. After the death of the marquise Casanova reflected with no great contrition, "I saw there was nothing I could do but to encourage her mania and to profit by it."

Casanova was an ardent Freemason and as such could usually rely upon a welcome at the Masonic lodges that had opened in numerous European cities in the course of the century—in London, Paris, Florence, Berlin, Budapest, St. Petersburg, and elsewhere. (The New World had lodges in a half dozen American cities.) Although the Masons often claimed a history dating as far back as the days of Solomon, the rise of so many lodges in this modern guise was a typically eighteenth-century phenomenon. Many illustrious men were attracted to the order, among them Frederick the Great, Goethe, "Bobby" Burns, Mozart, Voltaire, Washington, and Franklin, to name but a few. With such distinguished membership of intellectual and socially minded men, the Society exercised untold influence at the time. One of Franklin's first moves on coming to Paris was to join the important lodge there, whose members could be of such inestimable help to him in propagandizing for America.

In its program Masonry combined philanthropy and wealth. With its mysterious rituals and its membership which, however select, was drawn from all social classes, it created a unique international fellowship of men of different stations who were bound together by their common interests in liberty, progress, and reform. The dogmas and moral principles espoused by the Masons closely resembled those of Christianity, and indeed were derived from them, but they were oriented toward man and this world rather than toward God and eternity. Generally speaking, Masonry was a humane, utilitarian, and rationalistic appreciation of Christian ideas and discipline. The Mason took the priest's place as a professor of morals, the lodge took the place of the church, and the order thereby won the enmity of the clergy. It also won the resentment of women, who were excluded from its ranks and some of whom, at least, believed that its meetings were likely to be occasions for orgies rather than for earnest deliberation. The movement had its aberrations, to be sure (as Cagliostro had demonstrated with his peculiar order Egyptian Masonry, which, like a number of others, was Masonic in name only); but in general the order played a unique role in spreading liberal ideas through its hundreds of lodges and many thousands of members.

In that part of the Masonic creed that called attention to the essential brotherhood of man and implemented such feelings with charitable works can be detected the pangs of conscience. The world in 1776 was definitely not the best of all possible worlds; in many unfortunate respects it was very far from that. Everywhere the eye turned, there was dismal evidence that the evils of society, or at the very least its deficiencies, alluded to in so many enlightened tracts of the time, were terribly real and persistent. There were many who felt that by itself rationalism offered a program that was too arid to effect the improvement of mankind; that as a necessary corrective the benevolent promptings of the heart must be consulted. The Age of Reason had barely run its course before this feebleness of reason as an instrument of betterment was widely conceded; the Age of Reason was becoming the age of sentiment, the cult of sensibility was replacing the cult of logic.

Rousseau was by no means altogether responsible for those attitudes, but his influence in making such thoughts a popular vogue was enormous. When in 1761 he published *La Nouvelle Héloise*, he immediately became the idol of ardent spirits everywhere the book could be found. One reporter tells of people snatching it from one another's hands for a chance to look at its pages. It is a novel written in the form of letters, according to a fashion of the time, describing the passionate affair of a young girl with her tutor and of her subsequent mildly happy marriage to a friend of her father's. Haunted by the remembrance of her premarital lapse, the young wife, now the mother of two sons, confesses to her husband. He knew all about the affair in the first place and was now forgiving enough to hire the earlier lover as a tutor to the young boys. When the reinstated tutor tries to revive the old passion he is properly repulsed. Shortly afterward the mother becomes ill with pneumonia contracted while saving one of her children from drowning. On her deathbed she is surrounded by adoring husband, sons, and lover.

This reads like what we refer to today as a soap opera. However, it so aptly expressed a growing mood of the time—a mood still with us, obviously, that recognized the imperious demands of passion and sought some means of reconciling them with the obligations of virtue—that it fascinated a huge audience. Readers wept copious tears over the pages of Rousseau's book; in fact, weeping became a fashionable indulgence as an indication or proof of delicate sensibilities. Even the cynical Frederick the Great openly gave way to tears when his feelings were moved to the right pitch by his reading or conversation. In France the cult of sensibility reached almost hysterical proportions following the publication of *La Nouvelle Héloïse*. The book ran through seventy-two editions before its popularity waned. Superficial as Rousseau's plot appears to us, its theme was deeply rooted in larger considerations of the day. It laid bare emotions that were leading men and women to be more sensitive to one another's heartfelt needs as individual human beings in a complex and often restrictive society.

However mawkish the approach, Rousseau's story pointed in the direction of a more humane and benevolent civilization. In one of his plays Diderot gave as a measure of the growing enlightenment of the century the fact that "books that inspire benevolence are practically the only ones read." Courtesy and kindness, or at least their semblances, became a vogue. A queen might leap from her carriage to aid an injured postilion; a king might put his shoulder to the wheel to help a workman whose cart was stuck in the mud. Such demonstrations of noblesse oblige were no doubt self-conscious, but at least they showed an awareness of new concepts that could in time replace traditional social attitudes and discriminations as a norm of human intercourse and understanding; although that time was long in coming.

There was another side to the coin. To release the emotions too freely was to induce excesses that would in the end undo society. Anticipating Freud's theory of the Oedipus complex by a century and a half, in *Le Neveu de Rameau*, or *Rameau's Nephew*, Diderot pointed out (with an oblique reference to Rousseau's theories) that if a child "were left to himself and his native blindness, he would later combine the infant's reasoning with the passion of a man of thirty —he would cut his father's throat and sleep with his mother." The eminent Scots philosopher David Hume, who was Rousseau's patron when he sought refuge in England and who was influenced by the Frenchman's philosophy, went so far as to pronounce that "reason is and ought to be only the slave of the passions and can never pretend to any other office than to obey them." It was a pronouncement with unintentional implications.

As the slave of the passions, reason might be forced in strange directions. If the heart was to rule the head, if all "natural" impulses were good, and if individual satisfaction was an ultimate goal of life—and these several propositions were all countenanced by various men of wisdom—then it might be possible to conclude that the removal of the false and artificial restraints of society could lead to sheer hedonism. As in nature, the strong animal could satisfy his desires at the expense of the weak. The possibility was clearly demonstrated by that mad child of the Enlightenment, that ultimate libertine, the Comte de Sade (often called Marquis), who gave his name to the perversions he practiced. In his novels as in his life Sade shocked the contemporary world with his complete philosophical amoralism. Since there was no ever-watchful God to hinder, Sade argued, the sensible man will gratify every desire, however uncommon, so far as he can without incurring punishment by human custodians of law and morality here on earth. The word "abnormal" was not in his lexicon. Such were his irregularities, however, that he did not escape earthly punishment. He wrote his chief works while imprisoned in the Bastille for his homosexual offenses. Although he escaped from there, he was committed to a lunatic asylum as an incurable case, and there he died.

Sade was an extreme aberration of the romantic spirit that in so many ways fired the cult of sensibility. That spirit, which would come to full flower only in the nineteenth century, had had an early birth in England. More than twenty years before the appearance of Rousseau's *La Nouvelle Héloïse*, Samuel Richardson had already carried the sentimental novel to a dizzy height with his *Pamela*, subtitled "or Virtue Rewarded," soon followed as a sort of supplement by another novel, *Clarissa Harlowe*. As the title page of the latter book discloses, it was intended as a warning of "the Distresses that may attend Misconduct both of Parents and Children in relation to Marriage." Even Vol-

The infamous Marquis de Sade, seen above in the only known contemporary portrait, served twelve years in the French army before being arrested and condemned to death for homosexual offenses in 1772. He escaped that punishment, but while confined to the Bastille and later an insane asylum, wrote shocking novels and plays detailing his amoral philosophy.

taire, the supreme satirist, was moved by the cause of virtue as expounded in Richardson's novels to prepare a dramatization of *Pamela*. He also wrote a sentimental comedy, *Nanine*, in much the same vein, a piece that served that cause so well that Rousseau was constrained to praise it, his rival's work, "Because in it honor, virtue, and pure natural sentiments are preferred to the impertinent prejudices of rank." Diderot, with extravagant approval, said he would put Richardson's works on the same shelf with Moses, Homer, Sophocles, and Euripedes.

At home in England Richardson's attraction was enormous, even among the most sophisticated and reticent of Britons. The famous bluestocking Lady Mary Wortley Montagu succumbed to the sentimental appeal of his work. "I was such an old fool as to weep over Clarissa Harlowe," she wrote her daughter, "like any milkmaid of sixteen over the Ballad of the Lady's Fall. To say truth, the first volume softened me by a near resemblance of my maiden days; but on the whole 'tis most miserable stuff. . . . [Clarissa] follows the maxim of . . . declaring all she thinks to all the people she sees, without reflecting that in this mortal state of imperfection, fig leaves are as necessary for our minds as our bodies, and 'tis as indecent to show all we think as all we have." In another letter she philosophically concluded, "All that reflection and experience can do is to mitigate, we can never extinguish our passions. I call by that name every sentiment that is not founded upon reason." Even the dour and intransigeant Dr. Johnson, the foremost literary critic of the day, gave way to Richardson's persuasive fiction. "If you were to read Richardson for the story," he commented, "your impatience would be so fretted that you would hang yourself. But you must read him for the sentiment."

The spirit that gave birth to the sentimental novel was persistent and pervasive. In Germany it found its perfect expression in Goethe's *The Sorrows of the Young Werther*, first published in 1774. For Goethe the heart was the source of "all power, all happiness, and all suffering." His character Werther, a young man totally absorbed in his feelings, falls in love with a girl he cannot have, and ends his wandering, brooding life a suicide. As an exploration of morbid sensitivity, the book was a remarkably skillful performance that so conveniently suited the temper of the times it won a huge success. It was read in translation as eagerly in England and France as it was in its original form in Germany. (The impressionable young Corsican Napoleon Bonaparte read it seven times, he claimed, weeping profusely at each reading.) A "Werther fever" swept across the land. Young German intellectuals affected Werther costumes (sky-blue coat, yellow breeches, and jackboots); there were Werther engravings, embroideries, and medallions, and a perfume called "Eau de Werther." There were even dramatic and needless suicides à la Werther. The government attempted to discourage this raging sentiment, but to no avail. In his second edition Goethe himself added a cautionary introduction to his book, indicating that the impact of the tale might have unfortunate consequences—which provided an additional inducement to new readers.

With the publication of *Werther*, the younger generation of German writers, in their passionate revolt against contemporary conventions, began to be taken seriously by other European intellectuals. *Werther* was at the center of a brief literary revolution that lasted through most of the 1770's and that revivified the German language and German letters, although Frederick the Great, devoted as he remained to French cultural tradition, seemed quite unaware of

In 1772, at the age of twenty-three, Johann Wolfgang von Goethe wrote Götz von Berlichingen, *a play that glorified German heroism and national pride and won wide popularity, although Frederick the Great condemned it as a "detestable imitation" of Shakespeare's "barbarism." This sketch of Goethe was done in the 1780's in Rome, where Goethe had retreated to study art.*
GOETHE MUSEUM, FRANKFURT

145

the development. These authors spoke with the voice of outraged, discontented, and confused youth, somewhat more eloquently than we have heard similar protests in recent years. Historians have dubbed this brief period the "Storm and Stress" period, the *Sturm und Drang*, a phrase taken from the title of a play by Friedrich von Klinger that was performed in 1776. Here was planted the seed of the romanticism that flourished so extravagantly in Germany in the following century.

It is not easy for us today to read these romantic novels with any serious interest or just appreciation. They suggest stilted performances of adolescent fantasy. Even in their own time they were rejected by some because of their sickly sentiment. J. H. Plumb has remarked that John Cleland wrote his very candidly erotic novel *Fanny Hill*, first published in 1749 (and in modern times so long withheld by official censors from American readers), out of destestation for Richardson's *Pamela*. Cleland seems to have lived a wild bohemian youth, finding adventures in Asia as well as in Europe, and he may have discovered in exotic places a franker approach to sexual matters than was generally condoned in Christian England. (His book, incidentally, has more literary style than any of Richardson's tales.) By implication, at least, *Fanny Hill* is a criticism of the morality of eighteenth-century England where sex was conventionally regarded as either a sacrament or a sin, with all the hypocrisy and dissimulation that have always attended scrupulous codes of behavior. Fanny, the outright whore, reaches the respectability of Pamela not by preserving but by losing her virginity. "A not uncommon road even in eighteenth-century England," writes Plumb.

However, it is possible to find in the sentimental novel historic signposts that pointed toward new social concepts. In so unreservedly revealing intimate thoughts and feelings, it tended to break down old distinctions between what was public and what was private, to close the artifical gaps that traditionally separated one class of society from another, to promote democratization of human relations. It was "escape" literature, but the best of it underlined a conviction that escape from current realities could take the road of constructive social reforms—might lead to a world where the holy Church would be more mindful of its trust and its priests more observant of their vows and obligations, the military more responsive to civilian rights and needs, the wealthy less insistent on their privileges, monarchs more observant of their duties than of their prerogatives.

But for a while yet, such a world remained a largely visionary prospect. It would only be realized by making basic changes in long-established patterns of life; and at a time of intense international rivalries, any disturbance of the social order might affect the security of the state. Tranquility and stability at home provided necessary protection against hostilities from without, and this discouraged serious reforms that otherwise might have been more readily considered at the expense of long-standing traditions. For all the enlightenment shed by philosophers in different nations, and for all the tears shed over heartfelt human needs, life in the world of 1776 still had large, dark aspects immune to all but the most modest change—until revolutionary forces suddenly turned important parts of that world quite upside down.

In that age of remarkable contrasts those dark areas were scarcely discernible from within the glittering circles where the wealthy and the privileged were for the most part content to move in rounds of polite activity, without peering too intently beyond the confines of their closed society. Looking back from the turbulent days following the French Revolution, the French statesman Talleyrand remarked that those who had not lived before 1789 did not know how pleasant life could be. For those of Talleyrand's rank, life indeed had been pleasant during the closing decades of the ancien régime. In most countries of Europe the aristocratic way of life was then as pleasing as any that mankind has ever developed. Delicately poised at the apex of the social structure, a highly privileged few enjoyed advantages known to no other group. Their exclusiveness was favored by law and custom. The patrimonial rights they exercised on their landed estates entitled them to dues and services from others of lower caste. To abstain from any productive work was a necessary condition to the preservation of their status and their privileges. They were often legally exempt from certain obligations, such as compulsory military duties and the payment of a share of public taxes commensurate with their means—or frequently enough of any taxes at all; obligations that consequently fell more heavily on the rest of society.

These aristocrats, or nobles, were often entrenched in high positions of state administration and in important offices of cultural or religious character. Throughout Europe they were bound by an international solidarity, secured by marriage alliances, in what appeared to be a self-perpetuating system. They advertised their distinction in their dress, their behavior, and their speech, as well as in the quarterings of their heraldic escutcheons. They were granted reserved places, apart from ordinary people, at public performances and ceremonies in church and theater alike. At the universities their sons were set apart in separate sections of lecture halls and separate dining and sleeping quarters; and along with the wealthy gentry such youths traveled about

TEXT CONTINUED ON PAGE 150

William Hogarth satirized high-life fashions in this mid-century engraving of a room full of ridiculousness: the effeminate man of the house, a black servant boy, the hoop skirts, the tasteless artwork, and an exotic menu being studied by an elegant pet monkey.
NEW YORK PUBLIC LIBRARY, PRINT DIVISION

A View of the Urban Poor

Early in his career William Hogarth was a highly successful "phizmonger," his term for a society painter. He rebelled against portraying his patrons idealistically, and believing that humanity was "placed between the sublime and the grotesque," set about satirizing the human condition. His subjects were the urban poor. Nowhere in Europe could a workingman expect to earn more than he needed for himself; consequently, women and children, from the age of six, had to contribute to their own sup-

port. The working poor lived daily from hand to mouth, with no provision for sickness or old age. The inevitable result was widespread thievery, violence, drunkeness, vagabondage and prostitution. Governments tended to idealize the poor as honest, hardworking, God-fearing people. Hogarth's paintings made that somewhat difficult. *An Election Entertainment*, shown above, attacked the politicians' seduction of the lower classes to obtain votes. By the 1770's more people had begun to agree with Dr. Johnson that a "decent provision for the poor is the true test of civilization."

Europe on expensive grand tours as a necessary extension of their education. (Quite aside from the pursuit of edifying experiences, it was considered preferable for young gentlemen inclined to pleasures of another sort to sow their wild oats abroad rather than at home.) Referring to the arrogant young noblemen of Bohemia, a statesman high in the counsels of Joseph II complained: "I wish that young men of distinguished families would . . . set an example of zeal and industry by their mode of life. . . . I would then be the first to support their claims [to political prerogatives]. But I know from many years of experience where the nobly born young gentlemen find their pleasures!"

However, that picture of an especially privileged, aloof, and idle minority, true as it may often have been, presents but one side of a complex matter. As was suggested in the first chapter, it had long been felt by men of serious mind that a responsible aristocracy was essential to the stability of the state. As early as 1719 the English statesman Robert Walpole had pronounced what he termed the "most certain maxim of politics . . . that a monarchy must subsist either by an army or a nobility; the first makes it a despotic, the latter a free government." Some thirty years later Montesquieu made a corollary observation in his *The Spirit of the Law*. "Nobility enters in a sense into the essence of monarchy," he wrote, "of which the fundamental maxim is: *No monarch, no nobility; no nobility, no monarch*." "There are always in a state some people distinguished by birth, wealth, or honors," he added, "but, if they are confounded with the rest of the people, if they have only one vote like others, the common liberty will be slavery for them, and they will have no interest in defending it. . . . Their share in legislation should therefore be proportionate to their other advantages in the state."

Although Montesquieu believed that "the rest of the people" should have some voice in government, he also believed that the "great" should have the largest share of responsibility and power. It was the nobility that, with its long-established dignity and inherited authority, would be immune to the fear by which despots ruled and would thus be the custodians of political liberty for all. *The Spirit of the Law* went through a half-dozen editions in France within a few years. It was immediately translated into English, and repeatedly issued in that language over the next quarter of a century. As early as 1751 a Latin translation was published in Hungary (Latin was the official political language of the Magyars). A Dutch edition appeared in 1771. It was translated into Italian in 1777, into German in 1789, and into Russian in 1801. No other modern French work was better known in America. Classes in politics at Yale and Princeton used the book as a text, and the library at Harvard owned at least one copy.

In the last decade of the eighteenth century Edmund Burke, who had been a staunch apologist for the grievances of colonial America, summarized his argument for a responsible and vigorous aristocracy to combat the threat of egalitarian despotism, which he viewed as the alternative. "To be bred in a place of estimation," he wrote, "to see nothing low and sordid from one's infancy; to be taught to respect oneself; to be habituated to the censorial inspection of the public eye . . . to take a large view . . . in a large society; to have leisure to read, to reflect, to converse . . . to be habituated in armies to command and to obey; to be taught to despise danger in the pursuit of honor and duty; to be led to a guarded and regulated conduct, from a sense that you are considered as an instructor of your fellow citizens in their highest concerns,

More than forty years before it happened, Charles de Montesquieu, shown above in a contemporary caricature, predicted the revolt of the American colonies.

and that you act as a reconciler between God and man; to be employed as an administrator of law and justice . . . to be a professor of high science . . . to be amongst rich traders, who from their success are presumed to have sharp and vigorous understandings . . . these are the circumstances of men that form what I should call a *natural* aristocracy, without which there is no nation.''

Burke clearly did not equate aristocracy with nobility. Those two terms are at best elusive in their meaning. They represent abstract categories that were not so much empty as overfull and that overlapped. Neither one denoted a homogeneous group; their constituency and their importance varied not only from country to country but also in different districts within a single country. Burke used the word ''aristocracy'' in its original Greek sense, meaning the best and most highly qualified citizens who could be called upon to serve and guide the state, some of whom might be nobles, others not. In virtually every country there were relatively poor, undistinguished, and insignificant members of the nobility who had no voice in affairs of state, but who clung pitifully to vestiges of some past glory. And in every country there were prestigious, cultured, wealthy, and influential persons—aristocrats—who held no patents of nobility. Even in colonial America, where there was no nobility at all, during the years approaching 1776 there was what could be called an aristocracy, composed of intermarried families, members of which had for three or four generations held seats on the governors' councils and who played a continuing influential role in public affairs—and who enjoyed profitable advantages in securing land grants. Governor replaced governor over the years, but the colonial councilors sat until incapacitated by old age or until removed from the scene by death, often to have their places taken by their relatives. In 1775 ten of the twelve members of the Virginia governor's council occupied seats that had been held by their fathers or grandfathers. The situation was not far different in the other colonies. Those particular circumstances ended, of course, with the Declaration of Independence and the following years of conflict and decision.

The ''natural aristocracy'' of America was by no means eliminated by the departure of the Loyalists during and after the Revolution, but its numbers were considerably reduced; and by specific prohibitions in the Constitution any likelihood of its emergence as a formal institution in the American society of the future was definitely ended. In discussing the form the new Constitution should take, John Adams declared, ''The rich, the well-born and the able acquire an influence among the people that will soon be too much for simple honesty and plain sense, in a house of representatives. The most illustrious of them must, therefore, be separated from the mass, and placed by themselves in a senate; this is, to all honest and useful intents, an *ostracism* (emphasis added).'' Later in life he wrote Jefferson, ''Your *aristoi* are the most difficult animals to manage in the whole theory and practice of government. They will not suffer themselves to be governed.'' With those Constitutional restrictions, one of the most traditional and characteristic institutions of the Old World, a hereditary nobility with social and legal claims to privilege and deference, was thus flatly rejected. The bold claim that *all* men had a right to life, liberty, and the pursuit of happiness, without regard for birth or rank or monarchical dispensation, was the most novel and radical assertion of America's independent republican polity. That ideal, so stated, by itself gave the eighteenth century a measure of greatness. The supreme social art, it seemed possible, was

Edmund Burke, seen here addressing Parliament, made every effort to dissuade his countrymen from employing force against the American colonies.
BRITISH MUSEUM

going to be achieved in America.

Until long after the American Revolution was concluded, thoughtful Europeans continued to believe that a hierarchical form of government and society was essential to the welfare of the state; that an organized, select, and small element of the population provided a necessary bulwark against the despotic intentions of the monarch on the one hand and the unruly will of the populace on the other. Unfortunately, the system was open to corruption, as Adams would observe. Positions within the restricted group, delegated to preserve a proper balance in government, could be bought as well as earned. As Turgot, the appointed minister of Louis XVI, anticipating Adams, pointed out, privileges thus acquired could easily be unjust and unworthy of respect. "Where nobility can be acquired by a payment of money," he once said, "there is no rich man that does not speedily become a noble, so that the body of the nobles includes the body of the rich, and the cause of the privileged is no longer the cause of distinguished families against a common class, but the cause of the rich against the poor." There could be a despotism of the aristocracy as well as a despotism of royalty, and Turgot, among many others of his time, advocated a strong monarchy as the only agency by which the interests of the many could be protected from those few whose influence and power were all too frequently asserted in their own self-interest, and who could become an oppressive force in society.

In 1770, when the young Swedish crown prince Gustavus came to France for political advice and backing, he was seriously counseled by some to assert his royal authority when he became king, for his own advantage and for that of his state. Voltaire so advised him when Gustavus searched him out at Ferney. In Paris Gustavus heard of his father's death, and he hurried back to Sweden to assume the crown. For decades past Swedish affairs had been controlled by a diet largely dominated by the nobility, with little regard for royal prerogatives. Many of its members were accustomed to receiving bribes from foreign powers to influence their judgment in decisions of state policy. In a remarkable coup d'état Gustavus seized the reins of power. Shortly after his return to Sweden, in 1772, he addressed the Riksdag, boldly declaring his intention to deliver his state from the "insufferable aristocratic despotism" to which the land had been so long subjected. The country at large accepted his royal leadership with relief. However, in Sweden as in France and elsewhere, the coming decade would see a resurgence of the aristocracy. Gustavus' days ended when he was assassinated at a masked ball by a member of the nobility —a murder that was commemorated years later in an opera by Giuseppe Verdi.

It was about the time of Gustavus' visit to France that a royal pamphlet issued in Paris referred to the "monstrous hereditary aristocracy" that was then threatening to thwart the French king's will, although that stupid and kindly person had only the most flaccid will of his own. In 1776, when Turgot as both a philosophe and a practical politician attempted to introduce economic reforms in France that might help to bridge gaps between the classes and enhance royal authority in the process, the king summarily dismissed him. "Your nation has no constitution," Turgot had advised the king. "It is a society composed of different orders, imperfectly united, and of a people whose members have very few social links among themselves, with the result that each one is concerned exclusively with his own interests." Louis ex-

"A well-born young man who wishes to travel and know not only the world, but also what is called good society, who does not want to find himself, under certain circumstances, inferior to his equals, and excluded from participating in all their pleasures, must get himself initiated in what is called Freemasonry, even if it is only to know superficially what Freemasonry is."

Giovanni Casanova

plained that it was not his purpose to mix the orders of society, and thus disrupt the traditional establishment of his realm. His queen and his courtiers were too closely attached to the privileges they shared to wish for any change in that established order, and the king followed their lead. Monarchist though he was, Voltaire was appalled by this royal rebuke to one of the most enlightened statesmen of the day. "The dismissal of this great man crushes me . . . ," Voltaire wrote. "Since that fatal day, I have not followed anything, I have not asked anyone for anything, and I am waiting patiently for someone to cut our throats." Meanwhile, the state moved toward political and economic bankruptcy. Louis was no master of a crisis and in the end he was overcome by the aristocracy—which then quickly had to give way to the proletariat. The cutting of throats would soon become a commonplace in revolutionary France.

In Prussia, despot as he was, Frederick relied heavily on his Junker aristocracy to run the state, and this group was more firmly entrenched in its privileged position at the end than at the beginning of his reign. That the crushing burden of taxation fell on the peasantry because of the exemptions enjoyed by the Junkers was of little concern to Frederick. Even his "enlightened" program of primary education was designed principally to teach the youngsters religion and morals in order to "keep them in the villages." In Russia Catherine could not and would not do anything to lessen the absolute authority the nobles exercised over the serfs, even though this enormous majority of the population was being reduced to virtual slavery. Public auctions normally included the sale of serfs along with horses, dogs, and cattle. Thus, at one point a notice in the Moscow *Gazette* offered for sale "two plump coachmen, two girls eighteen and fifteen years, quick at manual work. Two barbers: one, twenty-one, knows how to read and write and play a musical instrument; the other can do ladies' and gentlemen's hair."

In Great Britain such gross abuse of privilege was, of course, unthinkable. Yet even in that advanced society the last third of the eighteenth century witnessed a consolidation of important aristocratic factions within the government. "It is our business . . . to maintain the independency of Parliament," observed Charles James Fox in 1771; "whether it is attacked by the people or by the crown is a matter of little consequence." (Members of the Paris parlement obviously felt the same way, as did spokesmen for similar bodies in Holland, Belgium, and other states.) The success of the American Revolution did little to encourage reform of a parliamentary system that favored the substantial landed aristocracy; and the subsequent excesses of the French Revolution and the wars that followed called for a further closing of the ranks against the sinister forces of change. The aristocratic world was menaced, and that danger provoked a self-protective determination to survive with a minimum loss of power.

In 1776 the liberal English nonconformist Richard Price viewed the matter dimly from the side of the middle classes. "In this hour of danger," he wrote in his book *Observations on Civil Liberty and War with America*, "it would become us to turn our thoughts to Heaven. This is what our brethren in the Colonies are doing. From one end of North America to the other they are fasting and praying. But what are we doing?—shocking thought.—We are running wild after pleasure and forgetting everything serious and decent in Masquerades. —We are gambling in gaming houses: trafficking in boroughs: perjuring ourselves at elections: and selling ourselves for places—which side is Providence

Named finance minister by Louis XVI in 1774, Anne Robert Jacques Turgot alienated the nobility when he tried to abolish some of their feudal privileges and was dismissed in 1776. This bust of Turgot is by Jean Antoine Houdon.
MUSEUM OF FINE ARTS, BOSTON,
ARCHIBALD CARY COOLIDGE FUND

The "Extravaganza," or the "Mountain Head Dress," fashionable in 1776
THE H. F. DU PONT WINTERTHUR MUSEUM

likely to favour?" As a measure of the temper of the times, Price's book immediately sold sixty thousand copies and double the number in a cheap edition.

Almost everywhere, whatever the degree of their political influence, the patricians or nobles who occupied the highest stratum of society formed a highly self-conscious class, ever sensitive to any threat, real or imaginary, to their exclusive station by members of other classes. That self-consciousness was intensified by the rapid growth of the bourgeois in various countries. In the years around 1776, society was, in fact, becoming both more aristocratic and more bourgeois at one and the same time. The growing exclusiveness of the aristocracy (as its own bourgeois origins receded into the past) and the mounting aspirations of the more newly formed bourgeoisie emphasized the distinctions that separated the two classes. However, so long as the principle of a hierarchical society was upheld, class consciousness did not necessarily imply class conflict. For a while, at least, the members of the middle class, far from resenting aristocracy or nobility as an institution, wanted nothing more than to rise into that upper class, to share its privileges and perquisites, its advantages and distinctions—even its mannerisms. (Such pretensions had been lampooned even a century earlier in Molière's *Le Bourgeois Gentilhomme.*) To participate in all this they may have felt that they had the proper qualifications—wealth, education, upbringing—except for the necessary heraldic quarterings that testified to an exalted lineage.

An unexpected reflection of those aspirations can be found in a visit paid by Gibbon to Paris, a city he knew very well. His reception on this occasion was cordial, but it irked him that he was lauded as an accomplished man of letters instead of being honored as "a man of rank for which I have such indisputable claims," as he wrote. He insisted on the need and desirability of class distinctions, and he wanted to have it known that he belonged in the upper social crust. The prestige he had earned by his literary talents was another matter.

From a distance of two hundred years such social conceits appear trivial to a point of absurdity. What once may have seemed important degrees of distinction have fused with time into a general pattern of fashionable appearance and endeavor. Style in dress, decoration, manners, and diversions filtered down the social scale, mainly from a summit at Versailles through most of the other courts of Europe to a respectable public at large, reaching a level of uniformity that characterized the age. Ladies and gentlemen with an interest in what was *à la mode* could turn to such handsomely illustrated fashion journals as *La Galerie des modes* and *Le Courrier des modes*, first published in Paris in the 1770's and soon copied and imitated in other large cities. The letters of Goethe's mother to her son indicate the impatience with which successive issues of *Journal der Luxus und der Moden*, a German periodical of fashions, were anticipated. New styles in coiffures, the most important element of a lady's toilette, were awaited with raging interest. To illustrate the attention lavished on such passing fancies, in 1772 one French journal contained 96 different styles of headdress in each issue, totaling 3,744 by the end of the year. Paris alone boasted of six hundred ladies' hairdressers. Every lady aspired to emulate the queen in these matters. So it was with hats. One visitor to the fashionable shop of Mademoiselle Bertin, "the minister of fashions," was disappointed when she was shown models that were a month old. She was advised she would have to wait for anything more recent since the queen and Mademoiselle Bertin had decided not to show the latest fashion for another week or so.

As the American revolutionary cause became more popular in France, the ladies referred to their hats and hairdresses by such terms as *à la Philadelphie, à l'Independance,* and *à la Bostonienne,* but these were, of course, transient affectations. Those names had no connection whatsoever with the events and places to which they referred, and certainly did not reflect anything like republican simplicity in the designs they were associated with. On the other hand, in 1776 when Franklin appeared on the streets and in the salons of Paris in his simple costume he did start a vogue that led Parisians for a while to dress "*à la Franklin,* in coarse cloth . . . and thick shoes." It was in a similar spirit that Marie Antoinette liked to play at rustic simplicity in her separate little village apart from the formidable splendors of Versailles, and that Louis XVI had himself pictured behind a plow like any ordinary farmer (see page 31).

That high fashions should become so easily available to a public of lesser rank galled the aristocracy. Throughout the eighteenth century various laws regulating forms of dress were passed by authorities who could not tolerate the possibility that external class distinctions might disappear. In some places, for example, the middle class was forbidden to flaunt gold and silver galloon, trimming, and embroideries. Elsewhere, only the patriciate were allowed to carry plumed hats and swords, and what the other ranks of society, down to maids and other menials, might wear was specifically detailed. Swiss women were so restricted by sumptuary laws that they took every opportunity to visit foreign spas where they could dress as splendidly as they pleased; and so on. The attempt to legislate distinctions in dress was, of course, a losing cause, as was the cause of an overweening aristocracy itself. The time was soon coming when it would be difficult to tell a man's class by his manner of dress. In part, the trend toward simpler (and more comfortable) dress was allied to a vogue for "natural living." "Everybody that have [sic] country seats is at them," reported Arthur Young, a widely traveled English observer, from France, "and those who have not visit those who have. This revolution in French manners is certainly one of the best features they have taken from England. The introduction was the easier because of the magic of Rousseau's writings."

Uniformity in the styles of decorative art and architecture was encouraged by the publication of widely consulted pattern books and manuals with engraved illustrations of examples "in the modern taste." In 1754, the same year that Washington suffered his sharp defeat on the western frontier, Thomas Chippendale of London issued the first edition of *The Gentleman and Cabinet-Maker's Director.* (The title runs on to say, *Being a large collection of the most elegant and useful designs of household furniture in the . . . modern taste . . . the whole comprehended in one hundred and sixty copper plates, neatly engraved, calculated to improve and refine the present taste and suited to the fancy and circumstances of persons in all degrees of life.*) This was the most complete and comprehensive furniture manual that had appeared to date, and it provided a stimulus to craftsmen—in the American colonies and in other countries, as well as in England—that endured for a generation after its publication. It was only one of a number of such books to be published in the second half of the eighteenth century, but probably the one most commonly remembered today. Numerous others on architecture were widely distributed, copied, and adapted with the result that structures might be found in areas as far apart from one another as London, Virginia, Italy, France, Russia, and elsewhere that bore a strong family re-

The elegant evening gown of a French jeune dame de qualité *in 1779*
Galerie des Modes, 1779

semblance in their style and plans.

In every country those who could afford any serious interest in the current patterns of fashion and culture represented only a small fraction of the total population. Throughout the eighteenth century the world remained overwhelmingly a world of peasant farmers; people whose way of life was deeply rooted in timeless, unchanging customs, and whose mere struggle for subsistence demanded their complete attention and exhausted their human energies. There was no place in their restricted lives for modishness. Their dominating concern was the quest for tomorrow's crust of bread.

It is, of course, impossible to generalize about the varied circumstances that ruled their lot in separate areas. The freemen who worked the land in England, where serfdom had long since disappeared, were at a polar extreme from the chattel slaves who served as the base of contemporary Russian society. The hard-working farmer of France who in good years might hope for a modest sufficiency from his land was hardly comparable to the listless Spaniard who could find no incentive but irresistible want to bestir himself to any form of industry. In his *Confessions* Rousseau tells of a stop he had made, tired and hungry on his vagrant way, at a countryman's house in France, where at first he was offered the most meager fare; but when it was learned that he was not an agent of the tax collector, as had been feared, his relieved host provided an ample meal from hidden supplies. It seems all too likely that here Rousseau imagined an incident he wished might have happened to justify his theories; rustic simplicity must have its own just rewards. However, other historical evidence indicates that a meal such as he described, of meat, eggs, bread, and wine, could probably have been provided only at tables of the wealthy. Had Rousseau stopped at a typical hut in Brittany he would have been offered only a bowl of gruel made of buckwheat, without apologies or substitutions. In Spain the repast would have been a piece of rye bread soaked in oil.

Whatever the variety of experience that distinguished the lot of the peasant in one country from that of his counterpart in another, it is all too clear that for most of them what we choose to recall as the Age of Enlightenment was actually a time of darkness and depression; a time of ignorance and indigence, of superstition and fear. The recurrent plagues and widespread famines that had brought such misery to the preceding century, so vividly recounted in Daniel Defoe's *Journal of the Plague Year*, had for no discernible reason abated. Still, millions of people died annually from typhus, small pox, and other diseases, as many as 10,000 or 12,000 a year in Sweden alone. The dwellings of the poor, in city and country alike, with whole families often confined to a single room (and in the country, often with some of the livestock), were breeding places of disease—especially in the cold weather when those rooms for the sake of a little warmth were sealed off as best they could be from any suspicion of fresh air from the outside. Bishop Berkeley, the Irish clergyman and philosopher, left a grim picture of an Irish peasant's hut filled with stinking children and pigs and littered with excrement, and with an absolute unawareness of the most elementary hygiene. It was a picture that could have been drawn with little variation wherever unrelieved poverty afflicted the land. The miserable peasant who endured such conditions, if he survived them, would not have recognized any likeness in the sugar-coated portrayals of the eighteenth-century painter Jean Baptiste Greuze who was encouraged by Rousseau's writings to paint moral lessons revealing that simple things and poor people are inherently noble—paintings that in their gross distortions and sentimentality appealed not only to aristocrats far removed from the bitter facts of poverty (Catherine the Great purchased some of them).

Nevertheless, for reasons that have not been completely explained, in most countries population increased significantly as the century progressed, especially in northern rural areas. This brought problems of a different nature, for unless the land could be made more productive it could not support the growing numbers who depended upon it for sustenance, in city or country; or, as another consequence, with increasing demand the price of food would rise to prohibitive levels. In either case the addition of one or two unwanted children could reduce a peasant family from poverty to destitution. That threat, at least, was reduced by the appallingly high rate of infant mortality. It took a measure of luck to survive the ministrations of ignorant midwives followed by the unsanitary conditions that attended the especially susceptible early years of childhood. A pathetic number of babies were blinded, crippled, or physically handicapped for life by those "well-meaning murderesses" who helped at childbirth. Until a baby had outlived those particular hazards, its parents would regard it with some dispassion as a highly problematical addition to the family, for better or for worse. Countless numbers of newborn children were simply abandoned, possibly to be cared for by charity (d'Alembert was one of those), or shipped off to foundling hospitals, piled upright into paniers

William Hogarth exposed the self-destructive world of lower-class gin drinkers in a *1751* engraving titled Gin Lane. *Amidst the brawling and dying (a drunken mother is unconcerned about her child falling to its death), the pawnbroker's shop is the only sign of prosperity. At left is one of Hogarth's preliminary sketches; in the final engraving he added an infant being force-fed gin and a crazed father impaling his own child. The same year the engraving was issued, Parliament passed a law that stiffened the regulations on the sale of gin.*
PIERPONT MORGAN LIBRARY, NEW YORK

strapped to donkeys—a murderous trip for many of them.

One of the characteristic aspects of the century was the migrant laborer, male or female, who seasonally or permanently quit the land hoping to earn a pittance elsewhere. Most conspicuously, during the dead of winter men and women from mountainous regions would leave their upland dwellings in search of remunerative work in more active areas. Every year men drifted down from the Pyrenees and the Massif Central into more clement parts of France or Spain to hire themselves out as rough laborers. It is said that in Marseilles the settled population of 106,000 supported a floating population of 30,000. Some journeyed to Portugal to serve as woodcutters, or to Normandy and Brittany to peddle pins and needles, or to Paris and other French cities to sweep chimneys. Women from North Wales trudged to Middlesex to help harvest the fruit, which they then carried on their backs to London markets, sometimes covering fifteen miles a day to deliver their loads and return for more. London and other large English cities swarmed with migrants, many of them lousy and tubercular, from inhospitable parts of Ireland. Peasants from Belgium and Luxembourg were even prepared to walk their way to Hungary when opportunity beckoned from that distant land.

Many of the mobile rustics who trekked to the cities in an effort to tide over a difficult season stayed on, joining the hapless poor already there and aggravating urban woes that already were grave. In the opening lines of this book the eighteenth century was characterized as a time of remarkable contrasts. This was nowhere more apparent than in European cities. Never before had society been so sharply divided into the few rich and the many poor, a division dramatically outlined when with intensified urbanization the two elements were forced so closely together with little contact and less understanding between them. Every city of consequence had its splendid buildings, public and private, that testified to the dignity of state and the power of property. And nearby most of them exhibited the almost indescribable squalor, easily matching the worst of rural conditions, that encompassed the life of the poor and that spilled over into the purlieu's of the well-to-do. Lice and rats showed no respect for social barriers; the stench caused by inadequate drainage, faulty sewage, and accumulated refuse was carried by the winds in all directions without discrimination. It has been said that one could smell Berlin

from six miles away, and other cities must have been similarly malodorous, and pestiferous. The great Swedish botanist Linnaeus compared the stench of Hamburg to that of an open sewer. Venice, for all its elegant facades, was engulfed by stagnant waters that invited typhoid and malaria, as were Amsterdam and Stockholm. Dr. Johnson, a man whose own standards of personal hygiene were not elevated, once described London as fit only for a colony of Hottentots.

If the hovels of the poor were breeding places of disease, the sordid neighborhoods where they congregated in the larger cities were hotbeds of crime. Except for a few districts where new industries were thriving, no city in Europe offered the workingman much hope of improving his lot during a lifetime. For a family to make ends barely meet, all its members were commonly put to work—or to begging or stealing. In 1767 a concerted national drive against beggars and vagrants in France netted some 50,000 of them.

Children were expected to become self-supporting almost from infancy. Obliged to live by its wits, at an early age a child, girl or boy, learned the tricks of begging and petty thievery, laying the foundations for a life of crime. In any European city a gentleman making the Grand Tour could expect to be besieged by hordes of children plaintively and persistently clamoring for coins to relieve their misery. With their parents' blessing they might act as decoys or agents for more mature criminals. In one French court alone in 1773–74 more than twelve thousand children were arrested for smuggling contraband across a regional boundary.

The mothers of such miscreant youngsters had little time for their upbringing, except perhaps to coach them in their devious pursuits or to teach them to share their own exhausting menial labor in the mills or mines, or vending in the streets. No working man was likely to marry a woman who would not and could not contribute to the family budget. In areas where there was a demand for such labor the housewife could supplement the family income at home by spinning cotton or wool or by making lace on assignment, a domestic industry that vanished with the introduction of the factory system of production.

To be poor and in want and to remain virtuous and honest was frequently more than could be expected of human nature. Those who did not have to face the dilemma could find some comfort in the belief that innate depravity led to

The Italian economist and criminologist Cesare Beccaria (his statue by Grandi) argued against capital punishment and inhuman treatment of criminals in his book Essay on Crimes and Punishments, *which stimulated demands for penal reform throughout the Continent.*
MUSEO ARCHEOLOGICO, MILAN

poverty, without concern for the possibility that unrelieved and inescapable poverty led almost inevitably to vice and crime. Vagrancy and beggary, brigandage on the highways and pillaging in the towns, were alternatives to desperate need or starvation. There was enough support for the feeling that the destitute were naturally given to unbridled license to result in a savage intensification of the laws dealing with crimes against property. Even in England a child could be hanged by the neck until dead for stealing a handkerchief worth one shilling, if it were removed privily from a person. Elsewhere, sentences of torture and death were meted out with horrible regularity for crimes that today would be considered relatively minor breeches of the law. A person could be hanged if he shot a rabbit or cut down a young tree on another's lands. To be mercilessly broken on the wheel, their bones shattered with an iron bar, was a common fate of criminals in France and Germany. For his alleged crime Jean Calas, whose name was later cleared by Voltaire's efforts, was tortured, each of his limbs broken in two places, strangled, and finally burned at the stake.

Under Frederick the Great in Prussia the severity of the punishment for certain crimes was reduced. As one example, the crime of infanticide was to be punished by beheading instead of by drowning in a leather sack which the culprit had often been forced to stitch up himself. Infanticide was more difficult to detect than many other crimes, a fact of which there were ghastly reminders in the tiny skeletons discovered when disused drains were occasionally dug up. In 1771 an official of Brussels claimed that he received daily reports of infant bodies found in drains, rivers, cellars, and other places. Many of those doomed babies were, no doubt, unwanted bastards; in equal probability others were the remains of new-born infants whose legitimate parents could not face the intolerable strain of having to feed one more mouth.

At the lowest levels of society life was obviously cheap. Death could be an occasion for celebration. In London one observer reported the defiant acceptance amongst prisoners facing public execution in whatever form, and the general air of festivity that attended those gruesome events. "When the day of the execution is come," he wrote, "among extraordinary sinners and persons condemned for their crimes who have but that morning to live, one would expect a deep sense of sorrow with all the signs of a thorough contrition. . . . But the very reverse is true . . . the substantial breakfasts that are made . . . the seas of beer that are swilled: the never ceasing outcries for more. . . . But what is most shocking to a thinking man is, the Behaviour of the condemned whom, (for the most part) you'll find, either drinking madly or uttering the vilest ribaldry. . . . At last out they set and with them a Torrent of Mob bursts through the gate. Amongst the lower Rank and working people, the idlest and such as are most fond of making holidays, with prentices and journeymen to the meanest trades, are the most honorable part of these floating multitudes. . . . All the way from Newgate to Tyburn is one continued fair for whores and rogues of the meaner sort. Here the most abandoned of rakehells may light on women as shameless; here trollops all in rags, may pick up sweethearts of the same politeness. . . ."

For many the day of execution never came; they simply rotted away in jails where they were indiscriminately crammed—those "prototypes of hell," as one magistrate termed the English prisons, where juvenile delinquents, debtors, and prostitutes were confined along with murderers and the insane, all at the mercy of jailers who were often brutal keepers. The great English jurist Sir William Blackstone was meanwhile boasting that English law was "with justice supposed to be more nearly advanced in perfection than in any other land." Blackstone's complacency, which irked Jeremy Bentham and other reformers, was countered by Beccaria, whose famous *Essay on Crimes and Punishments*, published in 1764, provided one of the first arguments against capital punishment and inhuman treatment of criminals. That work was as great a landmark of eighteenth-century liberalism as Adam Smith's *The Wealth of Nations*. In preparing his important little treatise, Beccaria drew upon many of the ideas earlier proposed by a number of the philosophes, including Voltaire, Hume, Rousseau, Montesquieu, and several others. He considered the prevention of crime more important than its punishment. Any reasoning person who knew from the criminal code that his punishment would outweigh any benefits derived from wrongdoing, Beccaria believed, would thereby be deterred from doing evil. That observation led one wit to comment that presumably a criminal was to consult Beccaria's prescriptions for punishment before committing a crime.

Since the insane were considered insensitive to such normal human feelings as hunger, thirst, cold, or pain, they were treated with complete indifference or outright cruelty. The English artist William Hogarth has left an unforgettable depiction of the horrors of Bedlam (the name is a corruption of "Bethlehem" hospital), London's notorious asylum where for an admission charge

Despite the growing demands for reform, conditions within prisons and insane asylums changed very little. Filth, brutality, and hunger characterized prison life for the poor. Not until 1792 did an asylum—Pinel, in Paris—release lunatics from their chains. Public executions were still considered deterrents to crime. Right, the sick men's ward at Marshalsea prison, London; left, an insane man under restraint at London's Bedlam asylum; below, the scaffold at the Old Bailey in London, used to execute ten prisoners at a time.

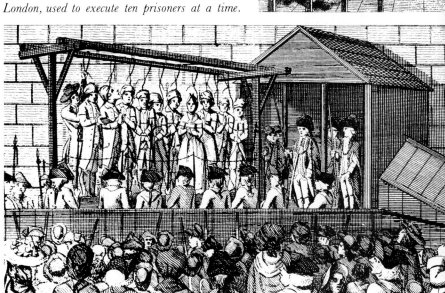

persons of quality might come as a form of amusement to observe the antics of the wretched inmates as though they were so many sideshow freaks. During the night the weird noises created by those abject creatures, "rattling their chains and making terrible out-cry," carried across the otherwise silent city. Hospitals for the physically ill were often no less primitive in their treatment of patients. An English visitor to the municipal hospital in Paris, the Hotel-Dieu, with its several thousand patients, saw four patients in one bed and heard of more crowded scenes where those struggling to stay alive lay mingled with those already dead. "The sufferings of hell," wrote the eminent scientist Baron Cuvier of a similar situation, "can hardly surpass those of the poor wretches crowded on each other, crushed, burning with fever, incapable of stirring or breathing, sometimes having one or two dead people between them for hours."

For all its enlightenment the eighteenth century brought only modest relief to the human degradation that stemmed from poverty, underemployment, filth, diseases, and their corollary, crime. The pictures of contemporary reality painted and engraved by Hogarth, the most brilliant satirical artist of the century, with their gin-soaked harlots and wastrels, their scenes of frightful human neglect and debauchery and corruption, were commentaries drawn to the life. On the other hand, there were many with cool heads and warm hearts who were acutely sensitive to those anguishing problems. Indeed, probably never before in the history of the world were so many at one time moved by feelings of compassion to bring social justice to bear on those problems; not only philosophers with their lofty and often distant perspectives, but humanitarians with very practical and immediate concerns about human welfare. The retired British sea captain Thomas Coram dedicated his entire life after 1739 to the London Foundling Hospital, the most memorable achievement of English philanthropy in the century. (In 1756 the hospital was given a parliamentary grant.) As the appointed High Sheriff of Bedfordshire, the "eccentric but truly worthy" John Howard, as he was picturesquely described by a contemporary, took the opportunity in the mid-1770's to visit almost every jail in England and found in nearly all of them such a chaos of cruelty and immorality (noticed by others long ago but left unredressed by Parliament) that his vivid reports aroused keen indignation wherever they were read. He tested the foul darkness of cramped cells where prisoners were kept by shutting himself up in the worst of them as long as he could bear it, and until he could readily understand why an inmate would beg for hanging as a mercy. He visited the prisons of Holland and Germany to document his studies and was still engaged in such investigations when in southern Russia he was stricken by a malignant fever and was "laid quietly in the earth," as he wished.

Reformers like Coram and Howard did not live long enough to see the evils and injustices they complained of corrected in their lifetimes. Dr. Johnson could fulminate that "a decent provision for the poor is the true test of civilization," but that test had not been fairly passed before the century ended. Nevertheless, the ideals propounded by philanthropic spirits, and the humanitarian efforts they encouraged, betokened an advance toward the realization of social responsibilities that our own age is still trying to bring to terms in the welfare state.

With very little question the single most effective reformer of the eighteenth century was the minister John Wesley, founder of Methodism. He may truly

In an age characterized by an attitude of apathy toward established religion, John Wesley led a profound religious revival in Great Britain. Although he wanted to retain a connection with the Church of England, his followers founded the Methodist Church. Wesley is shown above in a 1766 portrait by Nathaniel Hope.
NATIONAL PORTRAIT GALLERY, LONDON

be called one of the greatest Englishmen of his time, and his influence was international. Wesley had no particular desire to change the structure of society; he thought the existing class order was natural and just. He preached rather resignation to the established social system, with all its hardships and injustices, and he directed his message principally to the poor, the overburdened, and other unfortunates. He spoke not so much about the external conditions of life as about the inner nature of men's souls.

At the time of Wesley's emergence as an evangelist, the established religion in England was in a state of decline. "There never was an age since the death of Christ," solemnly declared Bishop Watson, "never once since the commencement of this history of the world, in which atheism and infidelity have been more generally confessed." Under the weight of its complacent dignity and the doubts so widely spread by deism, the Anglican clergy found little inspiration to fire their congregations (when they attended services) with religious zeal and conviction. Voltaire described a typical English sermon as a "solid but sometimes dry dissertation which a man reads to the people without gesture and without particular exaltation of voice." Oliver Goldsmith denounced even the better types of clergymen for their "insipid calmness." Those of the population with little to expect in the way of material rewards in life yearned for religious experience that would fill their otherwise arid lives with deeply felt excitement, passionate conviction, and some sense of individual consequence in the divine order of things. As the century advanced, increasing numbers of thousands found the satisfaction of such yearnings in the preachments of Wesley—not only throughout Great Britain, but in the New World and elsewhere.

Methodism as preached by Wesley was not an isolated phenomenon of the time. The contemporary German pietists, who prospered under the generous patronage of Count Nikolaus Ludwig von Zinzendorf, equalled Wesley and his followers in the fervor of their religious life and observances. Indeed, on his

Ferment in the Catholic Church centered on the Jesuits, members of the Society of Jesus. For centuries they had served as confessors to kings and queens and shared in royal policymaking in areas ruled by Catholic monarchs. As the monarchs' power increased, they grew to resent the influence of the Jesuits. In 1759 Joseph I of Portugal, at the urging of his chief minister, Pombal, expelled all Jesuits from Portugal and Brazil. Their property was confiscated, and they were herded on to ships and sent to Italy, in a manner not far removed from the satirical representation below. Similar expulsions took place in France (1764–67) and Spain (1767). Under pressure from rulers threatening further expulsions, Pope Clement XIV abolished the Society of Jesus in 1773. It was not restored until 1814.

journey to America in 1736 in the company of a group of Moravian immigrants, Wesley wondered at the profound and dedicated spirits of his German shipmates, which he felt excelled his own and which spurred him on with new determination to witness God's truth. (With their missionary zeal, gentle demeanor, and peculiar devotions, the Moravians were welcome newcomers to colonial America. Their settlements at Bethlehem, Pennsylvania, Salem, North Carolina, and elsewhere in the New World flourished in a manner that made these communities show-places of the back country.)

In the Age of Reason Wesley repudiated all appeal to reason. He looked to divine inspiration and inner conviction as the only guides to man's behavior on earth and to his path toward salvation. Between the Methodist preacher and his congregation there were no social or intellectual barriers. Wesley himself shared the commonplace superstitions and delusions of his time. He believed in ghosts, the diabolical origin of eerie noises, the reality of witches; to give up a belief in witchcraft, he pronounced, was to give up belief in the Bible. He led his followers through a world of portents and miracles, and made them feel with immediate intensity the sense of sin, the terror of hell, and, above all, the love of Christ. In every audience he could witness a proved miracle as sinners who heard his fervid appeals were reduced to hysteria and convulsions—and then were moved to rapture when they felt their sins had been forgiven.

Rarely has a man driven himself with such unsparing intensity as did Wesley. For forty years he traveled indefatigably at the rate of four thousand miles a year, by foot, on horseback, or by coach. He was on the move, exhorting, praying, preaching almost to his dying day in 1791 at the age of eighty-eight. Through those all but superhuman exertions he made the daily lives of thousands upon thousands of poor and simple folk—peasants, miners, criminals—seem to be part of a great, universal drama in which their precious individual souls were the scenes of a mighty contest between Satan and Christ. He gave the mass of otherwise unguided people an ethical code that worked for the moral rehabilitation of England. In providing the suffering and the underprivileged with an emotional release for their discontents, Wesleyanism also diverted them from any course of violent social protest. Wesley himself was a magnificent organizer and long before his death Methodism was the most highly coordinated body of opinion in Britain, and the most dynamic and spirited. "Had it been bent on revolution in Church or State," writes J. H. Plumb, "nothing could have stopped it. But then Methodism was not a religion *of* the poor but *for* the poor."

Even so England was not spared from sordid violence. In 1779, during the savage Gordon Riots, London was for days at the mob's mercy. The riots had originated in religious fanaticism directed against Roman Catholics, but they served as an outlet for the discontents of the wretched and vicious elements of the population. Destruction was widespread. The Newgate prison was sacked and set on fire, and all its prisoners freed. Other buildings, public and private, were attacked and set ablaze. An attempt was even made to seize the Bank of England, until regular troops were brought in to quell the disturbances. However, the country was spared such horrors as revolution would soon bring to France. England's revolution was already taking place thousands of miles away in America, and compared with the French holocaust that was a relatively bloodless affair, although by no means of less consequence.

English Connoisseurs in Rome

THE GRAND TOUR

By 1776 the Grand Tour—a journey through European cities culminating in Rome—had become a necessary final step in a wealthy gentleman's education. It was popular in all circles of European nobility, but particularly among the English. "Where one Englishman traveled in the reigns of the first two Georges," noted an observer in 1772, "ten now go on a grand tour." The results varied. Adam Smith thought most "returned home more conceited, more unprincipled, more dissipated, and more incapable of any serious application. . . ." But many aristocrats acquired a lasting appreciation of classical antiquity and a much heightened sense of taste and elegance.

THE FIRST LEG

The shortest and most popular route abroad for an Englishman was from Dover to Calais. Adverse winds could prevent a Channel packet from sailing for days, and the crossing itself was often rough (opposite, a contemporary cartoon shows nervous travelers being rowed from shore to the packet). One tourist wrote after ten hours at sea: "I arrived about five of the clocke in the afternoone, after I had varnished the exterior parts of the ship with excremental ebullitions of my tumultuous stomach, as desiring to satiate the gormandizing paunches of the hungry Haddock. . . ." The journey to Paris by coach (like the one seen below at a Paris station) took on the average a week. After renting rooms and hiring servants, the next order of business was a new wardrobe. The novelist Tobias Smollett found the custom degrading: "When an Englishman comes to Paris he cannot appear until he has undergone a total metamorphosis. [He] finds it necessary to send for the tailor, peruquier, hatter, shoemaker, and every other tradesman concerned in the equipment of the human body."

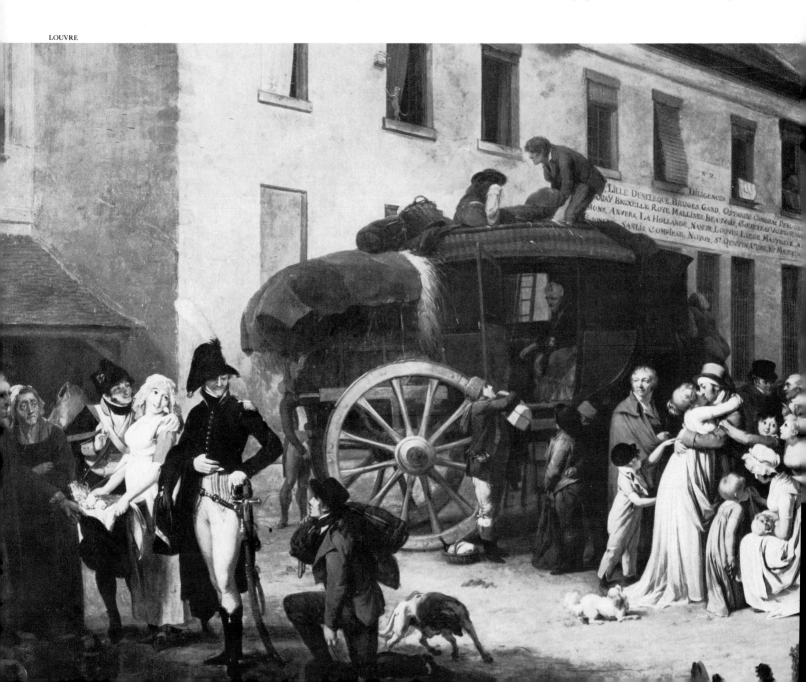

BULLOZ

THE PARIS SCENE

Once in Paris, the young noblemen—under the supervision of a tutor—took lessons in fencing, riding, and French conversation. Armed with letters of introduction, they were welcomed in French aristocratic circles. Most sought after was an invitation to Madame Geoffrin's salon—the most brilliant of its day—attended by noblemen and scholars from all over Europe. Even tourists who spent nearly all of their time in Parisian taverns or brothels made obligatory visits to the Louvre (seen above as it appeared in 1773), the Palais Royal, the Opéra, and the theaters. On his trip to Paris in 1775, Samuel Johnson was particularly impressed with the Tuileries, where only the upper classes, and no "mean persons," were permitted to stroll. Along with "inferior" or "mediocre" French food, a common complaint in the letters and diaries of English tourists concerned the experience of being accosted by the poor seeking work as servants (opposite) and the numbers of beggars: "The whole kingdom swarms with beggars. This observation was confirmed at every inn I came to by crowds of wretches. I have often passed . . . to my chaise through a file of twenty or thirty of them."

A VISIT TO VERSAILLES

The French royal palace was on every tourist's itinerary. A coach left Paris twice each day for Versailles. It was designed to carry sixteen, but, as seen in the sketch below, frequently carried twice as many. The tourists, looking forward to seeing "one of the finest palaces in Europe," were generally disappointed. They, and ordinary Frenchmen as well, were free to wander about the palace unattended, observing members of the royal family leading their lives in public. An English visitor in 1773 commented: "The apartments are dirty, which cannot be wondered at when you are told that all the world rove about the palace at pleasure. I went from room to room as my choice directed me, into the king's bedchamber, dressing-room, etc. in all of which there were numbers of people, and many of them indifferently clad." Usually, foreign tourists were more impressed with the gardens than the palace; but by 1776 the gardens had fallen into such a state of decay that Louis XVI was spending huge sums for replanting and redesigning. The painting opposite is a view of the work in progress.

171

CROSSING INTO ITALY

Before leaving France, those lucky enough to be granted an audience with Voltaire journeyed to his estate at Ferney, four miles west of Geneva. He received all visitors—tourists, kings, statesmen—in bed, clothed in a blue and gold satin robe and a nightcap (opposite). Although a visit with Voltaire was not to be sniffed at, Italy was the culmination of every Grand Tour, and all routes there from France promised adventure. The two most traveled paths were by sea from Antibes to Genoa or over the Mont Cenis Pass to Turin. Pirate crews roaming the Mediterranean made the sea route less popular; but the trip over the Alps was dangerous too. The tourist went by coach until it could go no farther; the vehicle was then dismantled and packed on the backs of mules. He then moved to a sled (below left), which porters could carry like a sedan chair as the caravan made its treacherous way along snow-covered rocks. Few arrived in Turin, capital of Piedmont, without having suffered some mishap. Turin was noted for its beautiful streets and magnificent buildings (right), but most tourists found it dull. Edward Gibbon wrote sardonically to a friend: "The principal amusement seems to be driving about in Your Coach in the evening and bowing to the people you meet. If you go when the royal family is there you have the additional pleasure of stopping to salute them every time they pass. I had that advantage fifteen times one afternoon. . . . If there is any pleasure in watching a play which one does not understand, in listening to Piedmontese jargon of which one does not take in a word, and in finding oneself in the midst of a proud nobility who will not speak a word to you, we had an amusing time in this assembly."

OVERLEAF: Venice was anything but dull. Samuel Johnson had said, "If a young man is wild, and must run after women and bad company, it is better this should be done abroad," and Venice was notorious for its women. The major tourist attraction, however, was Carnival time, when the city was jammed with 30,000 visitors, attracted by countless masquerade balls, operas, and regattas. The height of the social season was an elaborate Ascension Day ceremony, presided over by the doge, seen atop his richly decorated craft in the center of this painting.

FLORENCE & ROME

Florence—with its medieval charm, beautiful countryside, hospitable nobility, and unsurpassed art galleries—was a favorite of English tourists. The living was inexpensive, and many chose to remain a year or more. The Uffizi palace, where the more serious tourists studied art and the treasures of its Tribuna room, became such a gathering place for Englishmen that the royal family commissioned a painting by Johann Zoffany. Completed between 1772 and 1778, his work (seen at right) included famous paintings by Raphael, Rubens, Holbein, Rembrandt, and Michelangelo, as well as portraits of English tourists, diplomats, and art collectors.

OVERLEAF: Rome offered something for every taste. The antiquities in 1776 were not what they are today. The Colosseum was rented to citizens who kept animals there; the Palatine Hill was overrun by weeds; the Forum (left, a detail from a Canaletto painting) was a market for cows and oxen twice a week. Yet, it was there in 1764 that Gibbon was inspired to write his masterpiece: "I trod, with lofty step, the ruins of the Forum; each memorable spot where Romulus stood, or Tully spoke, or Caesar fell, was at once present to my eye . . ." Students of architecture thrilled to St. Peter's (right, a Pannini painting); one tourist wrote of the interior, it "is all airy magnificence, and gigantic splendor; light and sunshine pouring in on every side; gilding and gay colours, marbles and pictures, dazzling the eye above, below, and around."

176

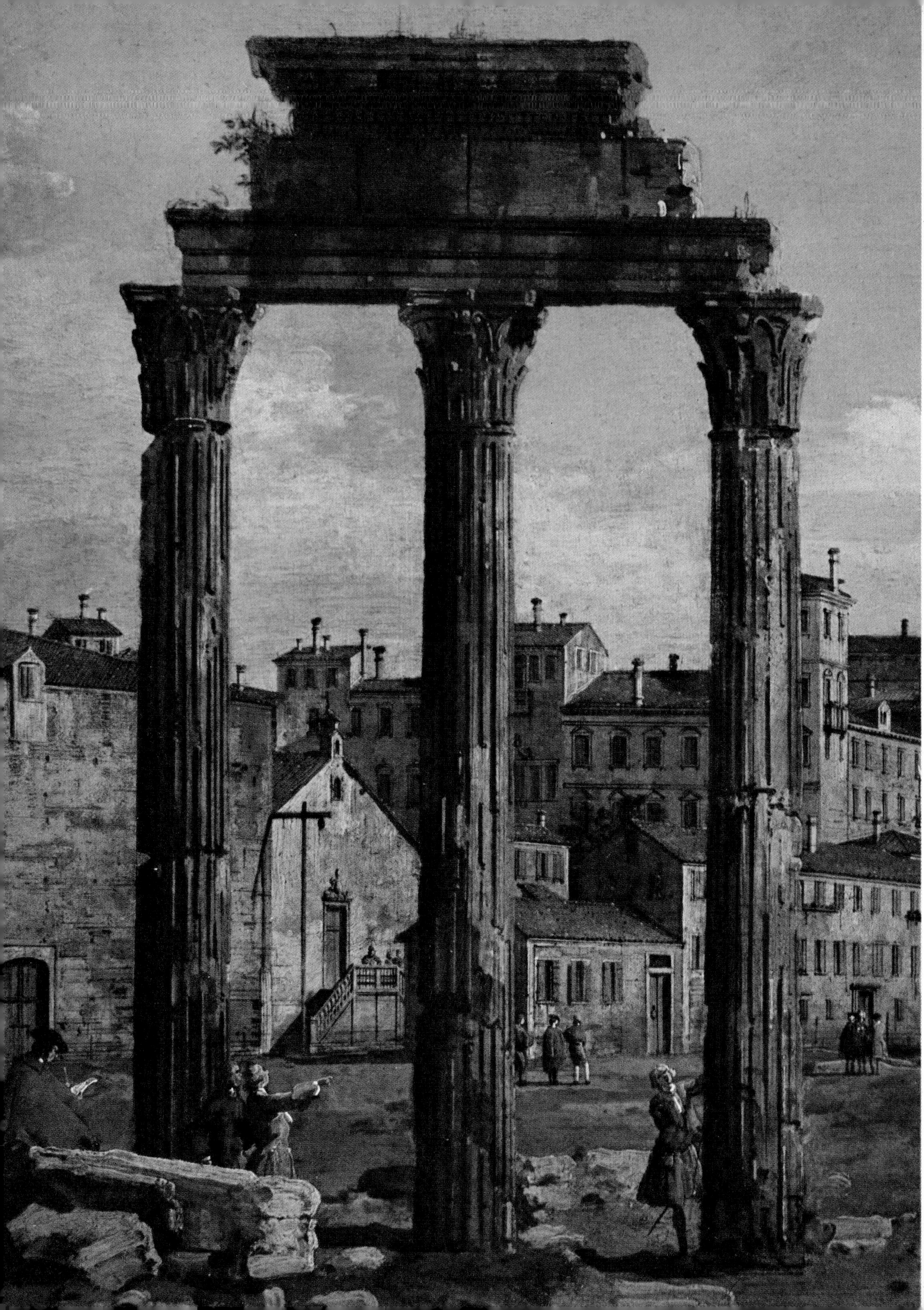

A ROMAN HOLIDAY

The Piazza di Spagna was the meeting place for touring Englishmen in Rome. It even contained several English inns and cafés, and was always crowded with cognoscenti selling their dubious "masterpieces" to the gullible, newly arrived visitor (a scene depicted in the contemporary cartoon below). The discerning tourist, however, frequently received more value than he had bargained for. Tour guides—often Anglo-Roman expatriates—could be contacted in the English coffeehouse. Edward Gibbon hired James Byres, who took him on an 18-week tour of Roman antiquities that left Gibbon exhausted. James Boswell began his ambitious tour by insisting that he and his guide speak only Latin in the Forum, but soon discovered that his guide's enthusiasm for ancient ruins far exceeded his. Usually these guides also had close contacts with Italian art dealers and painters, and managed to collect a double commission, from the patron and the patronized. Giovanni Pannini was one of the most popular artists among the English nobility. In his painting opposite, crowds of European tourists are shown climbing the stairs of the Campidoglio to admire the square designed by Michelangelo in 1536 on Capitoline Hill, site of the ancient Roman Capitol.

ANCIENT CITIES

Herculaneum and Pompeii, buried by an eruption of Mount Vesuvius in A.D. 79, were rediscovered in the eighteenth century—Herculaneum first and Pompeii in 1748. Tourists flocked to the digging sites, sparking a neoclassical revival in England. Pompeii, where systematic excavation had begun in 1763, offered the better opportunity for sightseeing. (Above, tourists survey the ruins of Pompeii; opposite top, a detail from a Piranesi drawing showing a tourist sketching at Pompeii.) When Robert Adam went to Herculaneum in 1775, it seemed to him "like a coal-mine worked by galley slaves." After visiting the excavations, the more courageous made the difficult, sometimes dangerous ascent of Mount Vesuvius: "I had five men to get me up, two before whose girdles I laid hold of; and three behind who pushed me by the back. I approached quite to the opening from whence issues the sulphureous smoke . . . I endeavored to go quite around but was almost suffocated by the smoke. . . . You descend with great difficulty, sometimes almost up to the knees in ashes. . . ." (Opposite bottom, an eyewitness sketch shows King Gustavus III of Sweden and his party during their 1784 ascent.)

183

A COGNOCENTI contemplating y̆ Beauties of y̆ Antique.

TRINKETS & TREASURES

No traveler would think of returning home from the Grand Tour without a collection of impressive souvenirs—paintings, statuary, bronzes, books, prints. With such a ready market, the naive tourist was frequently saddled with fakes (in the cartoon above by James Gillray, a self-professed art connoisseur inspects his purchases). Thomas Jenkins, a shrewd Welshman who became the leading art dealer in Rome, specialized in creating instant antiques by staining statues with nicotine. But it was rare that a tourist returned without at least one genuine work of art as a memento. Charles Towneley, the noted antiquarian, bought the entire contents of Emperor Hadrian's villa, and then celebrated his coup by commissioning Zoffany to paint the collection—and Towneley—on a single canvas (opposite).

'WELLADAY! IS THIS MY SON TOM?'

NEW TASTES

The effects of the Grand Tour were at once amusing and significant. Many parents feared their sons would return with affected manners (above, a horrified father greets his elaborately coiffed son). Some Englishmen who had traveled in Italy formed the Macaroni Club, leading a 1770 magazine to complain: "There is indeed a kind of animal, neither male nor female, a thing of neuter gender, lately started up amongst us. It is called a Macaroni. It talks without meaning, it smiles without pleasantry, it eats without appetite, it rides without exercise, it wenches without passion." More importantly, the Grand Tour sparked an interest in reviving the concepts of classical architecture. Upon his return from four years of study in Italy, Robert Adam emerged as England's leading architect. The entrance hall to Syon House (opposite), in Middlesex, is typical of the Adam style evident in so many English country homes of the period. The neoclassical influence was evident on the Continent as well, notably in new public buildings.

AN AGE OF

In the years between 1763 and 1793 crucial chapters were written in the history of science and technology. The "reckless search for truth" that engaged men and women of the Enlightenment led in all directions. There was promise that the hidden secrets of the whole of nature might sooner or later be revealed. The Age of Reason had given way to a new age of faith, of faith in science—a conviction that Nature did act according to the general laws by which scientists suggested it *must* act. Science could furnish dependable answers to all manner of practical as well as philosophical problems. Sailors who wanted to know at what longitude their ship was at sea, shipbuilders who wanted to know how to gauge the stress on the beams they used, surveyors and others who looked for precise measurements of distance or size—all these and others of different concerns looked with confidence to the answers science could provide for their questions. This new faith preached very little, it persecuted not at all, and used neither threat nor force to win its converts; but it conquered Western civilization—and that of most of the rest of the world in the centuries to come. As the British mathematician and philosopher Alfred North Whitehead has observed, the spirit of scientific inquiry seemed even to open the secret workings of the very heavens for scrutiny. And in a very real sense this is what actually happened. It was during the years surrounding 1776, for example, that William Herschel, exploring outer space with his great reflecting telescope, discovered 2,500 nebulae and clusters, 848 double

RECONNAISSANCE

stars, a new planet (Uranus, the first planet to be discovered since ancient times), and four moons. With his discoveries the diameter of the known solar system was doubled. Some of these celestial bodies, he reported, were 11,750,000,000,000,000,000,000 miles (in sextillions) from the earth. Herschel was the first man to describe the universe essentially as we know it today.

We are accustomed to think of scientists as highly specialized and more or less detached from the commonplace realities of life as they pursue their esoteric interests in the isolation of their laboratories. That is, of course, a stereotype, but a popular one, and it serves to throw into contrast the eighteenth-century scientist who was more often than not a man of affairs pursuing science as a gentlemanly avocation, or at least as a part-time diversion from other important concerns of his life. Herschel himself is an example. Born in Hanover, he served as a musician in the first campaign of the Seven Years' War before going to England to seek his fortune in the musical world. At fashionable Bath he made his way as oboist, conductor, organist, and teacher, using his limited spare time to study calculus, optics, and, finally, astronomy. (He is still recorded in the major musical encyclopedias as the composer of a symphony and two concertos for wind instruments.) With the help of his brother and sister, whom he had brought over from Germany, he constructed the gigantic telescope through which he made his sensational observations, grinding and polishing the lenses he needed. In the end, urged to do so by

George III, he abandoned his career as a musician and became astronomer to the king. He secured his financial independence by marrying a rich widow, and then with single-mindedness pursued his career as a dedicated astronomer until he died at the age of eighty-eight, heaped with honors. With his far-reaching observations he had reduced our own solar system to a mere speck in an unimaginably vast cosmos of light. In the future men would think more of infinity and less of immortality. (His sister, whom he had taught to keep his records, became an astronomer in her own right and lived on with well-earned honors until her ninety-eighth year.)

There were many who dabbled in scientific matters because it had become a fashionable thing to do—and diverting at the same time. The Marquise de Pompadour made a hobby of astronomy, as did King John V of Portugal; and the Paris socialite Mademoiselle de Coigny was an amateur anatomist. George III enthusiastically studied botany, and Dr. Samuel Johnson conducted chemical experiments in his home. Voltaire's mistress wrote on gravitation. Popular lectures on science were delivered by those who were qualified, and by those who were not. Telescopes, microscopes, models of the solar system, and similar scientific tools and appurtenances, many of them exquisitely wrought, furbished fashionable drawing rooms. Private and public demonstrations were staged to entertain or to enlighten, according to the spirit of the occasion. It is said that Louis XV found particular delight in the sight of a long line of monks leaping into the air simultaneously upon the application of an electric shock. A fun-loving German professor charged a pretty girl with static electricity before inviting a group of men to step up and kiss her, whereupon they got a shock that, as he joyfully put it, almost "knocked their teeth out."

Some of the greatest strides in physics during the eighteenth century were made in the field of electricity. However, until its essential properties were better understood, it was widely considered to be chiefly a means of indoor and outdoor sport that provided novel amusement. In the early days of his experiments even Benjamin Franklin, who was to contribute so much to the science of electricity, played games with its novel currents of excitation and power. "Chagrined a little that we have been hitherto able to produce nothing in this way of use to mankind," Franklin wrote in a long letter to the English botanist Peter Collinson in 1746, "and the hot weather coming on, when electrical experiments are not so agreeable, it is proposed to put an end to them for this season, somewhat humorously, in a party of pleasure on the banks of the Schuylkill. Spirits, at the same time, are to be fired by a spark sent from side to side through the river, without any other conductor than the water; an experiment which we some time since performed, to the amazement of many. A turkey is to be killed for our dinner by the *electrical shock*, and roasted by the *electrical jack*, before a fire kindled by the *electrified bottle*; when the healths of all the famous electricians in England, Holland, France, and Germany are to be drunk in *electrified bumpers*, under the discharge of guns from the *electrical battery*."

Franklin's experiments, his very considerable contributions to science in general, were made in precious hours stolen from the many other activities and concerns that filled his long life. Had he altogether ignored science, Franklin would still be remembered as an illustrious citizen of the eighteenth-century world. Were his other accomplishments forgotten, he would

When William Herschel (shown above at the age of fifty-six) discovered a new planet in 1781 he named it Georgium Sidus, in honor of King George III. Later, the name was changed to Uranus.
YERKES OBSERVATORY, UNIVERSITY OF CHICAGO

still be honored for his work in science alone. In Franklin scientific understanding was perfectly blended with a broad sense of social responsibility. He
enriched the life of his time wherever he touched it with his genial and practical wisdom. If he was unique in his eminence, he did not stand alone in his
time as a versatile man of affairs with a distinguished scientific reputation.
Among others, Franklin's English friend Joseph Priestley was also just such a
man. He, too, touched the history of civilization at many points, and is one of
its most inspiring characters. Priestley, the son of a Dissenting Yorkshire
cloth-dresser, was a voracious student of philosophy, theology, and languages,
as well as of science. He learned Latin, Greek, French, German, Italian, Ara-
bic, and even some Syriac and Chaldee, as he taught others and served as a
preacher of the Dissenters. Franklin met Priestley in 1765 "at the House of a
philosophical friend" in London and encouraged him in his scientific studies.
The next year Priestley won a fellowship in the Royal Society.

Priestley recalled that when he was in London scarcely a day passed when
he and Franklin did not meet. With the older man's sympathetic urging,
Priestley undertook to write the story of electricity. From writing about the
discoveries of others he began seriously to experiment himself and made many
important discoveries in pneumatic chemistry, the most important being the
discovery of oxygen, which he announced in 1775. (Oxygen had already been
identified as a separate element by a Swedish scientist, but Priestley's discov-

*Electrical experiments like the one
shown in this painting by Charles van
Loo were popular parlor entertainments.*
ARKHANGELSKOY MUSEUM, MOSCOW, ROGER-VIOLLET

Dr. Joseph Priestley, a discoverer of oxygen, was a friend of Wedgwood, who struck this cameo medallion of him.

ery was independent of that study, which was not reported until several years later.) Settled in Birmingham as a minister of a large Dissenting congregation, he there joined a "Lunar Society," a club at whose meetings he discussed the latest developments in sciences, technology, and philosophy with such prominent contemporaries as Erasmus Darwin, Josiah Wedgwood, James Watt, and Matthew Boulton.

For Priestley, as for Franklin, science was not an end in itself but rather a device, subject to indefinite refinement, that might serve human welfare. Besides being a scientist Priestley was a humanitarian, and in this he personifies the scientific spirit of his age at its highest level. With careful thought of the services scientific advances could perform to such ends, he preached the religion of progress and the perfectibility of Christian brotherhood. "All knowledge will be subdivided and extended," he wrote; "and knowledge . . . being power, the human powers will in fact be increased; nature, including both its materials and its laws, will be more at our command; men will make their situation in this world abundantly more easy and comfortable; they will probably prolong their existence on it, and will daily grow more happy, each in himself, and more able (and, I believe, more disposed) to communicate happiness to others. Thus, whatever was the beginning of this world, the end will be glorious and paradisaical beyond what our imaginations can now conceive. . . . Happy are they who contribute to diffuse the pure light of this everlasting gospel."

Unfortunately for his own welfare, Priestley believed that government as well as science must contribute to this new and more perfect world, and in doing so he espoused radical political views that earned him violent opposition from his conservative fellow countrymen. He favored the revolutionary cause first of the Americans and then of the French. In Parliament Edmund Burke denounced him—this mild-mannered, studious, Christian apologist—as a heretic. Dr. Johnson regarded him as a menace. Infuriated by Priestley's liberal opinions, a mob stormed his Birmingham home (and those of some of his friends and colleagues) and burned it to the ground. His laboratory with all his instruments and his library with all its books and papers went up in the flames. Priestley fled to a brief sanctuary in London, whence he addressed his ex-townsmen with a message that reveals as nothing better could the Christian charity that was the spiritual base of this extraordinary man:

> After living with you eleven years, in which you had uniform experience of my peaceful behavior in my attention to the quiet duties of my profession, and those of philosophy, I was far from expecting the injuries which I and my friends have lately received from you. . . . Happily the minds of Englishmen have a horror of *murder* and therefore you did not, I hope, think of that. . . . But what is the value of life when everything is done to make it wretched?
>
> You have destroyed the most truly valuable and useful apparatus of philosophical instruments. . . . You have destroyed a library . . . which no money can repurchase except in a long course of time. But what I feel far more, you have destroyed manuscripts which have been the result of the laborious study of many years, and which I shall never be able to recompose, and this has been done to one who never did, or imagined, you any harm.

You are mistaken if you imagine that this conduct of yours has any tendency to serve your cause, or to prejudice ours Should you destroy myself as well as my house, library, and apparatus, ten more persons of equal or superior spirit and ability would instantly spring up. If those ten were destroyed, an hundred would appear. . . .

In this business we are the sheep and you the wolves. We will persevere in our character, and hope you will change yours. At all events, we return you blessings for curses, and pray that you may soon return to that industry, and those sober manners, for which the inhabitants of Birmingham were formerly distinguished.

At the age of sixty-one, finding the life he was forced to live in England intolerable, Priestley emigrated to America, to live out his years on the banks of the Susquehanna River in Franklin's Pennsylvania.

To cite only one further example of those men whose interest in science was but part of a wider participation in the life about them, Antoine Laurent Lavoisier, the noted French chemist, paid with his life for his involvement in public affairs unrelated to his scientific pursuits. Among his other substantial achievements Lavoisier, an acquaintance of Priestley's, was the first to enunciate the law of the indestructibility of matter. This, and his further contributions to science, will be discussed later. It is enough to point out here that he was born to wealth and that he increased his fortune with his highly successful business enterprises. He was at the same time seriously interested in public affairs, and he lent both his intelligence and his resources to governmental activity and social reforms. In many ways Lavoisier's career was the sort to win him a wide following. He was awarded a gold medal in 1766 by the French scientific academy for a paper on the lighting of towns, and he was active in promoting the economic well-being of his countrymen through forms of insurance and through the establishment of savings banks. He advised the government on military matters and on taxation. He advocated public education and public hygiene. And his work as a member of a commission to set up a uniform system of weights and measures is still considered an important contribution to the formulation of the metric system. As late as 1788, during a period of famine, he aided two French towns through interest-free loans of his own money.

Lavoisier did what he could to avert the French Revolution by suggesting ways to correct the abuses. At his urging a wall was built around Paris, with new customhouses and barriers, to check the smugglers who were evading tolls on the goods they brought into the city. In the course of his professional work in chemistry, Lavoisier had won the enmity of the revolutionary Jean Paul Marat by refusing to take seriously one of the latter's "discoveries" in chemistry. When his time came, Marat, the "Friend of the People," struck back at his wealthy adversary, denouncing him for having put Paris in a prison by cutting off the city's fresh air with the wall that had cost the poor so much money in taxes. In 1794 Lavoisier was guillotined in what is now the Place de la Concorde and dumped into a communal grave. "It took only a moment to cut off his head," observed one dismayed contemporary, "and a hundred years may not give us another like it."

Among those who took to "scientific" demonstration were frauds and charlatans intent on exploiting popular interest in the subject, and others who

Priestley's political and religious views were quite controversial. In this 1790 cartoon, Charles James Fox asks, "Pray, Doctor, is there such a thing as the Devil?" When Priestly denies it, the devil appears immediately at his right.

were simply misled into blind alleys by their uninformed enthusiasm. Some of the performances of such adventurers as Cagliostro have already been noted. Early in the eighteenth century, in his account of the third voyage of Lemuel Gulliver, as related in his famous *Travels*, Jonathan Swift poked fun at the learned scientists of a "Grand Academy" who conducted experiments in building houses from the roof downward, in feeding colored flies to spiders as a means of producing gaily colored webs, and in extracting sunbeams from cucumbers. Until well into the eighteenth century alchemy remained the pursuit of men of honest intent, some of whom enjoyed royal patronage. The great Sir Isaac Newton had not been above experimenting with the possibilities of transmuting base substances into more precious ones. As late as 1782 James Price, an English physician, professed to have changed mercury into gold with white and red powders. However, when he was asked to repeat his first apparently successful experiments, he was unable to do so and committed suicide.

The Austrian physician Franz Anton Mesmer was probably the most outstanding quack of the century. In 1766 he earned a doctor's degree in Vienna with a thesis claiming that by magnetic waves human beings were subject to astrological influences, which could be channeled through the proper hands with beneficial results to the ill and indisposed. About 1775 he coined the term "animal magnetism" to describe this healing power that he claimed emanated from him, and that he could control. Convinced that he was actually practicing magic, Viennese authorities asked him to quit their city, and he retreated to Paris, where for a while he found a more hospitable and profitable base for his operations. There, in the spacious salon of his hotel, magnificently furnished and provided with mysterious and half-concealed apparatus, he daily received swarms of patients upon whom, with magic wand, he appeared to work with miraculous effect. Using music and incense for their power of suggestion, and a form of hypnosis, or "mesmerism," he treated cases of hysteria and other presumed diseases of the mind. He not only became the rage of the fashionable world (the Marquis de Lafayette was one of his patients) but made some converts among men of repute in scientific circles. The French government at one point actually offered him a handsome pension for his secret, but ultimately appointed a commission (which included Lavoisier and Franklin, then in Paris) to investigate such strange proceedings. Although the committee admitted some of his claims and cures as a "mesmerizer," he was labeled a quack, his fortune was confiscated, and he was banished from France. Mesmer undoubtedly did anticipate the benefits of hypnosis and suggestion, later used with more authority in psychotherapy.

Johann Lavater, a Swiss preacher of philosophical leanings (he corresponded with Immanuel Kant), earnestly believed in the science of physiognomy, that the outward appearance of all living things, from men to elephants, indicated their underlying character. He not only discerned the fundamental nature of the eagle and the camel by studying their profiles, but he also swore he could spot a criminal by the same means; in the light of his perception, he advised judges to dispense with normal jurisprudence and simply draw their conclusions from the laws of appearance that he had with good faith established. Were it not for the amusement provided later generations by the illustrations in his treatise, Lavater would long since have been forgotten.

Eighteenth-century science came to its tasks with a rich heritage from the

Franz Mesmer and his disciples built up a large clientele by claiming to possess a mysterious healing power called "animal magnetism." In this eighteenth-century etching a mesmerist puts a woman into a trance while his assistant holds a candle to fix the patient's attention.

PRECLARISSIMUS·ISAACUS·NEWTON·EQUES

ECCE PHILOSOPHORUM PRINCEPS

See the great *Newton*, He who first Survey'd   O wond'rous Man! in whom the heav'nly Mind
The Plan, by which the Universe was made;   Shines forth distinguish'd, and above Mankind;
Saw Natures Simple, yet Stupendous Laws,   Whilst here on Earth, how humble, wise and good!
And prov'd the Effects tho' not explain'd the Cause   In Heav'n a Star of the first Magnitude!

LONDON: Sold by John Bickham, Engraver, at the Seven-Stars in King's-Street, Covent-Garden.   Sold by H.Overton, at ye White Horse with.

195

preceding two centuries. Such titans as Francis Bacon, Johannes Kepler, Galileo Galilei, Christian Huygens, and René Descartes—men whose brilliant genius would be unsurpassed by any who followed them—had turned away from the time-worn precepts of Aristotle that had for so long dominated and misled scientific investigation. These great investigators had changed man's notions about the universe they inhabited once and for all. Newton lived on into the eighteenth century, his reputation and his influence growing along with the passing years as popularized versions of his works (by Voltaire, among others) spread and clarified his message. Even granting the genius of these predecessors and contemporaries just listed, it might fairly be said that he was the greatest scientist who ever lived. Newton had presented the results of his study of light to the Royal Society of London in 1672, not modestly, as "the oddest if not the most considerable detection wch hath hitherto beene made in the operations of Nature." But he was then only a young and obscure professor of mathematics, and his "detection" was not immediately accepted by older and more experienced scientists. Even fifteen years later, when he issued his *Principia* (*Philosophiae naturalis principia mathematica*), the greatest single work in the history of science, Newton encountered skepticism among the learned. But time was on his side. Before his death at the age of eighty-four, in 1727, he had become virtually a semi-deity. Such had become his renown that at his funeral six peers of the realm carried his coffin to his final resting place in Westminster Abbey among the immortals.

Newton's greatest legacy was his concept of a world governed by physical laws that were not only demonstrable but that could be determined by close observation and experiment. In a letter written to the secretary of the Royal Society of London, one of the earliest scientific organizations, he advised that "the best and safest method of philosophizing seems to be, first, to inquire diligently into the property of things and to establish those properties by experiments, and to proceed later to hypotheses for the explanation of things themselves. For hypotheses ought to be applied only in the explanation of the properties of things, and not made use of in determining them."

Newton's scientific method of patient and skeptical inquiry could be applied to all men's endeavors to reach the truth—in history, theology, morals, and politics—with reliable and certain results. And it was this hopeful conclusion, as it was widely understood, that set the stage for the Enlightenment. With science as a license, men felt free to investigate all fields of knowledge with critical purpose. The eighteenth century may not have seen accomplishments commensurate with those of Galileo and Newton, but it did generate a galaxy of stellar scientists whose research and discoveries vastly expanded the limits of knowledge—knowledge that accumulated at a faster rate than ever before in history. "The diffusion of a general knowledge, and of a taste for science, over all classes of men, in every nation of Europe," declared one chemist of the time, "seems to be the characteristic feature of the present age."

It was that compelling spirit of inquiry that gave rise to the various scientific academies, the earliest of which were the Royal Society in London and the Académie des Sciences in Paris, founded as far back as the 1660's. Such organizations proliferated in the century to come, and broadened their bases by increasing their membership and engaging in cooperative enterprises. The interchange of scientific ideas on an international scale was stimulated through congresses and published journals, establishing a community of interest in

This painting by Charles Lebrun commemorates the founding of the French Académie des Sciences. Louis XIV is seated at the center; to his right is his finance minister, Jean Baptiste Colbert, a strong supporter of the Académie.
MUSEE DE VERSAILES—GIRAUDON

scientific developments that extended across national boundaries, not only to most of the major cities of western Europe, but to the little "cities in the wilderness" along the Atlantic seaboard of North America. In 1743 Benjamin Franklin wrote letters to his learned friends in the other colonies suggesting that they form a society to promote the exchange of scientific and other ideas that would contribute to the public interest and the advancement of knowledge. As the American Philosophical Society, it remains the oldest learned society in America; its membership has included the leading scientists, scholars, statesmen, and public servants of the country, and some of the most illustrious of foreign lands as well.

The subjects Franklin proposed for consideration provide an insight into his own encyclopedic interests as well as an index of the immediate, practical purposes that science then accepted as its mission: "Newly discovered plants, herbs, trees, roots, their virtues, uses, methods of propagating them, and making such as are useful but particular to some plantations, more general; improvements of vegetable juices, as ciders, wines; new methods of curing or preventing diseases; all new-discovered fossils in different countries, as mines, minerals, and quarries; new and useful improvements in any branch of mathematics; new discoveries in chemistry, such as improvements in distillation, brewing, and assaying of ores; new mechanical inventions for saving labor, as mills and carriages, and for raising and conveying of water, draining of meadows; all new arts, trades, and manufactures, that may be proposed or thought of; surveys, maps, and charts of particular parts of the sea-coast or inland countries; course and junction of rivers and great roads, situation of lakes and mountains, nature of the soil and productions; new methods of improving the breed of useful animals; introducing other sorts from foreign countries; new improvements in planting, gardening, and clearing land; and all philosophical experiments that let light into the nature of things, tend to increase the power of man over matter, and multiply the conveniences or pleasures of life."

From this, and from what has earlier been said, it is clear that science and technology were closely associated in the minds of men, although, strangely, the practical application of science to technology was slow in developing. Such societies as the one Franklin proposed, and those earlier established in Europe, provided open forums for the unlimited discussion of ideas to "improve useful knowledge." This was at a time when universities were not always hospitable to some of the advanced theories of the day. In 1744 the eminent French naturalist Georges Buffon, generally considered the founder of modern geology and a developer of the theory of evolution, was obliged by the Sorbonne in Paris to retract his views, which seemed to the orthodox to contradict the biblical account of creation.

Views of any nature could and did circulate more freely at informal meeting places. In France the salons provided an open environment as did the coffee houses of England. Lectures by prominent scholars were given at the Marine Coffee House in London. The clientele who gathered there for enlightenment along with rounds of coffee ranged from navigators, naturally interested in mathematics, to insurance brokers, naturally concerned in the laws, or theories, of probability. At similar informal places doctors might meet their patients and apothecaries glean information from the specialists in their field. At London's Rainbow Coffee House botanists who often met there formed the Botanical Society and there, also, was founded the Society for the Encourage-

" . . . I have laid down the principles of philosophy; principles not philosophical but mathematical: such, namely, as we may build our reasonings upon is philosophical inquiries. These principles are the laws and conditions of certain motions, and powers or forces, which chiefly have respect to philosophy . . . I have illustrated them here and there with some philosophical scholiums; such as the density and the resistance of bodies, spaces void of all bodies, and the motion of light and sounds."

Isaac Newton

ment of Learning, "with the general aim of promoting the Arts and Sciences." There were numerous congregations devoted to different branches of inquiry throughout the city. As one reporter has suggested, the coffee house offered "a rite of communion with the liberal spirit of the times." He went on to say that science, far from stemming from the puritan spirit, rose from the hedonistic atmosphere that enabled "the senses to take a place at least the equal of intellect and intuition as a means of knowledge."

At a more formal level universities increasingly admitted science to their curriculums. This happened sooner in Germany and Italy than in the rest of Europe. However, between 1702 and 1750, Cambridge established chairs in anatomy, astronomy, botany, chemistry, and "experimental philosophy," or physics. Before the middle of the century a small college was founded in Philadelphia (with strong support from Franklin); it became the first institution of higher learning in colonial America to provide instruction in physics and mathematics. In 1765 it also established the first school of medicine in North America. In the following decades it became America's first university.

In spite of these various new facilities for learning, progress in scientific education was erratic throughout much of the century. With men all over Europe and in parts of America turning their attention to the same kinds of scientific problems, there was growing danger that a man in one country might waste a lifetime exploring questions that, unknown to him, had already been satisfactorily answered in another part of the world. Because of the increasingly apparent interrelationships of the various sciences, a small clue in one field might provide a key to an obstinate problem in another field of inquiry. It was this grave difficulty that was alleviated by the interlocking membership of scientific societies, by the publication of their proceedings and transactions and learned journals, and by the correspondence between individual scientists of different cities and different countries. For some time the independent societies contributed more to the advancement of scientific learning than did the academic programs at the universities. A barometer of the relative importance of the societies was the support they received from governments, which looked to them for new information that would promote the interests of the state— usually, if not always, meaning the improvement of military prowess, by one means or another, on land and sea. Thus it was, for instance, that Lavoisier as the appointed commissioner of gunpowder (in 1775) improved the quality and increased the production of that explosive to the point where it could be exported in large quantities to the American revolutionary forces, very considerably enhancing their ability to wage a successful war. "French gunpowder," Lavoisier observed shortly before he lost his head to the guillotine, "has become the best in Europe. . . . One can say with truth that to it North America owes its liberty." It was also a significant factor in the victories of the French revolutionary armies. (It was Lavoisier's improved gunpowder that early in the next century the émigré Eleuthère Irénée du Pont de Nemours started to make in his powder mill on the banks of the Brandywine in Delaware, which was the seed of today's gigantic Du Pont enterprises.)

Lavoisier's great contribution was in the field of chemistry. As late as 1750 the workers in that science continued to subscribe to the idea that the elementary components of the universe consisted of, or included, earth, air, fire, and water. These were considered irreducible fundamentals, a concept that goes back not only to medieval cosmologies but to the reasoning of the ancients.

Eighteenth-century scientists met informally at coffee houses (although in London tea was the popular beverage) to discuss the latest theories and experiments.
BRITISH MUSEUM

This view of an eighteenth-century classroom experiment in Navarre, France, on the conduction of electricity first appeared in a book by Abbé Jean Antoine Nollett entitled Research in Physics.
BIBLIOTHEQUE NATIONALE. ROGER-VIOLLET

From the chemist's point of view nature still seemed extraordinarily simple. Bit by bit during the second half of the eighteenth century this traditional notion—it was little more than that—was analyzed, picked apart, and reconstituted as something closely resembling our current understanding of these matters. Earth, air, fire, and water, it was gradually learned, could be separated into identifiable components or explained in terms of demonstrable chemical action. By the end of the century the first tentative listing of basic chemical elements was charted, suggesting the complex interrelationships of all matter, organic and inorganic, in a manner never before conceived. This may have been the single most important scientific development of the Age of Enlightenment.

Although a number of "airs" had earlier been distinguished as part of the ordinary atmosphere, according to their inflammable nature or their inability to sustain life, some of them had been clearly described in terms commonly used in modern chemistry. Fire was explained on the basis of a hypothetical substance called phlogiston, an essential part of all combustible matter that was released in the process of burning; fire and its accompanying heat, in other words, was a substance detached from burning matter, although no one could explain why, if this were the case, metals weighed more after burning than before. The phlogiston theory was part of a spurious chemical philosophy, closely allied to alchemy, that had earlier been elaborated by German scientists, and it died a slow death.

The role in combustion of what we now know as oxygen was only gradually determined, but with the isolation of that element a new world of chemistry was opened. The colorless, odorless, and tasteless oxygen is the most abundant of all elements—the basic resource of life on earth, the essential constituent of protoplasm itself. Until its true nature was understood, progress in most of the sciences was held in a strait jacket of ignorance. Several men were responsible for the identification of oxygen as a separate element and the determination of its distinguishing characteristics; three of them stand out most prominently. A Swedish chemist, Karl Wilhelm Scheele, may have been the first. About 1772 he discovered what he termed "empyreal air" or "fire air," which was, in fact, oxygen, but he did not officially report his findings for several years. (It was but one of dozens of new substances he was discovering in time-consuming experiments that delayed his publications.) In the meantime, on August 1, 1774, Joseph Priestley heated mercuric oxide with a burning glass and produced what he termed "dephlogisticated air." He still considered this the necessary raw ingredient of all fire. It clearly supported combustion vigorously when applied to the flame of a candle. He had, in fact, discovered oxygen's true role in combustion without completely understanding what he had done. And he went to his grave in 1804 without realizing all the implications of his discovery.

However, Priestley correctly observed that the new gas might be "peculiarly salutary for the lungs," and busied himself with the "purification of air by plants and the influence of light on that process." His dephlogisticated air not only speeded combustion but improved respiration as well. As early as 1771 he had observed that green plants immersed in water restored the ordinary air of the atmosphere; through exhalation they produced the vital element. This discovery was the basis of photosynthesis. It was another contemporary scientist, the Dutch-English chemist Jan Ingenhousz, who in 1779 revealed that sunlight is the key to the interchange of gases between plants and the atmosphere, a finding he set forth in a report entitled *Experiments on Vegetables, Discovering Their Great Power of Purifying the Common Air in Sunshine, but Injuring in the Shade or at Night.*

It remained for another to prove that combustion was not a release of the hypothetical substance phlogiston, but the result of a combination of burning matter with oxygen. Not long after Priestley had made his own great, if misunderstood, discovery in 1774, he began a tour of the Continent, and in Paris had a historic meeting with Lavoisier in which the two discussed matters of common interest. In the following several years the Frenchman extended Priestley's work, and by his experiments conclusively demonstrated that air was not a simple element but rather a mixture of two unlike gases, one conducive to respiration, the other quite the opposite. He took the further step of naming the beneficial gas, a true element, *oxygine* and then *oxygène,* after the Greek word for "acid-maker," in recognition of one of the properties of that element.

What is called pneumatic chemistry, the isolation of separate gases on a scientific basis, had been studied as early as the 1750's by the Scottish chemist, physician, and anatomist, Joseph Black. By experiment he had learned of the existence of another gas that was different from the ordinary atmosphere— carbon dioxide (carbonic acid gas), which he called "fixed air," and which he had discovered incidentally while seeking a remedy for gout. He showed that this gas is contained in human exhalations, and he thereby cleared the way for the discovery of oxygen (the acid-maker) without however going on to that discovery himself.

A bit later, in 1766, Henry Cavendish, a wealthy and uncommunicative

English recluse who fits the stereotype of an eccentric scientist, established the identity of what he called "inflammable air," which he subsequently determined united with oxygen to produce water. Lavoisier named it hydrogen, a word derived from the Greek term meaning "maker of water." Cavendish's chief object in life seems to have been to avoid attention, and he did not share his discovery with his fellow scientists or report it to the Royal Society. Men in the same field were obliged to repeat his experiments to rediscover what he had originally accomplished.

Lavoisier's greatest legacy to chemistry was still to come. Thanks to his very considerable wealth, he was able to equip the most complex and extensive laboratory of the time with hundreds of instruments, thousands of containers and chemical preparations, and three precision balances, which would later help him to establish the gram as the unit of weight in the metric system. By the careful and precise weighing of substances he changed chemistry from a qualitative to a quantitative science. (It was by such measures that he had exploded once and for all the myth of phlogiston.) He made valuable contributions to biochemistry, thermochemistry, and the chemistry of agriculture. Two of his monumental published works laid the foundations of modern chemistry. With a group of French colleagues, in 1787 he issued *Méthode de nomenclature chimique*, which set the pattern for naming substances on the basis of their chemical composition—both substances that are elements and those that are compounds. Two years later appeared his *Traité élémentaire de chimie*, which not only elaborated the principle of elements but provided the first available listing of them. This work also introduced the chemical equation as such and set forth the principle of the indestructibility of matter, earlier mentioned. "Nothing is created in the operation either of art or nature," he propounded, "and it can be taken as an axiom that in every operation an equal quantity of matter exists both before and after the operation." More than one respected authority has likened the *Traité* to Newton's *Principia* as a landmark

This rough drawing by Madame Lavoisier (seen at right, sketching) shows an experiment being performed in her husband's laboratory on human respiration.
MUSEE DU CONSERVATOIRE NATIONAL
DES ARTS ET METIERS

of scientific progress. Had he not tragically met his death at such an early age (he was forty-five) he might well have proceeded to ever greater accomplishments.

In the meantime Joseph Black continued his own endless experiments in the comparative safety of the University of Edinburgh. He had been born in Bordeaux in 1728, the son of a Scot who was in the wine business in that city. As a young man he received a degree from the University of Edinburgh, which at the time was one of the great centers of scientific education, and it was there that he became a celebrated lecturer. He was one of the rare men of science in that day who became famous as a teacher—and his fame endures, not only as a teacher.

Black's discovery of carbon dioxide has already been mentioned. He was concerned with the problem of heat, a subject little understood when he first undertook his studies in the late 1750's. Such basic matters as the difference between temperature and quantity of heat were still mysteries to be solved. Black's theory of latent heat, now solidly established, deals with that quantity of heat absorbed or released by a substance as it undergoes transformation—from solid to liquid, as in the case of ice changing to water, or from liquid to steam, as in the case of boiling water. He had observed that the application of heat to ice does not cause immediate liquefaction, nor does a like application of heat to boiling water cause immediate evaporation. These findings form the basis of a demonstration now familiar to all students of elementary physics, but it was a revelation at the time of Black's experiments.

From his observations Black evolved his theory of latent heat. Thus, when a substance is in the process of changing from a solid to a liquid state, or from a liquid to a gas, the changing substance absorbs from the atmosphere an amount of heat not detectable as a change of temperature. This latent heat is then returned to the atmosphere when the change is completed. In other words, when heat is applied to a container holding a mixture of ice and water at 32 degrees Fahrenheit, the ice begins to melt, but there is no change of temperature in either ice or water until the ice completely melts. The heat thus absorbed by a solid at its melting point to effect its change to liquid form is known as the latent heat of fusion. This latent, or hidden, heat is employed by the solid to overcome the force that keeps its molecules together.

Again, when water is boiling, both water and steam remain at 212 degrees, Fahrenheit (the boiling point) until all the water has evaporated. The heat that must be added to any liquid at its boiling point to vaporize it is the latent heat of vaporization. Unlikely as this seemed to many of his contemporaries, Black's theory was clearly demonstrable. The idea was of almost immediate help in developing the condensing steam engine of James Watt, who was one of Black's pupils. With the refinement of such a power engine, made of iron and steel and using coal, England completed the first stage of a profound revolutionary process. As earlier noted, for the first time in history man was no longer dependent on the natural sources of power.

Black taught the doctrine of latent heat in his lectures from 1761 until his death at the end of the century, although he never published any detailed account of it, and others were able to claim the credit for his results. In the course of his various inquiries into the nature of heat he also noticed that different bodies in equal masses required different amounts of heat, measured in calories, to raise them to the same temperature, and went on to establish the doc-

Experiments such as the one shown in this detail from a 1768 painting by Joseph Wright were performed to prove that oxygen was vital in respiration. The lark, placed in a glass bell over an air pump, slowly suffocates as the air is removed. The assembled "students" seem at once horrified and fascinated.
TATE GALLERY, LONDON

trine of specific heats. Until he died at the end of the century at the age of seventy-one, he retained an almost morbid horror of hasty generalizations or of any pretense of developing a full-fledged system based on his discoveries.

Although experiments in electricity attracted widespread interest because of their diverting novelties, they did not produce any very coherent system of knowledge until late in the century. Even then practical application of electricity's peculiar properties was realized only in rudimentary fashion. How little general understanding there was of this new science is suggested by the fact that John Wesley hailed the medical properties of electricity as useful in the treatment of a wide variety of maladies. Electricity, he believed with more faith than reason, supplied that *élan vital* without which life was incomplete.

At the time Benjamin Franklin turned his attention to the subject in the 1740's, experiments were largely confined to static electricity, produced by friction, or to charges stored in an early form of capacitor, or condenser. The distinction between conductors and insulators had only recently been recognized through the work of Stephen Gray, an irascible old pensioner in a London almshouse. Having identified the conductive properties of some substances, Gray managed to send an electrical current (he called it "virtue") for 666 feet along a strong thread suspended from a series of poles. With that operation he had, in effect, anticipated the telegraph by about a century. Somewhat earlier another Englishman, Francis Hauksbee, had demonstrated a primitive method of generating electricity by rotating a glass globe against human hands. The obvious need to find some way of storing electricity for use at will led to the invention of the Leyden jar just before mid-century. (It was frequently referred to as "Professor Muschenbroek's miraculous bottle," after one of its inventors.)

It was at this time that Franklin began his serious work with electricity. He was not yet as deeply involved in affairs of state as he soon would become, and the study of electrical phenomena for a time completely absorbed his interest. "I never was before engaged in any study that so closely engrossed my attention and my time as this has lately done," he wrote early in 1747; "for, what with making experiments when I can be alone, and repeating them to my friends and acquaintances, who, from the novelty of the thing, come continually in crowds to see them, I have, during some months past, had little leisure for any thing else." The next year he put the foreman of his printing shop in charge of the business so that he could concentrate on his electrical studies.

In May, 1751, a pamphlet entitled "New Experiments and Observations in Electricity, made at Philadelphia, in America," and containing Franklin's reports was issued in London. Buffon recognized the importance of this document and translated it into French. German, Italian, and Latin translations quickly followed. Louis XV directed that a letter be written to the Royal Society of London expressing his admiration of Franklin's ingenuity and learning. The report was without doubt one of the first works in any field by an American to gain wide international recognition. In 1753 Franklin received the Copley medal from the Royal Society and was elected to membership not only in that organization but in like societies throughout Europe. Both Yale and Harvard conferred upon him the honorary degree of Master of Arts. (In passing, Franklin coined at least four terms that have continued to the present day to identify basic ideas or objects concerned with electricity: "positive," "negative," "conductor," and "battery.")

Like a number of other scientists, Franklin was fascinated by lightning. As early as 1749 he became convinced that this was an electrical phenomenon, and that its charges could be drawn off the atmosphere. In 1752, just before he conducted his own experiment with a kite during a thunderstorm, unbeknownst to him a Frenchman brought lightning down from the sky with an iron rod. Franklin's procedure was to bring electricity out of a cloud, down a wet kite string to a key, and then into a Leyden jar. (Another experiment along the same lines electrocuted a scientist in St. Petersburg.) With this novel and risky experiment he established the identity of lightning and static electricity. It led Franklin to conclude that clouds can be positively and negatively charged; it proved as well that electrical charges could be drawn off the atmosphere by means of a pointed iron rod; and this had its immediate practical application in the development of the lightning rod.

This novel device was not universally accepted on its obvious merits. Just as years before insuring houses against fire was denounced as an interference with the prerogatives of the Deity, so now the installation of a lightning rod was considered by some to be an act of impiety. In 1755 an earthquake shock was felt in New England. One Boston clergyman contended in a sermon that it was caused by the fact that lightning rods had accumulated electricity in the earth. Fifteen years later another Boston divine concluded that since lightning was one of the means of punishing the sins of mankind, and of warning men from the commission of such sins, it was impious "to prevent its full execution." However, the truth prevailed, and Franklin again found himself the object of nearly universal applause. "It is well we are not, as poor Galileo was," he wrote in one of his letters, "subjected to the inquisition for philosophical heresy." His successes in these and other fields contributed to the favorable reception Franklin received when he came to France to seek aid for the rebellious American colonists. When, with France's substantial help, the War of Independence was won, Franklin's achievement was summed in an unforgettable line: *Eripuit coelo fulmen sceptrumque tyrannis* ("He snatched the lightning from the sky, and the scepter from the tyrants").

There were, of course, many others who also contributed to a better understanding of the properties of electricity, Priestley and Cavendish among them. Later in the century Luigi Galvani, an Italian physiologist, formulated his idea of "animal electricity," using as a basis for his reasoning his observation of a frog's leg. He noticed that a frog's leg muscle contracted when a nerve was touched by a brass or copper wire at the same time that an iron wire on the muscle came in contact with the other wire, and concluded that this came about through electricity already present in the frog's body. His countryman Allessandro Volta disputed the thesis, and later proved that the presumed animal electricity had, in fact, been produced by contact of the metals. It was, in other words, no different from the electricity generated by inanimate things. By the time Franklin was laid to rest, the way had been opened for electricity to brighten the future of mankind in ways that even he had never dreamed.

While some men were trying to catch lightning in bottles, others were combing the earth for specimens of plant and animal life, the study of which would throw new light on the nature of the organic world, and seeking to classify all biological knowledge into those orderly and systematic arrangements

A The chimney.
B An iron bar continued from D, and F
faftened to the brick wall, which it
touches all the way, by iron clampsCC
o o o o o Five iron wires at the top of
the bar B, tipped with filver.
E A wire tied to the bar at D, and continued into the ground.
F A wooden frame round the wire, to
prevent the wire from being touched,
left it fhould deftroy the perfon that
touched it. G

This explanation of a lightning rod is from a 1756 Gentleman's Magazine.

so dear to the Age of Reason—and to modern science. One of the greatest of these was the Swedish botanist Carl von Linné, better remembered by the Latinized version of his name, Carolus Linnaeus. He was the son of a Lutheran pastor, a fact that may partly explain the course of his life-long research and the conclusions he drew from it. As a young man in Uppsala he helped compile the *Hierobotanicum*, which described the plant life mentioned in the Bible. As a result of a tour in Lapland in 1737, he published *Flora Lapponica*. (The best-known likeness of Linnaeus shows him in the garb of a Laplander.) Two years earlier he had been awarded a medical degree in the Netherlands, and for a time he was a practicing physician in Stockholm, then professor of medicine at the University of Uppsala. There, in 1742, he became a professor of botany and eventually one of the most respected figures in the academic world of his country. He was granted a patent of nobility by Gustavus III.

Botany was Linnaeus' passionate interest, allied with his equally passionate interest in names. Of his many writings *Systema Naturae*, which appeared between 1735 and 1758, is the most widely known and is rightly considered a landmark in the development of biological studies. It went through a dozen editions in Linnaeus' own lifetime. The original catalogue for this work included, among the animals, an entry for man—modern man—and Linnaeus is credited with originating the designation of *homo sapiens* for this creature. He classified not only plants and animals but minerals and diseases. Of living things, more than twelve thousand examples, for which his students had foraged all over the world, were meticulously grouped in four divisions: classes, orders, genera, and species. The last two have survived in modern taxonomy. Although some of his predecessors in the field had tried to classify organisms systematically, and had even used a combination of two Latin terms to describe plant life, Linnaeus was the first to formalize binomial nomenclature for the genus (family) and the species (individual); the first to list inclusively according to a single, grand design all the known world of living things, painstakingly identified and consistently named. It was a monumental accomplishment. (Most of the names earlier designated had been coined at the will of individual collectors and specialists.)

In grouping plants, Linnaeus used sexuality as a classifying principle, taking as criteria the stamens and stylus. Apparently Linnaeus came to realize the rather arbitrary nature of such a basis, for toward the end of his career he varied it. At the outset he had denied the possibility of new species evolving from the old, for he considered species immutable. All of them, he believed, had "issued in pairs from the hands of the creator," a position still in vogue when Charles Darwin undertook his memorable studies in the next century. But in the end he did consider the possibility of hybridization and the consequent emergence of new species. However, Linnaeus was no prophet of evolution. He remarked that God had suffered him to "peep into His secret cabinet," a privilege he treasured.

The world at large had become the province of naturalists. Thanks in good measure to global trade, to colonization, and to exploration, it was a changing world ecologically. Merchants and mariners brought to Europe and to North America wide varieties of plant and animal life from distant places. From the earliest days of settlement, the American colonists had of necessity introduced plants and animals that were not native to the New World, and such imports and transplants from all over multiplied as the eighteenth century advanced.

The most famous portrait of Linnaeus shows him in Lapland dress. Several years earlier he had traveled to Lapland and published Brief Lapland Flora, *the first written work in which he used his sexual system of classification. One contemporary thought the portrait "most grotesque," the only resemblance to Linnaeus being the "piercing eyes."*
BETTMANN ARCHIVE

European wheat, oat, rice, and rye were naturalized in America, as were wool-bearing sheep, chickens, horses, mules, oxen, plugs, goats, and dairy cattle, none of which were indigenous. On the other hand, in time the Americas contributed to the diet of the Old World with staples that had not previously been known overseas. As a prime example, the potato, immemorially grown by Peruvian Indians, was carried to Spain in the early sixteenth century, naturalized there, and taken back across the ocean to Florida by Spanish colonizers. There it was discovered by English marauders who took it to the British Isles, where it flourished. Early in the eighteenth century Irish settlers carried it back across the Atlantic to the English colonies, where the "Irish potato" soon became a basic dietary ingredient.

Such great shifts in the earth's vegetable and animal life, barely outlined here, were not only noted but actively encouraged by scientists of the eighteenth century, like Linnaeus, who longed to include everything that could be discovered in the world in their summaries of human knowledge. Naturalists sailed with Captain James Cook on his historic voyages of exploration that were organized by the Royal Society of London, and brought home a wealth of new botanical and zoological data to be recorded and classified. Hundreds of dedicated scientists of different nationalities, amateurs and professionals, carried on the quest for new specimens and additional information. In 1735 the French botanist Joseph de Jussieu had accompanied the mathematician Charles de La Condamine on an expedition to South America and sent back plants hitherto unknown in Europe for transplantation in the Jardin du Roi (Jardin des Plantes) in Paris, where his brother was then director. This extraordinary institution had been founded as early as 1635 and was the most celebrated of several such European centers of research for biology and other sciences.

The Jardin des Plantes—its collections included animals and minerals as well as plants—practically tripled in size during the course of the eighteenth century. In 1739 Buffon was appointed as the new director, a post he held for forty-nine years. Buffon has been called the greatest naturalist of the century. He was also a very well-to-do socialite and a public official. But with his appointment he made biology his great enterprise. From then until his death in 1788 at the age of eighty-one he devoted his life, with the help of several colleagues, to the preparation of his *Histoire Naturelle*, which was nothing less than an encyclopedia of the sciences. This stupendous and beautifully illustrated work finally ended with forty-four volumes published between 1749 and 1804. It was the first natural history of such scope that had ever been attempted, and since Buffon expressed his ideas in a clear and attractive manner, its appearance in successive parts was met with wide acclaim. (In 1753 Buffon used the occasion of his admission to the French Academy to deliver his celebrated inaugural address, *Discours sur le style*, in which he observed that, regardless of the importance of their contents, the only books that would influence posterity were those that were well written—ending his address with his unforgettable phrase, "the style is the man himself.")

Primarily, Buffon's weighty work dealt with the earth and its development —as such, it ranks as one of the earliest studies of geology—and with the natural history of birds and quadrupeds. Here, as in other books, Buffon advanced an idea of the earth's great age and suggested the different geologic periods that covered that vast span of time. It was with his *Théorie de la Terre*,

Carolus Linnaeus proved his controversial theory of the existence of sexuality in plants and based his binomial classification system on it.

On the sexes of plants

I am no poet, but something, however of a botanist; I therefore offer to you this fruit from the little crop that God has granted me. . . . In spring, when the bright sun comes nearer to our zenith, he awakens in all bodies the life that has lain stifled during the chill winter. See how all creatures become lively and gay, who through the winter were dull and sluggish! See how every bird, all the long winter silent, bursts into song! See how all the insects come forth from their hiding places where they have lain half dead, how all the plants push through the soil, how all the trees which in winter were dormant now break into leaf! Why even into man himself new life seems to enter. . . . Words cannot express the joy that the sun brings to all living things. . . . Every animal feels the sexual urge. Yes, Love comes even to the plants. Males and females, even the hermaphrodites, hold their nuptials (which is the subject that I now propose to discuss), showing by their sexual organs which are males, which females, which hermaphrodites. . . . The actual petals of a flower contribute nothing to generation, serving only as the bridal bed which the great Creator has so gloriously prepared, adorned with such precious bed-curtains, and perfumed with so many sweet scents in order that the bridegroom and bride may therein celebrate their nuptials with the greater solemnity. When the bed has thus been made ready, then is the time for the bridegroom to embrace his beloved bride and surrender himself to her. . . .

Although the earliest observers of nature could not possibly be ignorant of the sexes of plants, it has been left for the philosophers of the present age to demonstrate them. And so abundant are the proofs of this phenomenon, that not a single vegetable can be found, which does not offer them to our consideration. . . . In the month of April, I sowed the seeds of hemp (*Cannabis*) in two different pots. The young plants came up so plentifully, that each pot contained thirty or forty. I placed each by the light of a window, but in different and remote apartments. The hemp grew extremely well in both pots. In one of them I permitted the male and fe-

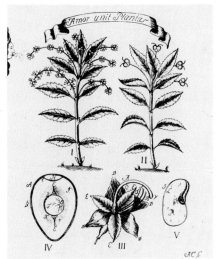

NEW YORK BOTANICAL GARDEN

male plants to remain together, to flower and bear fruit, which ripened in July, and being macerated in water, and committed to the earth, sprung up in twelve days. From the other, however, I removed all the male plants, as soon as they were old enough for me to distinguish them from the females. The remaining females grew very well, and presented their long pistilla in great abundance, these flowers continuing a very long time, as if in expectation of their mates; while the plants in the other pot had already ripened their fruit, their pistilla having, quite in a different manner, faded as soon as the males had discharged all their pollen. It was certainly a beautiful and truly admirable spectacle, to see the unimpregnated females preserve their pistilla so long green and flourishing, not permitting them to begin to fade, till they had been a very considerable time exposed, in vain, to the access of the male pollen. . . . I am perfectly convinced that the circumstances which authors have recorded, of the female hemp having produced seeds, although deprived of the males, could only have happened by means of pollen brought by the wind from some distant place. . . .

On the study of Nature

While we turn our minds to the contemplation of the beauties which surround us, we are also permitted to employ them for our benefit. . . . The Creator has given us *eyes*, by the assistance of which we discern the works of creation. He has, moreover, endowed us with the power of *tasting*, by which we perceive the parts entering into the composition of bodies; of *smelling*, that we may catch their subtle exhalations; of *hearing*, that we may receive the sound of bodies around us; and of *touching*, that we may examine their surfaces; and all for the purposes of our comprehending, in some measure, the wisdom of his works. The same instruments of sensation are bestowed on many other animals who see, hear, smell, taste, and feel; but they want the faculty which is granted us, of combining these sensations, and from thence drawing universal conclusions. . . . We must therefore necessarily ascribe this prerogative to something altogether immaterial, which the Creator has given to man alone, and which we call *soul*. If therefore the Maker of all things, who has done nothing without design, has furnished this earthly globe, like a museum, with the most admirable proofs of his wisdom and power; if, moreover, this splendid theatre would be adorned in vain without a spectator; and if he has placed in it Man, the chief and most perfect of all his works, who is alone capable of duly considering the wonderful economy of the whole; it follows, that Man is made for the purpose of studying the Creator's works, that he may observe in them the evident marks of divine wisdom.

in 1744, that he proposed the hypothesis about creation that was at odds with the Bible and that brought him into confrontation with the authorities at the Sorbonne. The experience did not change his outlook, which clearly forecast the evolutionary theories of Charles Darwin, although there is no definite statement of such principles in his writings. These do, however, reject the idea that the species of organic life were fixed and unchanging. A number of animal organs no longer have apparent use, he reasoned, and they thereby recall earlier circumstances and types of organisms. Both Diderot and Erasmus Darwin were in general agreement with Buffon's position—clear signs that these studies were taking a new direction.

Late in his life, in 1778, he elaborated his earlier theme that the earth was much older than was commonly thought and set forth the proposition that it had resulted from the cooling and condensing of incandescent matter torn from the sun in a collision of the sun and a comet. He proceeded to divide the earth's history into seven epochs, totaling about sixty-five thousand years up to the time of his publication; he estimated the habitable future of our planet at ninety-three thousand years. Large animals, he claimed, had appeared in the fifth epoch and man in the sixth, which had ended about five thousand years before he was writing. Anticipating further trouble with the theologians, Buffon left Paris for a while. However, this time the only outspoken disagreement he encountered was from other scientists with contrary theories about the original formation of the earth's crust, which have since proved to be wrong in their basic particulars. Out of the controversy between the several schools of thought there nevertheless emerged a systematic classification of minerals and a demonstration of how the earth's rocks have a chronological relationship, following one another in classifiable order. The German geologist Abraham Gottlob Werner, whose theories about the formation of rocks, opposed to those of Buffon, have long since been completely disproved, made such a solid contribution to mineralogy that he has been called "the Linnaeus of the rocks." In any case, the ingenious and ingenuous calculation of Bishop James Ussher, who had a century earlier than Buffon set the date of creation at exactly 4004 B.C., had been reduced to a pious fable.

An English contemporary of Linnaeus and Buffon, Sir Joseph Banks was a distinguished example of the wealthy benefactor of science. An amateur naturalist in his own right, Banks was a patron of the Botanic Garden in Chelsea, the English equivalent of the Jardin des Plantes. After his death, his valuable herbarium and his extensive library went to the British Museum, where they have continued to serve botanical studies. Among other things, Banks was founder of the Association for Promoting the Discovery of the Interior Parts of Africa, and he sent numerous collectors to the so-called Dark Continent to glean what they could. He was himself active in remote places, including Iceland. It was Banks who equipped Captain Cook's *Endeavour* for its wide-ranging voyage of 1768–71, and he accompanied the expedition as its naturalist.

Sir Joseph had a wide vision of the worlds he explored. "On the Island of Tahiti where love is the chief occupation," he observed, "both the bodies and the souls of the women are moulded into the utmost perfection." It was such remarks that Diderot had in mind when he unfavorably contrasted the civilized European to the uninhibited "natural" man of the South Seas paradise. Banks, however, was not distracted from the main purpose of his venture. The findings of his expensive, lengthy, and pioneering journey paid handsome dividends to scholarship. He had taken with him the artist Sydney Parkinson, whose numerous sketches of plant and animal life proved to be invaluable records. Sadly, Parkinson paid for the work he accomplished with his life. He died of malaria before the *Endeavour* arrived back at its home port.

Colonial America added its fair share of fact and theory to this busy ferment of scientific inquiry and speculation—over and above the major contributions made by Franklin, although his influence seems omnipresent in the colonial scene. Before the Revolution the best minds of the colonies had been brought to a focus in Philadelphia by the activity of the American Philosophical Society. From Philadelphia the society not only fed back a synthesis of American intellectual and scientific accomplishments to the other cities and villages of North America but relayed it across the Atlantic to European illuminati, many of whom were pleased to accept membership in the Philadelphia organization. The botanical gardens of John Bartram in the Quaker City were known to amateur and professional naturalists at home and abroad, including the king of England, the queen of Sweden, and the scientists of remote Russia—and, of course, to Linnaeus, with whom he exchanged plants and who referred to the American as the foremost "naturalist botanist" of the time. In 1743 he received a commission to explore the territory of the Indian tribes of the League of Six Nations and the area in Canada near Lake Ontario. Some twenty years later he was dispatched by the crown (he was a fellow of the Royal Society) to the remote parts of the Carolinas and Georgia and then to Florida, accompanied by his son William, who carried on his father's work. The journal that he published (in 1769) after the Florida expedition is considered an early classic of American botany. The plants gathered in their wide-ranging travels and transplanted in their garden constituted a microcosm of the American wilderness. The seeds and specimens Bartram sent overseas to his numerous correspondents were responsible for the naturalization in England alone of more than one hundred fifty American plants. Parenthetically, Bartram was hybridizing flowering plants at least as early as was the elder Darwin in England.

Foreigners came to America to see for themselves what remained for science to conquer in the vast provinces of the New World. The Swedish naturalist

The English naturalist Sir Joseph Banks, seen in a portrait by an anonymous artist, was president of the Royal Society from 1778 until his death.

209

Peter Kalm, for example, came to America in 1748 on such a mission, and John Bartram gave him lessons in botany. On his travels through the colonies Kalm was constantly amazed at the spectacle that unfolded before him. "Whenever I looked to the ground," he reported, "I everywhere found such plants as I had never seen before. When I saw a tree, I was forced to stop and ask those who accompanied me how it was called. I was seized with terror at the thought of ranging so many new and unknown parts of natural history." Nevertheless, between 1753 and 1761 he published an account of his travels in the New World, the first account of its kind by a trained scientist.

As a postscript to the story of John Bartram, his idea of a survey of the western territory eventually resulted in the historic expedition of Lewis and Clark overland to the Pacific Ocean. He died in 1777, but his son lived on to be as famous as the father. William Bartram's delineation of the American scene in his *Travels*, published in 1791, with its precise descriptions and colorful evocations of the wilds of America, a world barely imaginable to most European minds, provided a literal stage for their thoughts and dreams. It reached far beyond the realm of scientific interest. The English poet Samuel Taylor Coleridge read the book, and it fired his hope of founding an ideal colony of poets and philosophers in the unspoiled land, where human virtue would hold sway as it could never do in the worn environment of the Old World. Many of the vivid images that Coleridge wove into *The Ancient Mariner, Kublai Khan*, and his other poems were inspired by the younger Bartram's book. Coleridge's fellow poet Robert Southey also made use of the book in his own writings, as did William Wordsworth. Vicomte François René de Chateaubriand, the most popular French author of his time, came to America briefly the year Bartram's *Travels* was published, and he subsequently made imaginative use of the American's material to invent passages in *Atala* and *Les Natchez*, tales of romantic agony set in the primeval forest and amongst the innocent and virtuous aborigines of America, that thrilled a wide European public. By that time the eighteenth century was history, but the early concept of the noble savage was more popular than it ever had been. The Age of Reason had almost im-

From 1773 to 1777 William Bartram traveled through Florida, Georgia, and the Carolinas. Three of his drawings are reproduced below: a bobolink with a speckled snake and a green tree frog; a golden canna flower with a snail and a pipe given to Bartram by an Indian chief; and two views of a black vulture.
ALL: BRITISH MUSEUM

perceptibly dissolved into the Romantic era with its fresh currents of thought and feeling.

Both the Jardin du Roi and the Chelsea Gardens (more precisely the Physic Garden at Chelsea) originated as gardens for the study of medicinal plants. Botany, like biology and chemistry, contributed to advances in the healing art, although the connection was not always apparent. It was apparent, however—or is now—that as the eighteenth century entered its last quarter, medicine was not meeting the basic needs of an age that prided itself on its enlightened approach to the problems of mankind. For most people the movement of the planets, the hybridization of plants, the combustion of gases, and other such scientific matters were of only the most remote interest. However, the problems of disease and infirmity, of accident and pain, of life and death, indeed, were obviously of immediate and unavoidable concern. Unfortunately, for a large part of the eighteenth century the medical world was still hemmed in by unreliable theories and practices, by mysticism and quackery —an incongruous mixture of faith and reason that was conducive neither to personal nor to public health, not to mention the alleviation of simple physical discomfiture. Voltaire estimated that in his time the average life expectancy was a mere twenty-two years, although he himself lived to be eighty-eight. (As late as 1800 the estimated figure for Americans was only thirty-five years.)

It was difficult for the ordinary person to determine what a really qualified physician was. A practicing doctor was frequently also a drug seller, that is, a purveyor of herbal concoctions or mineral salts that were allegedly curative but often dangerous and rarely inexpensive. Many reputable doctors charged for the prescriptions they had concocted, rather than for their visit, and some got rich from their patented formulas—"Stoughton's Elixir," "Betton's British Oils," Ching's "Worm Lozenges," and the like. Bloodletting long remained a standard panacea, often resorted to with such excessive zeal that patients died of the "cure" by the thousands. In the absence of aseptic surgery and of anesthesia, surgery involved formidable treatment that was reserved for emergencies. (It was only in the last year of the century that Sir Humphrey Davy discovered the anesthetic properties of "laughing gas," or nitrous oxide. Before that the favorite anesthetic had long been drunkenness.) Surgeons were traditionally associated with barbers. In the Prussian army, for example, it was the job of the regimental surgeon to shave officers. In both England and France the two "arts" were formally separated just before the middle of the century. However, in provincial Great Britain the apothecary continued to be the general practitioner, often combining those roles with that of a surgeon. In the American colonies conditions were even less promising. Aside from a handful of European-trained doctors, practitioners were largely men and women grounded only in folk medicine (including Indian cures), who rounded out their income with a variety of nonmedical pursuits; perhaps one in nine had medical degrees. As late as 1786 a directory for New York City contained listings for doctors and surgeons, and along with them surgeon-barbers, surgeon-apothecaries, surgeon-dentists, and physician-apothecaries. Wherever it was practiced, medicine made only limited attempts to treat specific maladies; instead the doctor concerned himself with the state of the patient's "system," which might be classified as "bilious" or "feverish," and treated by the standard prescriptions described above, in addition to purging, sweating, or perhaps electric shock. To all intents there was little specialization as we understand that term today, although serious and successful efforts in that direction were being made.

In spite of that summary list of discouraging details, the second half of the eighteenth century gave increasing evidence that the health of both the individual and the public was showing some signs of improvement, because of advances in medical sciences or for reasons only indirectly related to medicine that can be read in statistics. By mid-century the death rate was declining steadily if slowly in the more advanced areas of Europe, and the birth rate increasing. The unprecedented growth of population coincided with the dawn of the Industrial Revolution and was in a real sense a prerequisite of that revolution, since increased production was dependent upon greater demand for goods from more people. The population of England and Wales doubled between 1750 and 1832, doubling the domestic market for consumer goods available to English industry, which helps to explain why Britain was the first country to industrialize. In turn, the social and economic benefits that might be reaped from preventive medicine and measures to safeguard public health became obvious. The welfare of children in England was a matter of increasing concern, evidenced in advances in midwifery and the establishment of new lying-in hospitals and orphanages. Just before the Industrial Revolution got under way, about 1740, some three-quarters of the newborn died before the age of five. Two generations later such fatalities had been reduced almost by one-half. The approaching new order also meant increasing urbanization, which caused fresh problems for young and old. Improvement acts were adopted in London and other English cities, and these produced significant advances in sewage disposal, as well as in street paving and lighting and other matters vital to the public welfare.

In 1756 Victor Riqueti, Marquis de Mirabeau (father of the French revolutionary leader and disciple of the physiocrats), laid down the principle, remarkably advanced for the time, that the health of the people is a responsibility of the state. However, the greatest single figure in the emerging science of public health was the German physician Johann Peter Frank, who began life as a poor child abandoned at a street door. In 1777 he issued the first installment of his six-volume work, *System Einer Vollstandigen Medicinische Polizei (A Complete System of Medical Policy)*, in which he surveyed all the medical topics affecting the human being from cradle to grave, from childbirth to the disposal of the dead. He dealt with the measures that the community should take to dispose of waste, to guard the purity of water and food, to maintain hygiene in school and factory, and to protect the health of women in industry. He also prescribed the taxation of bachelors, advised on conjugal hygiene, and demanded the education of children in the principles of health. Frank had unusual opportunity as an administrator to put at least some of his pioneering theories into practice. He held appointments at the courts of several German princes and eventually served Czar Alexander I of Russia as personal physician. In addition, he held important posts at five universities, including those in Pavia and Vienna. Among those who esteemed Frank's ideas was Napoleon Bonaparte, who begged him to come to Paris; but the doctor demurred and remained in Vienna. He was a man far in advance of his own time, but a prophet of better times to come for all men.

Nevertheless, public officials were becoming increasingly aware of the im-

John Brown and his followers, called Brunonians, believed that ill health was caused by a maladjustment of physical and emotional stimuli. The Brunonians soon won a reputation as believers in massive doses of drugs, particularly opium. This caricature of John Brown appeared in a magazine during the 1780's.
BRITISH MUSEUM

portance of sanitation and hygiene. Epidemics in general were becoming less frequent and severe than in earlier centuries, although the curse of smallpox, most contagious of diseases, with its high mortality rate and its humiliating disfigurement, remained a horrible menace. As a youth, the revolutionary younger Mirabeau was so shockingly disfigured by the disease that he lost his father's favor. As it often had in the past, the disease reached epidemic proportions in various parts of Europe in the eighteenth century—in London as late as 1766 and 1770. A cure for this recurrent and ravaging plague had top priority in medical circles all through the eighteenth century. In the vanguard of those determined to find such a cure was that remarkable woman Lady Mary Wortley Montagu. Early in the century she spent several years in Constantinople in the official capacity of wife of the English ambassador to Turkey, while adding to her literary stature by writing *Letters from the East* (published after her death). In that city she had observed demonstrations of inoculation for smallpox. She herself had narrowly survived an attack of the disease in 1715. She had apparently not read descriptions of the operation that had appeared a year earlier in *Transactions of the Royal Society*, but she was so convinced of its safety and efficiency that she determined to have it done to her "dear little son" when she could. In March, 1715, she undertook this on her own initiative, which required not only conviction but courage. The embassy surgeon, Dr. Charles Maitland, performed the operation "with so little Pain to [the child], that he did not in the least complain of it." A few days later Lady Mary could write her husband, then at the grand vizier's camp near Sophia, that the boy was "singing and playing, and very impatient for his supper." "I am patriot enough to take pains to bring this useful invention into fashion in England," she wrote in a letter to a friend; "and I should not fail to write to some of our doctors very particularly about it, if I knew any of them that I thought had virtue enough to destroy such a considerable branch of their revenue for the good of mankind. . . . Perhaps, if I live to return, I may, however, have courage to war with them. Upon this occasion admire the heroism in the heart of your friend." Upon the Montagus' return to England she also had her daughter so immunized.

The practice was indeed stoutly resisted by a wide segment of the public as something "unnatural and even impious." A few years after Lady Mary's brave gesture a similar situation arose in Boston, where a smallpox epidemic had broken out in 1721. Eight hundred and fifty persons out of a population of twelve thousand died of the disease that year. The Reverend Cotton Mather had read of the Turkish practice of immunization in the *Transactions of the Royal Society*, which he received regularly, and urged its adoption by local physicians, as did his venerable father Increase Mather. Once again there were protests in which other members of the clergy and physicians joined against this unusual procedure. Young Benjamin Franklin was then setting type for his brother's newspaper, *The New England Courant*, which with wit and spirit opposed the Mathers' support of immunization. However, at Cotton Mather's urging, Zabdiel Boylston, a well-regarded physician, inoculated his son and several other persons, with satisfactory results. Irate mobs attacked his house, and like Mather, he was abused in print. It is said that he had to adopt a disguise in making his rounds; but before the crisis passed, he had treated well over two hundred patients with great success.

Fifteen years later, in Philadelphia, Franklin had occasion to regret what-

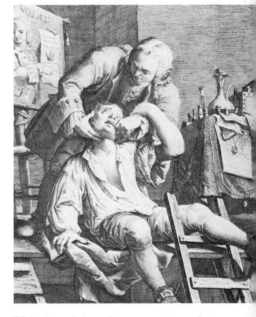

This late-eighteenth-century view of a dentist attempting to extract a tooth in Venice indicates that dentistry was not yet a profession. Most learned their trade through apprenticeship to other dentists or technical craftsmen. Tooth extraction often caused serious injury to the jaws.
BRITISH MUSEUM

ever part he may have played in the campaign against the Mathers and Boylston in their program. Soul of the Enlightenment though he was, Franklin could not bring himself to expose his beloved second son, Francis Folger Franklin, even to the slight peril of inoculation against smallpox, although he knew the fearful havoc made by the disease earlier in Boston and now in Philadelphia. The child died at the age of four in 1736. "I long regretted him bitterly," Franklin later wrote, "and still regret that I had not given him the disease by inoculation."

A detailed study of inoculation published by the eminent English physician Richard Mead in 1747 helped in the long effort to overcome opposition to the practice from both medical and public quarters. Finally, about 1775, another Englishman, Edward Jenner, began to investigate forms of cowpox as possible preventive agents against smallpox. He had recently completed medical studies with John Hunter, a noted surgeon, and had then prepared for exhibit the zoological specimens brought back by Banks from Cook's first voyage. The final breakthrough for Jenner came in 1796 when he inoculated an eight-year-old boy with matter taken from cowpox blisters on the hands of a milkmaid, and subsequently with smallpox. The dreaded disease did not develop. Two years later Jenner published the results of his work, containing the announcement of the discovery of vaccination. Even then, however, this method of controlling the great scourge of the century did not gain immediate widespread acceptance.

In 1796, also, the German physician Samuel Hahnemann formally announced the results of his long experiments with the quinine-yielding Peruvian bark, cinchona, which he had noted produced in healthy persons symptoms resembling those of the disease for which the bark was used as a cure.

A doctor and his assistant, binding swollen legs, visit a patient suffering from gout. The doctor inspects a glass that contains the devil, symbolizing gout's main cause, an excess of uric acid.

From that came the system he named homeopathy, based on the principle that the way to attack some diseases is by administering small quantities of drugs which, in larger doses, cause in the healthy symptoms similar to the diseases to be guarded against.

The evolution of the reputable doctor from the barber-surgeon of earlier days was due in large part to the increasingly high level of university medical training. At the beginning of the eighteenth century Padua and Leyden were among the leading centers in this field. While at Leyden the great physician and teacher and a pioneer in chemical medicine Hermann Boerhaave helped to organize a school at Vienna. Leyden was also instrumental in establishing a medical school and hospital at the University of Edinburgh in 1729. Because of the rapid growth of its reputation, Edinburgh soon attracted aspiring physicians on both sides of the Atlantic. (At an early date its curriculum was broadened to include the study of mental illness.) Alexander Monro, generally considered the founder of the school, was its first systematic teacher of medicine and surgery.

With the advantage of greater opportunities to study anatomy, comparative anatomy, physiology, and pathology, surgery was gradually achieving dignity as a special branch of medicine, ranking with the older branches. An Academy of Surgery was established at Paris in 1731, an institution that set high standards from the start. In London and Edinburgh private dissecting rooms and anatomical theaters were instituted. The most notable of these was the school of Dr. William Hunter in London. Hunter was physician to Queen Charlotte Sophie and the first professor of anatomy at the Royal Academy. His more famous younger brother, John, began to lecture on surgery in 1773, but spent much of his career in the British army. In 1776 he became surgeon to George III. It was he above all who, with his distinguished reputation, is given credit for converting the trade of barber-surgeon into a specialized science. "More than any other man he helped to make us gentlemen," remarked another surgeon in a eulogy delivered a century later.

During the revolutionary generation, that is to say, from 1758 to 1788, sixty-three Americans were graduated from the University of Edinburgh. Among the most famous were John Morgan and Benjamin Rush. Working in conjunction with the College of Philadelphia, Morgan set up the pioneer American medical school there in 1765, and both he and Rush were leading members of the faculty. By 1768 the school had graduated ten bachelors. Morgan had also studied in London, Paris, and Italy and was elected to the Royal Society. In Philadelphia he wrote a paper, the first of its kind in America, in which he recommended the separation of drug selling from the practice of medicine, and the separation of both from surgery. He also proposed the establishment of liberal studies for medical students. During the Revolution, from 1775–77, he was director-general of hospitals and physician in chief of the American army, but his program of exacting reforms made him enemies through whose influence he was summarily dismissed from both posts. Subsequently, Congress completely cleared Morgan of all the charges that had been brought against him and he was further exonerated by George Washington.

Rush was a man of many parts. He, too, served in the revolutionary army as surgeon general, and he, too, was removed from his command, for ill-advisedly joining a cabal that sought to remove Washington as commander in chief. Nevertheless, for the rest he enjoyed a distinguished career in and

English country doctor Edward Jenner, seen at right in a portrait by James Northcote, happened to overhear a farm girl boasting that she could not get smallpox because she had had cowpox. That remark spurred him to find a way to rid humanity of that terrible scourge.
NATIONAL PORTRAIT GALLERY, LONDON

out of his professional field. Aside from his scientific pursuits and his medical practice, in 1776–77 he was a member of the Second Continental Congress and a signer of the Declaration of Independence; he was active in prison reform and strongly urged the abolition of slavery and capital punishment; and he recommended broadening educational opportunities for women and the poor. In 1786 he established the first free dispensary in the United States, and he wrote the first systematic treatment of mental disorders. It was through his mediation late in his life that his two old friends John Adams and Thomas Jefferson were reconciled after both had retired from active political lives in the course of which they had often had bitter disagreements. And withal he remained a generally esteemed doctor and teacher. He was, inevitably, a friend of his fellow Philadelphian Benjamin Franklin. To our everlasting loss Rush never fulfilled his intention of writing out and publishing a volume of Franklin's conversations. Had he done so he might have been remembered for this above all else.

In general, the Revolution had a disastrous effect on American colleges. Indirectly, however, the war led to the establishment of a medical faculty at Harvard College by John Warren of Boston. After his graduation from Harvard in 1771, Warren studied medicine privately, taking time out to participate in the Boston Tea Party of 1773, then serving in the medical department of the revolutionary army until he started private practice in Boston, in 1777. (His older brother Joseph, also a doctor, had dispatched Paul Revere to Lexington to warn of the approaching British troops and then, on June 17, 1775, was killed by enemy fire in the battle of Bunker Hill.) Shortly after the Revolution he helped to establish a medical school at Harvard, where he served as professor of anatomy and surgery. He lectured on cadavers, for which the revolutionary army hospital, located in a Boston pasture, provided the specimens. The dissection of corpses aroused as much public opposition as had smallpox inoculation and he prudently conducted his anatomical course behind locked doors. (A few years later the need of corpses for dissection by students at King's College in New York, later Columbia University, led to grave robbing, which fired public indignation to the point where the militia had to be called out to quell the ensuing riots. John Jay was among the injured in the disorder.)

Underlying the many advances that were being made in the sciences was the development of more sophisticated and accurate instruments and the refinement of mathematical calculations. Early in the century Anton van Leeuwenhoek devised microscopes with which he conducted his revealing investigations in physiology. As a draper's apprentice he had used lenses in examining cloth, an experience that led him to make lenses of his own. He assembled more than 247 microscopes, some of which magnified objects 270 times. By means of such superior instruments he was able to provide the first complete descriptions of bacteria, protozoa, and red blood corpuscles. Early in the century also the Swede Celsius, the French physician Réaumur, and the Danzig physician Fahrenheit produced accurate thermometers, so essential to clinical practice, among other things.

With the improvement of telescopes, much larger worlds were brought into view. Nothing quite like Herschel's gigantic reflector telescope, mentioned earlier in this chapter, had ever been seen before. The English novelist Fanny (Frances) Burney, whose diaries recorded so many interesting details of life in the eighteenth century, left an engaging account of her visit to Herschel's home to see the instrument. "This great and extraordinary man received us with almost open arms . . . ," she reported with undisguised amazement. "I took a walk . . . through his telescope and it held me quite upright, and without the least inconvenience; so would it have done had I been dressed in feathers and a bell-hoop—such is its circumference." Few young ladies have ever been privileged to take a walk under such unique circumstances. Through that immense tube with its four-foot-wide mirror Herschel drew within his

Scottish physician William Hunter headed a school and museum of anatomy where many noted doctors, including his brother John, were trained. Rowlandson depicted the London school in this cartoon.

John Ledyard, an American who sailed with Captain Cook in 1776, was inspired to continue looking for the northwest passage. He did not succeed, but his hike through Europe and across Siberia was one of the most remarkable journeys in history. When he died in Cairo, Ledyard was making plans to explore Africa's unknown interior.

vision the Milky Way, not as a cloud of glowing matter but, with the new magnification, as an almost unimaginably great aggregation and succession of single luminous entities.

Astronomy not only fired the imagination of men, it also loosened the purse strings of state treasuries. Observatories were built at Leyden early in the century and at Uppsala some years later. (Two had already been constructed at Nuremburg and Greenwich in the preceding century.) Not long before the American Revolution, the Pennsylvania House of Representatives gave the American Philosophical Society one hundred pounds toward the construction of an observatory on the lawn of the State House together with a grant of land "forever free from taxation" as the site of a library and museum. Small planetariums and orreries abounded, not only in institutions of learning and studios of professional scientists, but as status symbols in parlors of the wealthy. The orrery, a mechanical model of the solar system named after a Scot, Charles Boyle, fourth earl of Orrery, was featured in a well-known painting by Joseph Wright (see page 225), as one indication of the popular enthusiasm for astronomical studies.

Newton's work on the telescope had been a great stimulus to those studies. He was one of many scientists whose attention had been directed to the moon. In the mid-eighteenth century a German scientist published lunar tables that were of great aid in the determination of longitude at sea. As early as 1713 the British government had offered £20,000 for the invention of a satisfactory marine chronometer that could be depended upon for establishing longitude at sea. Determining latitude by astronomical observation was no longer a problem, but setting longitude was a different and crucial matter. During a thirty-year period beginning in 1691, the British had lost five naval squadrons because of the lack of satisfactory instruments for this purpose. In addition to accurate lunar measurements a precise chronometer was required for computing the difference between local time on shipboard and standard time at a fixed meridian, recorded in tables of reference—a chronometer that would not be affected by changes of temperature or the motions of the sea. It was more than fifty years later before the reward was collected by John Harrison, a Yorkshire clockmaker. The fifth chronometer he made passed the government's standard for accuracy when it was tried on a voyage to Jamaica in 1761–62.

Captain Cook used a chronometer on his second voyage in 1772–75, during which he ranged from the ice fields of the Antarctic to Tahiti, the New Hebrides, and New Caledonia. (By strictly observing newly developed principles of hygiene and by dietary controls, Cook was able to limit loss of life on this three-year expedition to a single crew member.) In 1776 Cook set forth again on his last voyage. He sought a passage around North America from the Pacific Ocean. This he did not find, but he did succeed in charting the western coast of North America as far north as the Bering Strait. With him on this trip were William Bligh, later master of the *Bounty*, and young George Vancouver, who was subsequently to make a more detailed survey of the northern Pacific coast of America—and to establish the fact that there was no northwest passage from the Atlantic to the Pacific. The expedition ended tragically for Cook in Hawaii, where he was murdered by natives of the island.

With Cook also was John Ledyard of Connecticut, a corporal of marines, who had joined the crew just before the Declaration of Independence was issued and whose imagination was kindled by what he saw on the journey. When he and his companions landed at Nootka Sound in what was to become Vancouver Island, Ledyard was "painfully afflicted" with nostalgia at the sight of the American coast, he later wrote, although it was "more than 2,000 miles distant from the nearest part of New England." However, he noticed that the Indians of the region, who had never before seen a white man, nevertheless carried European-made knives and bracelets. "No part of America," he concluded, "is without some sort of commercial intercourse, immediate or remote."

After his return to America (on the east coast this time) Ledyard made plans to revisit the Pacific Northwest and make his fortune dealing in the valuable furs that could be procured there from the natives for a few pence worth of iron and sold at an enormous profit in the Orient. Unable to find financial backing in America, Ledyard went to Europe, where he fared no better, although he talked over his plans with John Paul Jones, Benjamin Franklin, Thomas Jefferson, and others.

Finally, encouraged by Jefferson, Ledyard decided to make his point by walking back home via Siberia and Kamchatka to a port where he could board a ship for Nootka Sound, and from there continue overland to the east coast. He had actually reached Yakutsk in distant Siberia, with "but two long frozen stages" between him and his first main objective, when Catherine of Russia had him brought back, putting an end to his dreams and to the most heroic hike in history. He died in Cairo the next year, leaving for other men (such as John Jacob Astor) the very practical business of making fortunes in the northwest fur trade.

Meanwhile, exploration of the heavens continued to attract the interest of astronomers and scholars of all nations, and of high-minded men of state. In 1761 and 1769 the transit of Venus across the sun prompted the governments of Great Britain and several Continental nations to send expeditions to various parts of the globe to measure the distance between the earth and the sun. In 1769 there were 151 observers posted at 77 localities, among them members of Captain Cook's first expedition on Tahiti. The occasion turned out to be a particularly important one for American science. Under the sponsorship of the American Philosophical Society the colonies participated in this early example of international scientific cooperation. David Rittenhouse of Pennsylvania and John Winthrop of Massachusetts were among the American astronomers who joined the vigil, and the results of their measurements of the transit (especially those of Rittenhouse) were among the most accurate recorded up to that time. Excellent weather conditions in America on the day of the transit, June 3, 1769, favored their observations. Both men were amateur astronomers, but their skill in building and manipulating the devices they used contributed largely to the success of their operations. As one consequence of their accomplishments, the international reputation of The American Philosophical Society was justly enhanced.

Winthrop was the great great-grandnephew of John Winthrop, who was the first governor of the Massachusetts Bay Colony, himself one of America's first scientists and industrialists. (On New Year's Day, 1641, he resolved to give up his habit of inventing things, in a moment of reflection having doubted whether any technological improvements he could devise would help him, or any one else, to salvation.) The later Winthrop was one of the first American

David Rittenhouse, a Philadelphia clockmaker by trade, also emerged as a talented astronomer and instrument-maker. He surveyed, with his own instruments, the boundaries of several states and part of the Mason-Dixon Line. In 1777 Rittenhouse became the treasurer of Pennsylvania, a position he held for twelve years.
FREE LIBRARY OF PHILADELPHIA

astronomers worthy of the name. He is also credited with having built the first laboratory for experimental physics in the colonies, in 1746, and it was he who instituted courses in differential and integral calculus in the Harvard curriculum.

But it is the name of his younger colleague, Rittenhouse, that is most closely associated with the triumph of 1769. He was the great-grandson of the Prussian immigrant William Rittenhouse, a clergyman-industrialist who in 1690 built the first paper mill in America and who in 1703 became bishop of the first Mennonite church in this country. The Rittenhouses were among the earliest settlers of Germantown, Pennsylvania, and David was born there in 1732. His love of mathematics, manifest at an early age, was reflected in his first adult enterprise, the making of clocks and mathematical instruments. He also became a skilled surveyor. In 1763 he laid out an area along the boundary between Pennsylvania and Maryland, and did it so well (with instruments of his own making) that his results became a permanent record. When the proprietors of these colonies brought over the English astronomer Charles Mason to survey the whole of a disputed common boundary, Mason and his partner Jeremiah Dixon accepted Rittenhouse's findings and incorporated them in their famous Mason-Dixon Line, which they established between 1763 and 1767.

In 1768 Rittenhouse built an observatory near his home, and about the same time he constructed what is thought to have been the first telescope made in America. Both were put to excellent use a year later in the observation of Venus. (The Pennsylvania legislature donated the sum of £200 to this enterprise.) He built more telescopes and was the first to use cross hairs in their focus, using spider webs for the purpose, to improve the accuracy of measurements. In 1770 he finished work on another major project, an orrery intended to incorporate all that was then known about the solar system. (It became the property of Princeton University.) He made a second orrery that was purchased for what had become the University of Pennsylvania. A representation of it was incorporated into the seal of the state of Pennsylvania. (Both celebrated instruments displayed the planetary movements "for a period of 5,000 years, either forward or backward.")

During the Revolutionary War he supervised the manufacture of arms and munitions and designed a chain intended to protect harbors against invasion fleets. In the final years of the war he served as professor of astronomy at the University of Pennsylvania and with the peace he became treasurer of Pennsylvania and then, reluctantly, first director of the United States Mint. His versatility led him in numerous directions. He constructed a barometer and a metallic thermometer, and kept detailed meteorological records. He made a reading glass and a pair of spectacles for George Washington and in 1791 succeeded Franklin as president of the American Philsophical Society. "As an artist he has exhibited as great proof of mechanical genius as the world has ever produced," Jefferson wrote. "He has not made a world, but he approached nearer its Maker than any man from the creation to this day." At the time of his death near the close of the eighteenth century, it seemed that in the pattern of Rittenhouse's scientific accomplishments and intellectual interests America had produced "a brilliant child of Newton," whose discoveries had a century earlier laid the foundation of scientific and philosophical thought of the Age of Enlightenment.

An eighteenth-century allegory on science

FRONTIERS OF SCIENCE

Isaac Newton's *Principia* captured the imagination of the public more completely than any scientific revelation before or since. Within a century after its publication in 1687, science had become a kind of religion among European intellectuals. As knowledge increased, so did professionalism and specialization. Naturalists collected and classified thousands of plants and animals. Chemists explained combustion, the nature of air, the composition of water. Physicists experimented with electricity. Astronomers revealed the universe basically as we know it today. To the world in 1776 it seemed that science could provide the answers to all questions worth asking.

A NEW DISCIPLINE

The progress made in the seventeenth century had engendered confidence in the practical value of science, and the eighteenth century opened in an atmosphere of optimism. Most European rulers were supporting scientific academies, where students could work in relative peace with few financial worries, in the hope that the research would yield useful military or social advances. Still, the pursuit of science was little more than a gentleman's hobby. Even Isaac Newton had not devoted himself exclusively to mathematics and physics, but had studied theology, history, and alchemy as well. Few universities included science in their curriculums, and most students were forced to rely on books tucked away in school libraries (above, the Oxford library) and tutors. As the century progressed, universities—first in Germany and Italy—added science to their curriculums. Information was exchanged informally at the coffee houses in London and the salons in Paris. Science became fashionable, even a craze; countless amateurs adopted scientific hobbies. Oliver Goldsmith, visiting France, wrote: "I have seen as bright a circle of beauties at the chemical lectures of Rouelle as gracing the court of Versailles." Ladies and gentlemen bravely tackled Buffon's forty-four volume *Histoire Naturelle*, or peered into telescopes, sometimes through the wrong end, as in the 1750 engraving opposite, or rubbed iron rods with cloth and gave each other electric shocks. Astronomy and mathematics were beyond the level of most laymen, but amateurs could, and did, contribute to physics, chemistry, and medicine.

KUNSTSAMMLUNG DER VESTE. COBURG

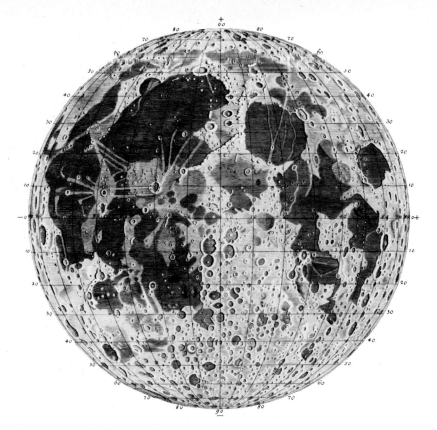

Eighteenth-century astronomers concentrated their studies on the solar system. William Herschel's discovery of Uranus in 1781 doubled the diameter of the known solar system. Appointed court astronomer by George III the following year, Herschel gave up a promising career in music, and devoted himself full time to scientific research. He built the reflecting telescope seen below (it was forty feet long with a four-foot aperture), the largest then in existence. The remarkably accurate map of the moon, above, was published in the memoirs of German scientist Johann Mayer in 1775. Model solar systems, called orreries, were fashionable in wealthy homes. Joseph Wright's *The Orrery* (opposite) shows a family fascinated by the workings of astronomy.

UNLIMITED

HORIZONS

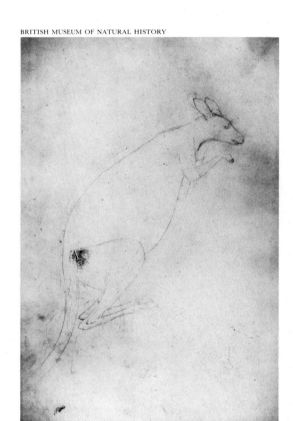

The three voyages led by Captain James Cook, and co-sponsored by the Royal Society and the admiralty, charted much of the Pacific and enriched botany and zoology with hundreds of new specimens and volumes of research. As the purpose of the first voyage (1768-71) was to observe the transit of Venus, explore and chart the islands of the Pacific, and "observe the Nature of the Soil and the Products thereof, the Beasts and fowls that inhabit or frequent it . . . ," Cook's crew included a number of eminent scientists and artists. The kangaroo (above right) was among a host of new discoveries sketched by artist Sidney Parkinson. On the second voyage (1772-75) William Hodges painted Cook's two ships in Matavi Bay, Tahiti (opposite). Descriptions of Tahiti led to its idealization as an island paradise, peopled with the innocent children of nature. The purpose of the second voyage, however, was primarily scientific; above is a sketch of the Forster father-and-son natural science team. Cook's third voyage (1776-79), which included exploration of the North Pacific, ended when he was killed by natives in Hawaii.

CAPTAIN

COOK'S

TOURS

ANDERSON. *Captain Cook's Travels, London, 1784*

MORE PACIFIC
EXPLORATIONS

Exploration of the Pacific was considerably more purposeful than earlier voyages of discovery. Government-sponsored expeditions had scientific, as well as imperial, goals. In 1764 an experienced French soldier and seaman, Louis Antoine de Bougainville, established a colony in the Falkland Islands (opposite bottom). But Bougainville, himself a mathematician and member of London's Royal Society, was primarily interested in promoting French science. Accompanied by naturalists and astronomers, he commanded the first French voyage around the world (1766–69). (Bougainville, the largest of the Solomon Islands, and the bougainvillea vine are named for him.) In 1785 Louis XVI asked Admiral Jean de La Pérouse to lead an expedition to the Pacific. La Pérouse discovered a strait between Hokkaido and Sakhalin Islands and studied the sculptured heads on Easter Island (above) before he and his entire crew were shipwrecked off New Hebrides in 1788. The following year Spain commissioned an Italian, Alessandro Malaspina, to lead an expedition to the Pacific. While searching for a northwest passage along the Alaskan coast, Malaspina and his men investigated an ancient Indian burial ground (opposite top).

CLASSIFYING NATURE

Exploration led to the discovery of thousands of previously unknown plants and animals. Carolus Linnaeus, a Swedish doctor, devised a system of classifying the flora and the fauna. Greatly aided by microscopes with compound lenses, such as the rococo one at the left, he identified 12,000 species of living things. Linnaeus developed the system, but Georges Buffon popularized natural history with his brilliantly written *Histoire Naturelle*, a compendium of data interspersed with his own speculations and theories, some of which anticipated Darwin. Buffon was the superintendent of the *Jardin des Plantes* from 1739 until his death in 1788. The *Jardin* sponsored research in zoology, chemistry, and astronomy, as well as botany. The view seen above shows the seedling garden; the building on the left housed delicate plants and experiments; the frames on either side were for seedlings of tropical plants and those in front for bulbs and tubers from the Cape of Good Hope. The "new" plants opposite were discovered on Captain Cook's first voyage by its leading naturalist, Joseph Banks. *Banksia Serrata*, at left, was found in Australia in 1770; the blossom at far right was found growing on trees near Rio de Janiero.

232

THE BARTRAMS
OF PHILADELPHIA

The British colonies in America contained innumerable plants never before seen in Europe. English scientists and rich amateur naturalists coveted these plants for their botanical gardens. A self-taught botanist from Philadelphia, John Bartram traveled all over the colonies collecting, labeling, and packing plants for export to Europe. Linnaeus considered Bartram the finest botanist in the world. William Bartram carried on his father's work and added his artistic and literary talents to it. Dr. John Fothergill, an eminent London physician interested in natural history, employed William from 1766 to 1776 to collect plants and seeds for his botanical garden. Bartram not only collected specimens, but kept an extensive journal and made numerous sketches of plants and animals. At left is Bartram's painting of the spotted turtle and the milk snake. Joseph Banks purchased all of Bartram's illustrations in 1780. With the publication of *Bartram's Travels* some years later, William Bartram also impressed European intellectuals with his descriptive prose.

HARNESSING ELECTRICITY

Electrical experiments fascinated the public. One man amused Louis XV and his court by shocking 700 monks so that they all jumped into the air at the same time. Benjamin Franklin's experiment in 1752 (opposite, a Benjamin West painting) proved that lightning was, indeed, electricity. An Italian anatomy professor, Luigi Galvani, asked, in experiments seen below, why dead frogs' legs contracted violently when the nerve was touched by a brass or copper wire and the muscle by an iron wire in contact with the first. He erred in deciding that the metals conducted "animal electricity" already present in the frog; Volta later proved that contact between the two metals produced the charge. The search for electricity's practical application yielded very little. The engraving above, from a magazine called *Electrical Medicine* (1766), suggested electric shock to treat rheumatism or paralysis.

GALVANI. *De Viribus Electricitatis In Motu Musculari Commentarius, 1791*

THE MEDICAL ARENA

Eighteenth-century medicine slowly came to reflect the age's growing reliance on scientific methods, initiating trends which subsequently made it a true science. In 1729 the University of Edinburgh opened the first hospital and faculty of medicine in Britain. More medical schools were opened in Britain as well as Europe. Medical school curriculums included surgery, heretofore practiced by uneducated barbers. Anatomy won acceptance as a science. Opposite, in a 1775 painting by Zoffany, an anatomy instructor lectures to the Royal College of Physicians with the aid of models. For the first time the importance of studying symptoms and case histories was recognized. Traditional cures, such as bloodletting, came into question. Pharmacists, like the ones in France seen at left, worked more closely with doctors. Serious research into contagious diseases, such as smallpox, was undertaken. For centuries the Chinese had protected themselves against smallpox by blowing the powdered scabs that fell from infected people into the nostrils of healthy ones. It was common practice in Europe for much of the eighteenth century to prick the skin of a healthy person in three different places with a needle that had been pushed in a fresh smallpox pustule. Those who survived this process, known as variolation, were immune. In 1795 Edward Jenner introduced a safe and effective vaccine (below, a drawing that appeared in Russia to urge the people to protect themselves by vaccination).

BY KIND PERMISSION OF SIR ALFRED BEIT— PHOTO: JOHN WEBB (BROMPTON STUDIO)

AN EMERGING
PROFESSION

At the beginning of the eighteenth century pursuit of science was a hobby for rich dilettantes (opposite, a detail from a painting of Bonnier de la Mosson and his impressive collection of scientific objects); as time went on, it became a profession based upon observation and experimentation. Chemists were the greatest empiricists of all, yet by the middle of the century they still thought water, fire, and air were individual elements. Then the years of weighing, measuring, and testing began to pay off. Henry Cavendish isolated hydrogen, and discovered it was lighter than air in 1776. Joseph Priestley isolated oxygen in 1774, but it took Antoine Lavoisier (below, with his wife in a portrait by Jacques Louis David) to appreciate the significance of Priestley's discovery. He proved that water was a compound of hydrogen and oxygen. Further tests with oxygen by Lavoisier showed that fire results when oxygen unites rapidly with matter. In a famous experiment in 1776, Lavoisier combined a measured volume of oxygen with mercury and later recovered the same volume by heating the mercuric oxide; this and other similar tests led to his conclusion that matter cannot be created or destroyed, the basis of modern chemistry.

BULLOZ

DESIGNS FOR THE FUTURE

The scientific revolution held the promise of spectacular changes in the way people traveled. With the successful launching of the first hot-air balloon by the Montgolfier brothers in 1783, a ballooning craze swept Europe. The painting opposite depicts the first crossing of the English Channel in a balloon on January 7, 1785. It was manned by an American loyalist, Dr. John Jeffries, and a Frenchman, Jean Pierre Blanchard. They left from Dover, but were soon so threatened by the balloon's fast descent that they began to throw everything overboard, including their clothes. They avoided final disaster by emptying their bladders shortly before landing, nearly frozen, some twelve miles from Calais. Earthbound inventors were challenged to find a way to use the steam engine to power a boat. The design seen below, drawn by American John Fitch, received a patent from Louis XVI in 1791, the same year that Fitch received an American patent. Fitch ran steamboats more than two thousand passenger-paying miles in America, but his boats lost money and he could not raise the funds to refine his design.

THE TASTE

"*This search and study of the history of the mind, ought not to be confined to one art only. It is by the analogy that one art bears to another, that many things are ascertained, which either were but faintly seen, or, perhaps, would not have been discovered at all, if the inventor had not received the first hints from the practices of a sister art on a similar occasion.*"

Joshua Reynolds in *Discourses on Art*, 1776

To the understanding eye, the prints and paintings, the music, the drama, the sculpture, and the architecture of the eighteenth century are varying expressions of the same attitudes and aspirations that have been noticed in other aspects of the social and intellectual activity of the time —with all the conceits and convictions, the follies and accomplishments, and the ambiguities, contradictions, and insights that were such vital phases of that changing world. We can also find a growing cosmopolitanism and at the same time a burgeoning romantic spirit as artists in all mediums looked toward faraway places and distant times—and to the world of nature—in search of new truths and fresh inspirations. So much was true at least for the Continent, the British Isles, and England's North American colonies. Most of the rest of the world was not yet prepared to question the permanent value of old, fixed, and indigenous habits of expression.

We are undoubtedly better able to see the broad significance of the arts of the period of 1776 than men of the time could have done. Thanks to the wide-ranging eye of the camera and the proliferation of photomechanical reproductions both in black and white and in color (and thanks also to the faithful re-creations of music of the past in concert hall and on high-fidelity discs and tapes), we can get reasonably accurate impressions of more works of art than would have been possible even for the most determined and fortunate traveler two centuries ago. It is doubtful that any young gentleman on the Grand

OF THE TIMES

Tour, however assiduous and privileged he may have been, would have seen the variety of contemporary evidence that is presented by the illustrations in this book, limited as these must be for practical reasons. Nor would he, obviously, have been as aware, as we are today, of the relative and lasting importance to be found in that variety.

Even before the eighteenth century dawned, French culture had won leadership in most parts of Europe. Louis XIV had planned the great complex of buildings and gardens of Versailles to astonish the whole world with its grandeur. It was meant to be, and indeed was, an inimitable declaration of the "Sun King"'s eminence, an eminence no European monarch had attained since the days of Rome's greatness. For many decades Versailles remained the supreme model which envious monarchs of other states sought to emulate with their own extravagant constructions. "Little Versailles" sprang up everywhere, from London to Naples and from Madrid to St. Petersburg. In 1716 Peter the Great lured the French architect Jean Baptiste Leblond from Paris to construct the great country palace of Peterhof; with its formal gardens and flowers it was an impressive translation of Versailles into Russian splendor. Peter's daughter Elizabeth brought an Italian-born architect who had studied in France to Russia to build the Winter Palace at St. Petersburg and the summer palace called Tsarkoye Selo just outside that city. Maria Theresa completed the huge imperial residence at Schönbrunn, which Emperor Leopold I

Purchased by Louis XIV in 1662, the Gobelins Manufactory in Paris produced tapestries, furniture, and jewelry for the royal family and for other customers throughout Europe. After 1700 Gobelins specialized in tapestries; above, a detail.
MALTA GOVERNMENT TOURIST BOARD

had conceived as a palace that would surpass Versailles in size and magnificence. It failed to reach that ambitious goal, but its vast scale and spacious park amply advertised Hapsburg pretentions—and bore witness to the control of state finances by the absolute monarchy for its own glorification. The list of such imitations of Versailles' glory is all but endless.

The glory of Versailles was not simply in the magnitude of its conception. At the command of Louis XIV, or with his assent, and under his lavish patronage, his very capable minister Jean Baptiste Colbert had established royal academies (and reinvigorated existing ones), which gave direction to the arts as well as to science and letters. The Academy of Architecture was founded in 1671. Colbert reorganized the Academy of Paintings and Sculpture, an institution that would control the character of French art for two centuries to come. He also founded an academy at Rome where French students of the arts were to be integrated into a system of tutelage and performance under royal patronage. Under Colbert's command, indeed, the arts became virtually a national industry and, in effect, a vast propaganda machine for the French crown. And Versailles was the first great showplace for those enterprises.

The Gobelins Manufactory was a royal establishment that was commissioned to supply, in addition to its celebrated tapestries, all the other furnishings and decoration required by the king for his various palaces. Here was produced everything from hardware and bric-a-brac to the richest furniture and the most elaborate mural paintings. The director of the Gobelins, the celebrated Charles Le Brun, who had a genius for organization, was charged with the total decoration of Versailles and of other large projects that included the magnificent system of fountains and the fêtes and fireworks that celebrated special occasions. As it has often been said, Le Brun virtually created the Louis XIV style, a style of almost overwhelming splendor and of a unity unequaled in the history of art. It was under such circumstances that France assumed leadership in the arts on the Continent—a pre-eminence that was not challenged until the last quarter of the eighteenth century when England's claims were voiced with new authority.

French had become firmly established as the language of international diplomacy. It was also the dominant language of European scholarship, culture, and polite society. "The French language has succeeded the Latin and Greek languages," one writer observed as early as 1697, ". . . it has become so general that it is spoken today throughout almost the whole of Europe and those who frequent society feel a kind of shame if they do not know it." Almost a full century later one Frenchman confessed, "We entertained so high an idea of ourselves that we looked upon foreign idioms as the jargon of barbarians: accordingly we neglected to learn them" (At one point Voltaire expressed alarm at the corruption of French taste by Shakespeare's writings.) Frederick the Great, as earlier remarked, would speak nothing but French unless compelled to by circumstances. In 1743 he ordered that the learned theses presented to the Academy of Sciences at Berlin be published in French. As late as 1794 this academy awarded its highest prize to a discourse on the "Universality of the French Language."

During the middle years of the eighteenth century a wave of Gallomania swept over Russia. Catherine the Great, for example, commissioned the French sculptor Etienne Falconet to model a colossal bronze equestrian statue of Peter the Great, to be placed in Senate Square as a memorial to that emperor. This monument was the epitome of imperial Russian sculpture and the model for a vast body of civic statuary which, as one historian has observed, "encouraged the pretentions of one ruler in the guise of commemorating another." (Falconet enjoyed the favor of the empress for a dozen years before quarreling with her and her ministers, at which point he quit Russia in a huff and returned to Paris.) Peter himself had visited Paris shortly after the death of Louis XIV (partly to negotiate a marriage between his son and the daughter of the French regent, the duke of Orleans, or, failing that, between the czar's daughter and the boy-king Louis XV—marriages which proved to be non-negotiable), and he was enchanted by what he saw. The tapestry workshops at the Gobelins fascinated him, and he engaged skilled artisans to establish similar manufactories in Russia. He made repeated visits to Versailles, Fontainebleau, and St. Cloud to study the art and architecture of those palaces and their gardens. During his stay he recruited craftsmen of every kind to take back to St. Petersburg. Catherine's consuming interest in French culture has already been described. It remains to note that French influence pervaded not only the atelier and the school, the court and the parlor, but the boudoir and the kitchen as well.

There were some pockets of resistance to that influence. The secular and skeptical attitudes of the French were distrusted in Spain, where the Church played such an important and reactionary role in the dissemination of culture. Italy with its rich historic legacy could afford to rest on the dignity of its own accomplishments; in many ways, indeed, it could well serve as a school for French artists, as for the English, American, and others who came to pay tribute to and to learn from its venerated treasures of antiquity and the Renaissance. England, as ever, had its own insular traditions. A large proportion of the Englishmen who visited France returned home with an unchanged conviction that their native land enjoyed a civilization superior to that of their neighbors across the Channel. The French themselves were not altogether indifferent to the amenities of life in England. One Frenchman, making the Grand Tour in an opposite direction to the usual one, described England as "the finest country in Europe, for variety and verdure, for beauty and richness, for rural neatness and elegance—a feast for the sight, a charm for the mind." However, it seems evident that by early in the eighteenth century Paris was the most sophisticated and cosmopolitan city of Europe. Here the arts flourished in a variety and with a vigor unmatched elsewhere; and here was an ample body of amateurs, those men and women of considerable cultivation who understood art and often wrote critically on the subject, who collected art and encouraged artists with their patronage, demanding a high standard of performance in return. "From Paris," Leopold Mozart advised his young son Wolfgang, urging him to go there, "the name and fame of a great talent resounds through the whole world. There the nobility treat men of genius with the greatest deference, esteem, and courtesy; there you will see a refined manner of life, which forms an astonishing contrast to the coarseness of our German courtiers and their ladies. . . ."

For a score of years around the middle of the century France had no more discriminating, active, and influential patron of the arts than the Marquise de Pompadour, sometime actual and long titular mistress of King Louis XV. After she had been replaced in the royal bed by other paramours, until her death, Pompadour remained the king's confidante and adviser. With affection

With the active support of Madame de Pompadour, a royal porcelain factory was opened at Vincennes in 1745. After the factory was moved to a chateau in 1756, it was called Sèvres. The exquisite figurine of Madame de Pompadour, above, is a product of the famed Sèvres works.
WADSWORTH ATHENEUM, HARTFORD, CONN.

and gratitude he squandered a large fortune upon her, and this, in turn, she used in profligate measure to encourage and improve the arts. Hardly had she been installed as the royal favorite when she established a little theater in her private apartments, and there the proudest members of the nobility competed with one another for the smallest parts. From that enterprise she proceeded upon a career of organizing and directing the arts of the nation.

Pompadour might well be called the Colbert of her day. With her approval, the Gobelins, Beauvais, and Aubusson factories continued to receive the royal patronage that enabled them to produce tapestries of unexcelled quality. At her instigation the porcelain factory at Sèvres, just outside Paris, was established to match the exquisite fabrications of the Meissen works in Germany. Ambassadors and rulers throughout the world, from Turkey to China, received presents of Sèvres from Louis XV; and among the large orders which poured in from foreign countries was one from Catherine the Great for a service of 744 pieces in *bleu turquoise*, for which she paid a formidable sum (328,000 livres). Pompadour patronized and won commissions for the foremost painters, sculptors, and architects of her day. At her suggestion some of the paintings from the king's collection were hung in the Luxembourg palace. It was the first free public exhibition of them ever to be held. She would have liked to transform the *grand galerie* of the Louvre into a museum of the principal paintings from the royal collections, but in this she was thwarted by her enemies at court. Not wishing to see her popularity grow in any way, they objected, saying that it would strip Versailles of its treasures—and that it would be an unwise concession to the public to enable them to see pictures which were by custom reserved for the king and the nobility. She had plans for the completion of the Louvre itself and for renovating areas of Paris, but these were also blocked by the same inimical factions.

However, it was at the height of Pompadour's influence that the plans were drawn up for the Place de la Concorde, which when completed twenty years later would become—and remain—possibly the most celebrated urban space in the world. Meanwhile, with her all but unlimited budget she frequented the shops of craftsmen along the fashionable rue Saint Honoré and bought, there and elsewhere, such an abundance of treasures that upon her death it took two notaries an entire year to catalogue her possessions.

Across the Channel the English monarchs never encouraged such purposeful support or patronage of the arts. It might be said that any encouragement that was provided was generated in spite of the House of Hanover rather than because of it and was undertaken by the aristocracy and a middle class that was steadily gaining importance. Neither George I nor George II could speak the king's English nor did they have any measurable interest in English art, or in any other art for that matter, although during the reign of the first, the Royal Academy of Music was formed at London under the direction of George Frederick Handel, another immigrant from Hanover. George II once remarked, "I hate bainting and boetry," a statement that elicited a lash from Alexander Pope, "You by whose care in vain he cursd'/Still Dunce the Second reigns like Dunce the First."

Frederick Louis, son of George II, and the prince of Wales, did not outlive his father and thus never became king. However, during his relatively short life he secretly encouraged artists and bought their works. He also studied and catalogued the pictures that had come into the royal collections during earlier reigns, and added to them by purchasing works by Rubens, Van Dyck, Claude, Poussin, and other masters of the past. "I have something of every kind," he remarked to the connoisseur George Vertue, "because I love the arts and curious things." Some of his taste seems to have passed on to his son, who became George III; or perhaps, as has been observed, the latter was so bored by official life that he listened to good advice on art in order to avoid listening to it on political matters. In any case, none of the three monarchs shared the taste that fired Pompadour to the point of chauvinism in maintaining and furthering the contemporary arts and crafts of France in all their forms.

Before the middle of the eighteenth century the grandiose visions that had inspired Versailles and the rigidly formal styles that had been imposed by that spirit had given way to less pretentious and ostentatious forms and attitudes that reflected a more flexible and intimate manner of living. Art, which had been in the service of magnificence and power, could now be used to make at least some men more at home in the world. With the death of Louis XIV the court itself had moved back from the crowded and controlled discomforts of Versailles to the freer atmosphere of Paris. Young Louis XV was installed in the Tuileries at the west end of the Louvre; the nobility built or bought their own private residences in the city as a welcome change from the "dormitory" accommodations of Versailles. High life in the capital quickly forgot the rigid etiquette that had been taught at Versailles as it cultivated the lighter modes and manners that were to prevail in royal and other privileged social circles until the French Revolution brought a day of reckoning.

Princes and kings built residential retreats to which they gave such suggestive names as Mon Repos ("my rest"), Sans Souci ("without care"), Bagatelle ("a trifle")—much in the manner that Americans name their vacation cottages at lakeside or on mountaintop to indicate a temporary withdrawal from the wear and tear of workaday life. In these and the private houses built by people of wealth and taste, new rooms were designed to accommodate a new style of living: the salon, for the pleasure of conversation and friendly hospitality; the study, for reading and contemplation; the dining room, for the delights of the table; the boudoir (literally, "a place for pouting"), for ladies to retire to and dress in with privacy—or to whisper sweet nothings with their admirers; and so on. At Versailles Louis XV found the immense ceremonial rooms that had served his grandfather unbearable, and built a number of small apartments where he might cease to act the king and rather be himself when the spirit moved him. During the generation or so leading up to 1776 the Louis XV style, with all its delicate grace, had been brought to its ultimate degree of refinement. To give further examples of the new spirit of liberation, chairs that had been straightbacked and thronelike, lined up against the walls of a room or hall like so many symbols of place and station, were replaced by a wide variety of graceful forms with such suggestive names as *bergère* (or "sheperd's chair"), *gondole, confidante,* and so on, suggesting the ease and comfort they promised. Curvilinear designs gave an effect of life and movement to such seating accommodations, which were, in fact, meant to be moved—to be pulled about in groupings that would facilitate small, intimate conversational groups that played a vital part in the social and intellectual life of France in the closing days of the ancien régime. And so it was with other domestic arrangements designed to further convenience and privacy.

Following the French lead, similar developments took place in other coun-

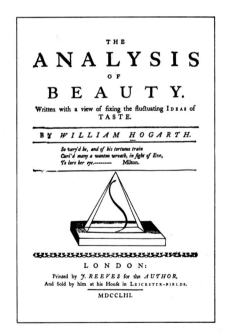

The title page of The Analysis of Beauty (1753) *by William Hogarth, a book that won respect from intellectuals but was the subject of much derision from the London art world*

247

tries. The Louis XV style was variously adapted in different lands. It could broadly be termed the rococo style. "Rococo" is derived from *rocaille*, a word that refers to the rock and shell forms and similar intricately carved patterns that were so popular in French ornament during the reign of Louis XV. (The word was applied to the style only after its vogue had passed.) At an early date this kind of ornament invaded England, where it was naturalized, and assumed a character that won the approval of much of the gentry. In his *Analysis of Beauty*, published in 1753, the English artist William Hogarth paid tribute to the grace of curvilinear lines in furnishings and decorations; he deemed them essential to beauty. "There is scarce a room," he wrote at the time the vogue was approaching a peak in England, "where one does not see the waving-line employ'd in some way or other. How inelegant would the shapes of all our moveables be without it? how very plain and unornamental the mouldings of cornices and chimney-pieces without the variety introduced by the *ogee* member, which is entirely composed of waving lines."

The elegant palace at Versailles, built by Louis XIV between 1661 and 1682, inspired imitations by numerous princes as well as among his rivals. The grandiose Nymphenburg Palace (opposite) was built by the ruler of Bavaria. Schönbrunn Palace (above) was begun in Vienna in 1695, but not finally completed until late in the reign of Maria Theresa. Bernardo Belloto, a nephew of Canaletto, painted these views in the mid-eighteenth century.

For Hogarth, the S-curve was the "line of beauty," and he discerned it at every hand among those things that pleased the eye (leading it a "wanton kind of chase"), from the curved stays that gave proper shape to a woman's figure to the "winding walks and serpentine rivers that graced the English countryside. He also remarked that "the lines that form a pleasing smile about the corners of the mouth have gentle windings" (but not excessive laughter which distorted such graceful patterns). A year after Hogarth's book appeared, Thomas Chippendale published his famous *Director*, in which he provided patterns for numerous furniture forms in the rococo style. When he referred to them as in the "Modern Taste" he meant the French taste. Chippendale's designs and others by his English contemporaries quickly reached America, where they were translated into a provincial idiom by colonial craftsmen in various mediums, only distantly recalling the earlier French inventions in the rococo style.

As a style, the rococo, with its asymmetrical patterns and whimsical details, was in itself an additional repudiation of the symmetry and straight lines of the preceding style. In a real sense it was a reflection of the frivolous mood of Louis XV's pleasure-loving court, so different in spirit from the overwhelming formality that had been favored by the "Sun King." It was this exuberance, its impish perversity and gaiety, that offended some staid Englishmen. However, in spite of such reservations, the style was used as decoration in some very dignified places in England, as on the ceilings of the Bodleian Library at Oxford and in the Christ Church Library, for example, as also in the most modern country residences and city apartments. English design in general gave way to the vogue, as can be seen in everything from silver teapots to Spitalfields silks, as well as in porcelains and other miscellaneous furnishings of the period. This was the case even though English Francophobes continued to deplore the corruption of native taste by such caprices, which had originated across the Channel, as one critic observed, merely to "please the light eye of the French, who seldom carry their observation further than a casual glance." Since the French influence seemed so difficult to conquer, the same critic continued, "Let us rouse in every sense the national spirit against them, and no more permit them to deprave our taste in

this . . . than to introduce among us the miseries of their government, or fooleries of their religion."

It was in Germany that the rococo style, somewhat belatedly, reached its most unrestrained exuberance. As the Duchesse d'Orléans observed from Paris, "Germany not only imitates France but always doubles what is done here." When the ruler of Bavaria turned his Italianate summer villa, the Nymphenburg Palace, into a rococo extravaganza, he started a trend that soon swept across Germany. In spite of the small size of their domains, virtually every prince of the land began trying to imitate such a display. In the palace at Potsdam and at the Residenz at Würzburg, these endeavors reached an apogee. This lavish aping of majesty quickly established a contrast between overprivileged rulers and their underprivileged subjects that was more conspicuous in Germany than elsewhere on the Continent precisely because the German kingdoms were so small.

In spite of its prevalence, the rococo was by no means the exclusive trend of the time. Never before, indeed, had there been so many disparate influences contending for favor. The classical tradition that had been revived during the Renaissance underwent modifications, but its basic, ancient, and orderly discipline—directly contrary to the spirit of the rococo—was a constant motivation in the arts of the eighteenth century. In fact, in the second half of that century, and especially in the years just before 1776, it enjoyed a fresh revival that was to be almost universally accepted as fashionable.

In many of its phases the rococo itself was a mélange of variant inspirations, an eclectic blend of elements that evoked incongruous historic and geographical associations. The practice of incorporating ornamental motifs derived from Oriental and medieval sources was, indeed, an essential characteristic of the rococo style. It was during the several decades leading up to 1776 that Europe's appreciation of Chinese art found its happiest expression. The porcelains, lacquers, ivories, wallpapers, and silks that since the sixteenth century had been imported from the Far East were considered treasures to marvel at. That appreciation had been nurtured over the years by the reports on China made by visitors to that distant and exotic land, many of which confirmed the opinion that the Chinese were unsurpassable craftsmen. Those reports typically went on to laud everything about Chinese culture and civilization in terms which made many readers wish they were born Chinese. (It occurred to one enthusiast that it might be better to send a young Englishman to Peking rather than to the Continent to acquire the elegant refinements of a complete education. What a sensation he would create, wrote this reporter, when milord returned to his homeland with "a dress and equipage à la Chinoise!") As earlier noted, it was such reports that gave Voltaire and his brother philosophes the material they wanted to point out the contrasting inadequacies of Western thought and practice. (Voltaire, it seems, wrote his classical tragedies in a room lined with Chinese wallpaper.) On the other hand, with his

usual common-sense approach to all matters, Dr. Johnson denied the Chinese any such exceptional status. One will find "no *Chinese* perfectly polite, and completely skilled in all sciences," he expostulated; "[one] will discover what will always be discovered by a diligent and impartial inquirer, that wherever human nature is to be found, there is a mixture of vice and virtue, a contest of passion and reason; and that the Creator doth not appear partial in his distribution, but has balanced in most countries their peculiar inconveniences by particular favors." And John Wesley, with moral indignation worthy of his calling, declared that to contrast the heathen Chinese with Christians was "a mere pious fraud."

However, regardless of such dissident voices, Europe's initial astonishment at the extraordinary and previously unheard of rarities brought in from the East gave way to a spreading desire to collect and own them—a desire which quickly found its way to the American colonies. To Europeans and the colonists these collectors brought a fresh aesthetic experience; ideas of beauty to which Western eyes were unaccustomed and a display of techniques and materials which were new and exciting. The asymmetry of Oriental designs (so congenial to the spirit of the rococo), its indifference to perspective, its disregard for proportion, its free use of line in rendering and framing naturalistic motifs—all this tended to liberate European taste from its attachment to the restraints and regularities that had conditioned the artistic expressions of earlier years. Representations of odd flora, of even stranger human and animal figures, and of scenery (as represented), unlike anything known in the Occident, also lent this imported art grotesque, bizarre, and mysterious qualities that enhanced its appeal to Western eyes and imagination. Such was the mood cast by the Oriental image that in one eighteenth-century play an English lord who affected a knowledge of women boasted that all that was necessary to seduce a lady of quality was "a jaunt or two in a hack to an Indian House, a little china, an odd thing for a gown or so."

Unfortunately for collectors of Oriental wares, supplies of such imports were for a long time too limited to satisfy the demand, and for would-be collectors prices remained too high. (In the Elizabethan period examples of blue-and-white Chinese porcelains were deemed so precious they were provided with handsomely wrought English silver-gilt mounts.) For both reasons efforts were early made in Europe to duplicate or approximate the various types of Oriental wares—except in Spain and Portugal, countries that had first been intimately connected with the China trade. Possibly they had imported sufficient quantities of Oriental commodities to supply local demands. The potters of France, Holland, Germany, England, and other countries, including Mexico, simulated Oriental porcelains by coating their earthenware forms, often molded and turned in Oriental shapes, with opaque white glazes decorated with designs in the Chinese and Japanese manner.

But pottery was not porcelain; it lacked the glittering whiteness of the real thing, the translucency, the fine texture of the basic material. Also, pottery chipped easily. Meanwhile, throughout Europe, innumerable alchemists were vainly trying to transmute base metals into gold. One of them, Johann Friedrich Böttger, was hired by Augustus II, king of Poland, to attempt that impossible task and was put to work at Dresden, with a threat of various punishments should he fail. When, perforce, he did fail he was thrown into prison. Upon his release he was charged with a new task: to discover the Chinese

The chinoiserie craze that swept Europe in the latter half of the eighteenth century gave birth to a wide variety of "Chinese" objets d'art. The items pictured opposite are a japanned cabinet, a textile of the Great Pagoda at Kew in Surrey, a porcelain serving tray, a tea caddy, and a porcelain centerpiece, made in Germany and showing Ch'ien Lung attended by a courtier, an artist, and a scholar. The chair shown below was fashioned in the Chinese style by Chippendale in the late 1760's.

The Sèvres porcelain factory produced this bowl and saucer especially for the dairy at Rambouillet.

secret of true, hard-paste porcelain. To be converted from a "goldmaker" to a potter seemed to him demeaning and humiliating. However, by 1710 he had indeed produced a true porcelain so hard that it could be cut like a jewel and with a brilliantly clear white glaze. The quest was over; a factory was established under the patronage of Augustus at Meissen, twelve miles outside Dresden, and its wares were soon intoxicating Europe. Orders poured in from Edinburgh, Moscow, Stockholm, and Cadiz. Those who were wealthy enough began to eat off it, drink from it, wash in it, and even spit in it. Silver became commonplace in comparison. Although in an effort to guard the secret formula that Böttger had discovered, the workmen at Meissen were watched over with the same concern shown to nuclear physicists in our own day, there were renegades among them. Inevitably, the secret leaked out, and in the decades to come factories for making the precious ware spread throughout Europe.

When Louis XV gave porcelain his royal favor, interest in the ware raged more fiercely than it earlier had. Sèvres, the factory to which Pompadour paid such devoted attention (but which, of course, was owned by the king) produced porcelain of such quality that even the Chinese emperor Ch'ien Lung deigned to accept a vast service from Louis as a gift. Because of its brilliance of color, the splendor of its decoration—lavishly accented with gold (an embellishment forbidden to other French factories)—and its almost intolerable cost, Sèvres porcelain came to dominate the taste of Europe in the 1750's and 1760's. Louis gave a further impetus to the fashion by personally conducting a sale of the factory's products at the end of each year in the galleries of Versailles. When the king acted as auctioneer, the courtiers were virtually obliged to buy. Nothing better suggests the reverence with which European aristocracy regarded the ware than that the Most Christian King of France, who could not socially meet a bourgeois, should have been willing to act as huckster for the products of his factory.

The porcelain craze was only one aspect of the pervasive Oriental influence on Western art. Practically every phase of decoration was affected, from architectural "follies" to bowls of Chinese goldfish, from tapestries to bibelots. In 1738 Thomas Hancock of Boston, as he was building his new mansion in Beacon Street, wrote a London stationer requesting enough wallpaper in the Chinese style to cover the walls of two rooms—a fashion which he observed "takes much in the Town." Hancock referred to the wallpaper recently imported by a friend of his, which he considered very handsome, with its "Great Variety of Different Sorts of Birds, Peacocks, Macoys, Squirril, Monkys, Fruit and Flowers, &C." So-called "japanned" furniture was made to simulate, more or less effectively, the original lacquerwork of China, Japan, and India. Crude imitations were made in the American colonies early in the eighteenth century; remarkably fine examples were fashioned for Marie Antoinette by the foremost *ébénistes* (cabinetmakers using fine woods) of France in the 1780's. Fabrics inspired by imported examples were woven at Lyons, Spitalfields, and elsewhere in enchanting and endless variations on Oriental themes. Once the techniques and practices which inspired these efforts were mastered, the designers freed themselves from their models and developed a strong Western accent in their work. From the beginning the Western knowledge of Far Eastern art had been but a distant, dimly understood vision. Just how vague were European notions about China is revealed by the delightful hoax of one impecunious but resourceful Frenchwoman who succeeded in convincing an important bloc of French society that she represented one of the best families of China. (In 1756 a Chinese man named Loum Kiqua actually came to London, via Portugal, and excited so much interest that he was received by the royal family and "was much caressed" by the nobility.) In his fictional account of a Chinese citizen of the world, Goldsmith suggests how baffled an Oriental would have been if confronted by European interpretations of Chinese art. When asked by a lady of taste to examine the beauties of a Chinese temple in her garden, the bewildered visitor replied: "I see nothing, madam . . . that may not as well be called an Egyptian pyramid as a Chinese temple; for that little building . . . is as like one as t'other."

China rarely exported its finest work to the Occident. At the same time, this was a period of consummate craftsmanship in Paris and in some other European capitals. When skilled and creative European artists and artisans interpreted the models of Oriental wares that were available to them, their work not only assumed an independent style, referred to as chinoiserie, but it often achieved a quality superior to that of the originals that may have inspired them. As a corollary to this, from an early date, eager to take advantage of Oriental craftsmanship, Europeans were busy encouraging Eastern workmen to carry out European patterns in native materials for sale in Western markets, frequently with amusing results. Eastern craftsmen understood the Western scene no better than their European counterparts understood the Orient, and their misinterpretations of the models they copied reveal once again how far apart the two worlds were in spirit and tradition. Western art had no serious impact on the East, nothing comparable to the reverse influence of East on West over the centuries. As one further result of this curious interrelationship of different cultures, Western craftsmen were sometimes moved, or commissioned, to reproduce examples of Chinese reproductions of European designs, in what began to resemble an endless game of shuttlecock.

Europe also turned to its own past to find such exciting strangeness as it had discovered in the arts of the Chinese. The Gothic past seemed as far away in time as China was in distance, but it was exotic in a different way. Motifs culled from the Gothic style, dimly understood as they often were, could be incorporated into rococo decoration to add a further fantasy to the effect. The results have been termed gothic rococo. "The modern Gothick," reported one eighteenth-century English builders' guide, ". . . is known by its Disposition, and by its affected Lightness, Delicacy, and over-rich, even whimsical Decorations." Quite apart from any association with the rococo, "modern" Gothic designs were used, above all in England, for their own intrinsic interest as wayward parodies of medieval sources. In 1753 another English writer observed: "A few years ago everything was Gothic; our houses, our beds, our books, our couches were all copied from some parts or other of our old cathedrals." Almost anything was called Gothic, or Chinese, or "modern," as fancy dictated.

The secure and relatively tranquil society of eighteenth-century England found in the Middle Ages the stuff of reveries, compensating dreams of a time when chivalric knights sprang to action and pious monks pursued their spiritual goals with passionate intensity. Out of this craving for self-dramatization emerged the sham ruins that dotted the English countryside and even whole houses constructed in the supposed image of medieval structures. It was in this spirit that Horace Walpole went on the "Gothic pilgrimages" through the

English countryside, so brilliantly described in his letters, hunting out tumbled ruins of monasteries and castles and parish churches, and then built his own extraordinary "Gothic" mansion, Strawberry Hill, the most notable document of its time in the medieval manner. In creating this structure, Walpole had no intention of denying himself conveniences and refinements of luxury unknown to the Middle Ages. "Every true Goth must perceive," he explained, "that they [my rooms] are more the works of fancy than imitation." (The American clergyman William Bentley referred to Strawberry Hill as "a Gothic mouse-trap.")

In France the playful exuberance of mingling styles was a dramatic departure from the grand and heavy manner that had been favored by the "Sun King." His successor Louis XV was a lazy, indifferent, and in many ways an incompetent monarch; but in matters of art and culture, as earlier observed, he clearly found a strong-minded, ardent, and sensitive surrogate in Madame de Pompadour. She, rather than the king, was the arbiter of taste. The marquise had artistic talents of her own. Some of her etchings and engravings survive to testify she had almost professional abilities. (Voltaire addressed a poem to her, suggesting she draw a self-portrait, for never could a more beautiful hand create such a beautiful image.)

Pompadour had known the artist François Boucher before she had become the king's mistress. When she started her little theater she chose Boucher as her designer and stage director, a post he occupied in the professional theater as well for sixteen years. She also chose him as her tutor, and as her favorite painter. He, in turn, was devoted to the marquise, as his various glowing portraits of her seem to reveal. Boucher was a versatile artist who, with Pompadour's encouragement, spread his talents among many of the projects she favored. Aside from his stage designs for the opera and ballet, he drew cartoons for tapestries and designed objects and decorations for Sèvres porcelain. But he is best remembered, of course, for his paintings.

Boucher was the perfect artist for Pompadour and the courtly circle in which she moved with such unquestioned authority. It was her contemporary, the Marquise du Châtelet, who succinctly expressed the mood of that circle with the memorable statement she is said to have made: "We have nothing else to do in this world but seek pleasant sensations and feelings." Boucher's sensual art was admirably fashioned to excite such sensations and feelings, to titillate the jaded society he addressed. It has been said that he brought the gods into the boudoir and the bedroom, with his brush transmuting Venus, Diana, and their attendants into nubile and seductive grisettes. Well connected and capable as he was, Boucher was named painter to the king and president of the Royal Academy. It was he who, at a critical moment in Pompadour's relations with the king, produced the erotic pictures that hung in the *cabinet secret* where she received Louis and which caused His Majesty to regain his good humor.

Years later the brothers Goncourt, the most perceptive critics of eighteenth-century French art, wrote: "Prettiness, in the best sense of the word, is the symbol and seduction of France at this airy moment of history." "Boucher," they further observed, "was one of those men who indicate the taste of a century, express, personify, embody it. In him French eighteenth-century taste was manifest in all the peculiarity of its character. Boucher was not only its painter but its chief witness, its chief representative, its very type." In Boucher's own lifetime Diderot assailed the artist for doing just that—at least for suggesting the depravity, dissoluteness, and debauchery of life among the members of the *haut monde* who commissioned his paintings. "What can a man have in his imagination who passes life with the lowest kind of prostitutes?" Diderot asked with all the earnestness of a dedicated reformer; where in all this were those ideas of honesty, innocence, and simplicity, extolled by the enlightened thinkers of the day? The answer was all too obvious to critics of such a society. Yet even Diderot could not help being beguiled by Boucher's concoctions. "*C'est un vice si agréable,*" he was obliged to confess—"it is such an agreeable vice." Boucher's art, Diderot added, lacked only the truth.

Pompadour died in 1764, Boucher six years later. There were other patrons and other artists who continued to serve the ancien régime as it frittered away its remaining years. In his *Nymph and Satyr*, his *Bacchanals*, and other compositions, the "boudoir sculptor," Clodion, suggested the ecstasy of the flesh quite as unreservedly as Boucher had ever done in his paintings; and through the sale of these skillfully modeled figures he achieved an ample prosperity. Boucher's sometime assistant, Jean Honoré Fragonard, became a far better painter than his master. As a relatively young man, "Frago," as he was called by his friends, had a brilliant success not only in his own amorous pursuits but in producing happy and luscious paintings that were colorful reminders of the delights of such pursuits. He was apparently at home in the

"*. . . His Majesty, always prompt to recompense those who excel, by their talents, in the Fine Arts and wishing to make known his particular benevolence towards those who, by consistent application, have achieved perfection and proved themselves worthy of his esteem and that of his country, considers that no one is more worthy to exercise the function of Chief Court Painter . . . than the Sieur François Boucher . . .*"

Certificate of Boucher's appointment, signed by Louis XV, 1765

François Boucher (top, a sketch by an unknown artist) and Jean Honoré Fragonard (above, a self-portrait) painted for the French upper classes. Jean Baptiste Greuze (below, a self-portrait) painted moralistic genre scenes, popular with intellectuals.

demimonde and the darling of fashionable, kept ladies whose friends were members of the court, rich financiers, and others with reputations as *bons vivants*; and in such circles he found appreciative patrons. The patronage of art had spread far beyond the king and his immediate court. Above all, it included women—pretty women, or women made to look pretty—and those who paid tribute to their charms. Art was in their service to a degree unthought of in the previous century and to a degree not ever again to be equaled. To please women, to celebrate their attraction, and to affirm their influence in society, and on the intelligence that guided it, had become in the works of men like Boucher and Fragonard a dominant motive. It was also the purpose of Elisabeth Vigée-Lebrun (see illustration on page 277), who by the time she was sixteen was proficient enough to earn a good living from her pleasing portraits of sentimental, affected beauties, whom the artist endowed with grace and charm. When Vigée-Lebrun was twenty-four she painted Marie Antoinette, who was so flattered by the results that she sat for the artist twenty times. The two became fast friends and sang tender airs together. With such exalted patronage and her obvious facility, Madame Vigée-Lebrun won an ample clientele of fashionable and wealthy ladies who craved to be made beautiful by her brush, and she thereby became very fashionable and wealthy herself. She lived on well into the next century, painting her way from Paris to Rome and to Vienna, Berlin, and St. Petersburg.

But Fragonard outlived his popularity and his success. As Diderot's criticism of Boucher strongly indicated, the temper of the times was radically changing. The art historian and critic John Canaday has observed that Fragonard's art summarized the ills of the decaying society he served. "He reflects its frivolity, its licentiousness, its preoccupation with superficial effects, its refusal to think ahead or to look back," writes Canaday. "It was a corrupt society but one of abundant charms, and insofar as these supplied material for an ideal expression, Fragonard performed one important historical function of the artist in any society; he presented its virtues intact and with a conviction of their legitimacy."

Even while Boucher was enjoying his greatest success, there was a growing and outspoken conviction that art had a larger purpose than to amuse, that it had a serious moral and social function to perform. In the vanguard of the critics, Diderot pointed out that the mission of art was "to show virtue as pleasing, vice as odious, to expose what is ridiculous." This didactic approach to art is completely out of fashion today when the artist's freedom to express whatever he feels or chooses is virtually sacrosanct. But Diderot was writing in an entirely different context. In the first place he made his judgments as the spirit of the Enlightenment was approaching a crest. The reformist ideology of the philosophes was influencing an ever-increasing number of intelligent and thoughtful people, art patrons among them; and now, for the first time in history, periodic art exhibitions were being held, and the large public they attracted, drawn from many stratums of society, was exposed to varieties of paintings and sculptures that were otherwise inaccessible. From such experiences new tastes could be formed.

In the Salon of 1775 the work of a young and relatively obscure artist, Jean Baptiste Greuze, who has been called "the Rousseau and the Diderot of the brush," won an enthusiastic reception. The title of his canvas, *A Father Reading the Bible to his Children*, indicates clearly enough the character of his painting—anecdotal and sentimental, and with its very obvious moral overtones, in accord with the new taste of the times. As a measure of its appeal, the painting was bought by an influential collector and hung in his home before it was shown at the Salon. With that success Greuze proceeded to paint other subjects in the same vein, narratives in paint that usually described simple, rustic settings and that brimmed with emotional content. Their titles are all equally self-descriptive—*Young Girl Weeping over a Dead Bird, The Village Bride, The Prodigal Son,* and so forth—and for the most part they attracted a rapturous audience.

Diderot was among the first to hail Greuze's talent. He was, observed that philosopher (who was then writing periodic essays on art), "the first of our artists who gave morals to art, and arranged pictures to tell a story." Such paintings, Diderot reported in a significant commentary on his approach to painting, "could quite well be turned into a novel." To make sure that the point of his canvases would be clearly understood, Greuze took to announcing their appearance with detailed explanations of their meaning in letters addressed to the principal gazettes. He was a very vain man and practically demanded his due of appreciation. That trait led him to defy the Academy which, he felt, did not accord him full recognition. Like Courbet long afterward, in his protest against official painting, Greuze showed his work in his own studio at the same time as the Salon exhibitions. Meanwhile, his domestic life was troubled. The woman he had married turned out to be unrestrainedly promiscuous, and her amorous exploits were everywhere rumored.

Greuze was a very good artist, as many of his portraits especially reveal. But his genre paintings did not wear very well even in his own lifetime. Diderot himself wearied of them, realizing that however simple were the truths that the artist set out to tell, he gave them such a heavy sugar coating of sentimentality that the results were as specious as Boucher's amorous idylls. There was also in them a barely disguised salaciousness that robbed them of any purity of thought they professed. The bodices of his otherwise innocent-looking young women tended to slip, showing nicely rounded white shoulders and a bared breast. (Toward the end of his life Greuze himself was disturbed by such disclosures, and he was led to destroy "all his studies of women and all else that might be offensive to modesty.")

Tired of the painter's pride and insolence, and disenchanted by what seemed a betrayal of the trust he had put in Greuze, Diderot turned away from him. "I no longer like Greuze," he wrote in 1769. When a plan was broached to send Greuze to Petersburg as court painter to Catherine the Great, who admired his paintings, Diderot, whom the queen highly respected, wrote to a correspondent: "Listen, my friend, all things considered, I think we shall not be sending Greuze to Russia. He is an excellent artist but a bad-tempered fellow. One should collect his drawings and his pictures and otherwise leave him alone. And then his wife is by universal consent—and when I say universal I include both herself and her husband—one of the most dangerous creatures in the world. I still have hopes that one day Her Imperial Majesty will send her off to Siberia."

Greuze outlived his fame and was soon forgotten by his contemporaries. In 1780 it was noted that the public already showed little interest in his studio exhibitions. Twenty-four years later, when he belatedly tried to woo back an audience by re-exhibiting his work, his efforts met with complete indifference.

He had shortly before written to the minister of the interior to solicit a pension or some other form of relief, remarking that he was an old man (he was then in his late seventies) who had "lost everything, talent as well as courage," and that he did not have a single painting on order. He died penniless in 1805.

The reputation of his close contemporary Jean Baptiste Chardin has fared much better over the last two hundred years. Chardin also painted pictures of quite ordinary daily life, and still lifes of objects that were accessories to that way of living, but in an entirely straightforward fashion. And Chardin, too, won Diderot's appreciation from the start. His art, Diderot wrote, "is nature itself; the objects stand out of the canvas with a truth that deceives the eye." This was a form of deception quite different from that of Greuze. It sprang from an accomplished artistry that conveyed the semblance of things, the forms and textures of reality, with remarkable fidelity but without resorting to photographic exactitude. In this respect it recalls the work of earlier Dutch and Flemish little masters, as his contemporary Nicholas de Largillière, an esteemed portrait painter, observed. But in Chardin's work there is rarely the gleam of crystal, the glitter of silver, or the sheen of rich fabrics. Rather, he depicted the solid and sometimes rough substance of ordinary pottery and the stuffs of ordinary clothing and household textiles. The men, women, and children who people his canvases are plain, usually serious, and of the middle class (as he himself appears to be in his self-portrait—a good, average man of no commanding distinction). He accepted the simplest things as the most profound because they seemed to him to represent the goodness and truth upon which all else depends.

In his unpretentious way Chardin was a revolutionary artist. His interior scenes, and his still lifes particularly (a not very popular genre in his day), reflect a world that is at the same time both natural and orderly—qualities dear to the philosophical temper of the age. In his representations of people and objects he achieved harmonious patterns of texture, line, color, and light, such as were not again so successfully mastered until Cézanne launched his own revolution more than a century later. (When someone asked him what colors he preferred to use, Chardin responded, "My friend, one does not paint with colors but with one's feelings.")

Chardin's canvases were sufficiently esteemed to earn him an apartment in the Louvre by royal warrant. His ample list of prosperous patrons included members of the nobility. Painting at the same time as Boucher, Chardin worked toward entirely opposite ends. In his own quiet and distinctive manner he proclaimed the nobility of the commonplace, the dignity of the simple life and of simple things, without a trace of Greuze's mawkishness; and it is no great exaggeration to say that, without any apparent intention of being philosophical about it, he did this more convincingly than did Rousseau with his revolutionary preachments.

The idea that art had a serious, didactic function won increasing acceptance in the third quarter of the eighteenth century. It was in that spirit that the young Louis XVI, only shortly after Boucher's death, in a fit of moral indignation denounced the paintings that artist had created for Pompadour's boudoir and that had so charmed Louis XV, and ordered them destroyed. He considered them indecent. (Happily, the order was quietly destroyed, and some of them are still preserved.) Even at the French court the views of Diderot and his associated reformers were winning the day. And with this general renunciation

of art as frivolous, as nothing much more than a plaything of the senses, the spell of the rococo was completely broken.

At about the same time that Greuze and Chardin were earning their reputation in Paris, the extraordinary young English artist William Hogarth was starting his career in London, the city that was to be his universe throughout the sixty-seven years of his lifetime. In his character and in his art he was a strictly insular figure. He left England only once, and then only to find that he loathed France (on his brief excursion to that country he never even got as far as Paris). With excellent reason, he has been called the first truly great English painter. (The American expatriate artist James McNeill Whistler called him "the only great English painter.") Most of the important artists who had practiced in England before his time had beem emigrants from other lands— such men as Hans Holbein, Peter Lely, and Godfrey Kneller from Germany, Van Dyck from Belgium, Largillière from France, and others.

Hogarth died twelve years before 1776, but he cleared paths in English painting that led to developments long after that date. Like Diderot, Hogarth believed that painting should have a didactic message; echoing Diderot in his praise of Greuze, Hogarth once remarked that he wanted his pictures to be

Jean Baptiste Simeon Chardin was invited to join the French Academy of Painting after two of his works were selected for display (one was The Rayfish, *shown above). Chardin was the master of the still-life genre in the eighteenth century, and his honest portrayals of the French bourgeoisie were unrivaled.*
LOUVRE—GIRAUDON

read like books. With Greuze, he thought art should serve a moral purpose, inculcate an uplifting message. But, for the cloying sweetness of Greuze's painted tales and the earnestness of Diderot's strictures, Hogarth substituted satire, often very cutting and merciless satire. He attacked the evils of English society by illustrating their most bitter consequences. In a series of pictorial sequences—*Harlot's Progress, Marriage à la Mode, Rake's Progress*—he followed the corruption of his characters, lowborn and highborn together, as they were caught up in the vice and dissoluteness common to the age. In these "morality plays" in paint (Hogarth wished to be judged as a dramatist; "I treat my subjects as a dramatic writer," he wrote, "my picture is my stage, and men and women my players.") he exposed the sordid examples of the innocent country girl who succumbs to the temptations of fashionable London; of the aristocratic rake who dissipates his fortune, or the fortune he married, in riotous living; of wastrels of various stripe who were ruined by overindulgence. Occasionally he hinted broadly at political corruption. Laws that had been passed early in the century encouraged the consumption of cheap gin by making licensing easy and by putting a very low tax on spirits. As Daniel Defoe pointed out, distilling called for corn that could be supplied at an ample profit by the landed gentry so well represented in Parliament. In *Gin Lane* Hogarth illustrated how this plentiful flow of inexpensive intoxicant reduced a mass of people to poverty and degradation, while the pawnbroker and the undertaker did a good business.

Such obvious themes could have resulted in banality if it were not for the ebullient spirit, the fervor, and the skilled artistry that Hogarth brought to these self-imposed assignments—an approach not free of mercenary incentives. He planned to live, as he remarked, "by small sums from many by means of prints which I could Engrave from my Picture myself." The engravings he made of his paintings for popular consumption were, in fact, an immediate and great success. Thanks to the British freedom of the press, his works were not subject to censorship, and were circulated widely not only in England but on the Continent, where they set the style for some French engravings and furnished themes for French and German writers. In England, justifying Hogarth's claim to be a dramatist, *Harlot's Progress* was quickly staged as a pantomime and as a ballad opera, thus increasing the already large audience he had won with the prints. How widespread that audience was is suggested by an anecdote that tells of an English lord who saw a coachman ill-treating his horses. "You rascal," he is said to have shouted, "haven't you seen Hogarth's pictures?" (In 1768 Benjamin Franklin, in behalf of the Philadelphia Library Company, issued a "draft in favour of Jane Hogarth [widow] for prints, £6,6c., £14.11.0," to cover the price of a full set of Hogarth's engravings.)

Hogarth's lasting influence on English art was also important in an entirely different way. He called the attention of his countrymen to their neglect of the arts and artists of England. When Voltaire visited England between 1726 and 1729 he was amazed at the young nobles who with their wealth patronized letters and sciences. He was filled with admiration of their "great rural palaces filled with pictures brought from Italy and furniture from France, of the editions of Italian, French and Latin authors that lined their bookcases." Hogarth, on the other hand, complained that in England paintings were considered as pieces of furniture, and that there, as elsewhere in Europe, surfeit of

Enter Servant.

Serv. Madam, Mrs. Candour is below, and if your ladyship's at leisure, will leave her carriage.

Lady Sneer. Beg her to walk in.—[*Exit* Servant.] Now, Maria, here is a character to your taste; for though Mrs. Candour is a little talkative, everybody allows her to be the best natured and best sort of woman.

Maria. Yes, with a very gross affectation of good nature and benevolence, she does more mischief than the direct malice of old Crabtree.

Joseph S. I' faith that's true, Lady Sneerwell: whenever I hear the current running against the characters of my friends, I never think them in such danger as when Candour undertakes their defense.

Lady Sneer. Hush!—here she is!

Enter Mrs. Candour.

Mrs. Can. My dear Lady Sneerwell, how have you been this century?—Mr. Surface, what news do you hear?—though indeed it is no matter, for I think one hears nothing else but scandal.

Joseph S. Just so, indeed, ma'am.

Mrs. Can. Oh, Maria! child—what, is the whole affair off between you and Charles? His extravagance, I presume—the town talks of nothing else.

Maria. I am very sorry, ma'am, the town has so little to do.

Mrs. Can. True, child: but there's no stopping people's tongues. . . .

Maria. 'Tis strangely impertinent for people to busy themselves so.

Mrs. Can. Very true, child: but what's to be done? People will talk—there's no preventing it. Why, it was but yesterday I was told that Miss Gadabout had eloped with Sir Fili-

Richard Sheridan's The School for Scandal, *which opened to rave notices in 1777, is generally considered to be the best comedy of manners in the English language (below, from an early edition of the play, a scene from Act IV). This excerpt is from Act I, Scene 1, and features the hypocritical Joseph Surface and the hilarious gossips Lady Sneerwell and Mrs. Candour.*

CULVER PICTURES

gree Flirt. But, Lord! there's no minding what one hears; though, to be sure, I had this from very good authority.

Maria. Such reports are highly scandalous.

Mrs. Can. So, they are, child; shameful! shameful! But the world is so censorious, no character escaped. Lord, now who would have suspected your friend, Miss Prim, of an indiscretion? Yet, such is the ill-nature of people, that they say her uncle stopped her last week, just as she was stepping into the York diligence with her dancing-master.

Maria. I'll answer for't there are no grounds for that report.

Mrs. Can. Ah, no foundation in the world, I dare swear; no more, probably, than for the story circulated last month, of Mrs. Festino's affair with Colonel Cassino; though, to be sure, that matter was never rightly cleared up.

Joseph S. The license of invention some people take is monstrous indeed.

Maria. 'Tis so; but, in my opinion, those who report such things are equally culpable.

Mrs. Can. To be sure they are; tale-bearers are as bad as the tale-makers; 'tis an old observation, and a very true one. But what's to be done, as I said before? How will you prevent people from talking? Today, Mrs. Clackitt assured me Mr. and Mrs. Honeymoon were at last become mere man and wife, like the rest of their acquaintance. And at the same time Miss Tattle, who was by, affirmed that Lord Buffalo had discovered his lady at a house of no extraordinary fame; and that sire Harry Bouquet and Tom Saunter were to measure swords on a similar provocation. But, Lord, do you think I would report these things! No, no! tale-bearers, as I said before, are just as bad as the tale-makers.

Mrs. Can. I confess, Mr. Surface, I cannot bear to hear people attacked behind their backs; and when ugly circumstances come out against our acquaintance, I own I always love to think the best. By the by, I hope 'tis not true that your brother is absolutely ruined?

Joseph S. I am afraid his circumstances are very bad indeed, ma'am.

Mrs. Can. Ah! I heard so—but you must tell him to keep up his spirits; everybody almost is in the same way: Lord Spindle, Sir Thomas Splint, Captain Quince, and Mr. Nickit—all up, I hear, within this week; so if Charles is undone, he'll find half his acquaintance is ruined too, and that, you know, is a consolation.

Joseph S. Doubtless, ma'am; a very great one.

Even the most prestigious artists added to their incomes by making engravings of their paintings. Here, fashionable Londoners in search of works by their favorite artist crowd an eighteenth-century printshop.
BRITISH MUSEUM

works of art of past ages existed, and copies of them as "countless as the sands on the seashore." These, he pointed out, were bartered back and forth by those who preferred expensive imported items to anything of native production. "Who can be expected to give forty guineas for a modern landscape," he asked, "though in ever so superior a style, when we can purchase one which, for a little more than double the sum named, is warranted original by a solemn-faced connoisseur?" (To illustrate his point he drew a caricature of a fop in the form of a monkey assiduously watering dead plants representing the old masters.)

"Whether it is to our honor or disgrace," Hogarth wrote, "I will not presume to say; but the fact is indisputable, that the public encourages trade in mechanics rather than painting or sculpture. Is it then reasonable to think that the artist . . . will follow this tedious and laborious study merely for fame, when his next-door neighbor, perhaps a porter brewer, or haberdasher of small wares, can, without any genius, accumulate an enormous fortune in a few years, become a Lord Mayor, or a Member of Parliament and purchase a title for his heir? Surely no; for as very few painters get even moderately rich, it is not reasonable to expect that they should waste their lives in cultivating the higher branches of the arts, until their country becomes more alive to its importance, and better disposed to reward their labors. These are the true causes that have retarded our progress."

The insignificance of the court as a patron of the arts, or as a cultural stimulus of any sort, put the fashionable world on its own during the reigns of the first two Georges. There were none of the continuing traditions of the royal collections that existed in Paris. In fact, there was virtually nowhere that the artist could go to see fine works of art. England seemed to be composed of many minor courts which centered around the life peculiar to the country houses of the landed gentry. But, as Hogarth pointed out, the fashionable world of the time had only limited interest in encouraging "modern" English art—except for portraiture. "In Holland selfishness is the ruling passion," he explained; "in England vanity is united with it. Portrait painting, therefore, ever has, and ever will succeed in this country better than in any other." As one English collector observed, he could hardly be expected to hang a picture by a contemporary English artist unless, of course, it were a portrait. Hogarth was himself a superb portraitist, as he so fully demonstrated with his *Shrimp Girl*. But the unflattering forthrightness of his characterization did little to attract the aristocracy to his studio. (Hogarth's antipathy to any form of pretension is indicated by the fact that he dedicated his *Analysis of Beauty* not to a prince or potential high-ranking patron but "to everybody.")

The situation in England had its very close parallel in England's North American colonies. A somewhat disillusioned English painter, Benjamin Robert Haydon, once sourly observed that "portraiture is always independent of art and has little or nothing to do with it. It is one of the staple manufactures of the empire. Wherever the British settle, wherever they colonize, they carry, and will always carry, trial by jury, horse racing, and portrait painting." By far the most numerous surviving examples of colonial art are portraits (although they were by no means all by English-born artists or of colonists of English descent). John Singleton Copley, the best of colonial American painters, voiced the same complaint about the status of the artist that Hogarth had made before him. Just before he quit America on the eve of the Revolution to try his talents overseas, Copley expressed his mortification that "people regarded painting no more than any other useful trade . . . like that of a carpenter, tailor, shoemaker, not as one of the most noble arts in the world. . . ." In spite of such circumstances he became one of the first American artists to live by his brush alone and solely through his portraiture, and he prospered. "I am now in as good business as the poverty of this place [America] will admit," he wrote in 1767. "I make as much money as if I were a Raphael or a Correggio. . . ." However, in June of 1774, as war clouds gathered over the colonies, Copley sailed from America never to return, and soon established his reputation in a wider world.

The progress of English art in general was also discouraged by the fact that students had only the most limited opportunity to see paintings and sculptures that could guide, inspire, or excite their interest. Need for a solidly sponsored organization that would hold open exhibitions of representative work was obvious to those who cared about such matters. It was not until 1768, however, four years after Hogarth's death, that this need was met by the formation of the Royal Academy of Arts and the hanging of its first exhibition. Inevitably, the president of that institution was a portraitist, the recently knighted Sir Joshua Reynolds. Now, Reynolds observed in his opening address, "an Academy in which the polite arts may be regularly cultivated is at last opened among us by Royal munificence. This must appear an event in the highest degree interesting, not only to the artists, but to the whole nation. It is indeed difficult to give any other reason why an Empire like that of Britain should so long have wanted an ornament so suitable to its greatness, than that slow progression of things which naturally makes elegance and refinement the last effects of opulence and power. An institution like this has often been recommended upon considerations merely mercantile; but an academy founded upon such principles can never effect even its own narrow purposes. If it has an origin no higher, no taste can ever be formed, manufactured; but, the higher arts of design flourish, their inferior ends will be answered, of course. We are happy in having a prince who has conceived the design of such an institution according to its true dignity, and to promote the arts as the head of a great, a learned, a polite, and a commercial nation. . . ."

The Academy quickly became the fashion of London, and by this royal recognition the social status of the artist in England was assured. Superior students were awarded scholarships that enabled them to work for a year in Rome. Life classes were held with both male and female models. For pro-

This statue of Sir Joshua Reynolds stands in front of London's Burlington House, seat of the Royal Academy.
ROYAL ACADEMY OF ARTS

priety's sake, no one under twenty was permitted to draw from the female model unless he was married; and on days when a female was posing no visitor was admitted to the Academy, "the Royal family excepted." Membership in the Academy was a coveted distinction. Those elected were to be "painters, sculptors or architects, men of fair moral character, of high reputation in their several professions." Their responsibilities were "to examine the performances of the students, to advise and instruct them, to endeavour to form their taste." Each year an exhibition was held that was "open to all artists of distinguished merit." The works shown were for sale, and the proceeds were partly used to support the Academy.

Reynolds symbolized the new-found honorable station of the English artist. Whatever merits we may find wanting in them today, his portraits of members of the upper classes, the fine flower of the English race, painted in the "grand style," won him fame, knighthood, an honorary degree from Oxford, and opulence. The carriage that awaited him at the door of his great house on Leicester Square (then the most select quarter of London) was so fine that his servants could pick up extra shillings by letting members of the public sneak in to see it. That house became a meeting place for intellectuals, attracting such distinguished guests as Samuel Johnson, Edmund Burke, Oliver Goldsmith, Edward Gibbon, and others. Unlike his French counterparts, Reynolds was a "learned painter." Each year in a "Discours" he delivered a solemn message on the current state of the arts. He remained a bachelor, and when he died in 1792 he left his large fortune to a niece. Nine noblemen were proud to bear his remains to St. Paul's Cathedral.

Throughout his professional career Reynolds was constantly on the alert to recognize rising talents that he felt might challenge the supremacy he claimed as his own. To his ill-concealed discomfiture, in 1776 his acknowledged rival Thomas Gainsborough received a commission from the royal family to paint portraits of its members. He had become a favorite painter of the court. (It was in this period that Gainsborough also painted his celebrated portrait of Master Jonathan Buttoll, *The Blue Boy*, probably his most advertised picture.) Reynolds was the more irked because Gainsborough, out of sympathy with the academic routine imposed by Reynolds on studies undertaken at the Academy, had broken away from that institution. Gainsborough had a poetic sensibility completely alien to Reynolds; his work had a vivacity and lightness of spirit that brought him closer to the work of Boucher and Fragonard than to anything then being done in England. His education was superficial and included extensive research into the pleasures offered by life in London. (He once described himself as being "deeply read in petticoats.") Successful as he was with his portraits, he considered them as so much "potboiling" and expressed the wish that he could quit that trade and, taking his viola da gamba, walk off to some sweet village and paint "landskips." Critical of him to the end, Reynolds nevertheless brought himself to deliver a final eulogy to his rival: "If ever this nation should produce genius sufficient to acquire to us the honorable distinction of an English School, the name of Gainsborough will be transmitted to posterity, in the history of art, among the very first of that rising name." Gainsborough had only one—very obscure—pupil, and he had very little influence on contemporary art. But in the next century, as his work was reconsidered, he became the most influential of English painters who had worked in the eighteenth century.

Thomas Gainsborough painted this unaffected self-portrait when he was about twenty-seven in Ipswich.
MARCHIONESS OF CHOLMODELEY

Reynolds was succeeded as president of the Royal Academy, the highest post England could offer an artist, by the Pennsylvania-born Benjamin West. West had settled in England in 1763 after a visit to Italy; he was made a founding member of the Academy and in 1772 appointed "historical painter to the king." He not only became famous and wealthy, with his historical paintings he became the first English painter to lead the European avant-garde. In his painting of the death of Wolfe on the Plains of Abraham, he dared, over the objections of both the king and Reynolds, to show historical characters realistically and in modern dress—a radical departure from the firmly established convention of showing heroes of any period only in classical garb and in an allegorical manner. When the picture was exhibited publicly it was an immediate, spectacular popular success. Large crowds gathered to look at it and admire it. The king even asked West to paint a duplicate for him, and Reynolds conceded, "West has conquered . . . I retract my objections." Engravings of the subject were widely sold, far beyond England's shores. He had set off a revolution of sorts, just as his countrymen were about to set off a revolution of their own across the Atlantic. In spite of his outspoken regard for the American revolutionary cause, West remained the king's close friend and artistic adviser for the rest of that monarch's life. Attracted by his prodigious reputation, hopeful colonial artists of three generations flocked to West's studio for aid and advice, both of which he gave unstintingly. His home, indeed, became a veritable school of American painters—an American "academy" in miniature. Unfortunately, West's reputation quickly faded. The unkindest critical cut of all came from Lord Byron, who mercilessly referred to West as "Europe's worst, poor England's best."

Nevertheless, during the prime years of his professional career, West enjoyed extraordinary success—at least in England. That was more surprising since he had emerged from the colonial "wilderness" as an unheralded and virtually untutored youth, to be hailed in Europe almost immediately as the "American Raphael." Paradoxically, this quickly won renown as a "modern" master was largely due to the fact that he was the first painter anywhere in the world to apply the classical theories, then being propounded anew, in their entirety. (Thus Thomas Jefferson was in the vanguard of modern architects when he designed the Virginia State Capitol at Richmond in the image of an ancient Roman temple.)

Benjamin West painted this self-portrait when he was about thirty-two and had been in London for seven years.
NATIONAL GALLERY OF ART, WASHINGTON, D.C., MELLON COLLECTION

In one modified form or another the influence of classical antiquity had been a continuing factor in the development of European art, especially architecture, ever since the Renaissance. But in the second half of the eighteenth century this influence led to a new and dominant trend that swept away the rococo and all the free-flowing forms and designs with which that style was associated. The way had been opened for such a fresh revival just before the middle of the century with the excavations at Pompeii and Herculaneum (instigated by an interest in such matters that was obviously already active). In the long-buried cities were discovered unexpected and enchanting revelations of Roman design, as well as evidence of an ancient way of life that had been abruptly and eerily halted in the midst of a daily routine by a heavy fall of volcanic ash from Vesuvius in A.D. 79. The excitement caused by those remarkable discoveries led to fresh expeditions. Rome, Palmyra, Baalbeck, Spoleto (Split), and other ancient sites and ruins were examined with new enthusiasm and interest. Western Europe at large was seized by archaeological fervor.

Johann Winckelmann, not an artist but a scholar, was one of the most influential figures in the art history of the eighteenth century. The publication of his first book in 1755 marks the beginning of the neo-classical movement in modern art. His two books on Herculaneum and Pompeii, in 1762 and 1764, gave scholars the first orderly and scientific information about the excavated treasures. Although he never visited Greece, Winckelmann extolled Greek art over the more familiar Roman motifs. The portrait of Winckelmann reproduced at right was painted in 1768, the same year that he was murdered in Trieste by his traveling companion, Francesco Arcangeli. Arcangeli was captured and sentenced to "be broken alive on the wheel, from the head to the feet, until your soul departs from your body."

The French landscape painter Hubert Robert, a close friend of Fragonard, virtually built his professional career on picturesque renderings of classical ruins, sometimes quite literal, at other times imaginatively arranged like stage sets. At twenty-two years of age, returning to Paris from a visit in Italy, he was an immediate success with his canvases. "Robert of the Ruins," he was called. He sold as many of his scenes to foreign courts as he did to his French customers. Following the example of Catherine the Great, Russian noblemen purchased them in quantities; Russian museums are full of them to this day.

As the century progressed, a flow of books published in a number of different languages reported and illustrated the various discoveries made. And out of the evidence presented in this growing library of publication evolved the style of the new classical revival. Among the most important of such volumes were those produced by Johann Joachim Winckelmann, a poverty-stricken scholar, son of a German cobbler, who, struck by the decay of art in Germany and Italy, exhorted artists to take their models from Greco-Roman antiquity. In the first of his books, issued in 1755, he concluded that "the only way for us to become great, indeed to become inimitably great . . . is through imitation of the ancients." Finally, in 1764, after seven years of study and effort, he published the massive illustrated volumes entitled *History of Ancient Art*, a work accepted throughout Europe as an important event in the history of literature and art. (Frederick the Great invited Winckelmann to come to Berlin as superintendent of the royal library and cabinet of antiquities, but offered a salary Winckelmann considered unworthy of his great erudition.) The brand of neo-classicism promoted by his theories swept the Western world. By chance, West arrived in Rome on his circuitous way from America to London while Winckelmann was there, came to know the great man, and briefly studied with Winckelmann's earliest painter-disciple, the Bohemian-born Anton Raphael Mengs. West then proceeded to England to delight George III and other noted patrons with such paintings as *Agrippina with the Ashes of Germanicus*, *The Parting of Hector and Andromache*, *Regulus Leaving Rome*—and others with titles that read almost like a syllabus of ancient history. With these he led the way for the French artist Jacques Louis David, who, in the years following West's early triumphs, would paint re-creations of the classical world that were so popular among important elements of society that he became something of a dictator of art during the period of the French Revolution and the Napoleonic aftermath.

As might be expected, sculpture was a fruitful field for the neo-classicists, and the outstanding practitioner was Jean Antoine Houdon. As his fame grew, all the celebrities of the day—Voltaire, Rousseau, Diderot, Catherine the Great, Turgot, Louis XVI, Benjamin Franklin, and many others— were glad to sit or stand, to have their likenesses recorded in the classical repose of long-established heroes whose fame could never diminish with time. Houdon draped his seated figure of the scrawny, aged Voltaire in a classical toga that fitted the philosophe as casually as a dressing gown. He came to America to model George Washington, the modern Cincinnatus, whom he depicted once in classical costume, and again in modern dress but in a classical pose, his hand resting on the fasces that were the symbol of union.

In architecture and decoration, the neoclassical mode swept all before it. One of the earliest exponents, and the most influential, of the new style in England was the Scottish architect Robert Adam. As a young man Adam toured Italy and Dalmatia and examined the ruins at first hand. He took with him as draughtsman the great French classicist Charles Louis Clérisseau. In Rome he met Winckelmann and Giovanni Battista Piranesi, the extraordinary architect and etcher who produced nearly a thousand different plates dramatizing the grandeur that was Rome in views that were printed and reprinted by the tens of thousands, like the most popular postcards of today. With those theatrical but precise depictions he hypnotized the next several generations with the spell of Rome and, as A. Hyatt Mayor has written, "imposed a super-Roman scale on the architectural imagination that was to create our law courts, museums, and railroad terminals." In 1762 he dedicated his superb folio of the Campus Martius to Adam.

Then in the 1760's and 1770's, with his brother James, Robert Adam

Famed sculptor Jean Antoine Houdon is shown surrounded by his students in this painting by Louis Boilly. The busts of Washington, Jefferson, and Franklin are seen in the background.
ARCHIVES PHOTOGRAPHIQUES

created light and graceful adaptations of Roman forms and ornaments which almost immediately became the fashionable vocabulary of British architecture and design. A few years before the American Revolution, in 1773, the two brothers issued the first volume of *The Works in Architecture of Robert and James Adam, Esquires*, a publication that led to widespread copies and modifications of their inventions and that brought those, with different degrees of fidelity, to the attention of a wide audience. Some years later, in a lecture at the Royal Academy, Sir John Soane, one of Adam's most ardent admirers, quite truthfully remarked that "To Mr. Adam's taste in the Ornaments of his Buildings, and Furniture, we stand indebted in-as-much as Manufactures of every kind felt, as it were, the electric power of the Revolution in Art."

The Adam brothers designed some of the finest furniture of the day. In his later years Thomas Chippendale, whose *Director* had earlier been to the art of furniture what Reynold's pronouncements were to painting, became associated with the Adams and also worked in the light, classical manner they

This print, from The Works in Architecture of Robert and James Adam, Esquires, *shows the supper room and part of the ballroom in a pavilion designed by Robert Adam for a party in the garden of the earl of Derby at* The Oaks in Surrey in June, 1774.
SWARBRICK, *The Works in Architecture of Robert and John Adam*

had made so popular. And in the years that followed, those master designers George Hepplewhite and Thomas Sheraton were to continue in a similar vein. One of England's most eminent and successful classicists was Josiah Wedgwood, who in 1753 had started his own pottery works and built around it a town, near Burslem, which he named, significantly, Etruria. His output ranged from drainage pipes to the most exquisite tableware. For the latter, and for many other products, he frankly imitated classical models, but he also originated other forms, especially the famous jasper and basalt wares (which simulate natural stones used for decorative and useful objects in antiquity), with delicately embossed Greek figures. To provide such designs he employed John Flaxman, a very successful (and conventional) artist who went on from such assignments to illustrate Homer and Aeschylus, with drawings based on the art of the Greek vase painters, and to model imitations of classical statuary. From 1763 Wedgwood's potteries were exporting more than a half million items a year to the Continent and North America.

The impact of the new vogue was not fully felt in America until after the problems of war and peace with Britain were settled; but on the Continent architecture and decoration underwent much the same transformation as in England. What has become known as the Louis XVI style, with its avoidance of the sinuous irregularities and feminine delicacies of the rococo, and its insistence on straight, masculine lines and symmetrical proportions, was gaining way in the fashionable world at least a decade before that young monarch took to the throne in 1774. It was during the later decades of the century that England was assuming artistic leadership in Europe, at least in architecture, decoration, and gardening, and the development of the Louis XVI style was strongly influenced by English precedents.

That this was so was only natural. The deep historical tide of the eighteenth century was the rise of England. From Marlborough's victories early in the century through the "wonderful year" of 1759, the British steadily advanced in political, economic, and cultural importance. In 1762 a friend of Horace Walpole, just returned from Paris, told him, "our passion for everything French is nothing for theirs for everything English. There is a book published called the *anglomanie*." Not only France but Italy, Germany, and even Russia found in English institutions, English literature, and English customs and fashions worthy models to emulate. (As one small token of that enthusiastic admiration, Catherine the Great—as earlier noted—commissioned Wedgwood to provide her with an imperial dinner service decorated with views of English country seats.)

For artists and architects, as for dilettantes and amateurs, Italy remained a vast museum with irresistible appeal; one whose monuments and collections must be studied for culture's sake, and to learn invaluable lessons in the light of the past. But, except in musical matters, as a center of creative activity Italy's importance dwindled with the eighteenth century—compared, that is, with developments in northern countries. Many of the eighteenth-century Italian artists whose work is best remembered and most admired today had died or left the country before 1776. Giovanni Battista Tiepolo, whose illusionistic ceiling frescoes seemed to open a way to the sky above, brought to a glorious climax a century-old Venetian tradition. What is generally considered his masterpiece was painted on the ceilings of the Episcopal Palace in Würzburg with the aid of his two sons. He had earlier been proposed by the

This Wedgwood vase, manufactured at Etruria, is called "Dancing Graces."
WEDGWOOD COMPANY

Swedish minister in Venice as the perfect artist to decorate Stockholm's royal palace. "He is full of wit and zest," it was reported, "easy to deal with, bubbling over with ideas; he has a gift for brilliant color, and works at a prodigious speed; he paints a picture in less time than it takes another artist to mix his colors." Late in his life, when he was in his mid-sixties, Tiepolo was persuaded against his inclination to journey to Madrid, again with his sons, to work on the royal palace there; and there he suddenly died in 1770 without ever seeing his beloved Venice again. His sons continued to paint in his manner, but they lacked the father's genius.

Giovanni Antonio Canale, best remembered as Canaletto, was almost the exact contemporary of the senior Tiepolo, and also a Venetian. Half the world came to visualize Venice as he recorded the city in his *vedute*, or views. For nearly twenty-five years the British consul to Venice, Joseph Smith, acted as Canaletto's business manager, and in that capacity acquired for George III fifty-three of the artist's paintings and one hundred of his drawings. In 1745 the artist went to London and stayed there for the better part of ten years, demanding and getting stiff prices for his work and leaving his impress on a school of English landscape painting. Hardly a fashionable house in England was without its Canalettos. Almost to the day he died in 1768, at the age of seventy-one, and back in Venice, he was still hard at work ("without spectacles," as he boasted). Canaletto's nephew, Bernardo Belloto, who was at least the peer of his famous uncle as a scenic painter, left Venice as a young man and did the bulk of his work in the northern countries. He visited Dresden, where he was appointed court painter to Augustus II. He painted views of Munich and Vienna. Then, in 1767, on his way to Russia, he was invited by Stanislas II of Poland to remain in Warsaw, where he spent all the rest of his day. Belloto's depictions of that city were so precisely detailed that when the old part of the city was restored after the frightful destruction of World War II they could confidently be used as documentary evidence.

In his own lifetime Canaletto's former apprentice and Tiepolo's brother-in-law, Francesco Guardi, did not enjoy the fame of either of those masters. Most of his patrons were Englishmen living in Venice. Today, however, his shimmering visions of eighteenth-century Venice—its balls and promenades and water pageants, caught in their ephemeral moods and the evanescent atmosphere of that enchanted city—are valued far above the paintings of his contemporaries. Guardi found Venice lovely even in its decay; he noted glints of color and passages of poetry of the squalor of a crumbling tenement and the laundry that hung from its windows. Modern critics see in his sparkling landscapes (canalscapes, they could be called), with their bright highlights and free, suggestive brushwork, an anticipation of Impressionism.

The single eighteenth-century artist who speaks most directly to our own generation is unquestionably the Spaniard Francisco José de Goya y Lucientes, known the world over simply as Goya. He emerged from relative obscurity as a young man in the 1770's. It was a propitious time for the recognition and the blossoming of his singular talent. Charles III had come to the throne in 1759 eager to make Spain great once again, so that the country could play a prominent role on the international stage. For a while Spain felt the invigorating impact of the Enlightenment as the new monarch tried to release his kingdom from the bondage of its old and reactionary traditions. In 1767, following the lead of Portugal and France, Charles expelled the Jesuits from Spain and all its colonial holdings; a long step toward ending the strangle hold that the Church had for centuries maintained over the civil fabric of society—very importantly over the education of Spanish youth. The country felt a new spirit of secularization and cosmopolitanism as textbooks were finally modernized and experimental methods in science and in medicine, so long suppressed, were introduced.

For more than a century no native artist of any importance had emerged in Spain. To stimulate the arts Charles III brought to his capital not only Tiepolo, but Mengs, who became the director of the Royal Academy of San Fernando and virtual dictator of Spanish art. More disparate alien talents would hardly have been selected than the Italians, with their flamboyant oppression of a moribund tradition, and the Italianized German, with his bloodless formulas for a new classicism. However, the elder Tiepolo, as noted, died in 1770 and Mengs, his health broken, returned to Italy in 1777.

By then Goya's star was clearly rising. In 1776, defying—and transcending—the academic traditions so dear to Mengs, the young artist had produced for the Royal Tapestry Factory (whose work was directed by Mengs) a series of cartoons that portrayed the people of his own kind and time, rather than scenes from classical mythology and heroic history. With the boldest realism he showed bullfights and kite flying, games and markets and festivals, scenes to quicken the pulse of any contemporary Spaniard. Even Mengs was forced to recognize the vitality of this strictly unorthodox work, and before he quit Spain for good, he gave the young rebel further commissions. Goya was firmly established. He was soon enrolled as one of the court painters and admitted into the Academy.

In the middle of his life Goya was left stone-deaf by an illness. Yet his most enduring achievements were to fill his remaining years. He became the greatest printmaker to appear since Rembrandt, and with his series of etchings he produced the first Spanish works of art to stir the interest of the outside world. Locked in utter silence, his mind's eye released images unlike any that had ever been recorded. Goya became the castigating critic of cruelty and evil, of war and bloodshed, the bitter but humane reporter of human misery and suffering. From the farthest reaches of his muted inner world he projected nightmares that explored the most desperate realities of life. And with those visions he left the eighteenth century behind and prepared a bridge to the modern world.

The transformation of the musical arts was one of the more remarkable achievements of the eighteenth century. None of the other arts surpassed music in variety of invention or in sheer volume of production; none more clearly reflected the intellectual, social, and cultural growth of the age. At the risk of vastly oversimplifying matters, the changes that took place during the eighteenth century could be reduced to the history of the piano. That revolutionary keyboard instrument was introduced at the dawn of the century by the Italian Bartolommeo Cristofori. With its wide range of more than seven octaves, and particularly with its capacity to sound notes of any volume by using the keyboard to vary the pressure of its felt-covered hammers against vibrating, high-tension strings secured in a steel frame, the piano immeasurably increased the texture and variety that could be produced by a keyboard instrument. The harpsichord had a limited range, and its notes, sounded by plucking the brass strings fixed in a wooden frame, could not be varied in

The development of the piano (above, Bartolommeo Christofori's 1720 model) revolutionized the music world.
THE METROPOLITAN MUSEUM OF ART, THE CROSBY BROWN COLLECTION OF MUSICAL INSTRUMENTS, 1889

volume. (The piano was originally called the *gravicembalo col piano e forte*, "the gravity operated harpsichord with softness and loudness.") As it was developed and improved during the course of the century, the piano gradually rendered the harpsichord obsolete. The century ended with the earliest of Beethoven's great piano sonatas, harbinger of a new era in music.

That quick and limited glance at the musical scene does not, of course, even begin to suggest all the radical changes that had already revolutionized the art before the advent of Beethoven, and that made the flowering of his unique genius possible. The story must be very briefly told, for in its entirety it concerns a host of musicians whose names are hardly remembered by most of us today but who nevertheless made their important contributions. For most of the century Europe acknowledged the supremacy of Italian music, of Italian instruments, and of Italian performers. Everyone in that southern country seemed to have music in his very blood. "In the Piazza San Marco," one English traveler observed, "a man from the people—a shoemaker, a blacksmith—strikes up an air; other persons of his sort, joining him, sing this air in several parts, with an accuracy and taste which one seldom encounters in the best society of our Northern countries." To Italy went the music-minded amateurs and professionals of the northern countries—including such masters as Christoph Willibald Gluck and Wolfgang Amadeus Mozart—to observe, to listen, to study, and to learn. Johann Sebastian Bach studied Italian music, as did George Frederick Handel; Rousseau (himself a musician) and Goethe crossed the Alps to wonder at the music they heard in Italy; and Italian musicians, performers, conductors, and composers crossed the Alps in the other direction to entertain and charm northern audiences. Twelve hundred different operas

The finest musical instruments were made in Italy, where they were considered objects of art, precisely fashioned in precious wood and inlaid with ivory, enamel, or jewels. Pupils of Stradivari continued to produce violins, violas, and violoncellos in Cremona. The print seen below is an instrument-maker's workshop from Diderot's Encyclopédie.
GIRAUDON

were heard in the theaters of Venice alone in the course of the eighteenth century.

However, the conventions of opera were reaching a point of absurdity. Artificial, stilted plots of no consequence were used primarily to display the technical virtuosity of the performers and the ingenuity of the composer. A long coloratura passage could be devoted to the singing of a single word, heedless of any dramatic action or sensible narrative. Words and music became incompatible, the performance incomprehensible, and a clamor arose for reforms that would lead to productions that were more reasonable, simple, and natural—in the spirit of the Enlightenment. "There is nothing that has more startled our English Audience," Joseph Addison wrote in *The Spectator*, "than the *Italian Recitativo* at its first Entrance upon the Stage. People were wonderfully surprised to hear Generals singing the Word of Command, and Ladies delivering Messages in Music. Our Countrymen could not forbear laughing when they heard a Lover chanting out a Billet-doux, and even the Superscription of a Letter set to a Tune." (The fact that the language itself was alien and generally unintelligible was something else again.)

In 1728 the lyric poet John Gay pricked that balloon by presenting *The Beggar's Opera*, which was at once a satire on the standard Italian opera and on the political party in power. The beggar, professed author of the opera, announces in his introduction that "I have not made my Opera throughout unnatural, like those in vogue. . . ." The performance was a sensational success that ran for sixty-three nights. (Its producer was named Rich, and it was said that the opera made Gay rich and Rich gay.) As one consequence, in the face of such ridicule, the Royal Academy of Music, where traditional operas were staged, went bankrupt for lack of patronage.

In 1752 an Italian troupe journeyed to Paris to perform *opera bouffa*, comic opera, and set off what has been termed the "Buffoons' War" between those who admired the light-hearted simplicity of its presentation and those who clung to the traditional forms represented by the pompous French operatic tragedies of the time. Diderot, Rousseau, and other philosophes came out in favor of the Italian innovations. Rousseau caused a sensation by claiming that the French language in itself had no musical possibilities. "There is neither measure nor melody in French music," he wrote in a published pamphlet, "because the language itself is not susceptible of either; French song is nothing but a continual bark. . . ." He later changed his mind, but for the moment his comment so enraged the performers at the L'Opéra that they hanged and burned him in effigy.

Then, at Vienna in 1762, Gluck presented his *Orfeo ed Euridice*, and five years later *Alceste*, and with these performances he changed the history of opera. He was resolved "to divest the music entirely of all those abuses with which the vanity of singers, or the too great complacency of composers, has so long disfigured Italian opera and made the most splendid and most beautiful of spectacles the most ridiculous and wearisome. . . ." "I have striven to restrict music," he explained, "to its true office of serving poetry by means of expression . . . I believed that my greatest labor should be devoted to seeking a beautiful simplicity." He had *Orfeo* translated into French, and it won a substantial success when it was presented in Paris. It not only caused Rousseau to change his mind about the musical potential of the French language, but elicited from Marie Antoinette a pension of six thousand francs (to *mon cher*

The operas of Christoph Willibald Gluck (pictured at the spinet in this handsome 1775 portrait) presented a new integration of drama and music on the stage.
GIRAUDON

This eighteenth-century engraving shows the type of organ played by Johann Sebastian Bach. The hand-pumped bellows force air to the pipe under the keyboard. The finger keys release air to the small pipes at top center for the higher tones. The pedals control the low tones produced through the pipes at right.

Gluck). A dozen years later the composer died a rich and famous old man.

One distinguished contemporary considered Gluck the greatest composer of the eighteenth century, but it would be difficult to support such claims, preceded by Bach and Handel, both of whom left a deep impress on the history of music. Bach was primarily a Church composer; his object was to achieve "well ordered music in the honor of God." Among his many other works he composed some three hundred sacred cantatas, but since only a relatively few of his compositions were published in his lifetime he was not then well known except among fellow musicians. However, he brought to consummation the fugue form at a time when such contrapuntal, polyphonic compositions were passing out of fashion in favor of new combinations of harmonies and instrumental textures, and of music of more secular nature. More than a century would pass before the peculiar and powerful genius of Bach became generally acknowledged.

Beethoven thought Handel "the greatest, the ablest composer that ever lived," and Franz Joseph Haydn called him "the master of us all" when he heard his *Messiah* performed in Westminster Abbey—and wept in his rapture. Born in the same year as Bach, in 1685, and in the same province of Saxony (although the two men never met in their lives), Handel was as secular in his music as Bach was religious. Handel wrote for the living public, and he succeeded, both in the eyes of his contemporaries and the judgment of posterity. He went to England as a young man and lived there for the rest of his life. He had become embroiled in the arguments over Italian opera and had been in charge of the Royal Academy of music when it failed. That failure changed his musical life. With a stroke of genius he turned from opera to oratorio. Dispensing with all the lavish costuming and expensive scenery of the former, with acting and frivolous virtuosity and other such troublesome affectations, he would thenceforth simply assemble a chorus on stage and have them sing. With this development Handel, who never did quite master the English language, rose to fame as the most celebrated of English composers in the history of that country, and established the oratorio as the national art form. With his contrapuntal music Bach had summed up the past. With his masterful command of melody and broadly sweeping choral music Handel anticipated the future; he was a precursor of the Enlightenment. He liked writing for huge public audiences rather than for the elite. In 1727 Handel wrote an anthem for the coronation of George II, which had been used for all subsequent coronations. At his death in 1759 he was almost a public monument. Although born a foreigner, he was buried in Westminster Abbey.

The second half of the eighteenth century saw a revolution in the style of instrumental music, a revolution that freed music from its earlier bondage to other art forms. This came about as one aspect of the search for a more classical sense of form and balance that characterized developments in all the arts of the period. As it developed during these years, the sonata form influenced music of almost every description. It was what has been called the large architectural order of classicism in music, an instrumental design capable of great expansion, especially as expressed in string quartets and symphonies. The string quartet became the standard chamber music organization, with two violins, a viola, and a cello. New instruments were added to symphonic groups, mixing strings, woodwinds, brasses, and percussion in concerted compositions, thus broadening the range and swelling the volume of performances. The symphony, indeed, became an independent and uniquely expressive form of music on a scale never before imagined (although by no means the mammoth ensembles that came into being in the late nineteenth century). As earlier noted, the piano became the single instrument that probably attracted the most professional attention, and a vast library of music was composed for its performance.

Innumerable fertile talents contributed to this fundamental and exhilarating evolution of musical form and substance. Before the advent of Beethoven with his towering genius, Haydn and Mozart mastered the new concepts with a perfection that has brought them immortality. The accomplishments of these great composers were based on groundwork laid by a host of brilliant predecessors and contemporaries who are not mentioned here only for lack of space. Haydn was immensely prolific as a composer over the seventy-seven years of his life. He is credited with 106 symphonies, about 70 string quartets, 60 piano sonatas, 25 operas, 4 oratorios, and hundreds of lesser works. Most of his career he was in the service of two immensely wealthy Hungarian princes, the Esterházy brothers. Early in the years of this service he won the admiration of all Europe. In 1776 when asked for an autobiographical sketch he could truthfully answer, "I have had the good fortune to please almost everywhere."

The glory of Haydn's creative accomplishment rests on his contribution to the sonata form, on his greatness as the creator of the string quartet, on his reputation as the so-called father of the symphony, and on his great influence on the development of the modern orchestra. Haydn was the son of a Croatian

Thoroughly untemperamental, Franz Joseph Haydn befriended his competitors and suffused his music with gaiety. He hoped that in his music "the weary and worn, or the man burdened with affairs, may enjoy some solace and refreshment." This unusual portrait shows him standing while Mozart writes music at a table.

peasant, and the melodic strain of native folk songs runs through his sophisticated constructions. In his own words, he hoped that in listening to his music, "the weary and the worn, or the man burdened with affairs, may enjoy a few moments of solace and refreshment." Once, late in his life, when a group of musical amateurs wrote to thank him for the pleasure they had in performing one of his pieces, he responded, ". . . this is the greatest comfort to my declining years—that I am often the source from which you, and many other families receptive to heartfelt emotion, derive pleasure and satisfaction in the quiet of your homes." He well deserved to be known affectionately as "Papa" Haydn.

His sometime pupil and younger contemporary Mozart was hardly a less prolific composer, although his life span was less than half that of the older man. Almost incredibly, in the mere thirty-six years that he lived, Mozart composed 626 works, including 52 symphonies, 51 concertos, 77 sonatas, and 22 operas, among other pieces. He was off to an early start. Before he was six he was concertizing. He wrote his first symphony at the age of eight, and an opera when he was twelve. As a small child he played before the Empress Maria Theresa at Vienna, and when the performance was over he sat in her lap and "hugged and kissed her thoroughly." One day when he slipped on the polished floor of the palace the archduchess, later to become queen of France as Marie Antoinette, helped him up. "You are very kind," the child said, "when I grow up I will marry you."

As an extraordinary child prodigy Mozart was almost mercilessly exploited by his proud, loving, but inordinately ambitious father. However, in spite of his great gifts and his brilliant demonstrations of them, Mozart never won enough commissions or otherwise enjoyed a sufficient income to relieve him from the want of funds that plagued his life. At one point Haydn wrote young Mozart's father, "Before God and as an honest man . . . your son is the greatest composer known to me either in person or by reputation. He has taste and, what is better, the most profound knowledge of composition." Mozart believed as much of himself, and that knowledge bred an understandable but unfortunate arrogance that proved a disservice to a remunerative career. The archbishop of Salzburg, whom he served intermittently as court musician for almost ten years (and who treated Mozart as a servant in his retinue) was provoked by a show of the musician's arrogance to the point of having him literally kicked out of his service. His delightful opera, *The Marriage of Figaro*, is superficially a comical tale of a contest between servant and master. Essentially it extols the dignity of the common man and dares to question the morals and intelligence of the nobility. The plot was based on the comedy of the same title by Beaumarchais that was regarded as an attack on the privileges of aristocracy. Mozart died a pauper and was buried in an unmarked grave. No one knows where his remains lie.

Yet in his tragically short life Mozart lifted eighteenth-century music to giddy heights. In his dramatic operas he excelled in the delineation of personality. The serenity and clarity of his great string quartets and his matchless last symphonies provide enduring testimonials to his mastery of these forms. In the balanced, measured, and beautifully proportioned style of these and other works he expressed in musical terms an ideal of sophistication that was in the pure spirit of the Age of Enlightenment—innovative, rational, aspiring, and exquisitely ordered.

Madame Vigée-Lebrun, a self-portrait

THE ARTISTS' WORLD

The changing intellectual climate of the eighteenth century had a tremendous influence on the world of art. Until about 1750 boisterous, exuberant rococo art, subsidized by rich patrons, predominated. The Marquise du Châtelet expressed the prevailing attitude toward the arts: "We have nothing else to do in this world but seek pleasant sensations and feelings." By 1770 that attitude had undergone considerable revision. In the words of the painter Joshua Reynolds, "The wish of the genuine painter must be more extensive: instead of endeavoring to amuse mankind...he must endeavor to improve them by the grandeur of his ideas"—a view that led to the rise of neoclassicism and romanticism.

IN THE BAROQUE TRADITION

During the first half of the eighteenth century Italian painters and sculptors were the leading exponents and practitioners of baroque art. Dramatic ceiling paintings, evoking the miraculous, the supernatural, the ecstatic, were in demand in Italy and other parts of Europe. Giovanni Tiepolo was the recognized master of large-scale, decorative painting. Tiepolo believed that "painters must try and succeed in large scale works capable of pleasing the noble and the rich, because it is they who make the fortune of artists. . . ." As the painting below illustrates, he did just that. Commissioned by the Barbaro family, Tiepolo painted the *Glorification of Francesco Barbaro* between 1745 and 1750 for the ceiling of the Barbaro palace in Venice (the bearded man in the center is Barbaro). The Trevi Fountain (opposite) was completed in 1762 at the end of the baroque era. The largest fountain in Rome, its complex composition of sculpture and waterworks, designed by Nicola Salvi, dramatized the rebuilding of the city under the direction of Pope Clement XII. Numerous sculptors, notably Pietro Bracci, worked on the project, which took thirty years to finish.

Throughout Europe, public buildings and monuments were viewed as a gauge of royal power and prestige. Smaller kingdoms sought to emulate the most powerful monarchies. Turin, capital of Piedmont, had a tradition of impressive architectural accomplishment. In 1720 Piedmont, along with Savoy and Nice, became part of the kingdom of Sardinia. King Vittorio Amedeo II launched a building program in and around Turin under the direction of Filippo Juvarra. Part of Juvarra's baroque royal hunting lodge, completed in 1733, is seen opposite. Another Italian architect, named Giovanni Piranesi, was a major influence on a new art movement, which stressed the ideal of noble simplicity and the rational application of classical elements. Piranesi produced over a thousand copper-plate etchings of ancient Rome, which became extremely popular throughout Europe. He is most highly acclaimed for a series of fourteen etchings (above, number 6), completed in 1745, of imaginative designs for prisons. Piranesi considered these etchings a means of relaxation, and regarded his archaeological studies and reconstructions of Rome as his claim to greatness.

THE

GRAND

SCALE

THE POPULAR
THEATER

The theater world was in a period of transition in most European countries in 1776. Although condemned by the Church as immoral, extravagant theatrical productions captured the public's fancy as never before. Some of the finest actors in history graced England's stages, and yet there were only two dramatists of any significance: Richard Sheridan (*The Rivals*, 1775; *The School for Scandal*, 1777) and Oliver Goldsmith (*She Stoops to Conquer*, 1773). The *Comédie Française*, housed in the Théâtre-Français in Paris, was the best performing troupe in Europe. Their productions of two plays, *Eugénie* (1769) and *Le Barbier de Seville* (1775), had been a triumph for a new dramatist named Beaumarchais. Below, cast members from a 1778 production of Voltaire's *Irène* are shown honoring the author as France's greatest man of letters. In Italy comedy had dominated the theater since opera had driven tragic drama from the stage (opposite, an opera in progress at Turin). Except for plays by Carlo Gozzi and Carlo Goldoni, the *commedia dell'arte*, featuring character masks and improvised dialogue that often sank to slapstick and buffoonery, dominated Italian comedy.

MUSICAL REFINEMENTS

In the second half of the eighteenth century musical activity in Europe increased as never before. The rich and powerful maintained private orchestras, and many even mastered the playing of instruments. The middle classes followed suit; nearly every house contained a musical instrument (opposite, a family gathered to play at home by Pietro Longhi). The widening audience for concerts diminished the Church's domination of music, and also paved the way for new instruments and art forms—the piano, the symphony, the string quartet. Great composers, notably Gluck, Haydn, and Mozart (above, playing the harpsichord at the age of ten), flourished in this stimulating atmosphere.

MASTERS OF PORTRAITURE

The paintings of François Boucher and Jean Honoré Fragonard reflected society's values in mid-eighteenth-century France. Under the patronage of Madame de Pompadour, Boucher developed an artistic compromise between public aspiration toward classical learning and private taste for amorous adventure. Boucher's values were those of his clients, and neither they nor he cared to look deeper. His eroticism consisted simply in the frank enjoyment of the senses. His *Girl on a Couch* (above) is Louise O'Murphy, who was the mistress of Louis XV for some years and bore him several children. Boucher's students further developed the sensuousness and eroticism that he had exploited so successfully. Fragonard had a lighter touch than Boucher but his dedication to the frivolous, the rococo, the aristocratic remained the same. The *Hazards of the Swing* (opposite) is his most famous picture; the lover gazes in delight as his mistress swings higher and higher. Fragonard could not adapt to changing art tastes; he died, outmoded and barely tolerated, in 1806.

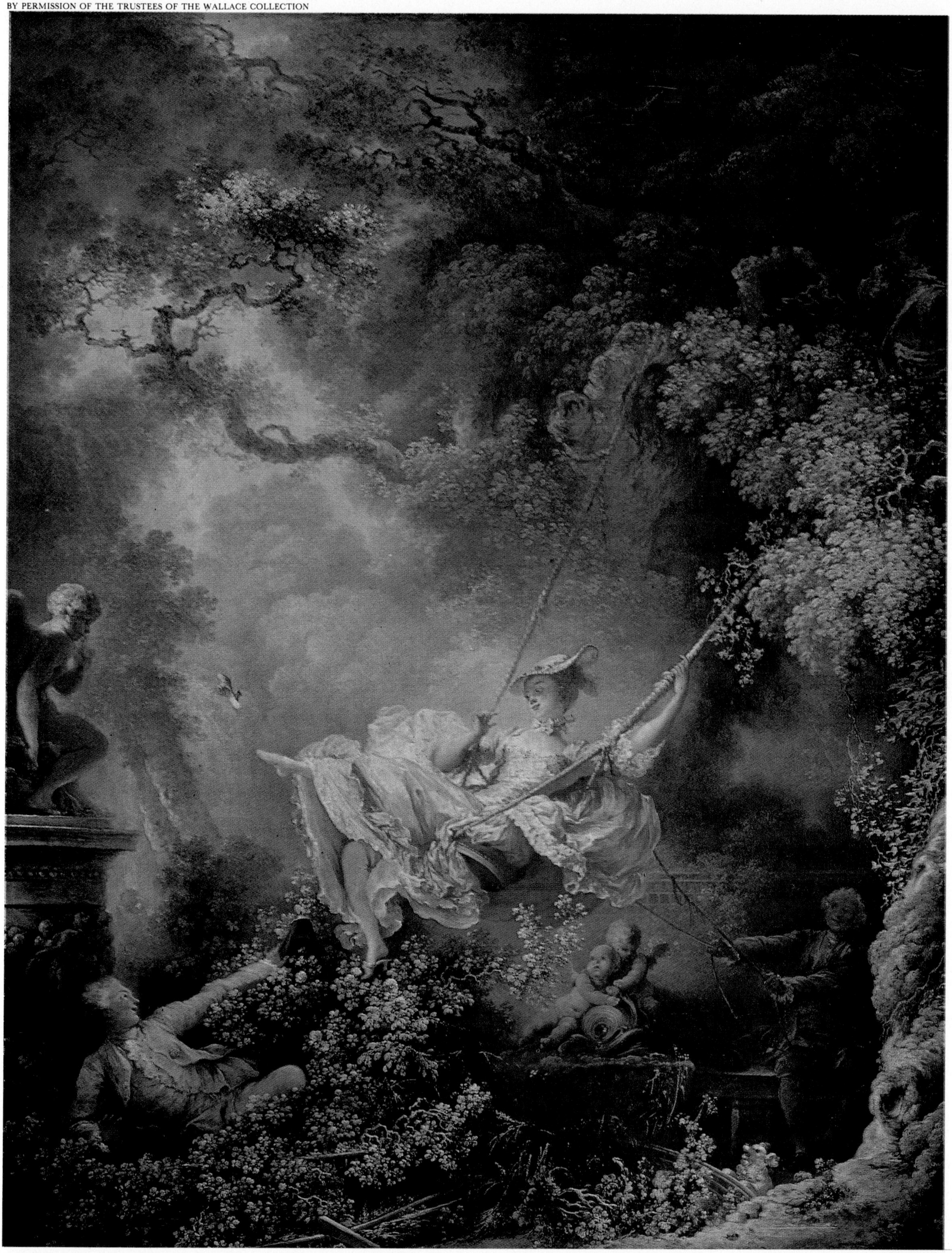

The duke and duchess of Atholl and their seven older children spend a quiet afternoon fishing as the family's pet lemur looks on.

Johann Zoffany painted the figures in London and another artist did the background at Blair Castle, the duke's Scottish seat.

290

Aristocrats were the chief patrons of the arts in England, and the latter half of the eighteenth century was the great age of portraiture. In order to support themselves, artists were forced to do portraits pleasing to the sitters, and Thomas Gainsborough, for one, resented it: "I make portraits for a living, landscapes because I love them. . . ." He often worked landscapes into his portraits, as is seen in the detail opposite from *Robert Andrews and His Wife*. Patronage had a broader base in France, and the art was more varied. Searching for an alternative to Fragonard and Boucher, Diderot praised the work of Jean Baptiste Simeon Chardin. To Diderot his paintings conveyed a sense of dignity, of human worth, of the values of ordinary life. His subjects were plain and of the middle class (top right, *Prayer Before Meal*), and Diderot wrote: "Chardin's genre is truth." Diderot was even more taken with the work of Jean Baptiste Greuze. At bottom, in *The Father's Curse*, a lower middle-class son is leaving home with a recruiting sergeant. Greuze seemed to have fused two ideals: Diderot's idea that art should teach a moral lesson and Rousseau's conviction that simple things and poor people are inherently noble. Before the end of the 1770's Diderot had condemned the theatrical disguise and make believe in Greuze's settings.

FAMILY SCENES

CLASSICAL REVIVAL

What Diderot really wanted was art that expressed heroic virtue in Roman style. Beginning with Benjamin West's *Death of Wolfe* (opposite) in 1770, paintings of historical events conveyed stoicism, fortitude, and courage. West's was the first history painting showing modern dress, and it represented the event as it ought to have been, not as it was. Jacques Louis David's pre-1789 paintings extol civic virtue and self-sacrifice. In *The Oath of the Horatii* (below) three brothers swear on their swords to "win or die for liberty." After the Revolution, David rose to virtual dictatorship of the arts in France. The most controversial statue of this period was one that European intellectuals chose Jean Baptiste Pigalle to make of a living subject—Voltaire. Suggested by Madame Necker in 1770, contributions came in from all over Europe. Even Rousseau contributed. The result (opposite) was a compromise between Pigalle's desire to do a classical nude and Voltaire's objection that his body was not a fit subject.

THE GENIUS
OF GOYA

The art of Francisco Goya went through remarkable transformations during his lifetime (1746–1828), and in 1776 he was just beginning. A year earlier he had started work at the Royal Tapestry Manufactory, under the direction of Anton Raphael Mengs. Mengs dropped the biblical and mythological themes that had predominated in Spain and ordered compositions based on the realities and pleasantries of country life. In 1777 Goya completed the first group of his tapestry cartoons, among which is *The Parasol* (above). For ten years the tapestries were Goya's major work, but he also began his career as a portraitist. Goya painted a number of court officials and members of the aristocracy in traditional eighteenth-century poses. *Don Manuel Osorio de Zuniga* (opposite), completed in 1788, is considered the best of his fashionable portraits. The cats hungrily watching the pet magpie suggest the creatures that emerged in Goya's *Los Caprichos*, a series of etchings in the nature of grotesque social satire, completed in the 1790's. Goya's later devastatingly human paintings of war made him the idol of nineteenth-century romantics.

ROMANTIC

RUMBLINGS

English artist George Stubbs' patrons included every nobleman and member of the royal family who owned a horse; an authority on anatomy—Stubbs lectured at medical schools—he was also a superb artist. Then, on a visit to North Africa, he saw a horse killed by a lion. Haunted by the vision, he painted a series of pictures, including *Lion Attacking a Horse* (above), completed in 1770. Although Stubbs chose not to pursue it, he had created a new type of animal painting, full of the Romantic feeling for the grandeur and violence of nature. The search for emotion also led to the dark recesses of the mind as in *The Nightmare* (opposite, a detail) by John Henry Fuseli. With a romantic's love of disorder, he rejected Joshua Reynolds' quest for perfection and declared that "the indiscriminate pursuit of perfection infallibly leads to mediocrity." Reynolds, however, was a major influence on art tastes, and the Swiss-born Fuseli was somewhat discouraged about the reception of his paintings: "There is little hope of poetical painting finding encouragement in England. The people are not prepared for it. Portrait with them is everything. Their tastes and feelings all go to realities."

297

AMERICAN

From what has been told in earlier chapters of this book, it is apparent that during the last four decades of the eighteenth century there was throughout much of the Western world a growing disenchantment with the prevailing and traditional social structure. There was indeed a groping toward a new kind of community that would be more egalitarian in its nature than the old order. Politically this implied that no established, privileged, closed, or self-recruiting groups of individuals or classes should control government or public power in general. In the new state that was envisioned, administrators and legislators would exercise only such authority as was duly designated to them by those they governed, and those representatives could be removed from their offices by proper legal measures and for good cause. It was, in sum, a revolutionary movement, or at least a revolutionary spirit, which manifested itself in different ways and with varying results in different countries, but with objectives and principles that were everywhere similar.

In referring to such tendencies, an eminent American historian has termed those last decades of the century—the decades on either side of the year 1776 —"the age of the democratic revolution," cautioning that the word "democracy" did not then mean, as it now generally does, that suffrage need be universal. However, it did signify "a new feeling for a kind of equality" in human relationships; a departure from the hierarchical divisions that had for so long put men more or less in their fixed place in society. None of the ideas that fired these revolutionary trends were unique to America; they were the common

HERITAGE

property of enlightened men of the time in all countries. But it was in the years before, during, and after the War of Independence that they were proposed, tried, and then realized on a practical basis and on a large scale in America for the first time since antiquity. There are those who look to our Pilgrim and Puritan forefathers as prophets of the present democratic society and government in America, a point that can be and has been nicely argued. The Mayflower Compact certainly appears to have been a voluntary agreement to establish a government by common consent (although it was signed only by the male passengers on that tiny vessel), in which the will of the majority would prevail in any case under dispute—an agreement that closely accords with democratic principles. It was in sympathy with some such interpretation of the Pilgrims' role in our history that on the eve of the Revolution the Sons of Liberty adopted Plymouth Rock as a symbol of American independence. A group of patriots undertook to use it as the base for a liberty pole in the town square at Plymouth, but they bungled the job; in trying to replace it, they broke the ten-ton boulder in two. They finally managed to install only one half of it in the new and more prominent location. However, the legend of the rock began to spread and its size accordingly to diminish. Egg-sized chunks were sold to souvenir hunters at $1.50 apiece. After a series of misadventures the two halves of the rock, or what was left of them, were finally reunited in 1920, inscribed with the date 1620, settled close to the high-tide mark (where it would have had to be in the first place to serve its legendary function), and enshrined in a modern Greek temple of white granite designed by the fashionable architects McKim, Mead, and White. There it remains today, revered as a threshold of the American experience. (It is interesting to speculate that had the *Mayflower* kept on to its original destination in Virginia, the history of the Pilgrims' adventure might have been altogether different; these "poor and humble men" might, in fact, have been quite forgotten.)

Ever since, Fourth of July orators, some historians, and sentimentalists of various stripes have praised both Pilgrims and Puritans for virtues that were not theirs—for what they would not have considered virtues in any case. They have been acclaimed as pioneers of religious liberty, which was a policy furthest from their minds, a point rudely demonstrated when those "schismatical factious" Quakers were whipped and dragged through the streets of Boston and hanged on the Common. To the pious and select men who guided these early settlers on their "errand into the wilderness," the concept of democracy, as we know the word, was actually anathema. "Democracy I do not conceive that God did ever ordain as a fit government for either church or commonwealth," protested John Cotton. "If the people be governors, who shall be governed? As for monarchy and aristocracy, they are both clearly approved and directed in the Scriptures. . . . He setteth up theocracy . . . as the best form of government in the commonwealth as in the church." John Winthrop, first governor of the Massachusetts Bay Colony, was no less adamant on the point. "A Democratie," he insisted, "is, amongst civil nations, accounted the meanest and worst of all forms of government." He reminded his compatriots that, among other things, there was no warrant for democracy in holy scripture. "A mixt Aristocracie, and no way as Arbitrary," Winthrop concluded, was best "fit to govern man in the name of God." These earnest pioneers may have set their face toward a distant democracy, but in their day and place they still wished to be governed by their best, not by their average, men.

Apparently the only person in our pre-revolutionary history to call explicit attention to the democratic potentialities in colonial religious experience was John Wise, a Massachusetts clergyman who thereby saved his name from obscurity. Wise was the first son of an indentured servant to be graduated from Harvard College. In 1717 this native-born and self-made man issued an unusual tract entitled *Vindication of the Government of New-England Churches*, which in a highly rational manner expressed principles that would be clearly echoed in the Declaration of Independence nearly sixty years later. He also anticipated the contention of Jeremy Bentham and like-minded reformers that the purpose of government was to assure the greatest happiness for the greatest number. Democracy, Wise maintained, was a government "most agreeable with the light of nature" (Jefferson would refer to the laws of "nature's god," although he never mentioned democracy, a word he did not favor) and that "the end of all good government is to cultivate humanity, and promote the happiness of all, the good of every man in his rights, his life, liberty, estate, honour etc., without injury or abuse to any." Wise's tract seems to have had little or no effect on colonial thinking, nor to have been cited in the debates that led up to the Revolution, but it was a clear-voiced harbinger of the subtle and tortuous changes in American attitudes that gradually converted the early Puritan ethic into a revolutionary mentality during the course of the eighteenth century. He was, it should be added, turning to the laws of Reason and Nature, and to the character of the social contract forty-five years before Rousseau published his *Social Contract*. Wise reminded his readers that he was writing in the light of several thousand years of history, "after the world had been tumbled and tossed from one species of government to another, at a great expense of blood and treasure"—and, he concluded, "it is as plain as daylight there is no species of government like a democracy. . . . " (Writing in the light of more than two hundred years of additional history, Winston Churchill once and for all described democracy as "the worst form of government except all those other forms that have been tried from time to time.")

The word "republic" does not appear in the Declaration of Independence, although it did not generally share the dubious connotations that clung to "democracy." By the time the Revolution got under way, no serious thought was given to the possibility of reinstituting monarchy in the New World. Nevertheless, as has been earlier observed, among experienced political thinkers it was widely held that except on a very small scale republicanism simply was not a practical system of government—republicanism, that is, denoting a regime of law directed by representatives of the people. Over the preceding century and a half, practically all experiments in establishing new republics had failed in the Old World. Yet, as the Revolution progressed, it became increasingly clear that the ex-colonists were attempting the awesome project of establishing, for the first time since ancient Rome, a large republican nation; and challenging the world's greatest empire, Great Britain, in the process. The bare possibility of re-creating the glory that had been Rome's on the American continent was a heady vision. The Revolution did arouse vague and often extravagant expectations as to the role this aborning nation might play in the political imagination and the political history of the human race. In October, 1776, one French journal took notice of the news from overseas and concluded that "this emergence of a new nation in the New World was one of the major events of modern history."

Just how those ex-colonists arrived at the point where they undertook to fight in common cause is wonder enough, with or without dreams of grandeur and glory. Up until the dawn of the Revolution no two persons reporting on the colonial scene saw it in quite the same light. Differences between colonies and differences within colonies seemed too many and too great for any pat summary of conditions. "Fire and Water are not more heterogeneous than the different colonies in North America," concluded one European traveler after an extended tour of the North Atlantic coast. Franklin, who understood the situation better than anybody else, pointed out that each colony had "peculiar expressions, familiar to its own people, but strange and unintelligible to others." From south to north, each colony presented a unique situation and history; each was born of different circumstances and shaped differently by its separate circumstances. The distinctive character of each was marked in its physical appearance, its social customs, and the nature of its enterprise. The bonds that would unite them proved in the end to be irresistible, but for a long time they remained barely visible in that world of differences. In 1758, at a crucial moment in the French and Indian War, Franklin complained, "Everybody cries, a union is absolutely necessary, but when it comes to the manner and form of the union their weak noodles are perfectly distracted." Thus, until virtually the last moment of resolve in 1776, the colonial world seemed to many to be a sadly disjointed fragment of empire.

Above is a detail from an eighteenth-century engraving of the harbor at Charleston, South Carolina. Colonial promoters used this and similar prints to attract capital and settlers.

Christian Remick dedicated this 1768 watercolor, showing the British army's 29th Regiment camped on the Common in Boston, to "John Hancock, Esq."

Those divergences in colonial experience were inevitable. At each point of original settlement life was conditioned in a different manner. At few points did the reality of New World experience jibe with preconceived notions of life in America that most colonists brought with them. The climate, the topography, the soil, and the disposition of the native savages all posed novel problems that varied from one latitude to the next and that had to be solved in different ways. To choose the wrong season or the wrong point of arrival could have tragic consequences, as the Pilgrims had good cause to realize (half that company died during the cruel winter that followed their arrival).

As a result, not one America but several different Americas sprouted in the New World wilderness, and each grew in its separate way. In many respects, indeed, colonial society was more varied than is American society in this century. There is no better witness to this than reports of the colonists themselves as they traveled from one area to another. Just before the Revolution, Josiah Quincy, Jr., of Boston visited Charleston, South Carolina, and found a disturbing warmth and excitement in the social life of that southern city. Within a generation after its founding in 1670, Charleston had won the reputation of a "wealthy place"; pirates swarmed about the port, and in that benign, subtropical climate a great mixture of peoples—Barbadians, French Calvinists, English Dissenters, Scottish Covenanters, Negroes, Dutchmen from New York and Holland, Quakers, New England Baptists, Irish Catholics, and Jews among others—had fused into a unique cosmopolitan society. Quincy admired the distinctive architecture of the city and enjoyed the music he heard there, although he resented southern pretensions. "It is the fashion to Send home [that is, to England] all their Children for education," one reporter wrote of South Carolinians, "and if it was not owing to the nature of their Estates in this Province, which they keep all in their own hands, and require the immediate overlooking of the Proprietor, I am of the opinion the most opulent planters would prefer a home life." (One opinionated and waggish historian has suggested that the explanation of the southern colonists' superior culture was that so many of them had been educated abroad, whereas in the north young men were sent to the provincial colleges of Harvard and Yale.) However, while he was in Charleston, Quincy took pains to copy the manuscripts of law reports of Edward Rutledge, a local leader who had attended London's Inns of Court. Quincy concluded from his travels that on the whole there was a "prevalent and extended ignorance" in the colonies about one another's concerns and that mutual prejudices and contrary interests discouraged the growth of any common feeling of Americanism.

In New England the foothills rolled down the countryside close to the sea, and the rivers were for the most part troubled by rapids and waterfalls just a few miles inland from the coast. The uneven and relatively unfertile soil could be profitably worked only by close personal attention to a small area. Consequently, there were no such large estates as could be found farther south, notably in Virginia, which provided the country seats of a landed gentry. In the tobacco country the rivers reached through alluvial plains for a hundred miles into the interior. The planters maintained their own wharves, and ocean-going vessels moved from one to another collecting tobacco in exchange for English manufactures. It was a land that could be profitably managed on a large scale and by the labor of hired servants or slaves. Here a minority favored by fortune and their own industry could play the part of country gentlemen in the English tradition, with rare freedom. From Westover, his magnificent residence on the James River, surrounded by his hard-worked library of 3,600 volumes, William Byrd ruled over his princely estate of 179,000 acres. "I have a large Family of my own," he wrote a friend in England, "and my Doors are open to Every Body, yet I have no Bills to pay, and half-a-Crown will rest undisturbed in my Pocket for many Moons together. Like one of the Patriarchs, I have my Flocks and my Herds, my Bond-men and Bond-women, and every Soart of Trade amongst my own Servants, so that I live in a kind of Independence on every one but Providence." His plantation was, in fact, a complete society in miniature, including within its bounds virtually all the trades and professions required for a civilized life.

Edmund Burke compared the Virginians and the Carolinians to the Poles (and he might have added the Hungarians), who enjoyed a certain high sense of liberty made more acute by the slavery that surrounded it. However, there was an essential difference. Not only were there many smaller landowning families in the south who owned no slaves, but there were many in the back country who, having recently moved in from Pennsylvania, Ireland, or Germany, had not yet accepted a view of life in which slavery seemed essential. Also, in spite of occasional class conflicts, in such a new country there was, among the whites, no sense of immemorial class separation and no feeling of inseparable hereditary apartness, as characterized life in Eastern Europe.

As a youth Byrd had been sent to England to be properly educated. He was graduated from the Middle Temple and became a member of the English bar, and a fellow of the Royal Society. (He had also studied in Holland and visited the French court at Versailles.) In London he had spent a number of rakehell years in the lingering atmosphere of Restoration gaiety and gallantry. He was the friend of Congreve and Wycherly, those masters of fashionable comedy. He read methodically in Hebrew, Greek, and Latin, sometimes in French, Dutch, or Italian, which he often did at five or six in the morning before saying his prayers. Once, after a visit to the nearby colonial capitol at Williamsburg as a member of the King's Council, he smugly reported, "Everybody respected me like a king." As a councilman, Byrd was the spokesman for the large planters in a struggle for power against the royal governor. He persistently sought that office for himself, although he never won the appointment, in spite of much wire-pulling with influential friends abroad.

Byrd was in the forefront of those colonial men of the world who were as

THE
SPANISH IN
THE WEST

Until 1769 America's west coast had no permanent European settlement. In that year Father Junipero Serra and a band of Franciscans founded a mission at San Diego to bring the civilization of Spain to the natives. Over the next fifty years Franciscans established twenty-one missions along the western coast. Above, the earliest-known view of California shows Indians, friars, and the explorer Malaspina at Carmel welcoming fellow explorer La Pérouse in 1786. Below is a view of Yakutat Bay in Alaska, discovered by Malaspina in 1791 and named Disappointment Bay, as it did not lead to the northwest passage.

much at home overseas as in their own province, but who rarely visited other parts of their native or adopted land. (He did complain, however, of the "banditti" from Massachusetts who anchored near his estate to traffic with his slaves, "from whom," he remarked, "they are sure to have good Pennyworths.") That staunchest of patriots John Adams, on the other hand, had never even been out of New England, no less to Europe, until he journeyed to Philadelphia in 1774 to attend the meetings of the First Continental Congress. He had even been thinking of quietly retiring to his Braintree farm when the explosive atmosphere in and about Boston (watchful redcoats camped on the Common that summer) thrust him from his own beleaguered part of the world into the main stream of large affairs—and into the most cosmopolitan, progressive, and affluent society in colonial America.

Adams' first opinions of the wider world that he observed along the way were not altogether charitable. Passing through New York en route to Philadelphia he had remarked that the inhabitants of the little city at the mouth of the Hudson River all talked "very loud, very fast, and all together." He confided to his diary that he had "not seen one real gentleman in that town." Taking Boston as his criterion, he felt that Philadelphia left much to be desired. To the delegate from Massachusetts the easy tolerance of Philadelphians was heterodoxy. Their general well-being was tainted by prodigality. Tested with the strong dye of Yankee Congregationalism, the city's confusion of religious sects, the medley of disparate cultures, and the babble of strange accents indicated grave impurities in the social body. "For all its trade and wealth and regularity," he concluded after a brief survey, Philadelphia was *not* Boston. "The morals of our people are much better," he wrote in his diary, "their manners are more polite and agreeable; they are purer English [an interesting observation from a patriot contesting English authority]; our language is better, our taste is better, our persons are handsomer [another interesting observation from a man who was physically not well favored]; our spirit is greater, our laws are wiser, our religion is superior, our education is better."

Local pride can be a useful social force, but Adams carried it to an extreme that "tinctured his judgment and clinched his prepossessions." His attitude does, however, emphasize the important fact that for most colonists, almost to the moment of revolution, loyalty to their own province and to the British empire outweighed their loyalty to the aggregate of colonies—to an "America" in short. Any sense of an American identity remained vague, unfocused, and weak.

Indeed, and somewhat paradoxically, during the quarter of a century before the Revolution, America depended on England more heavily than ever before or since for cultural models and standards. In matters of dress, literature, art, architecture, and home furnishings, London set a common standard that was generally accepted in all the colonies. Even the alien strains that had been added to the American melting pot were affected by the influence of English culture, and even such an ardent patriot as Benjamin Franklin, with his sure instincts for what was valid and special in American experience, looked to England for models and precedents in various departments of his life. During his prolonged stay abroad he felt so strongly the allure of life in England, that "petty island" with its "sensible, virtuous and elegant Minds," that he seriously considered moving there for good—if he could "persuade the

Philadelphia's public buildings and its craftsmen were outstanding in the colonies. Above, the House of Employment and Almshouse on the left, and Pennsylvania Hospital on the right. Below, the elegant trade card of Benjamin Randolph, who fashioned furniture in a wide variety of styles.

good Woman to cross the seas." However, he subsequently concluded that "*old Trees cannot safely be transplanted*," and his permanent home remained in Philadelphia. (In time, as he became more deeply engrossed in the question of American rights, his admiration for the older country diminished, although to his dying day he continued a spirited correspondence with a number of those "elegant Minds" as well as others in France and elsewhere abroad.)

Those regional peculiarities that distinguished habits and attitudes in the separate colonies can be read in the architecture and decorative arts of the times, even though the same British sources of design (such as Chippendale's *Director*) were generally and commonly used as a starting point. A cherished practice among antiquarians of our own day is to detect and catalogue the differences between a chair or a highboy made in Boston, let us say, and such a form made in Philadelphia—and, of course, the differences between any of those and an English-made prototype.

No one would have mistaken the flourishing city of Philadelphia, so neatly and spaciously arranged on its tree-lined, carefully planned checkerboard of streets, for the closed port of Boston, with its crooked, narrow streets echoing to the tramp of British soldiers' boots, its populace exasperated almost to the point of open revolt. As to morals, manners, and the other items in Adams' uncompromising list of particulars, it was evidently easier to detect the differences than to understand their meaning. As Montaigne long before had written of the disparaging reports he had heard of the New World, it is all too simple to call any divergence from familiar custom a barbarism and let it go at that.

Philadelphia was not like Boston to be sure. In many significant ways it was not like any other place on earth. It was, in fact, a prodigy among cities of the world. Within less than a century after its beginnings, William Penn's "green countrie towne" had become the most populous and consequential city in the British colonies, standing among the first half-dozen in the empire. No city in history had grown to maturity so rapidly and so handsomely. While Philadelphia was aborning, St. Petersburg was created by imperial fiat almost overnight on the swamp of the Neva (at an enormous cost in human suffering), so that Peter the Great might have a showplace that would serve as a window from which he might look out over western Europe. But St. Petersburg was a throwback to the creations of Louis XIV, the "Grand Monarch"; Philadelphia was a portent of the future.

Here the Quakers, that sect who had been earlier so mercilessly scourged in Boston, had opened the doors of Pennsylvania to the entire world. This would be, Penn promised, a "free colony for all mankind." Although all history and experience denied it, he cherished the notion that men of good will could govern themselves. By royal proclamation he was absolute proprietor, but he wrote his subjects: "You shall be governed by laws of your own making, and

live a free, and if you will, a sober and industrious people. I shall not usurp the right of any, or oppress his person. God has furnisht me with a better resolution, and has given me his grace to keep it . . . I am your true Friend."

Early reports about Penn's Society of Friends had made converts as far away as Russia. Penn himself had visited the Rhineland, and his letters and brochures, translated and widely circulated, had sent vast numbers of discontented German peasants swarming across the Atlantic. The Scotch-Irish Presbyterians from Ulster needed little encouragement to flock to this promised land where neither Irish "papists" nor the established Anglicans could hope to influence their lives and their convictions. In 1729 James Logan, secretary of the province, had begun to fear that these "Protestants of the Protestants" might take control of the province and the Quakers become victims of their own liberal policies. At mid-century Benjamin Franklin, himself a "refugee" from the heart of Boston, feared it would rather be the Germans who might take over. Why should the "Palatine Boors be suffered to swarm into our Settlements," he asked, "and by herding together establish their Language and Manners to the Exclusion of ours?" "Why should Pennsylvania, founded by the English, become a Colony of Aliens, who will shortly be so numerous as to Germanize us instead of our Anglifying them . . . ?"

At another point Franklin was concerned by intrusions of a different nature. In Pennsylvania, as elsewhere, class and sectional disagreements caused grave tensions that occasionally broke the peace. "Those from the westward," wrote one observer in the colony, "look upon the people in any of the commercial towns as little better than swindlers, while those of the east consider the western members a pack of savages." Infuriated by what they deemed eastern indifference to their claims for adequate frontier defenses, in 1764 six hundred armed "back inhabitants" marched in Philadelphia to force their claims. Armed resistance was planned in the east, but Franklin rode out to Germantown to reason with the invaders and persuaded them to turn back. "I became less a man than ever," Franklin remarked; "for I had by this transaction, made myself many enemies among the populace." In the elections of that year he did, in fact, lose his seat in the Assembly.

There was enough quarreling and contention among the various factions to keep the community in a healthy ferment. Nevertheless, virtually everyone, regardless of his individual persuasions, had a solid stake in this thriving society, and there was enough widely scattered good sense to recognize it and to keep the melting pot from boiling over. Penn had all but lifted the curse of the Tower of Babel. The revolutionary implications of that liberation were not lost on the philosophers of the eighteenth century. Philadelphia was the Enlightenment in a microcosm. At last, Voltaire exulted, there was reasonable proof for an age of reason that men of mixed origins and different beliefs could govern themselves and live together on terms of equality—and prosper.

"Philadelphia reaps the greatest profits from its trade with the West Indies. For thither the inhabitants ships almost every day a quantity of flour, butter, meat and other victuals, timber, planks and the like. In return they receive either sugar, molasses, rum, indigo, mahogany and other goods or ready money. . . ."

Peter Kalm in *Travels in North America*

Penn's experiment had, in effect, become a prospectus of the America to be.

The public buildings of Philadelphia were monuments to the humanitarianism and the enlightened spirit of the Quakers. "One of the principal Ornaments" of the city was its House of Employment and Almshouse—the so-called Bettering House—which was built and largely supported by private contributions and which was completed in the fall of 1767. The Pennsylvania Hospital, which had opened to patients eleven years earlier, quickly attracted medical students from all parts of the Continent. With its accommodations for lunatics, its sanitary arrangements, and its liberal administration, it was probably the most advanced institution of its kind then known. The Philadelphia doctor Benjamin Rush was the most prominent American physician of his day and the foremost teacher of medicine.

One of Rush's teachers, Dr. John Morgan, was another man of the world in science, a member of many distinguished foreign societies and a founder of the medical school in Philadelphia. With his wealthy companion Samuel Powel, Morgan made the Grand Tour in the grandest manner and studied in Paris and Italy as well as in London and Edinburgh. He first defined the separate concerns of the physician, the surgeon, and the apothecary, a degree of specialization that was at the time still considered revolutionary and that furthered his fame.

In 1763, on the first leg of his long and extensive tour of the Old World, young Powel was presented to George III, and delivered to him an address from his alma mater, the new little college in Philadelphia. During his stay in Rome he had numerous conversations with the duke of York and, exceptionally, an audience with the pope. At Turin he was presented to the king of Sardinia. As he circled back, he paid a visit to Voltaire before returning to London. From that city in 1765 he wrote home of his plans for bringing back to Philadelphia a quantity of furniture of fitting quality for the new mansion he proposed building there. In May of that year his uncle, Samuel Morris, wrote Powel advising him not to do this. The infamous Stamp Act had recently been passed, and as Pitt warned the ministry, America was almost in open rebellion. "In the humour people are in here," Morris wrote his nephew, "a man is in danger of becoming invidiously distinguished, who buys any thing in England which our Tradesmen can furnish. I have heard the joiners here object this against Dr. Morgan & others who brought their furniture with them." "Furthermore," he observed, "household goods may be had as cheap and as well made from English patterns." (That was a fair tribute to the superb craftsmanship being practiced in Philadelphia at the time.) Apparently, Powel went ahead with his plans, but he still remained popular enough to be chosen as Philadelphia's last pre-revolutionary mayor, and as such he played host to George Washington.

One evening during his sojourn in Philadelphia, John Adams was entertained at the "splendid seat" on South Third Street that Powel had by then completed. It was one of the occasions that seems to have seriously tried his New England conscience as he was drawn into local social life. He recorded "a most sinful feast again! every thing which could delight the eye or allure the taste; curds and creams, jellies, and sweetmeats of various sorts, twenty sorts of tarts, fools, trifles, floating islands, whipped sillabubs & Parmesan cheese, punch, wine, porter, beer, etc." However, he shortly made the necessary adjustments. Describing another comparable orgy at the "elegant and

Philadelphia physician Benjamin Rush (above, a portrait by Thomas Sully) was a representative to the Continental Congress and a surgeon in the Continental Army.

most magnificent" home of Benjamin Chew, chief justice of the Pennsylvania supreme court, Adams concluded his account of the affair triumphantly. "I drank Madeira at a great rate, *and found no inconvenience in it.*" A few weeks later, at the conclusion of this first visit, he bade adieu to "the happy, the peaceful, the elegant, the hospitable, and polite city of Philadelphia."

It is easy to believe that the social and intellectual climate of Philadelphia had a liberalizing influence, not only on Adams, but on a great many of his contemporaries. At Princeton in 1771 two young Philadelphia poets hailed their city as the "mistress of our world, the seat of arts of science, and of fame," an effusion which even a New England almanac of the same year virtually echoed. At the time of Adams' visit the city had become the indisputable art center of America (a distinction it would retain through the first decades of the following century). The local, self-trained painter Benjamin West had more than a dozen years before gone off to Europe, there to become possibly the most widely known American painter of all time—not excepting Grandma Moses, Alexander Calder, and Jackson Pollock. West never returned to his native land, but he sent back to it a host of aspiring colonial artists who visited his London studio for help, advice, and training, all of which he gave unstintingly. During the decade before the Revolution a number of them returned to Philadelphia, where the prosperous gentry provided abundant patronage. The city became a shining goal for painters—portraitists, mostly—from other parts of the colonies. More than three dozen of them found employment for their skills in the pre-revolutionary generation. John Singleton Copley, the greatest of them, wrote in 1771 before he went to England to vie with West as a New World genius, that Philadelphia was "a place of too much importance not to visit."

Philadelphia was the home of the Bartrams, father and son, whose gardens there and whose botanical studies, as earlier remarked, won international fame; and the home of the accomplished scientist David Rittenhouse; of Francis Hopkinson, the first American composer of secular music, including saucy ballads (he also wrote scholarly polemics and serious drama); of Thomas Godfrey, the first American dramatist to have his work performed professionally; and of still others who contributed importantly to the general enlightenment of their fellow colonists.

Philadelphia was also the home of John Dickinson, a prosperous, cultured, and studious man—a man of moderate temper and a consummate pamphleteer. In one of his essays he advised his fellow Americans that they could never be made an independent people, "except it be by *Great Britain* herself, and the only

This portrait of John Dickinson, probably after a 1771 engraving by Paul Revere, appeared opposite the title page of his best-selling pamphlet, Letters from a Farmer in Pennsylvania.

way for her to do it, is to make us frugal, ingenious, united, and discontented." All governments make mistakes, he declared, but they could be corrected and passions cooled. He hoped that it might "be impossible to determine whether an American's character is most distinguishable for his loyalty to his Sovereign; his duty to his mother country, his freedom, or his affection for his native soil." When Benjamin Rush visited Paris in 1769 he called upon the French publisher Barbeu-Dubourg, who was at that moment working out, at Franklin's suggestion, a translation of Dickinson's *Letters from a Farmer in Pennsylvania*, from which these quotations are taken. Voltaire applauded Dickinson's sentiments and Edmund Burke admired the author's cogent arguments.

It was finally, the home of Benjamin Franklin. In Franklin all the racial and religious differences, the sectional and intercolonial jealousies and rivalries, and the class prejudices that disturbed the social equilibrium were in some manner comprehended and reconciled. He has been called "the first American," and this he was in that he spoke and wrote so eloquently and with such authority for the new age and the New World. He was almost as old as the eighteenth century, and his life touched the developments of that age of enlightenment at practically every point. As a young printer's apprentice in Boston he had heard Increase and Cotton Mather preach; as an old man he stood beside Voltaire in Paris to be proclaimed the incomparable benefactor of mankind. He personified the intellectual revolution of the century that, in one sense, gave birth to the United States of America, a concrete kind of example of the ideal state philosophers of the age had envisioned. He had a practical grasp of the material and spiritual forces that were transforming the British colonists into a new and independent people. No one knew better than he, or viewed more tolerantly, the human imperfections that would have to be accommodated— and the risks that would have to be taken—before that transformation could be successfully completed.

The fifty-five delegates to the First Continental Congress who assembled at Philadelphia on September 5, 1774, had been summoned by popular demand. They came together from all but one of the colonies (only Georgia had no delegate), not to plan for independence, but to unite upon the most effective measures for defending what they considered to be their common rights. It was a body of able men who represented the division as well as the unity that prevailed in America (three of them would subsequently serve as presidents of the United States). Joseph Galloway of Pennsylvania and Isaac Low of New York would soon become Loyalists; Patrick Henry of Virginia and Samuel Adams of Massachusetts were already favoring independence; George Washington of Virginia and John Dickinson of Pennsylvania were among those for moderation. On his journey southward from Boston, John Adams had noted with surprise how greatly the middle colonies seemed to fear "the leveling spirit of New England"; and now he met many man at the Congress who would hear "no expression which looked like an allusion to the last appeal"; men who were content to limit the action of the Congress to protestation and negotiation.

But all agreed that in their disturbed relation with Britain the colonies had reason for complaint. That long period of "salutary neglect" on the part of England, which Burke claimed was responsible for colonial prosperity, had ended with the conclusion of the French and Indian War. Until then the colonists had, with certain exceptions, very much gone their own way. The Navigation Acts, which regulated trade within the empire, prescribed limitations that were binding on colonial commerce. However, those acts required the colonists to do very little that—for the time being—they would not have wanted to do in any case; and where some restriction proved irksome, either the law was not enforced or could be avoided by bribery and smuggling. Royal governors were often something more than a nuisance. In 1768 Franklin took it upon himself to explain to a London audience why these appointed officials were so generally resented in the colonies. They were, he pointed out, "not like Princes whose posterity have an inheritance in the government of a nation, and therefore an interest in its prosperity; they are generally strangers to the Provinces they are sent to govern, have no estate, natural connection, or relation there, to give them an affection for the country . . . they come only to make money as fast as they can; are sometimes men of vicious characters and broken fortunes . . . as they intend staying in the country no longer than their government continues and purpose to leave no family behind them, they are apt to be regardless of the good will of the people. . . ." However, those governors relied for their pay on appropriations of the colonial assemblies, and delaying their salaries could effectively dissuade them from an unwelcome excess of zeal in performing their duties.

With the peace that ended the Seven Years' War in 1763, those circumstances changed. As earlier told, Britain had now become an imperial power on an unprecedented scale. Running such a huge enterprise was enormously expensive and required new and urgent fiscal practices, and it was at this point that the American colonists began seriously to feel the weight of oppression. Freed from the menace of French border warfare by Wolfe's victory on the Plains of Abraham, and without overt menace from any other quarter, they had little interest in Britain's further foreign entanglements and no desire to share, through any form of taxation, the cost of maintaining Britain's imperial establishment, whose concerns seemed so remote from the western shores of the Atlantic. Taxation without representation was, in any case, simply not acceptable.

Then started that "long train of abuses" that were ultimately listed in the Declaration of Independence, and to which the Stamp Act of 1765 was but a brief if significant prelude. In England, where people were concerned enough about the question of their own liberties, the repeal of that ill-advised act within a year met such popular approval that one London artist made a small fortune satirizing the defeat of Parliament in a cartoon that sold for sixpence and that was immediately pirated in at least half a dozen versions by rival printsellers. (He was Benjamin Wilson, whose portrait of Franklin was taken by Major André as booty from Franklin's home when the British evacuated Philadelphia during the Revolution, carried back to England, and finally returned—to the White House—in 1906.)

The imposition and relatively quick repeal of the Stamp Act clearly revealed the indecisiveness and inconsistency of England's colonial policy. That the state needed to tap fresh sources of revenue was perfectly plain to the king and his ministers. However, during the 1760's each ministry in its turn differed as to how that revenue should be raised, and each had a separate solution for mollifying the American colonists' bitterness over the inept attempts that were made. Acts passed by one ministry were repealed by the next, until policy toward America became as changeable as the British climate. Political maneuvers of the contending parties seemed to have become more important than the fate of America.

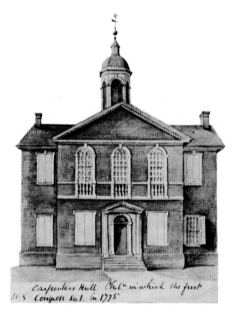

Meeting at Carpenter's Hall in Philadelphia in September, 1774, the First Continental Congress issued a declaration of grievances and resolves, amounting to a complete condemnation of British colonial policy for the preceding eleven years.

The Stamp Act of 1765 required that this particular stamp be placed on insurance policies and probates of wills.

But it was more than the question of revenue that riled the colonists. England's bumbling procedures betrayed an abysmal ignorance of American needs and American aspirations. Few if any Englishmen realized that the American colonies were moving toward a rapid expansion in trade, wealth, and power. On the other hand, very few Americans could conceive of the huge expenses of war that arose from Britain's vast imperial connections. In the meantime George III so closely identified himself with the English crown that any criticism of monarchical powers, any suggestion of reform or change, became for him a personal affront. He was simply too stupid to be able to distinguish between himself as a person and his constitutional position as ruler.

The various causes that finally brought the two countries to the point of separation will probably be argued with more or less scholarly contention in perpetuity. They quite certainly lay deeper than the hostile designs of ministers or the vindictive stubbornness of the crown on the one hand, or the ambitions of colonial agitators bent on revolution on the other. Burke would tell Parliament that the ultimate separation was, after all, deep in the nature of things; and what the "Laws of Nature and of Nature's God" would put asunder, neither men of patience and good will nor all the king's men and horses would be able to put back together again, although they tried in their different ways.

It has been said that the Revolution was the result of unfortunate misunderstandings, which in one sense it surely was. But, as the late historian Carl Lotus Becker observed, if by misunderstanding is meant lack of information, there is more truth in the famous epigram which claims that George III's minister George Grenville, the originator of the Stamp Act, lost the colonies because he read the American dispatches, which none of his predecessors had done. It seemed that during the decade before the Revolution every exchange of ideas drove the two countries farther apart, and that personal contact alienated the two peoples more often than it reconciled them. As late as 1771 Benjamin Franklin wrote of George III that he could "scarcely conceive a king of better dispositions, of more exemplary virtues, or more truly desirous of promoting the welfare of his subjects." (At the same time he predicted that the colonies would go their separate way, and outlined the way this would be done.) A year later he wrote expressing his disenchantment with English society. "Had I never been in the American colonies," he remarked, "but was to form my judgment of civil society from what I have lately seen, I should never advise a nation of savages to admit of civilization."

Two years after that the Boston-born royal governor of Massachusetts, Thomas Hutchinson, most aristocratic and most English of Americans, returned to England for the first time in more than thirty years. His conscientious, loyal interpretation of such unpopular measures as the Stamp Act had brought him into wide disfavor in and about Boston. At one point, in 1765, his elegant mansion had been sacked by a hostile mob, and he had to flee for his life. Subsequently he insisted on the unloading of the tea cargoes that resulted in the Boston Tea Party. He was virtually forced into exile, and sailed to England in 1774, shortly before the First Continental Congress convened, to serve as an adviser to George III and his ministry on American affairs—and to complete his valuable *History of the Colony and Province of Massachusetts Bay*. In England he mingled with the "best people," and like Franklin, was disillusioned by the experience. In the years before 1775 Englishmen had developed

In 1775 Samuel Johnson, England's outstanding literary figure, wrote Taxation No Tyranny, *a powerful argument against emancipation of the colonies.*

But hear, ye sons and daughters of liberty, the sounds which the winds are wafting from the Western Continent. The Americans are telling one another, what, if we may judge from their noisy triumph, they have but lately discovered, and what yet is a very important truth: *That they are entitled to Life, Liberty, and Property, and that they have never ceded to any sovereign power whatever a right to dispose of either without their consent.*

While this resolution stands alone, the Americans are free from singularity of opinion; their wit has not yet betrayed them to heresy. While they speak as the naked sons of Nature, they claim but what is claimed by other men, and have withheld nothing but what all with-hold. They are here upon firm ground, behind entrenchments which never can be forced.

Humanity is very uniform. The Americans have this resemblance to Europeans, that they do not always know when they are well. They soon quit the fortress that could neither have been mined by sophistry, nor battered by declamation. Their next resolution declares, that *their ancestors, who first settled the Colonies, were, at the time of their emigration from the Mother-country, entitled to all the rights, liberties, and immunities of free and natural-born subjects within the realm of England.*

This likewise is true; but when this is granted, their boast of original rights is at an end; they are no longer in a State of Nature. These lords of themselves, these kings of *Me*, these demigods of independence, sink down to Colonists, governed by a Charter. If their ancestors were subjects, they acknowledged a Sovereign; if they had a right to English privileges, they were accountable to English laws, and what must grieve the Lover of Liberty to discover, had ceded to the King and Parliament, whether the right or not, at least the power of disposing, *without their consent, of their lives, liberties, and proper-*

ties. It therefore is required of them to prove, that the Parliament ever ceded to them a dispensation from that obedience, which they owe as natural-born subjects, or any degree of independence or immunity not enjoyed by other Englishmen.

They say, That by such emigration they by no means forfeited, sur-

rendered, or lost any of those rights; but that *they were, and their descendants now are, entitled to the exercise and enjoyment of all such of them as their local and other circumstances enable them to exercise and enjoy.*

That they who form a settlement by a lawful Charter having committed no crime forfeit no privileges, will be readily confessed; but what they do not forfeit by any judicial sentence, they may lose by natural effects. As man can be but in one place at once, he cannot have the advantages of multiplied residence. He that will enjoy the brightness of sunshine, must quit the coolness of the shade. He who goes voluntarily to America, cannot complain of losing what he leaves in Europe. He perhaps had a right to vote for a knight or burgess; by crossing the Atlantick he has not nullified his right; but he has made its exertion no longer possible. By his own choice he has left a

country where he had a vote and little property, for another, where he has great property, but no vote. But as this preference was deliberate and unconstrained, he is still *concerned in the government of himself*; he has reduced himself from a voter to one of the innumerable multitude that have no vote. He has truly *ceded his right*, but he is still governed by his own consent; because he has consented to throw his atom of interest into the general mass of the community. Of the consequences of his own act he has no cause to complain; he has chosen, or intended to chuse, the greater good; he is represented, as himself desired, in the general representation.

But the privileges of an American scorn the limits of place; they are part of himself, and cannot be lost by departure from his country; they float in the air, or glide under the ocean. . . .

The colonists are the descendants of men, who either had no vote in elections, or who voluntarily resigned them for something, in their opinion, of more estimation: they have therefore exactly what their ancestors left them, not a vote in making laws, or in constituting legislators, but the happiness of being protected by law, and the duty of obeying it. . . .

But there is one writer, and perhaps many who do not write, to whom the contraction of these pernicious privileges appears very dangerous, and who startle at the thoughts of England free and America in chains. . . . This contest may end in the softer phrase of English Superiority and American Obedience.

We are told, that the subjection of Americans may tend to the diminution of our own liberties; an event, which none but very perspicacious politicians are able to foresee. If slavery be thus fatally contagious, how is it that we hear the loudest yelps for liberty among the drivers of negroes?

a profound contempt for "colonials"; and many of those Americans who visited the mother country found themselves regarded as "a little above a well-bred Negro in a gentleman's house," to quote Dr. Samuel Johnson. Hutchinson's one desire was to return to his homeland and be buried in the soil of his fathers. He "would rather die in a little country farmhouse in New England," he asserted, "than in the best nobleman's seat in old England." As Becker concluded, had Hutchinson lived earlier in England he might have died a patriot, whereas had Franklin seen as little of England as his Loyalist son he might have ended his days a Loyalist himself.

The ultimate fact was that the colonists were, in effect, free long before they were independent. In August, 1769, John Adams dined in an open field with three hundred and fifty Sons of Liberty and remarked how the inspiring popular songs of the day were promoting those "sensations of freedom" that had been noticed much earlier by travelers in the New World and that were now building up public excitement to a critical pitch. It took a long and wasteful war that nobody wanted to make the point clear and final.

In spite of the stirring events and the mounting feelings that led so inexorably to bloodshed at Lexington and Concord in 1775, there was surprisingly little violence during pre-revolutionary days. Contrasted with the bloody French and Russian revolutions of later years, the restraint and reasonableness on both sides of the growing controversy in America were extraordinary. The mobs of the Stamp Act days were soon brought to order by responsible men, the "Bloody Massacre" at Boston in 1770, a snow-balling lark that ended in the death of five townsmen, was immediately investigated by local authorities and the "murderous" British troops, defended by Josiah Quincy and John Adams, were honorably acquitted. That ardent Son of Liberty Paul Revere had great success with a picture he engraved that completely misrepresented the episode, showing the redcoats as cold-blooded slaughterers. Actually, one of the dying townsmen said he "never knew troops to bear so much without firing as these had done." Revere's engraving, copied many times over both in America and England, was such a hair-raising piece of propaganda leveled against the "bloody work in King's Street" that Quincy felt obliged to warn the jury which tried the British soldiers not to be prejudiced by "the prints exhibited in our houses" which had added "wings to fancy." Adams consented to act as Quincy's senior adviser, for as he later said, "I had no hesitation in answering, that counsel ought to be the very last thing that an accused person

In December, 1773, Boston colonists met at the Green Dragon tavern (below) to "plan the consignement of a few shiploads of tea." George III typified the British reaction to the Tea Party when he said, "We must master them or totally leave them alone." He opted for mastery, and Parliament passed three Coercive Acts. Paul Revere's engraving (below, right), titled "The Able Doctor, or America Swallowing the Bitter Draught," summed up the radicals' opinion of England's policy.

should want in a free country; that the bar ought, in my opinion, to be independent and impartial, at all times and in every circumstance, and that persons whose lives were at stake ought to have the counsel they prefer." The case, he explained, "compelled me to differ in opinion from all my friends, to set at defiance all their advice, their remonstrances, their raillery, their ridicule, their censure, their sarcasm, without acquiring one symptom of pity from my enemies." At the risk of his professional career, he helped to see that justice was done.

Even Boston's memorable Tea Party was conducted with "great order and decency," and not without a sense of high comedy as the actors played their roles very thinly disguised as Mohawk braves, with war whoops and "tommyhawks" to lend color to their resolute performance. "Not the least insult was offer'd to any person," wrote one witness, save to one man who tried to sneak some of the tea to shore, "and nothing but their utter aversion to make *any* disturbance prevented his being tar'd and feather'd."

The very next day a popular song was born to celebrate the momentous doings of the night before:

> Rally Mohawks! bring out your axes
> And tell King George we'll pay no taxes
>   On his foreign tea; etc.

What the tune of the song was probably nobody now knows, but it must have been cheering to hear it sung in the Green Dragon tavern, where plans for dumping the tea were worked out. The people of the little provincial town of Boston had thrown down the gauntlet to the British empire. They had "passed the river and cut away the bridge," and there was no retreat from the stand they had taken. To see the thing through, they would need support, and they dispatched their swiftest courier, the versatile Paul Revere, to test public opinion in other colonies, which were by no means always eager to view the local problems of New England sympathetically. However, Revere returned from New York and Philadelphia, as one diarist noted, "performing his journey in a much shorter time than could be expected at this Season of the year," and reporting that "the inhabitants of these Cities were highly pleased with the Conduct of the People here in destroying the Tea. . . . "

The other colonies were indeed sympathetic, but the king's ministers and Parliament took hasty action to answer Boston's naked challenge to imperial authority. As Hutchinson took sail for England, General Thomas Gage, military commander in chief for all America, arrived with four regiments of British troops to act as civil governor of the rebellious colony, to bring it to its knees by punitive acts, and by that example to chasten the other colonies out of any further thoughts of disobedience. In spite of the oracular arguments of Burke against such policies, the port of Boston was closed to all trade by sea; the Massachusetts charter was revamped to increase royal authority; royal officials were empowered to take to Great Britain all persons in Massachusetts accused of murder in connection with law enforcement; and the quartering of British troops in Massachusetts towns was specifically authorized. British cannon were installed on Boston's Common as a reminder of the enforcement authority that lay behind these laws—these "Intolerable Acts," as they were quickly and appropriately dubbed.

In its very sorry plight Boston got more than sympathy from the rest of the

Particularly after the Tea Party, the "American question" was a constant topic of conversation in London. This British cartoon, titled "The Bostonians in Distress," provided an acid commentary on the situation: city residents caged by the Port Act devour fish delivered by sympathizers from neighboring colonies.
THE NEW-YORK HISTORICAL SOCIETY

colonial world. Marblehead offered Boston merchants the gratuitous use of its harbor and all its facilities for the loading and unloading of goods. Early in June "the patriotic and generous people" of South Carolina sent two hundred barrels of rice to help alleviate any want on the part of the Bostonians, and promised eight hundred more. Two thousand pounds in currency were raised in Wilmington, North Carolina, in a matter of days, and one resident offered his vessel to carry a load of provisions freight free, and master and mariners volunteered to navigate her without wages to whatever destination might be chosen. One of the earliest "relief packages" came in the form of 258 sheep from Windham, Connecticut; and a "gentleman" from Norwich in that colony drove 291 more northeastward as a gift from that town. Throughout New England, towns sent rye, flour, peas, cattle, sheep, oil, fish, and occasional gifts of money. In Virginia, George Washington headed a subscription paper with a gift of £50. Even the French inhabitants of Quebec, joining with those of English origin, shipped a thousand and forty barrels of wheat to the beleaguered Bostonians.

Such was the immediate background against which the First Continental Congress staged its meetings in Philadelphia. "We must master them or totally leave them to themselves," George III had remarked of the colonists. It passed his regal understanding that the Americans should resent a measure which enabled them to buy their tea cheaper than he could buy it himself. An end must be put to such whimsical behavior. To review what has earlier been referred to in a broader context, in the spring of 1773 Parliament had passed a resolution to permit the East India Company to export tea stored in its English warehouses free of all duties except a three-pence tax in America, a resolution that had been backed by information obtained from certain American merchants who were considered reliable. The measure was solely in the interest of the Company, which had recently been rescued from bankruptcy by the interposition of the government. Parliament and the king's ministers had been assured that, although there would be strong opposition to that nominal tax, "mankind are in general governed by interest," and in line with the king's reasoning the fact that "the Company can afford their teas cheaper than the Americans can smuggle them from foreigners" put the success of the design beyond doubt.

It quickly became clear enough that those American informants had grossly misjudged the situation. Smugglers opposed the measure because it threatened to destroy their profitable Holland trade; the fair trader because it conferred a monopoly upon an English corporation which countered their legitimate interests. Beyond that, if the Company could thus sell its tea, the non-importation agreement, a favorite method of obtaining redress and one that was at once effective and legal, would have proved a useless expedient. Mankind might, in fact, be governed by interest; but there were substantial numbers of Americans who could see beyond the immediate interest of cheap tea to much broader interests. That insignificant tax of three pence rested upon the large and delicate question of Parliament's right to tax the colonists at all, and this touched American attitudes at many sensitive points. Unless the colonists were ready to take decisive action, the long struggle over this issue must end in submission. Britain had done for the colonists what it had never been able to do for its people: it brought them together in a semblance of unity. The long-spluttering fears that the colonies might one day unite against

TEXT CONTINUED ON PAGE 320

"As the Rebellion is general thro' the provinces, the friends of Governemt have no certain place to fly to for safety but to Eng."

Henry Caner, 1775

316

THE
LOYALIST
POSITION

After the battles of Lexington and Concord, those colonists remaining loyal to the king were, as a Virginian observed, "either obliged to go off or subjected to insult and danger" from their rebellious neighbors. Many fled to Boston, where they depended upon the British army for food and shelter. When the British evacuated Boston in March, 1776, they took some thousand Loyalists with them (above). All but one ship sailed to Halifax (left, the emblem of Nova Scotia Loyalists), where those who could not afford passage to London awaited the imminent British victory. Many less prosperous refugees established temporary camps in Canada (below, a settlement on the banks of the St. Lawrence River) and applied to the British government for land grants.

Many well-off colonists made it to London, where they petitioned the crown to compensate them for their loyalty. Governor Thomas Hutchinson so outraged the citizenry by upholding the law that he was forced to depart Massachusetts for England in 1774. He never returned to America, and led the Loyalist community in London until his death in 1780. William Franklin, the illegitimate son of Benjamin and the governor of New Jersey, was arrested and jailed as "a virulent enemy of this country." Released in 1778, he joined fellow Loyalists in London. Benjamin Thompson fled to England in 1776, launching a remarkable career, during which he was knighted by George III and made a count of the Holy Roman Empire. William Pepperrell had inherited an estate and a baronetcy from his grandfather, and left for England at the outbreak of the Revolution. John Eardley-Wilmot headed a committee of Parliament for settling Loyalist pension claims. His portrait by Benjamin West (opposite) includes in the background a picture portraying the Loyalists' gratitude to England for compensation and refuge. Franklin and Pepperrell lead the line of refugees. Other Loyalists, like the Mohawk leader Joseph Brant, were rewarded (in his case, with a land grant in Canada) for fighting on the British side during the war.

Joseph Brant, after a portrait by George Romney

Thomas Hutchinson, attributed to Copley

William Franklin by Mather Brown

Sir Benjamin Thompson (Count Rumford)
by Thomas Gainsborough

Sir William Pepperrell and his family by John Singleton Copley

John Eardley-Wilmot by Benjamin West

Britain were being realized. It had accomplished what it most wished to prevent, and in this sense America was originally Britain's idea. Only with great reluctance did the colonies finally accept it for themselves.

The time was inexorably coming for everyone to take sides in the crucial controversy; but there were many men of stout heart and hopeful vision on both sides of the Atlantic who were loath to recognize that this was the parting of the ways, which it soon proved to be. Even such a firebrand as Sam Adams suggested that liberty and loyalty to the king were not necessarily incompatible. The ties with "home" were, after all, long and strong—ties, by and large, of a common ancestry, a common tongue, a common culture, which could not be severed without causing grievous wounds that might never heal. "We are hastening on to desperate resolutions," wrote one Philadelphian, "our most wise and sensible citizens dread the anarchy and confusion that must ensue." There were some who thoughtfully considered that any such anarchy was preferable to tyranny.

If the Congress is unanimous, wrote Franklin from London in September, 1774, "you cannot fail of carrying your point. If you divide you are lost." In this opinion he was joined by informed English observers. In spite of many wide differences of opinion and tempestuous debates, the Congress finally agreed on a counter-offensive to the Intolerable Acts in the name of all the colonies. It "recommended" the adoption of nonimportation, nonconsumption, and nonexportation agreements to be everywhere superintended and enforced by local committees of inspection; measures that some of the influential congressmen believed would reduce England to bankruptcy, or at least win immediate concessions from Parliament. The Congress then passed a Declaration of Rights and Grievances addressed to the people of Great Britain as well as to the colonists, and a petition to the king for redress of the wrongs they felt they were suffering. "To your justice," the statements read, "we appeal. You have been told that we are impatient of government and desirous of independency. These are calumnies. Permit us to be as free as yourselves, and we shall ever esteem a union with you to be our greatest glory and our greatest happiness. But if you are determined that your ministers shall wantonly sport with the rights of mankind; if neither the voice of justice, the dictates of law, the principles of the constitution, or the suggestions of humanity, can restrain your hands from shedding human blood in such an impious cause, we must then tell you that we will never submit to be hewers of wood or drawers of water for any ministry or nation in the world."

Taken together, these papers led Lord Chatham to admit that "for solidity of reason, force of sagacity and wisdom of conclusion under a complication of difficult circumstances, no nation or body of men can stand in preference to the general Congress at Philadelphia." The Declaration of Rights conceded parliamentary regulation of strictly imperial affairs, but it also anticipated many of the grievances that would be finally summarized in the Declaration of Independence. Before adjourning in October, the Congress provided for a second Congress to be held in May of 1775 in case the situation then required such another assembly. The Congress had all but created a revolutionary government, extra-legal as it was in parliamentary terms, and at the same time had given birth to a Loyalist, as distinct from a Conservative, Party. Whether to submit to the Congress or the king became a fundamental question. Samuel Seabury of New York, who became an outspoken Loyalist, stated the issue

The losses on both sides at the Battle of Bunker Hill on June 17, 1775, made war inevitable. This contemporary engraving shows nearby Charlestown after bombardment by the British.

emphatically: "If I must be enslaved, let it be by a King at least, and not by a parcel of upstart, lawless committeemen." (His statement recalls Voltaire's remark made three years earlier that he would rather serve "under a lion of good pedigree [Louis XV] . . . than under two hundred rats of my own kind").

The nonintercourse policy proved a total failure. It injured America more than it injured England. In 1775 imports dropped by almost ninety per cent. The nonexportation agreement nearly brought business to a halt. There was a real dread that the colonists would feel that Congress was oppressing them more than Parliament. Unable "to do without trade," they were "between Hawk and Buzzard"; and on April 6, 1776, the American ports were opened to the world. However, so long as the colonists considered themselves British subjects, the world at large would not treat or trade with them, as Richard Henry Lee pointed out. A declaration of independence, it became increasingly clear to many, remained the only alternative to submission.

Events did not wait on the deliberations of the "wise and sensible citizens" who sat in the Congress. On April 19, 1775, the question of submission or defiance, of peace or war, was very simply and directly put to a few score of minutemen who gathered to the drumbeat on the Lexington green before the sun was up. "Too few to resist, too brave to fly," they stood up to a charge of musketry from red-coated British troops before those who were left standing (eight were killed and nine were wounded) returned the fire, with no immediate effect, and dispersed. This was not doctrinaire revolution drawn up by scheming philosophers; at this point it was revolution at the grass roots— an "outdoor" revolution that sprouted from seeds sown by immediate circumstances.

Those shots, "heard 'round the world," developed into a withering gunfire from the farmers who swarmed in from the countryside to worry the British all the long way back to Boston. At Concord, according to one of them, "We was all ordered to load and had stricked orders not to fire firs, then to fire as fast as we could." The London *Gazette* carried the news that His Majesty's soldiers had been "very much annoyed in the encounter." "Such was the cruelty and barbarity of the rebels," the account continued, "that they scalped and cut off the ears of some of our wounded men." Of those troops who had sallied out of the city the night before, blithely marching to the tune of "Yankee Doodle," 247 were killed, wounded, or missing—more casualties than in the battle before Quebec, where Wolfe had fallen.

Who could say that the consequences of this provincial skirmish were not greater than the great battles of Agincourt or Blenheim? The American Revolution had started. If there were any doubts that this was war they were settled just two months later at Bunker Hill, or more correctly, Breed's Hill, where the British lost more than eleven hundred men—almost one-third of their engaging force—before the colonists, their ammunition exhausted, reduced to clubbing their guns and hurling rocks, had to quit their redoubt. General Howe wept for the pity of it; he never forgot that carnage. Gage reported to England that the "rebels are not the despicable rabble too many have supposed them to be."

Was this war or self-determination? Nine months later, in January, 1776, Washington's officers still toasted the health of George III, while they kept the king's expeditionary army bottled up in Boston on short rations. But the

A number of Negroes fought with the colonists at Breed's Hill. The black man in this detail from a John Trumbull painting may be Salem Poor, whose bravery was praised by many officers.
YALE UNIVERSITY ART GALLERY, GARVAN COLLECTION

sound of gunfire had grown louder than the voices of statesmen. "The blood of the slain, the weeping voice of Nature cries, 'Tis time to part,'" wrote Thomas Paine. So it was unanimously resolved by the Second Continental Congress on July 2 and proclaimed to the world on July 4, 1776, fourteen troubled months after the morning at Lexington.

The ringing phrases of the Declaration of Independence left little more to say about American liberty, or, if it meant anything, about human liberty anywhere. "The decree has gone forth and cannot now be recalled," exulted John Adams, "that a more equal liberty than has prevailed in other parts of the earth, must be established in America." But during the years that followed, the men who pledged their lives, their fortunes, and their sacred honor to defend the principles of the Declaration often had too little to support their high hope and resolution. There were times, indeed, when the war seemed a pitiful anticlimax to the surging drama that had produced it.

Each side was still convinced that the other would not long stand firm before a strong show of force. "They will be lions while we are lambs," Gage had advised the king before he returned from a visit home to America—and to Bunker Hill, "but if we take the resolute part, they will be very meek, I promise you." Congress, on the other hand, earnestly hoped that serious armed resistance might shock the king and his counselors back to their proper senses. It was a bad misunderstanding on both sides.

Had either been truly united in its purpose and wholehearted in its efforts, the war could not have lasted long. But a substantial number of Englishmen would not support their king. "Is it common sense," asked John Wesley, "to use force towards America?" When William Howe was appointed general of the British expeditionary forces in America, the voters of Nottingham told him, "If you go, we hope you may fail." Howe apologized for following his orders, went away with a doubtful heart, and did indeed fail. On the other side, more than a hundred thousand Americans left the country during the war, rather than betray their king (a far higher percentage of the population than the number of emigrés who fled from France at the time of its revolution), and they were a small minority of the Loyalists. Some fifty thousand served with the British forces, many of whom honestly differed with their friends, their neighbors, and at times members of their own families on the question of loyalty. New York provided more troops for George III than for George Washington. Americans fought Americans with more fervor and with better effect than did the hired Hessians, as Tarleton's Legion and St. Leger's Loyal Greens demonstrated.

As the Second Continental Congress was preparing to sign the Declaration of Independence, the largest expeditionary force Great Britain had ever assembled, the largest certainly ever seen in the New World, gathered in the harbor off the port of New York under the command of Sir William Howe and his brother Admiral Lord Howe. There were approximately thirty-two thousand well-trained professional soldiers (including Hessians), completely armed and equipped, supported by a fleet that included ten ships of the line, twenty frigates, and about one hundred seventy transports of various sizes. To one observer, the bay looked like a forest of pine trees with their branches trimmed. With all this show of might the Howe brothers also carried an olive branch. The king would show clemency to the rebels if they would stop fighting. But this proposal was drawn up before the Declaration of Independence

This print shows the triumphal entry of British troops into New York City in September, 1776. They held the city until the peace treaty was concluded.
MORRISTOWN NATIONAL HISTORICAL PARK

322

was signed and did not recognize the United States as a political entity (and it had no guarantee of future liberty). Franklin, one of the three commissioners delegated to meet with the Howes, quietly pointed out that since they were not prepared to negotiate with a separate government their peace mission could not be considered. The Howes followed the olive branch with the sword, seized New York, and put Washington's inadequate little army to flight across New Jersey.

The long years of war that followed have become for many Americans the most familiar part of their country's history. In his old age John Adams recalled that the Revolution "was in the minds and hearts of the people" before the hostilities had started. Benjamin Rush, on the other hand, advised after the peace that the War of Independence should not be confounded with the American Revolution. "The American war is over," he wrote, "but that is far from being the case with the American revolution. On the contrary, nothing but the first act of the great drama is closed." Both men were right. In *Common Sense* Thomas Paine had reminded the colonists that what they undertook in their revolutionary cause was "not the affair of a City, a County, a Province, or a Kingdom; but of a *Continent*—of at least one-eighth part of the habitable Globe. 'Tis not the concern of a day, a year, or an age; posterity are virtually involved in the contest, and will be more or less affected even to the end of time, by the proceedings now."

One has to excuse Paine his emotional rhetoric, the rhetoric of a brilliant and infuriated pamphleteer. As one historian has remarked, it is not much of an exaggeration to say that one had to be a fool or a fanatic in early January, 1776, to advocate American independence. For many years past and for some years to come there were prophets on both sides of the Atlantic who foresaw that America would secure its freedom from England. There were as many more, also on both sides of the ocean, who predicted that should this come about it would end up in civil war or anarchy. The basis for the latter prediction was slim. There were, at least, no valid historical precedents by which to forecast the future of a nation that was taking shape under such unprecedented circumstances. As Paine wrote in another of his pamphlets, "the case and circumstances of America present themselves as in the beginning of a world. . . . We have no occasion to roam for information into the obscure fields of antiquity, nor hazard ourselves upon conjecture. We are brought at once to the point of seeing government begin, as if we had lived in the beginning of time."

There was no clear assurance that the war might not end, as would the French Revolution, in a military dictatorship, or that the old hostilities between the separate states might revive and drive some of them back into the secure shelter of the British empire. The defeat of Cornwallis did not eliminate such possibilities. Even while the war was waging, there were signs of discord that might be construed as symptoms of more trouble to come. When he had been in Massachusetts only a few weeks as commander of the American forces, George Washington reported back to Virginia that "the people of this government have obtained a character which they by no means deserved; their officers, generally speaking, are the most indifferent kind of people I ever saw, and as for the men, they are an exceeding dirty and nasty people." John Adams' nomination of the Virginian as commander in chief had been a masterly stroke of policy, for he knew that those in other colonies feared that New

"O ye that love mankind! Ye that dare oppose not only the tyranny but the tyrant, stand forth! Every spot of the old world is overrun with oppression. Freedom hath been hunted around the Globe. Asia and Africa have long expelled her. Europe regards her like a stranger, and England hath give her warning to depart. O! receive the fugitive, and prepare in time an asylum for mankind. . . ."

Thomas Paine in *Common Sense*, 1776

England would soon be full of veteran soldiers who might in time "conceive designs unfavorable to the other colonies." Once, later in the war at Ticonderoga, Pennsylvania troops came to blows with New Englanders. However, in the end the men from the different states stuck together in their common cause with enough enthusiasm to finish the war successfully.

That was a matter of fact England thoroughly miscalculated. Colonel James Grant, who had seen service in America as an "expert" witness, advised Parliament that Americans "would not fight." They would never dare face an English army, and did not possess any of the qualifications to make a good soldier. What he might more truly have observed was that the American soldier did not take kindly to discipline. The British army was recruited from the riff-raff of English society, and heavy-handed sergeants quickly brought any rebellious spirits to official order. British officers came largely from the upper class; they expected and they got submissive respect and unquestioning obedience from the regulars in the ranks. Understandably, they were confused by the fact that both officers and men in the colonial militia came from the same middle class of farmers, artisans, and shopkeepers—men who, against all military tradition, actually elected their own officers. As one French officer in the American army later remarked with incredulity, "our inn-keeper was a captain, and there are shoemakers who are colonels."

The first popular revolution in modern history was obliged to create its armed forces out of the civilian population that had at the start little time for drill and training but that persevered to perform military functions with the necessary authority, as was clearly demonstrated from Bunker Hill to Yorktown over the course of six long years. When General Burgoyne surrendered his entire army at the crucial battle of Saratoga on October 16, 1777, one Hessian observer reported that not one of the Americans was regularly equipped. "Each man had on the clothes he was accustomed to wear in the field, the tavern, the church and in everyday life. No fault, however, could be found in their military appearance, for they stood in an erect and soldierly attitude. They remained so perfectly quiet that we were utterly astounded. Not one of them made any attempt to speak to the man at his side; and all the men who stood in array before us were so slender, fine-looking and sinewy, that it was a pleasure to look at them. . . . The determination which caused them to grasp a musket and powder-horn can be seen in their faces, as well as that they are not to be fooled with, especially in skirmishes in the woods. . . ." Just how unmilitaristic the national temper was is indicated by the fact that after the treaty of peace the standing army stood at a mere 840 men and 46 officers—hardly enough to support a military dictatorship had such a thought entered anyone's mind.

Members of Congress, stimulated by the dignity and demands of their office, probably found it somewhat easier to think in national terms than could local recruits for the army, although they too had to learn their new and special functions. An article in a contemporary English journal remarked of those members generally: "From shopkeepers, tradesmen, and attorneys, they are become statesmen and legislators, and are employed in contriving a new system of government for an extensive empire, which they flatter themselves will become, and which indeed seems very likely to become, one of the greatest and most formidable that ever was in the world." A litigious French monarchist exiled in London, one Simon Linguet, echoed those thoughts with

The First Continental Congress established the Continental Association, a comprehensive, nonimportation, nonexportation, nonconsumption agreement that was to be enforced by special local committees. This British cartoon portrays one such committee using the threat of tar and feathers, hanging from the scaffold in the background, to force Virginians to sign the Continental Association in 1775.

considerable misgivings. Having gained power by a rapid revolution, he conjectured, Americans would amass not only wealth and power, but with the energy and immaturity of youth "they would be all the more terrible," and would eventually cross the Atlantic to crush a weakened and impoverished Europe. To return to problems outlined in the early pages of this book, by his forecast the comfortable balance of power and the European hegemony, so long regarded as a basic necessity of international survival and of Western civilization, would be ultimately threatened not from within Europe but from abroad.

Recently, one authority has described the American Revolution as "the first significant revolution of the modern era and . . . the only truly successful revolution, on a large scale, in the past two centuries." Alexis de Tocqueville referred to it as a revolution which "contracted no alliance with the turbulent passion of anarchy," but which followed its course "by a love of law and order." The observation of law and order is not generally associated with revolution, but it was just this that so largely gives peculiar importance and interest to the events that surrounded the year 1776 in this country. Blood was shed, of course, and soldiers died; there were some mob actions as well. But on and off the battlefield (except in the Indian warfare along the borders) there was little of the butchery that the idea of revolutionary warfare brings to mind. There were no bloodthirsty revolutionary tribunals to mete out "justice" to dissenters or unseated administrators in years to follow. (All the men who signed the Declaration of Independence died in bed, although seventeen of them saw military service, after having continued to serve the cause they sponsored in the first place during the remainder of their active days.)

It was a revolution, as Irving Kristol has pointed out, that was infused by mind to a degree never approximated since and perhaps never approximated before—by mind, not by dogma. The most fascinating aspect of the American Revolution is the severe way it kept questioning itself about the meaning of what it was doing. It was not a direct and inexorable march toward a clearly predetermined, fixed goal. Doubt, introspection, anxiety, skepticism, and intellectual sagacity attended the deliberation of those who guided its course, which was what made it a successful revolution in the end. Even the revolutionary pamphlets (such as Dickinson's), sermons, and newspaper articles were generally thoughtful and sober in tone, rather than inflammatory. And, it is well to remember, there was no official censorship to discourage outspoken opinion.

It was only after the war was definitely launched that the American people came to the decision that the time had arrived to establish a republican form of government. Once they "dismissed" George III they had no other option. By 1776 America was well prepared for republicanism. Although the word was not commonly used, republican traditions had long been a basic ingredient in colonial life, from the Mayflower Compact to the Declaration of Independence, as has already been observed. American political institutions, especially in New England, but also commonly elsewhere, had been close to republican in actual fact. In the months and years that followed the Declaration of Independence all the new states drew up separate constitutions, and in none of these were prescribed basic changes in prevailing political practices or institutions, or any significant alteration in existing legal, social, or economic institutions. Much that a revolution might have been expected to accomplish

Reactions to public readings of the Declaration of Independence (above) varied considerably. Charles Biddle wrote of the ceremony at the Philadelphia State House on July 8: "There were very few respectable people present." The following day the Declaration was read in New York to regiments of half a dozen states. Washington hoped that "this important Event will serve as a fresh incentive to every officer and soldier. . . ." Abigail Adams attended the reading at the State House in Boston on July 19 and wrote: "every face appeared joyfull. . . . Thus ends royal Authority in the State. and all the people shall say Amen."
COLONIAL WILLIAMSBURG

had already been accomplished before independence had been declared. In the recent words of one historian, the peculiar function of the Revolution was "to complete, formalize, systematize, and symbolize what previously had been only partially realized, confused, and disputed matters of fact."

A few years ago one university undergraduate concluded that the Revolution changed so little in the circumstances of American life that "it wasn't much of a revolution after all." Before it came about, at least half the (white) population already had enough property to qualify for the franchise in their local affairs. ("Everybody has property," wrote one British traveler in the colonies, "and every body knows it.") A beggar in America, it was said, was as rare as a horse on the streets of Venice, which for the time made for an unusually wide democratic participation in the conduct of the public business. In New England royal officials complained of "town meetings" where "the lowest Mechanics" could discuss "the most important points of government, with the utmost freedom." "Each individual," wrote one observer, "has an equal liberty of delivering his opinion, and is not liable to be silenced or browbeaten by a richer or greater townsman than himself; and each vote weighs equally whether that of the highest or lowest inhabitant." Except to a degree in England, Sweden, and some of the Swiss cantons, there was no such body politic in the rest of the world.

There was no need of a revolution to overthrow an entrenched aristocracy in America; there was none to overthrow. As one historian has remarked, colonial America was the land of the frustrated aristocrat. (In 1774 John Adams noted that British America has "a hereditary apprehension of and aversion to lordships, temporal and spiritual.") The ancient devices of primogeniture and entail by which a landed aristocracy could perpetuate its power never had enjoyed much reality in colonial America, and with the conclusion of the Revolution such traditional feudal customs were soon abolished by law in all the newborn states of the union. Democratic land-tenure was the natural thing in a new country like America, and made its way at once and completely when political revolution loosened the ties of old habits.

In none of the colonies was there an established Church that enjoyed power even remotely akin to that exercised by the religious establishments in most

European countries, and that might bar the way to revolutionary goals. In America, long before Rousseau startled the world with his paradoxes, men who could not agree on creeds or forms of government found common ground in thinking that the test of true religion was that it made good citizens, the test of rightly ordered society that it made good men. "I think vital religion has always suffered where orthodoxy is more regarded than virtue," wrote Franklin, "and the Scriptures assure me that at the last day we shall not be examined what we *thought*, but what we *did*; and our recommendation will be that we did good to our fellow creatures." Nevertheless, there were established religions of various kinds in separate colonies, which enjoyed special privileges, but these would be done away with. In Virginia it took Thomas Jefferson ten years of what he called the severest contest in which he was ever engaged to do away with such privileges. When in 1786 the Virginia legislature passed the Statute of Religious Liberty, which he had proposed seven years earlier, Jefferson considered this one of his three great contributions to his country (along with the Declaration of Independence and the establishment of the University of Virginia).

Jefferson's new University of Virginia was based on "the illimitable freedom of the human mind." By Old World standards education in America was already secularized, and there was no need of a revolution to relieve teaching or learning from the burden of undue religious prejudices and intellectual controls. Even in the seventeenth century a Baptist had been made president of Harvard College; and the trustees of the little college at Philadelphia, Presbyterians, Anglicans, and Quakers, sat on the board with the deist Benjamin Franklin as the first president of that body.

Until the time of the American Revolution, how to put their opinions into practical operation had defeated the liberal thinkers of Europe. It could not be done through suffrage, for suffrage on the required scale was virtually nonexistent in almost all countries. There was no way to make public opinion politically effective, had there been any means of determining just what public opinion was and a scheme for marshaling it in evidence. The Church and the universities were not sympathetic to any radical changes in the established order of things. And for those who seriously proposed such changes, there

327

were threatening consequences, as Voltaire, Diderot, and Rousseau, among others, had occasion to realize. Those who retained some positions of power were, like their "enlightened" princes and monarchs, frightened at the very prospect of translating liberal theory from philosophy to practical politics and daily endeavor.

Yet in America such deeds were done in the course of native experience, or the grounds were well laid for accomplishment in the future. "The foundation of our empire was not laid in the gloomy age of ignorance and superstition," Washington remarked in a letter of 1783, "but at an epoch when the rights of mankind were better understood and more clearly defined, than at any former period; the researches of the human mind after social happiness have been carried to a greater extent, the treasures of knowledge . . . are laid open for our use, and their collected wisdom may be happily applied in the establishment of our forms of government." On the occasion of Washington's death, the Reverend Samuel Miller preached a special sermon in which he referred to "our glorious emancipation from Britain," for which John Jay quickly took him to task. If Miller had consulted the statements of the Continental Congress in 1774 and 1775, Jay suggested, he would find that Congress "had regarded the People of this Country as being Free," and had resorted to arms only when England "recurred to arms to put a Yoke upon us." Under those circumstances, Jay admonished, the term "emancipation" was hardly applicable.

If a nation born of this rebellion could achieve stability; if a society made up of a mixed population with no ancient roots in the land and few, if any, common, time-hallowed traditions as a people could find some binding faith; if a people committed to the dangerous principle that freedom of religion, speech, assembly, and the press was not only permissible but desirable; if a nation thus conceived could survive conflicting ideas and unlimited criticism from within; if a nation could cast away the customary props of society—royalty, aristocracy, and an established national church; and if America could successfully demonstrate its ideas of social and political order on a continental scale, then by the unanswerable power of contrast, it would be a threat to every other existing form of government—and a model for those elsewhere who looked for a more promising future. Those were very large "ifs." In 1776, and indeed in 1787 or 1800, there were sober-minded men of the Revolution who had no real certainty that their experiments in war and peace would endure and flourish. "The preservation of the sacred fire of liberty and the destiny of the republican mode of government," Washington counseled his countrymen in his first inaugural address, "are justly considered, as deeply, perhaps as finally staked, on the experiment intrusted to the hands of the American people." He well knew that the world would watch with concern and wonder as the concept of popular sovereignty was put to practice.

The United States of America was the first society in history to be officially committed to "the pursuit of happiness" as the practical goal of politics and government, for all the lip service that had been given to the idea in years past. The Founding Fathers understood what they were undertaking when they took up arms in 1776. They imprinted their knowledge on the Great Seal of the United States: *Novus Ordo Seclorum* ("a new order of things"). They had fought not only to preserve their liberty but to justify their concepts of liberty itself. And so it was that the cause of America was set on a course toward becoming the cause of all mankind.

Ben Franklin's printing press

VOICE OF THE PEOPLE

The incidents that led to the outbreak of war between the colonies and Great Britain have been told and retold, interpreted and reinterpreted over the past two hundred years. At the time, however, these events were fresh news, and the public's impression of a particular happening was often formed by the views presented in magazines, newspapers, or broadsides (either hand-distributed or posted in public places). Propagandists on both sides used the printing press extensively. The documents on the following pages provide some insight into the diversity, as well as the depth, of feelings generated by the actions taken in America and Great Britain.

Repeal of the Stamp Act was popular in both England and America. The British cartoon above, published two weeks after the repeal in March, 1766, shows the Stamp Act author, George Grenville, carrying the coffin of his dead brainchild to the "Family Vault." On the Thames merchantmen await "Goods NOW Ship'd for America," as proclaimed on the warehouse at right. New Yorkers heard about the repeal from the "Joy to America!" broadside opposite, some two and a half months after the fact.

New-York, May 20, 1766.

Joy to AMERICA !

At 3 this Day arrived here an Exprefs from *Bofton* with the following moft glorious News, on which *H. Gaine* congratulates the Friends of *America*. *Bofton*, Friday 11 o'Clock, 16th May, 1766. This Day arrived here the Brig *Harrifon*, belonging to *John Hancock*, Efq; Capt. *Shubael Coffin*, in 6 Weeks and 2 Days from *London*, with the following moft agreeable Intelligence, *viz.*

From the LONDON GAZETTE.

Weftminfter, March 18.

THIS day his Majefty came to the houfe of Peers, and being in his royal robes, feated on the throne, with the ufual folemnity, Sir *Francis Molineaux*, Gentleman ufher of the black rod was fent with a Meffage from his Majefty to the houfe of commons, commanding their attendance in the houfe of peers. The commons being come thither accordingly, his Majefty was pleafed to give his Royal Affent to

An ACT to *Repeal* an Act, made the laft Seffion of Parliament, entitled, An Act for granting and applying certain ftamp Duties, and other Duties in the *Britifh* Colonies and Plantations in *America*, towards further defraying the Expences of defending, protecting, and fecuring the fame ; and for mending fuch Parts of the feveral Acts of Parliament relating to the Trade and Revenues of the faid Colonies and Plantations, as direct the Manner of determining and recovering the Penalties and Forfeitures therein mentioned.

When his Majefty went to the Houfe he was accompanied by greater Numbers of People than ever was known on the like Occafion ; many Copies of the Repeal were fent to Falmouth, to be forwarded to America ; and all the Veffels in the River Thames bound to America, had Orders to fail.

5 o'Clock, *P. M.* Since compofing the Above an Exprefs arrived from Philadelphia with a Confirmation of the Repeal, and that a printed Copy of it by the King's Printer lay in the Coffee-Houfe for the Perufal of the Publick.

As the most influential man in Massachusetts politics, Thomas Hutchinson was the target of vicious attacks in radical propaganda. The broadside opposite, published anonymously in the late 1760's, condemns him for secretly agreeing to the quartering of troops. The caricature of Hutchinson above ("Machiavel" is inscribed on the book at his feet) appeared on the cover of Gleason's almanac in 1774, the year that Hutchinson was forced to flee to England.

WHOEVER has candidly traced the rapid Growth of these Colonies from their little Beginnings to their present flourishing State in Wealth and Population, must eye the distinguished Hand of Heaven, and impress every Mind with a humble Confidence, that " no Design formed against us shall prosper :" The poor devoted Town of Boston has suffered, and is still suffering, all that the unmeritted Malice of Men and Devils could invent for her Destruction ; but although impoverished and distressed, she is not yet subjugated and enslaved ; though immured within the Fortresses of their Enemies, the free and generous Bosoms of the Inhabitants beat strongly in the Cause of Liberty : But it appears that the Measure of ministerial Wrath is not yet full : That detested Parricide Hutchinson, has vaunted to his few Friends, that should the People submit to the villainous Exactions of the present governmental Knot of Tyrants, * " yet still the Town of Boston would forever remain a garrisoned Town," as a Check upon the Country, lest they should hereafter be induced to clamour against the Edicts of their sovereign Lords and Masters, the British Parliament. The following Plan was providentially detected, and is now offered to the Public, with this solemn Question---Will the People sit tame and inactive Spectators of the hostile Designs of our inveterate Enemies, and exercise such Degrees of Moderation and Forbearance as to suffer those Enemies to compleat their Works, and so far effect their dangerous Purpose, that Resistance would finally be in vain ?

THE WATCHMAN.

Memorandums, for a Report.

WE have agreable to your Commands viewed and enquired what Cover can be hired with the Consent of the Proprietors for the Troops next Winter.

We find that Out-Houses, Distilleries and Store-Houses can be hired to contain the Serjeants, &c. and private Men of four Regiments. That as these want Fire-Places, Windows, and even Floors, the Expence of setting up these, and for Rent, and returning them in the Condition they now stand, will be nearly to One Thousand Pounds a Regiment. This Expence would be greatly lessened, and the Troops more comfortably quartered, if the public Buildings, such as the Manufacturing House, &c. can be appropriated for the Accommodation of the Troops.

It appears that Barracks can be built on a more thrifty Footing than they can be hired, and fitted up. But as no Body in this Place will aid such Works, Capt. Montrefor with the Assistance he can at present depend upon, thinks he cannot undertake to furnish Barracks before the End of November, for more than three Regiments ; the Officers of one of these Regiments to be quartered.

It appears on Enquiry, difficult to find Houses for quartering Officers of the Regiments, whose private Men are to be lodged in Out-Houses ; Lodging Money should be given to Officers who we cannot provide for.

In chusing Situations for the Barracks to be built, it might be wished to place them so as to make the present Erection part of some general Plan that may be found, with a View of commanding the Obedience of the Town on future Occasions; but if they are confined to Situations where the Ground is reputed to belong to the Public, we would propose to build Barracks for two Regiments, including Officers, on the Common, or on a Field near it, which could be hired or purchased from Mr. Brattle.

To put two Companies into a solid Barrack, or Block-House, on the Top of Bacon-Hill, which should be enclosed with a Trench and Palisade.

A Barrack should be built on Fort-Hill, which might lodge eight Companies and the Artillery.

As soon as it is proper to let each Regiment have its Quarters, their Efforts to get themselves lodged would contribute greatly to have the Work finished early.

* This is a Fact, founded on the Authority of a respectable Gentleman of this Town, lately arrived from London, who there had it from Mr. Hutchinson's own Mouth.

The tea tax aroused resentment throughout America. The Philadelphia Committee for Tarring and Feathering distributed the broadside opposite several weeks before the Boston Tea Party. When the Polly *arrived at Glouchester Point, the broadside was reissued at a protest meeting. Captain Ayres sailed back to England with his cargo intact. A year after the Tea Party in Boston, some forty men, disguised as Indians, seized a cargo of tea in Greenwich, New Jersey, and burned it in the public square. The engraving above, published in London in 1775, shows the women of Edenton, North Carolina, pledging not to drink tea.*

TO THE
Delaware Pilots.

WE took the Pleasure, some Days since, of kindly admonishing you *to do your Duty;* if perchance you should meet with the *(Tea,)* Ship POLLY, CAPTAIN AYRES; a THREE DECKER which is hourly expected.

We have now to add, that Matters ripen fast here; and that *much is expected from those Lads who meet with the Tea Ship.*----There is some Talk of A HANDSOME REWARD FOR THE PILOT WHO GIVES THE FIRST GOOD ACCOUNT OF HER.----How that may be, we cannot *for certain* determine: But ALL agree, that TAR and FEATHERS will be his Portion, who pilots her into this Harbour. And we will answer for ourselves, that, whoever is committed to us, as an Offender against the Rights of *America*, will experience the utmost Exertion of our Abilities; as

THE COMMITTEE FOR TARRING AND FEATHERING.

P. S. We expect you will furnish yourselves with Copies of the foregoing and following Letter; which are printed for this Purpose, that the Pilot who meets with Captain *Ayres* may favor him with a Sight of them.

Committee of Taring and Feathering.

TO
Capt. AYRES,

Of the SHIP *POLLY*, on a Voyage from *London* to *Philadelphia.*

SIR,

WE are informed that you have, imprudently, taken Charge of a Quantity of Tea; which has been sent out by the *Inaia* Company, *under the Auspices of the Ministry,* as a Trial of *American* Virtue and Resolution.

Now, as your Cargo, on your Arrival here, will most assuredly bring you into hot water; and as you are perhaps a Stranger *to these Parts,* we have concluded to advise you of the present Situation of Affairs in *Philadelphia*---that, taking Time by the Forelock, you may stop short in your dangerous Errand----secure your Ship against the Rafts of combustible Matter which may be set on Fire, and turned loose against her; and more than all this, that you may preserve your own Person, from the Pitch and Feathers that are prepared for you.

In the first Place, we must tell you, that the *Pennsylvanians* are, *to a Man,* passionately fond of Freedom; the Birthright of *Americans;* and at all Events are determined to enjoy it.

That they sincerely believe, no Power on the Face of the Earth has a Right to tax them without their Consent.

That in their Opinion, the Tea in your Custody is designed by the Ministry to enforce such a Tax, which they will undoubtedly oppose; and in so doing, give you every possible Obstruction.

We are nominated to a very disagreeable, but necessary Service.---- To our Care are committed all Offenders against the Rights of *America;* and hapless is he, whose evil Destiny has doomed him to suffer at our Hands.

You are sent out on a diabolical Service; and if you are so foolish and obstinate as to compleat your Voyage; by bringing your Ship to Anchor in this Port; you may run such a Gauntlet, as will induce you, in your last Moments, most heartily to curse those who have made you the Dupe of their Avarice and Ambition.

What think you Captain, of a Halter around your Neck----ten Gallons of liquid Tar decanted on your Pate----with the Feathers of a dozen wild Geese laid over that to enliven your Appearance?

Only think seriously of this----and fly to the Place from whence you came----fly without Hesitation----without the Formality of a Protest----and above all, Captain *Ayres* let us advise you to fly without the wild Geese Feathers.

Your Friends *to serve*

Philadelphia, Nov. 27, 1773   THE COMMITTEE *as before subscribed*

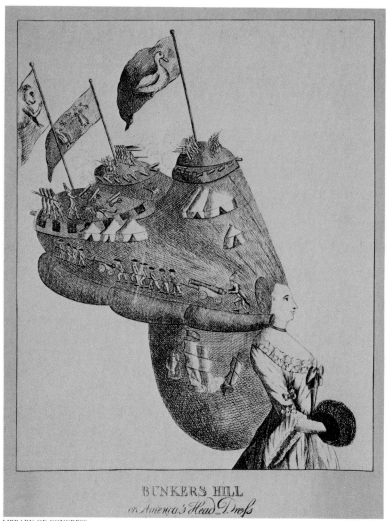

The Battle of Bunker Hill (which was actually fought on Breed's Hill) resulted in a narrow victory for the British—costing them 1,054 casualties out of 2,200 troops. However, the broadside opposite, showing a song composed by British soldiers to be sung to the tune of "Yankee Doodle," indicates that the rank and file expected little trouble in putting down the rebellion. Other British supporters were not so enthused. Above, a 1776 engraving published in London satirized the claim of a British victory at Bunker Hill as well as the day's fashionable, thoroughly ridiculous coiffures.

336

A SONG,

Compofed by the Britifh Soldiers, after the fight at

Bunker Hill, June 17, 1775.

IT was on the feventeenth by brake of day,
　The Yankees did furprife us.
With their ftrong works they had thrown up,
　To burn the town and drive us;
But foon we had an order come,
　An order to defeat them:
Like rebels ftout they ftood it out,
　And thought we ne'er could beat them.

About the hour of twelve that day,
　An order came for marching,
With three good flints and fixty rounds,
　Each man hop'd to difcharge them.
We marched down to the long wharf,
　Where boats were ready waiting;
With expedition we embark'd,
　Our fhips kept cannonading.

And when our boats all filled were
　With officers and foldiers,
With as good troops as England had,
　To oppofe who dare controul us;
And when our boats all filled were,
　We row'd in line of battle,
Where fhow'rs of balls like hail did fly,
　Our cannon loud did rattle.

There was Cop's hill battery near Charleftown,
　Our twenty-fours they played,
And the three frigates in the ftream,
　That very well behaved;
The Glafgow frigate clear'd the fhore,
　All at the time of landing,
With her grape fhot and cannon balls,
　No Yankees e'er could ftand them.

And when we landed on the fhore,
　We drew up all together;
The Yankees they all man'd their works,
　And thought we'd ne'er come thither:
But foon they did perceive brave Howe,
　Brave Howe our bold commander,
With grenadiers, and infantry,
　We made them to furrender.

Brave William Howe, on our right wing,
　Cry'd boys fight on like thunder;
You foon will fee the rebels flee,
　With great amaze and wonder.
Now fome lay bleeding on the ground,
　And fome full faft a running,
O'er hills and dales and mountains high,
　Crying, zounds! brave Howe's a coming.

They began to play on our left wing,
　Where Pegot he commanded;
But we return'd it back again,
　With courage moft undaunted.
To our grape fhot and mufket balls,
　To which they were but ftrangers,
They thought to come in with fword in hand,
　But foon they found their danger.

And when the works we got into,
　And put them to the flight, fir,
Some of them did hide themfelves,
　And others died with fright fir.
And then their works we got into,
　Without great fear or danger,
The work they'd made fo firm and ftrong:
　The Yankees are great ftrangers.

But as for our artillery,
　They all behaved dinty;
For while their ammunition held,
　We gave it to them plenty.
But our conductor he got broke,
　For his mifconduct, fure, fir;
The fhot he fent for twelve pound guns
　Were made for twenty-four, fir.

There's fome in Bofton pleas'd to fay,
　As we the field were taking,
We went to kill their countrymen,
　While they their hay were making;
For fuch ftout Whigs I never faw;
　To hang them all I'd rather,
For making hay with mufket-balls
　And buck-fhot mixed together.

Brave Howe is fo confiderate,
　As to prevent all danger;
He allows half a pint a day;
　To rum we are no ftrangers.
Long may he live by land and fea,
　For he's beloved by many;
The name of Howe the Yankees dread,
　We fee it very plainly.

And now my fong is at an end;
　And to conclude my ditty,
It is the poor and ignorant,
　And only them, I pity.
And as for their king John Hancock,
　And Adams, if they're taken,
Their heads for figns fhall hang up high,
　Upon that hill call'd Bacon.

Let us not Cut down the Tree to get at the Fruit.

Let us Stroke and not Stab the Cow; For her Milk, and not her Blood, can give us real Nourishment and Strength.

Conciliatory forces were at work in both America and England. The Second Continental Congress sent what John Adams dubbed the "Olive Branch" petition (opposite, the first page) to George III in July, 1775. Independence supporters gambled that the king would refuse it, thereby swinging moderates to the separatist cause. Moderates in England printed the cartoon above in 1775, urging that persuasion, not force, be used.

To the Kings most excellent Majesty

Most gracious Sovereign,

We your Majesty's faithful subjects of the colonies of New-hampshire, Massachusetts bay, Rhode island and Providence plantations, Connecticut, New-York, New Jersey, Pennsylvania, the counties of New Castle Kent & Sussex on Delaware, Maryland, Virginia, North-Carolina and South Carolina in behalf of ourselves and the inhabitants of these colonies, who have deputed us to represent them in general Congress, entreat your Majestys ~~gracious~~ attention to this our humble petition.

The union between our Mother country and these colonies, and the energy of mild and just government, produced benefits so remarkably important, and afforded such an assurance of their permanency and increase, that the wonder and envy of other nations were excited, while they beheld Great Britain riseing to a power the most extraordinary the world had ever known.

Her rivals observing, that there was no probability of this happy connection being broken by civil dissentions, and apprehending its future effects if left any longer undisturbed, resolved to prevent her receiving such continual and formidable accessions of wealth and strength, by checking the

growth

NEW YORK PUBLIC LIBRARY, MANUSCRIPT DIVISION

Although the 1775 cartoon seen above was published in London, it represents the attitude of the pro-independence people in America when the "Olive Branch" petition was drawn up. America is burning, while British political leaders fan the flames with various political measures. The petition was taken to England by William Penn's grandson, Richard. George III refused to see him and instead, on August 23, 1775, issued a proclamation ordering that the rebellion be suppressed. His language—referring to the rebel leaders as "traitorous," "wicked," and "desperate Persons within this Realm"—left no room for compromise.

By his EXCELLENCY

WILLIAM TRYON, Esquire,

Captain General, and Governor in Chief in and over the Province of *New-York*, and the Territories depending thereon in *America*, Chancellor and Vice Admiral of the same.

A PROCLAMATION.

WHEREAS I have received His Majesty's Royal Proclamation, given the Court at *St. James's*, the Twenty-third Day of *August* last, in the Words following:

BY THE KING,

A Proclamation,

For suppressing REBELLION and SEDITION.

GEORGE R.

WHEREAS many of our Subjects in divers Parts of our Colonies and Plantations in *North-America*, misled by dangerous and ill designing Men, and forgetting the Allegiance which they owe to the Power that has protected and sustained them, after various disorderly Acts committed in disturbance of the public Peace, to the Obstruction of lawful Commerce, and to the Oppression of our loyal Subjects carrying on the same, have at length proceeded to an open and avowed Rebellion, by arraying themselves in hostile Manner, to withstand the Execution of the Law, and traitorously preparing, ordering and levying War against us: And whereas there is Reason to apprehend that such Rebellion hath been much promoted and encouraged by the traitorous Correspondence, Counsels, and Comfort of divers wicked and desperate Persons within this Realm :---To the End therefore that none of our Subjects may neglect or violate their Duty through Ignorance thereof, or through any Doubt of the Protection which the Law will afford to their Loyalty and Zeal; we have thought fit, by and with the Advice of our Privy Council, to issue this our Royal Proclamation, hereby declaring, that not only all our Officers Civil and Military, are obliged to exert their utmost Endeavours to suppress such Rebellion, and to bring the Traitors to Justice; but that all our Subjects of this Realm and the Dominions thereunto belonging, are bound by Law to be aiding and assisting in the Suppression of such Rebellion, and to disclose and make known all traitorous Conspiracies and Attempts against us, our Crown and Dignity: And we do accordingly strictly charge and command all our Officers, as well Civil as Military, and all other our obedient and loyal Subjects, to use their utmost Endeavours to withstand and suppress such Rebellion, and to disclose and make known all Treasons and traitorous Conspiracies which they shall know to be against us, our Crown and Dignity; and for that Purpose, that they transmit to one of our principal Secretaries of State, or other proper Officer, due and full Information of all Persons who shall be found carrying on Correspondence with, or in any Manner or Degree aiding or abetting the Persons now in open Arms and Rebellion against our Government within any of our Colonies and Plantations in *North-America*, in order to bring to condign Punishment the Authors, Perpetrators, and Abettors of such traitorous Designs.

Given at our Court at St. James's the Twenty-third Day of August, *One Thousand Seven Hundred and Seventy-five, in the Fifteenth Year of our Reign.*

In Obedience therefore to his Majesty's Commands to me given, I do hereby publish and make known his Majesty's most gracious Proclamation above recited; earnestly exhorting and requiring all his Majesty's loyal and faithful Subjects within this Province, as they value their Allegiance due to the best of Sovereigns, their Dependance on and Protection from their Parent State, and the Blessings of a mild, free, and happy Constitution; and as they would shun the fatal Calamities which are the inevitable Consequences of Sedition and Rebellion, to pay all due Obedience to the Laws of their Country, seriously to attend to his Majesty's said Proclamation, and govern themselves accordingly.

Given under my Hand and Seal at Arms, in the City of New-York, *the Fourteenth Day of* November, *One Thousand Seven Hundred and Seventy-five, in the Sixteenth Year of the Reign of our Sovereign Lord* GEORGE *the Third, by the Grace of God of* Great-Britain, France *and* Ireland, *King, Defender of the Faith, and so forth.*

By his Excellency's Command,
SAMUEL BAYARD, Jun. D. Secry.

WM. TRYON.

GOD SAVE THE *KING.*

THE HORSE AMERICA, *throwing his Master.*

Pub.d as the Act directs Aug.t 1.t 1779. by M.rs White, Angel Court, Westminster.

The British cartoon above was printed in reaction to the news of America's Declaration of Independence. On July 2, 1776, Congress had passed a resolution declaring "That these United Colonies are, and of right ought to be, Free and Independent States. . . ." Two days later Thomas Jefferson's draft of the Declaration, as amended by John Adams and Benjamin Franklin (opposite), was submitted for approval. The representatives made some changes—the reference to slavery was omitted—but the Declaration that passed was almost entirely the work of Thomas Jefferson.

A Declaration by the Representatives of the UNITED STATES
OF AMERICA, in General Congress assembled.

When in the course of human events it becomes necessary for one people to
dissolve the political bands which have connected them with another, and to assume among the powers of the earth the separate and equal station to
which the laws of nature & of nature's god entitle them, a decent respect
to the opinions of mankind requires that they should declare the causes
which impel them to the separation.

We hold these truths to be self-evident; that all men are
created equal, that they are endowed by their creator with
inherent & inalienable rights; that among these are
life, & liberty, & the pursuit of happiness; that to secure these rights, governments are instituted among men, deriving their just powers from
the consent of the governed; that whenever any form of government
becomes destructive of these ends, it is the right of the people to alter
or to abolish it, & to institute new government, laying it's foundation on
such principles & organising it's powers in such form, as to them shall
seem most likely to effect their safety & happiness. prudence indeed
will dictate that governments long established should not be changed for
light & transient causes: and accordingly all experience hath shewn that
mankind are more disposed to suffer while evils are sufferable than to
right themselves by abolishing the forms to which they are accustomed. but
when a long train of abuses & usurpations [begun at a distinguished period
&] pursuing invariably the same object, evinces a design to reduce
them under absolute Despotism, it is their right, it is their duty, to throw off such
government & to provide new guards for their future security. such has
been the patient sufferance of these colonies; & such is now the necessity
which constrains them to expunge their former systems of government.
the history of the present king of Great Britain is a history of unremitting injuries and
usurpations, among which appears no solitary fact to contra-
dict the uniform tenor of the rest but all have in direct object the
establishment of an absolute tyranny over these states. to prove this, let facts be
submitted to a candid world, for the truth of which we pledge a faith
yet unsullied by falsehood.

Two Hundred Years Hence.

A Correspondent having favoured us with the following Picture of what he fears may be realized two hundred years hence, we submit it to the public just as we received it.

GREAT BRITAIN.	AMERICA.
LONDON—A Village supporting a few Fishermen, who make a wretched subsistence, by catching plaice, flounders, and other small fish.	PHILADELPHIA—An Imperial City, rich in all the products of the earth, and carrying on an immense commerce with half the globe.
Bristol—Ditto.	*Boston*—A large mercantile city.
Liverpool—Ditto.	*New York*—Famous for its shipping.
York—A turnip-field.	*Charles-Town, South-Carolina*—famous for its silk manufacture.
Edinburgh—A deserted rock.	*Newport, Rhode-Island*—A town famous for its fisheries.
Winchester—Formerly famous for its trade in corn—now a waste ground.	*Annapolis*—Remarkable for its amazing trade in tobacco.
Norwich—Consisting of three houses, in one of which they shew the remains of a machine for weaving stuffs.	*Reading*, in the Colony of *Massachusets*—famous for its extensive woollen manufacture.
Dover—In possession of the Prussians, who over ran France, and took this place, in the last century.	*Quebec*—A fortress commanding the whole district of *Canada*, and the adjacent countries.
Oxford— ⎰ Of about twenty houses *Cambridge*— ⎱ each: in either place is a ballad-printer's.	*New Jersey*—A collegiate city, famous all over the world for the learning of its members.
In what WAS *London*.	In what IS *Philadelphia*.
Buckingham-house—A dunghil.	—A Palace.
Westminster-hall—A Methodist meeting-house.	—A High Court of Justice.
St. Paul's Church—A brothel.	—A Cathedral.
Guildhall—A stable.	—Grand Mews.

General Face of the *Countries.*

Barren—waste—wild—with some few remains of its ancient splendor.	Rich—flourishing—cultivated — with new cities, towns, and villas, arising on every side.

POPULATION.

Seventeen thousand.	Seventeen million.

In July, 1776, a reader clearly sympathetic to the American cause contributed this dire bit of prognostication to London's Lottery Magazine.

ACKNOWLEDGMENTS

The Editors are especially grateful to the following individuals and organizations for their generous assistance, and for their cooperation in making available pictorial materials in their collections:

Peggy Buckwalter
City University of New York, City College
   Cohen Library, Donald Petty
Columbia University Libraries
Carla Davidson
Kaethe Ellis
Meryle Evans
Hershell George
The Grolier Club
Jerry Kearns
Pamela Lehrer
Library Company of Philadelphia
Library of Congress
Mercantile Library Association
The Metropolitan Museum of Art

National Gallery of Art
   Caroline Backlund
The New-York Historical Society
New York Public Library
New York Society Library
Eva Neurath
J. H. Plumb
Public Archives of Canada
   Georges Delisle
Charles J. Tanenbaum
Thames & Hudson, Ltd., London
   Elizabeth Clarke
Rene Trespalacios
Wan-go H.C. Weng

We gratefully acknowledge our debt to the authors and publishers of the following works:

Letters of Voltaire and Frederick the Great, translated with an introduction by Richard Aldington. Copyright © 1927 by Routledge, London. Reprinted by permission of Routledge and Kegan Paul, Ltd.

The Prodigal Rake: Memoirs of William Hickey, edited by Peter Quennell. Copyright © 1960, Poore, Ltd., London. Reprinted by permission of E. P. Dutton and Co., Inc., New York and Hutchinson Publishing Group, Ltd., London.

The Memoirs of Catherine the Great, edited by Dominique Maroger, translated by Moura Budberg. Copyright © 1955 by The Macmillan Company, New York and Hamish Hamilton, Ltd., London. Reprinted by permission of The Macmillan Company and Hamish Hamilton, Ltd.

Documents of Catherine the Great, edited by W. F. Reddaway. Copyright © 1931, Cambridge University Press, London. Reprinted by permission of Cambridge University Press.

Jan Compagnie in Japan, 1600–1817, by Captain C. R. Boxer. Published by Martinus Nijhoff, The Hague, 1936.

The Social Contract and Discourse on the Origin and Foundation of Inequality Among Mankind, by Jean Jacques Rousseau. Edited by Lester G. Crocker. Copyright © 1967 by Washington Square Press, New York. Reprinted by permission of Washington Square Press.

Diderot's Letters to Sophie Volland, translated by Peter France. Copyright © 1972, Oxford University Press, London. Reprinted by permission of Oxford University Press.

The Enlightenment: A Comprehensive Anthology, edited by Peter Gay. Copyright © 1973 by Simon & Schuster, Inc., New York. Reprinted by permission of Simon & Schuster, Inc.

Denis Diderot's The Encyclopedia Selection, edited and translated by Stephen J. Gendzier. Copyright © 1967 by Harper Torchbooks, New York. Reprinted by permission of Harper Torchbooks, New York.

Selected Letters of Voltaire, edited by Richard A. Brooks, copyright © 1973, New York University Press, New York. Reprinted by permission of New York University Press.

The Compleat Naturalist, A Life of Linnaeus, by Wilfred Blunt. Copyright © 1971 by The Viking Press, New York. Reprinted by permission of The Viking Press and William Collins Sons & Co., Ltd.

A Dissertation on the Sexes of Plants, by Linnaeus. Translated and published by J. E. Smith, London, 1786.

Reflections on the Study of Nature, by Linnaeus. Printed for G. Nicol, London, 1785.

The Literature of England, An Anthology and a History, edited by George B. Woods, Homer A. Watt, and George K. Anderson. Published by Scott, Foresman and Company, 1941, New York.

INDEX

Note: numbers in boldface refer to illustrations.